BEAU GESTE

BY
PERCIVAL CHRISTOPHER WREN
Author of
"The Wages of Virtue"

J. B. LIPPINCOTT COMPANY
PHILADELPHIA   **NEW YORK**

The Authorized American Edition
Published, 1925, by
J. B. LIPPINCOTT COMPANY

FORTY-SIXTH IMPRESSION

CONTENTS

PART I

MAJOR HENRI DE BEAUJOLAIS' STORY

PART II

THE MYSTERY OF THE "BLUE WATER"

PART I

MAJOR HENRI DE BEAUJOLAIS' STORY

CHAPTER I

OF THE STRANGE EVENTS AT ZINDERNEUF

TOLD BY MAJOR HENRI DE BEAUJOLAIS OF THE SPAHIS

TO

GEORGE LAWRENCE, ESQ., C.M.G., OF THE
NIGERIAN CIVIL SERVICE

"Tout ce que je raconte, je l'ai vu, et si j'ai pu me tromper en le voyant, bien certainement je ne vous trompe pas en vous le disant."

"The place was silent and *aware.*"

MR. GEORGE LAWRENCE, C.M.G., First Class District Officer of His Majesty's Civil Service, sat at the door of his tent and viewed the African desert scene with the eye of extreme disfavour. There was beauty neither in the landscape nor in the eye of the beholder.

The landscape consisted of sand, stone, *kerengia* burr-grass, *tafasa* underbrush, yellow, long-stalked with long thin beanpods; the whole varied by clumps of the coarse and hideous *tumpafia* plant.

The eye was jaundiced, thanks to the heat and foul dust of Bornu, to malaria, dysentery, inferior food, poisonous water, and rapid continuous marching in appalling heat.

Weak and ill in body, Lawrence was worried and anxious in mind, the one reacting on the other.

In the first place, there was the old standing trouble about the Shuwa Patrol; in the second, the truculent Chiboks were waxing insolent again, and their young men were regarding not the words of their elders concerning Sir Garnet Wolseley, and what happened, long, long ago, after the battle of Chibok Hill. Thirdly, the price of grain had risen to six shillings a *saa*, and famine threatened; fourthly, the Shehu and Shuwa sheiks were quarrelling again; and, fifthly, there was a very bad smallpox ju-ju abroad in the land (a secret society whose "secret" was to offer His

3

Majesty's liege subjects the choice between being infected
with smallpox, or paying heavy blackmail to the society).
Lastly, there was acrimonious correspondence with the
All-Wise Ones (of the Secretariat in "Aiki Square" at
Zungeru), who, as usual, knew better than the man on
the spot, and bade him do either the impossible or the
disastrous.

And across all the *Harmattan* was blowing hard, that
terrible wind that carries the Saharan dust a hundred
miles to sea, not so much as a sand-storm, but as a mist
or fog of dust as fine as flour, filling the eyes, the lungs,
the pores of the skin, the nose and throat; getting into
the locks of rifles, the works of watches and cameras, defiling
water, food and everything else; rendering life a burden
and a curse.

The fact, moreover, that thirty days' weary travel over
burning desert, across oceans of loose wind-blown sand
and prairies of burnt grass, through breast-high swamps,
and across unbridged boatless rivers, lay between him and
Kano, added nothing to his satisfaction. For, in spite of
all, satisfaction there was, inasmuch as Kano was rail-
head, and the beginning of the first stage of the journey
Home. That but another month lay between him and
"leave out of Africa," kept George Lawrence on his feet.

From that wonderful and romantic Red City, Kano,
sister of Timbuktu, the train would take him, after a three
days' dusty journey, to the rubbish-heap called Lagos,
on the Bight of Benin of the wicked West African Coast.
There he would embark on the good ship *Appam*, greet
her commander, Captain Harrison, and sink into a deck
chair with that glorious sigh of relief, known in its per-
fection only to those weary ones who turn their backs
upon the Outposts and set their faces towards Home.

Meantime, for George Lawrence—disappointment, worry,
frustration, anxiety, heat, sand-flies, mosquitoes, dust,
fatigue, fever, dysentery, malarial ulcers, and that great
depression which comes of monotony indescribable, weariness unutterable, and loneliness unspeakable.

And the greatest of these is loneliness.

§ 2.

But, in due course, George Lawrence reached Kano and the Nassarawa Gate in the East Wall, which leads to the European segregation, there to wait for a couple of days for the bi-weekly train to Lagos. These days he whiled away in strolling about the wonderful Haussa city, visiting the market-place, exploring its seven square miles of streets of mud houses, with their ant-proof *dôm*-palm beams; watching the ebb and flow of varied black and brown humanity at the thirteen great gates in its mighty earthen ramparts; politely returning the cheery and respectful *"Sanu! Sanu!"* greetings of the Haussas who passed this specimen of the great Bature race, the wonderful white men.

Idly he compared the value of the caravans of salt or of ground-nuts with that of the old slave-caravans which the white man thinks he has recently suppressed; and casually passed the time of day with Touareg camel-drivers, who invited him to hire or buy their piebald, brindled, or white camels, and, occasionally, a rare and valuable beast of the tawny reddish buff variety, so prized for speed and endurance. . . .

On the platform of Kano Station (imagine a platform and station at Kano, ancient, mysterious, gigantic, emporium of Central Africa, with its great eleven-mile wall, and its hundred thousand native inhabitants and its twenty white men; Kano, eight hundred miles from the sea, near the border of Northern Nigeria which marches with the French *Territoire Militaire* of Silent Sahara; Kano, whence start the caravan routes to Lake Tchad on the north-east, and Timbuktu on the north-west)—on this incredible platform, George Lawrence was stirred from his weary apathy by a pleasant surprise in the form of his old friend, Major Henri de Beaujolais of the Spahis, now some kind of special staff-officer in the French Soudan.

With de Beaujolais, Lawrence had been at Ainger's House at Eton; and the two occasionally met, as thus, on the Northern Nigerian Railway; on the ships of Messrs.

Elder, Dempster; at Lord's; at Longchamps; at Auteuil; and, once or twice, at the house of their mutual admired friend, Lady Brandon, at Brandon Abbas in Devonshire.

For de Beaujolais, Lawrence had a great respect and liking, as a French soldier of the finest type, keen as mustard, hard as nails, a thorough sportsman, and a gentleman according to the exacting English standard. Frequently he paid him the remarkable English compliment, "One would hardly take you for a Frenchman, Jolly, you might almost be English," a bouquet which de Beaujolais received with less concern by reason of the fact that his mother had been a Devonshire Cary.

Although the Spahi officer was heavily bearded, arrayed in what Lawrence considered hopelessly ill-fitting khaki, and partially extinguished by a villainous high-domed white helmet (and looked as truly French as his friend looked truly English), he, however, did not throw himself with a howl of joy upon the bosom of his *cher Georges,* fling his arms about his neck, kiss him upon both cheeks, nor address him as his little cabbage. Rather as his old bean, in fact.

A strong hand-grip, "Well, George!" and, "Hallo! Jolly, old son," sufficed; but de Beaujolais' charming smile and Lawrence's beaming grin showed their mutual delight.

And when the two men were stretched opposite to each other on the long couches of their roomy compartment, and had exchanged plans for spending their leave—yachting, golf, and the Moors, on the one hand; and Paris boulevards, race-courses, and Monte Carlo, on the other—Lawrence found that he need talk no more, for his friend was bursting and bubbling over with a story, an unfathomable intriguing mystery, which he must tell or die.

As the train steamed on from Kano Station and its marvellous medley of Arabs, Haussas, Yorubas, Kroos, Egbas, Beri-Beris, Fulanis, and assorted Nigerians from *sarkin, sheikh, shehu,* and *matlaki,* to peasant, camel-man, agriculturist, herdsman, shopkeeper, clerk, soldier, tin-mine worker, and nomad, with their women and *piccins,* the Frenchman began his tale.

Through Zaria, Minna Junction, and Zungeru, across the Jebba Bridge over the Niger, through Ilorin, Oshogbo, and mighty Ibadan to vast Abeokuta, with brief intervals during which Lawrence frankly snored, de Beaujolais told his tale. But at Abeokuta, George Lawrence received the surprise of his life and the tale suddenly became of the most vital interest to him, and from there to Lagos he was all ears.

And as the *Appam* steamed through the sparkling Atlantic, the Frenchman still told his tale—threshed at its mystery, dissected and discussed it, speculated upon it, and returned to it at the end of every digression. Nor ever could George Lawrence have enough—since it indirectly concerned the woman whom he had always loved.

When the two parted in London, Lawrence took it up and continued it himself, until he, in his turn, brought it back to his friend and told him its beginning and end.

§ 3.

And the story, which Major Henri de Beaujolais found so intriguing, he told to George Lawrence as follows:—

"I tell you, my dear George, that it is the most extraordinary and inexplicable thing that ever happened. I shall think of nothing else until I have solved the mystery, and you must help me. You, with your trained official mind, detached and calm; your *phlegme Britannique.*

Yes—you shall be my Sherlock Holmes, and I will be your wonder-stricken little Watson. Figure me then as the little Watson; address me as 'My dear Watson.'

Having heard my tale—and I warn you, you will hear little else for the next two or three weeks—you must unhesitatingly make a pronouncement. Something prompt and precise, my dear friend, *hein?*"

"Quite," replied Lawrence. "But suppose you give me the facts first?"

"It was like this, my dear Holmes. . . . As you are aware, I am literally buried alive in my present job at Tokotu. But yes, with a burial-alive such as you of the Nigerian Civil Service have no faintest possible conception, in the uttermost Back of Beyond. (You, with your Maiduguri Polo Club! Pouf!) Yes, interred living, in the southernmost outpost of the *Territoire Militaire* of the Sahara, a spot compared with which the very loneliest and vilest Algerian border-hole would seem like Sidi-bel-Abbès itself, Sidi-bel-Abbès like Algiers, Algiers like Paris in Africa, and Paris like God's Own Paradise in Heaven.

Seconded from my beloved regiment, far from a boulevard, a café, a club, far, indeed, from everything that makes life supportable to an intelligent man, am I entombed . . ."

"I've had some," interrupted Lawrence unsympathetically. "Get on with the Dark Mystery."

"I see the sun rise and set; I see the sky above, and the desert below; I see my handful of *cafard*-stricken men in my mud fort, black Senegalese, and white mule-mounted infantry whom I train, poor devils; and what else do I see? What else from year's end to year's end? . . ."

"I shall weep in a minute," murmured Lawrence. "What about the Dark Mystery?"

"What do I see?" continued the Major, ignoring the unworthy remark. "A vulture. A jackal. A lizard. If I am lucky and God is good, a slave-caravan from Lake Tchad. A band of veiled Touaregs led by a Targui bandit-chief, thirsting for the blood of the hated white *Roumi*—and I bless them even as I open fire or lead the attack of my mule-cavalry-playing-at-Spahis. . . ."

"The Dark Mystery must have been a perfect godsend, my dear Jolly," smiled Lawrence, as he extracted his cheroot-case and extended it to his eloquent friend, lying facing him on the opposite couch-seat of the uncomfortable carriage of the Nigerian Railway. "What *was* it?"

"A godsend, indeed," replied the Frenchman. "Sent of God, surely to save my reason and my life. But I doubt if the price were not a little high, even for that! The deaths of so many brave men. . . . And one of those deaths a dastardly cold-blooded murder! The vile assassination of a gallant *sous-officier*. . . . And by one of his

own men. In the very hour of glorious victory. . . . *One of
his own men*—I am certain of it. But why? *Why?* I ask
myself night and day. And now I ask you, my friend.
. . . The motive, I ask? . . . But you shall hear all—
and instantly solve the problem, my dear Holmes, eh? . . .

Have you heard of our little post of Zinderneuf (far,
far north of Zinder which is in the Aïr country), north
of your Nigeria? No? Well you hear of it now, and
it is where this incomprehensible tragedy took place.

Behold me then, one devilish hot morning, yawning in
my pyjamas over a *gamelle* of coffee, in my quarters, while
from the *caserne* of my *légionnaires* come the cries of '*Au
jus,*' '*Au jus,*' as one carries round the jug of coffee
from bed to bed, and arouses the sleepers to another day
in Hell. And then as I wearily light a wretched cigarette
of our beastly *caporal*, there comes running my orderly,
babbling I know not what of a dying Arab *goum*—they are
always dying of fatigue these fellows, if they have hurried
a few miles—on a dying camel, who cries at the gate
that he is from Zinderneuf, and that there is siege and
massacre, battle, murder, and sudden death. All slain
and expecting to be killed. All dead and the buglers blowing the Regimental Call, the rally, the charge; making
the devil of a row, and so forth. . . .

'*And is it the dying camel that cries all this?*' I ask,
even as I leap into my belts and boots, and rush to the
door and shout, '*Aux armes! Aux armes!*' to my splendid fellows and wish to God they were my Spahis. '*But,
no, Monsieur le Majeur,*' declares the orderly, '*it is the
dying goum, dying of fatigue on the dying camel.*'

'*Then bid him not die, on pain of death, till I have
questioned him,*' I reply as I load my revolver. '*And
tell the Sergeant-Major that an advance-party of the Foreign Legion on camels marches en tenue de campagne
d'Afrique in nine minutes from when I shouted "Aux
armes." The rest of them on mules.*' You know the sort
of thing, my friend. You have turned out your guard of
Haussas of the West African Frontier Force nearly as
quickly and smartly at times, no doubt."

"Oh, nearly, nearly, perhaps. *Toujours la politesse*," murmured Lawrence.

"As we rode out of the gate of my fort, I gathered from the still-dying *goum*, on the still-dying camel, that a couple of days before, a large force of Touaregs had been sighted from the look-out platform of Zinderneuf fort. Promptly the wise *sous-officier*, in charge and command since the lamented death of Captain Renouf, had turned the *goum* loose on his fast *mehari* camel, with strict orders not to be caught by the Touaregs if they invested the fort, but to clear out and trek with all speed for help—as it appeared to be a case of too heavy odds. If the Touaregs were only playful, and passed the fort by, after a little sporting pot-shotting, he was to follow them, I suppose, see them safe off the premises for a day or two, and discover what they were out for.

Well, away went the *goum*, stood afar off on a sand-hill, saw the Touaregs skirmish up to the oasis, park their camels among the palms, and seriously set about investing the place. He thought it was time for him to go when they had surrounded the fort, were lining the sand-hills, making nice little trenches in the sand, climbing the palm trees, and pouring in a very heavy fire. He estimated them at ten thousand rifles, so I feared that there must be at least five hundred of the cruel fiends. Anyhow, round wheeled Monsieur Goum and rode hell-for-leather, night and day, for help. . . .

Like *How we brought the good news from Aix to Ghent*, and *Paul Revere's Ride* and all. I christened the *goum*, Paul Revere, straight away, when I heard his tale, and promised him all sorts of good things, including a good hiding if I found he had not exceeded the speed limit all the way from Aix to Ghent. Certainly his 'Roland' looked as if its radiator had boiled all right. And, *Nom d'un nom d'nom de bon Dieu de sort!* but I made a forced march of it, my friend—and when we of the Nineteenth African Division do *that*, even on mules and camels, you can hardly see us go."

"Oh, come now! I am sure your progress is perceptible," said Lawrence politely. "Specially on camels, and all that. . . . You're too modest," he added.

"I mean you can hardly see us go for dust and small stones, by reason of our swiftness. . . . Any more than you can see a bullet, witty one," rebuked de Beaujolais.

"Oh, quite, quite," murmured the Englishman.

"Anyhow, I was away with the advance-party on swift *mehari* camels, a mule-squadron was following, and a company of Senegalese would do fifty kilometres a day on foot till they reached Zinderneuf. Yes, and, in what I flatter myself is the unbreakable record time between To-kotu and Zinderneuf, we arrived—and, riding far on in advance of my men, I listened for the sound of firing or of bugle-calls.

I heard no sound whatever, and suddenly topping a ridge I came in sight of the fort—there below me on the desert plain, near the tiny oasis.

There was no fighting, no sign of Touaregs, no trace of battle or siege. No blackened ruins strewn with muti-lated corpses here. The Tri-couleur flew merrily from the flag-staff, and the fort looked absolutely normal—a square grey block of high, thick mud walls, flat castellated roof, flanking towers, and lofty look-out platform. All was well! The honour of the Flag of France had been well defended. I waved my *képi* above my head and shouted aloud in my glee.

Perhaps I began composing my Report then and there, doing modest justice to the readiness, promptitude, and dispatch of my little force, which had maintained the glorious traditions of the Nineteenth African Division; giving due praise to the *sous-officier* commanding Zinder-neuf, and not forgetting Paul Revere and his Roland. . . . Meanwhile, they should know that relief was at hand, and that, be the Touaregs near or be they far, the danger was over and the Flag safe. I, Henri de Beaujolais of the Spahis, had brought relief. I fired my revolver half a dozen times in the air. And then I was aware of a small but remarkable fact. The high look-out platform at the top of its long ladder was empty.

Strange! Very strange! Incredibly strange, at the very moment when great marauding bands of Touaregs were known to be about—and one of them had only just been beaten off, and might attack again at any moment. I must offer the *sous-officier* my congratulations upon the excellence of his look-out, as soon as I had embraced and commended him! New as he might be to independent command, this should never have happened. One would have thought he could as soon have forgotten his boots as his sentry on the look-out platform.

A pretty state of affairs, *bon Dieu*, in time of actual war! Here was I approaching the fort in broad light of day, firing my revolver—and not the slightest notice taken! I might have been the entire Touareg nation or the whole German army. . . .

No, there must be something wrong, in spite of the peaceful look of things and the safety of the Flag—and I pulled out my field-glasses to see if they would reveal anything missed by the naked eye.

As I halted and waited for my camel to steady himself, that I might bring the glasses to bear, I wondered if it were possible that this was an ambush.

Could the Arabs have captured the place, put the defenders to the sword, put on their uniforms, cleaned up the mess, closed the gates, left the Flag flying, and now be waiting for a relieving force to ride, in trustful innocence and close formation, up to the muzzles of their rifles? Possible—but quite unlike brother Touareg! You know what *his* way is, when he has rushed a post or broken a square. A dirty fighter, if ever there was one! And as I focussed my glasses on the walls, I rejected the idea.

Moreover, yes, there were the good European faces of the men at the embrasures, bronzed and bearded, but unmistakably not Arab. . . .

And yet, that again was strange. At every embrasure of the breast-high parapet round the flat roof stood a soldier, staring out across the desert, and most of them staring along their levelled rifles too; some of them straight at me. Why? There was no enemy about. Why were they not sleeping the sleep of tired victors, below on their cots in the *caserne*, while double sentries watched from the high look-out platform? Why no man up there, and yet a man at every embrasure that I could see from where I sat on my camel, a thousand metres distant?

And why did no man move; no man turn to call out to a sergeant that a French officer approached; no man walk to the door leading down from the roof, to inform the Commandant of the fort?

Anyhow, the little force had been extraordinarily lucky, or the shooting of the Arabs extraordinarily bad, that they should still be numerous enough to man the walls in that fashion—'all present and correct,' as you say in your army—and able to stand to arms thus, after two or three days of it, more or less.

As I lowered my glasses and urged my camel forward, I came to the conclusion that I was expected, and that the officer in charge was indulging in a little natural and excusable *fantaisie,* showing off—what you call 'putting on the dog,' eh?

He was going to let me find everything as the Arabs found it when they made their foolish attack—every man at his post and everything *klim-bim*. Yes, that must be it. . . . Ah, it was! Even as I watched, a couple of shots were fired from the wall. They had seen me. . . . The fellow, in his joy, was almost shooting *at* me, in fact!

And yet—nobody on the look-out platform. How I would prick that good fellow's little bubble of swank! And I smiled to myself as I rode under the trees of the oasis to approach the gates of the fort.

It was the last time I smiled for quite a little while.

Among the palm trees were little pools of dried and blackened blood where men had fallen, or wounded men had been laid, showing that, however intact the garrison of the fort might be, their assailants had paid toll to the good Lebel rifles of my friends.

And then I rode out from the shade of the oasis and up to the gate.

Here half a dozen or so kept watch, looking out over

the wall above, as they leant in the embrasures of the parapet. The nearest was a huge fellow, with a great bushy grey moustache, from beneath which protruded a short wooden pipe. His *képi* was cocked rakishly over one eye, as he stared hard at me with the other, half closed and leering, while he kept his rifle pointed straight at my head.

I was glad to feel certain that he at least was no Arab, but a tough old legionary, a typical *vieille moustache,* and rough soldier of fortune. But I thought his joke a poor one and over-personal, as I looked up into the muzzle of his unwavering rifle. . . .

'*Congratulations, my children,*' I cried. '*France and I are proud to salute you,*' and raised my *képi* in homage to their courage and their victory.

Not one of them saluted. Not one of them answered. Not one of them stirred. Neither a finger nor an eyelid moved. I was annoyed. If this was 'making *fantaisie,*' as they call it in the Legion, it was making it at the wrong moment and in the wrong manner.

'*Have you of the Foreign Legion no manners?*' I shouted. '*Go, one of you, at once, and call your officer.*' Not a finger nor an eyelid moved.

I then addressed myself particularly to old Grey-Moustache. '*You,*' I said, pointing up straight at his face, '*go at once and tell your Commandant that Major de Beaujolais of the Spahis has arrived from Tokotu with a relieving force—and take that pipe out of your face and step smartly, do you hear?*'

And then, my friend, I grew a little uncomfortable, though the impossible truth did not dawn upon me. Why did the fellow remain like a graven image, silent, motionless, remote—like an Egyptian god on a temple wall, looking with stony and unseeing eye into my puny human face?

Why were they all like stone statues? Why was the fort so utterly and horribly silent? Why did nothing *move,* there in the fierce sunlight of the dawn? Why this tomb-like, charnel-house, inhuman silence and immobility?

Where were the usual sounds and stir of an occupied

post? Why had no sentry seen me from afar and cried the news aloud? Why had there been no clang and clatter at the gate? Why had the gate not been opened? Why no voice, no footstep in all the place? Why did these men ignore me as though I were a beetle on the sand? Where was their officer? . . .

Was this a nightmare in which I seemed for ever doomed to ride voiceless and invisible, round endless walls, trying to attract the attention of those who could never be aware of me?

When, as in a dream, I rode right round the place, and beheld more and more of those motionless silent forms, with their fixed, unwinking eyes, I clearly saw that one of them, whose *képi* had fallen from his head, had a hole in the centre of his forehead and was dead—although at his post, with chest and elbows leaning on the parapet, and looking as though about to fire his rifle!

I am rather near-sighted, as you know, but then the truth dawned upon me—they were *all* dead!

'*Why were they not sleeping the sleep of tired victors?*' I had asked myself a few minutes before. They *were*. . . .

Yes, all of them. *Mort sur le champ d'honneur!* . . .

My friend, I rode back to where Grey-Moustache kept his last watch, and, baring my head, I made my apologies to him, and the tears came into my eyes. Yes, and I, Henri de Beaujolais of the Spahis, admit it without shame.

I said, '*Forgive me, my friend.*' What would you, an Englishman, have said?"

"What about a spot of tea?" quoth Mr. George Lawrence, reaching beneath the seat for his tiffin-basket.

§ 4.

After a dusty meal, impatiently swallowed by Major de Beaujolais, that gentleman resumed his story, with serious earnestness and some gesticulation, while, on the opposite side of the carriage, George Lawrence lay upon his back, his clasped hands beneath his head, idly watching the smoke that curled up from his cheroot. But he was paying closer attention to the Frenchman's tale.

"But, of course, it soon occurred to me," continued that gentleman, "that someone must be alive. . . . Shots had been fired to welcome me. . . . Those corpses had not of *themselves* taken up those incredibly life-like attitudes. Whoever had propped them up and arranged them and their rifles in position, must be alive.

For, naturally, not all had been struck by Arab bullets and remained standing in the embrasures. Nine times out of ten, as you know, a man staggers back and falls, when shot standing.

Besides, what about the wounded? There is always a far bigger percentage of wounded than of killed in any engagement. Yes, there must be survivors, possibly all more or less wounded, below in the *caserne*.

But surely *one* of them might have kept a look-out. Probably the Commandant and all the non-commissioned officers were killed.

Even then, though, one would have expected the senior man—even if the survivors were all *soldats deuxième classe* —to have taken that much ordinary military precaution! . . .

Well, I would soon solve the problem, for my troop was approaching, my trumpeter with them. I was glad to note that my Sergeant-Major had evidently had a similar idea to mine, for, on coming in sight of the fort, he had opened out and skirmished up in extended order—in spite of the bravely-flying Flag.

When my men arrived, I had the 'rouse,' the 'alarm,' the Regimental Call, sounded by the trumpeter—fully expecting, after each blast, that the gates would open, or at least that someone would come running up from below on to the roof.

Not a sound nor a movement! . . . Again and again; call after call . Not a sound nor a movement!

'Perhaps the last one or two are badly wounded,' thought I. 'There may not be a man able to crawl from his bed. The fellow who propped those corpses up may have been shot in the act, and be lying up there, or on his cot,' and I bade the trumpeter cease. Sending for the *Chef,* as we

call the Sergeant-Major, I ordered him to knot camel-
cords, sashes, girths, reins, anything, make a rope, and
set an active fellow to climb from the back of a camel, into
an embrasure, and give me a hoist up.

That Sergeant-Major is one of the bravest and coolest
men I have ever known, and his collection of *ferblanterie*
includes the Croix and the Medaille given on the field, for
valour.

'It is a trap, *mon Commandant,*' said he. 'Do not walk
into it. Let me go.' Brave words—but he looked queer,
and I knew that though he feared nothing living, he was
afraid.

'The dead keep good watch, *Chef,*' said I, and I think he
shivered.

'They would warn us, *mon Commandant,*' said he. 'Let
me go.'

'We will neither of us go,' said I. 'We will have the
courage to remain in our proper place, with our men. It
may be a trap, though I doubt it. We will send a man
in, and if it is a trap, we shall know—and without losing
an officer unnecessarily. If it is not a trap, the gates will
be opened in two minutes.'

'The Dead are watching and listening,' said the *Chef,*
glancing up, and he crossed himself, averting his eyes.

'Send me that drunken *mauvais sujet,* Rastignac,' said
I, and the Sergeant-Major rode away.

'May I go, *mon Commandant?*' said the trumpeter,
saluting.

'Silence,' said I. My nerves were getting a little on
edge, under that silent, mocking scrutiny of the watching
Dead. When the Sergeant-Major returned with a rope,
and the rascal Rastignac—whose proper place was in the
Joyeux, the terrible Penal Battalions of convicted criminals
—I ordered him to climb from his camel on to the roof.

'Not I, *mon Officier,*' replied he promptly. 'Let me go to
Hell dead, not living. I don't mind joining corpses *as a*
corpse. You can shoot me.'

'That can I, of a surety,' I agreed, and drew my re
volver. 'Ride your camel under that projecting water-

spout,' said I. 'Stand on its back, and spring to the spout Climb into the embrasure, and then go down and open the gates.'

'Not I, *mon Officier*,' said Rastignac again. I raised my revolver, and the Sergeant-Major snatched the man's rifle.

'Have you *le cafard?*' I asked, referring to the desert-madness that, bred of monotony, boredom, misery, and hardship, attacks European soldiers in these outposts—especially absinthe-drinkers—and makes them do strange things, varying from mutiny, murder, and suicide to dancing about naked, or thinking they are lizards or emperors or clock-pendulums.

'I have a dislike for intruding upon a dead Company that stands to arms and keeps watch,' replied the fellow.

'For the last time—*go*,' said I, aiming between his eyes.

'Go yourself, *Monsieur le Majeur*,' replied Rastignac, and I pulled the trigger. . . . Was I right, my friend?"

"Dunno," replied Lawrence, yawning.

"There was a click, and Rastignac smiled. I had emptied my revolver when approaching the fort, as I have told you.

'You can live—to be court-martialled and join the *Batt d'Af*,' said I. 'You will be well placed among the *Joyeux*.'

'Better among those than the Watchers above, *mon Officier*,' said my beauty, and I bade the Sergeant-Major take his bayonet and put him under arrest.

'You may show this coward the way,' said I to the trumpeter, and, in a minute, that one had sprung at the spout, clutched it, and was scrambling on to the wall. He was *un brave*.

'We will proceed as though the place were held by an enemy—until the gates are opened,' said I to the Sergeant-Major, and we rode back to the troop and handed Rastignac over to the Corporal, who clearly welcomed him in the rôle of prisoner.

'*Vous—pour la boîte*,' smiled the Corporal, licking his lips. And then we watched and waited. I could see that the men were immensely puzzled and intrigued. Not an eye wandered. I would have given something to have known what each man thought concerning this unique experience. A perfectly silent fort, the walls fully manned, the Flag flying—and the gates shut. No vestige of a sign from that motionless garrison staring out into the desert, aiming their rifles at nothing—and at *us*. . . .

We watched and waited. Two minutes passed; five; six; *seven*. What could it mean? *Was* it a trap after all?

'*That* one won't return!' said Rastignac loudly, and gave an eerie jarring laugh. The Corporal smote him on the mouth, and I heard him growl, 'What about a little *crapaudine* [1] and a mouthful of sand my friend? . . . You speak again!' . . .

At the end of ten minutes, a very *Mauvaise quart d'heure*, I beckoned the Sergeant-Major. I could stand the strain no longer.

'I am going in,' said I. 'I cannot send another man, although I ought to do so. Take command. . . . If you do not see me within ten minutes, and nothing happens, assault the place. Burn down the gates and let a party climb the walls, while another charges in. Keep a half-troop, under the Corporal, in reserve.'

'Let me go, *mon Commandant*,' begged the *Chef*, 'if you will not send another soldier. Or call for a volunteer to go. Suppose you . . .'

'Silence, *Chef*,' I replied, 'I am going,' and I rode back to the fort. Was I right, George?"

"Dunno," replied George Lawrence.

"I remember thinking, as I rode back, what a pernicious fool I should look if, under the eyes of all—the living and the dead—I failed to accomplish that, by no means easy, scramble, and had ignominiously to admit my inability to climb up where the trumpeter had gone. It is sad when one's vile body falls below the standard set by the aspiring soul, when the strength of the muscles is inadequate to the courage of the heart. . . .

1 Torture. The hands and feet tied together in a bunch in the middle of the back.

However, all went well, and, after an undignified dangling from the spout, and wild groping with the raised foot, I got a leg over the ledge, scrambled up and crawled into an embrasure.

And there I stood astounded and dumbfounded, *tout bouleversé,* unable to believe my eyes.

There, as in life, stood the garrison, their backs to me, their faces to the foe whom they had driven off, their feet in dried pools of their own blood—watching, watching. . . . And soon I forgot what might be awaiting me below, I forgot my vanished trumpeter, I forgot my troop waiting without—*for there was something else.*

Lying on his back, his sightless eyes out-staring the sun—lay the Commandant, and through his heart, *a bayonet,* one of our long, thin French sword-bayonets with its single-curved hilt! No—he had not been shot, he was absolutely untouched elsewhere, and there he lay with a French bayonet through his heart. What do you say to that, my friend?"

"Suicide," replied Lawrence.

"And so did I, until I realised that he had a loaded revolver in one hand, one chamber fired, and a crushed letter in the other! *Does* a man drive a bayonet through his heart, and then take a revolver in one hand and a sheet of paper in the other? I think not.

Have you ever seen a man drive a bayonet through his heart, my friend? Believe me, he does not fumble for letters, nor draw a revolver and fire it, after he has done *that.* No. He gasps, stares, staggers. He grips the handle and the *forte* of the blade with both hands, totters, stretches convulsively, and collapses, crashing to the ground. . . . In any case, does a man commit suicide with a bayonet when he has a loaded revolver? . . Suicide? *Pouf.*

Was it any wonder that my jaw dropped and I forgot all else, as I stared and stared. . . . *Voyez donc!* A French fort in the Sahara, besieged by Arabs. Every man killed at his post. The Arabs beaten off. The fort inviolate, untrodden by Arab foot. The gates closed. Within—the dead, and one of them slain by a French bayonet while he held a loaded revolver in his hand! . . .

But *was* the fort inviolate and untrodden by Arab foot?
If so, what had become of my trumpeter? Might not the
Arabs be hiding below, waiting their opportunity to catch
the relieving force unawares? Might not there be an Arab
eye at every rifle-slit? Might not the *caserne,* rooms, offices, sheds, be packed with them?

Absurdly improbable—and why should they have slain
the Commandant with a French bayonet? Would they not
have hacked him to pieces with sword and spear, and
have mutilated and decapitated every corpse in the place?
Was it like the wild Touareg to lay so clever a trap with
the propped-up bodies, that a relieving force might fall
into their hands as well? Never. *Peaudezébie!* Had the
Arabs entered here, the place would have been a looted,
blackened ruin, defiled, disgusting, strewn with pieces of
what had been men. No, this was not Arab work.

These Watchers, I felt certain, had been compelled by
this dead man, who lay before me, to continue as defenders
of the fort after their deaths. . . . He was evidently a *man.*
A bold, resourceful, undaunted hero, sardonic, of a macabre
humour, as the Legion always is.

As each man fell, throughout that long and awful day,
he had propped him up, wounded or dead, set the rifle
in its place, fired it, and bluffed the Arabs that every wall
and every embrasure and loophole of every wall was fully
manned. He must, at the last, have run from point to
point, firing a rifle from behind its dead defender. Every
now and then he must have blown the alarm that the
bugler would never blow again, in the hope that it would
guide and hasten the relieving force and impress the
Arabs with the fear that the avengers must be near.

No wonder the Arabs never charged that fort, from
each of whose walls a rifle cracked continuously, and from
whose every embrasure watched a fearless man whom they
could not kill—or whose place seemed to be taken, at once,
by another, if they did kill him. . . .

All this passed through my mind in a few seconds—
and as I realised what he had done and how he had died

in the hour of victory, *murdered,* my throat swelled though my blood boiled—and I ventured to give myself the proud privilege of kneeling beside him and pinning my own Croix upon his breast—though I could scarcely see to do so. I thought of how France should ring with the news of his heroism, resource, and last glorious fight, and how every Frenchman should clamour for the blood of his murderer.

Only a poor *sous-officier* of the Legion. But a hero for France to honour. . . . And I would avenge him!

Such were my thoughts, my friend, as I realised the truth—what are yours?"

"Time for a spot of dinner," said George Lawrence, starting up.

§ 5.

Next morning, as the two lay awake on their dusty bedding, begrimed, tousled, pyjama-clad, awaiting the next stop, bath, and breakfast, de Beaujolais lit a cigarette, turned on his side, and fixed his friend with the earnest troubled gaze of his bright brown eye.

"Well, George, *who killed him*—and why?"

"Oh, Ancient Mariner!" yawned Lawrence.

"What?"

"I feel like the Wedding Guest."

"You look like one, my George," smiled the Frenchman.

"Get on with it, Jolly."

"How was the Commandant of that fort killed?"

"Someone 'threatened his life with a railway-share.' "

"Be serious, little George. I want your help. I *must* get to the bottom of this. Where did I leave off?"

"God knows. I was asleep."

"Ah! I was on the roof, pinning my Croix on the breast of the bravest man I have ever met. Your General Gordon in miniature! This obscure and humble soul had kept his country's Flag flying, as that great man did at Khartoum, and, like him, he had been relieved too late. But yes, and there it flapped above my head and recalled me to myself.

I rose, drew my revolver, loaded it, and walked to the door. As I was about to descend into that silence I had a little idea. I looked at each of the Watchers in turn. No. Each man had his bayonet, of course. I had not really supposed that one of them had stabbed his officer and then gone back to his post and died on his feet! He would have fallen—or possibly have hung limply through the embrasure. I raised my weapon and descended the stairs—expecting I know not what, in that sinister stillness—that had swallowed up my trumpeter. And what do you think I found there, my friend?"

"Dunno," said George Lawrence.

"*Nothing.* No one and nothing. Not even the man who had fired the two shots of welcome! . . . As I had felt sure, really, all along, no Arab had entered the fort. That leapt to the eye at once. The place was as tight shut as this fist of mine—and as empty of Arab traces. The *caserne* was as orderly and tidy as when the men left it and stood to arms—the *paquetages* on the shelves, the table-apparatus in the hanging cupboards, the *gamelles* and cleaning-bags at the heads of the beds, the bedding folded and straight. There had evidently been room-inspection just before the sentry on the look-out platform had cried, '*Aux armes! Aux armes! Les Arabes!*' and all had rushed to their posts.

No, not a thing was missing or awry. The whole place might just have been made ready by an outgoing garrison, to be taken over by the incoming garrison. No Arab had scaled those walls nor wriggled through the keyhole of the gate. The stores were untouched—the rice, the biscuits, bread, coffee, wine, nothing was missing . . ."

"Except a rifle," grunted Lawrence.

"My friend you've said it! Where was the rifle belonging to the bayonet that was driven through the heart of the murdered officer up above? That was precisely the question that my crazed mind was asking itself as I realised that the fort had never been entered.

Had a corpse bayoneted that *sous-officier,* returned to its post, and flung the rifle to the horizon? Scarcely.

Had an Arab—expert in throwing knife or bayonet as in throwing the *matrak*—possessed himself of a French bayonet, after some desert-massacre of one of our tiny expeditionary columns? And had he got near enough to the fort to throw it? And had it by chance, or skill of the thrower, penetrated the heart of the Commandant of the garrison?"

"Possibly," said Lawrence.

"So I thought for a moment," replied de Beaujolais, "though why a man armed with a breech-loading rifle, should leave the cover of his sand-hill, trench, or palm tree, and go about throwing bayonets, I don't know. And then I remembered that the bayonet went through the breast of the *sous-officier* in a slightly *upward* direction from front to back. Could a bayonet be thrown thus into the middle of a wide roof?"

"Sold again," murmured Lawrence.

"No, I had to abandon that idea. As untenable as the returning-corpse theory. And I was driven, against common sense, to conclude that the officer had been bayoneted by one of his own men, the sole survivor, who had then detached the rifle from the bayonet and fled from the fort. But why? *Why?* If such was the explanation of the officer's death—why on earth had not the murderer shot him *and calmly awaited the arrival of the relieving force?*

Naturally all would have supposed that the brave Commandant had been shot, like all the rest, by the Arabs.

Instead of fleeing to certain death from thirst and starvation, or torture at the hands of the Arabs, why had not the murderer awaited, in comfort, the honours, *réclame,* reward, and promotion that would most assuredly have been his? Obviously, the man who—lusting for blood and vengeance on account of some real or fancied wrong —could murder his superior at such a moment, would be the very one to see the beauty of getting a rich and glorious reward as a sequel to his revenge. Without a doubt he would have shot him through the head, propped him up with the rest, and accepted the congratulations

of the relieving force for having conceived and executed
the whole scheme of outwitting and defeating the Arabs.
Wouldn't he, George?''

"*I* would," replied George, scratching his head.

"Yes, you would. And I almost sent that theory to
join the other two wild ones—the corpse who returned
to its post, and the Arab who threw sword-bayonets from
afar. Almost—until I remembered that revolver in the
dead man's hand, and the empty cartridge-case in one
of its chambers. And then I asked myself, 'Does a man
who is conducting the defence of a block-house, against
tremendous odds, waste time in taking pot-shots *with a
revolver* at concealed enemies, two or three hundred yards
distant? Does he do that, with hundreds of rounds of
rifle ammuntion and a score of rifles to his hand?' Of
course not.

That revolver shot was fired at someone *in* the fort. It
was fired point-blank at the man who murdered him—
and the murderer must have been one of his own men,
and that man must have fled from the fort. But again,
why? Why? *Why?*

Why not have shot his officer, as I said before? He
would never have had even the *need* to deny having done
it, for no one would have dreamt of accusing him.

And then I had an idea. I suddenly said to myself,
'Suppose some scoundrel bayoneted the Commandant even
before the alarm was given or the attack began—and
then organised the defence and died at his post with the
others?'

Led a mutiny of the garrison, perhaps; took command;
and was shot and propped up in his embrasure by someone else. Yes, but who propped the last man up? He
did not do it himself, that was certain—for every single
corpse on that roof had been *arranged* before *rigor mortis*
set in. The only man who was not 'to the life' was one
who lay on his back. It was curious, that recumbent corpse
with closed eyes and folded hands, but I did not see that
it offered any clue. Whoever had been doing the ghastly
work of corpse-drilling had overlooked it—or, indeed, had

been going to set the dead man up when the final tragedy,
whatever it was, occurred.

It may have been that the brave *sous-officier* was going
to arrange this very corpse when he was attacked. Or,
as I say, the officer may have been dead the whole time,
or part of it, and the last survivor may have had this last
work cut short by a bullet, before he had put the man in
position.

But if so, where *was* he? . . . Was it the man who
had fired the two shots in answer to mine—and if so,
what had become of him? *Why had he fired if he wished
to hide or escape?*

My head spun. I felt I was going mad.

And then I said to myself, '*Courage, mon brave!* Go
calmly up to that terrible roof again, and just quietly
and clearly make certain of two points. First: Is there
any one of those standing corpses who has not quite obviously been arranged, propped up, fixed in position? If
so—*that* is the man who killed his officer and was afterwards shot by the Arabs. Secondly: Has any one of
those dead men been shot point-blank with a revolver?
(That I should be able to tell at a glance.) If so, *that*
is the man who killed his officer—(who lived long enough
to thrust his assailant into an embrasure). . . .'

"After himself being bayoneted through the heart?"
enquired Lawrence.

"Exactly what I said to myself—and groaned aloud
as I said it," replied de Beaujolais.

"Anyhow," he continued, "I would go up and see if
any man had been shot by a revolver, and if any man
lay *naturally* against the slope of an embrasure. . . . I
turned to ascend the stair, and then, George, and not till
then, I got the *real* shock of that awful day of shocks.
For, *where was my trumpeter?*

I had made a quick but complete tour of the place and
now realised in a flash that I had seen no living thing
and heard no sound.

'*Trompette! Trompette!*' I shouted. I rushed to the
door leading to the courtyard, the little interior, high-
walled parade ground.

'*Trompette!*' I shouted and yelled, again and again, till my voice cracked.

Not a sound. Not a movement.

And then, in something like panic, putting all else from my mind, I rushed to the gates, lifted down the great bars, pulled the heavy bolts, turned the great key, and dragged them open—just as the mule-squadron arrived and my good Sergeant-Major was giving them the signal to join the assault!

It was not that I had suddenly remembered that the time I had allowed him must be up, but that I needed to see a human being again, to hear a human voice, after a quarter of an hour in that House of Death, that sinister abode of tragic mysteries. I felt an urgent and unconquerable yearning for some . . ."

"Breakfast," said George Lawrence, as the train slowed down.

§ 6.

Bathed, full-fed, and at peace with a noisy world, in so far as choking dust, grilling heat, and the weariness of three days' close confinement in a stuffy carriage allowed, the two *compagnons de voyage* lay and smoked the cheroot of digestion in a brief silence. Brief, because it was not in the power of the impulsive and eloquent *beau sabreur,* of the Spahis, to keep silence for long upon the subject uppermost in his active and ardent mind.

"*Georges, mon vieux,*" he broke silence, "do you believe in spirts, ghosts, devils?"

"I firmly believe in whiskey, the ghost of a salary, and a devil of a thin time. Seen 'em myself," was the reply.

"Because the only solution that my Sergeant-Major could offer was just that. . . .

'*Spirits! Ghosts! Devils!*' he whispered, when he realised that the *sous-officier* had been murdered apparently by a corpse, and that the trumpeter had absolutely vanished into thin air, leaving not a trace of himself, and effecting the evaporation of his rifle as well as of his trumpet and everything else.

This was not very helpful, strongly as I was tempted to endorse it.

'Sergeant-Major Dufour,' said I, 'I am going to propound theories and you are going to find the weak points in them. The absurdities and idiocies in them.

Post vedettes far out, all round the place, and let the men fall out and water their beasts in the oasis. Sergeant Lebaudy will be in command. Tell him that fires may be lighted and *soupe* made, but that in an hour's time all are to be on grave-digging fatigue. He is to report immediately when mule-scouts from Lieutenant St. André's advance Senegalese arrive from Tokotu, or if anything happens meanwhile. If a vedette gives the alarm, all are to enter the fort immediately—otherwise no one is to set foot inside. Put a sentry at the gate. . . . You and I will look into this *affaire* while Achmet makes us some coffee'— and I gave the good fellow a cake of chocolate and a measure of cognac from my flask. We were both glad of that cognac.

While he was gone on this business I remained on the roof. I preferred the sunlight while I was alone. I freely admit it. I do not object to Arabs, but I dislike 'spirits, ghosts, and devils'—that commit murders and abductions. Perhaps I was not quite myself. But what would you? I had been enjoying fever; I had ridden all night; I was perilously near *cafard* myself; and the presence of those dead Watchers to whom I had spoken, the finding of that incredibly murdered man, the not finding of that more incredibly vanished trumpeter—had shaken me a little.

As I awaited the return of the Sergeant-Major I gazed at the corpse of the *sous-officier*. I stared and stared at the face of the dead man—not too pleasant a sight, George —contorted with rage, and pain, and hate—dead for some hours and it was getting hot on that roof—and there were flies . . . flies. . . .

I stared, I say, as though I would drag the truth from him, compel the secret of this mystery from his dead lips. hypnotise those dead eyes to turn to mine and—

but no, it was *he* that hypnotised and compelled, until I was fain to look away.

As I did so, I noticed the man who was lying near. Yes, undoubtedly someone had carefully and reverently laid him out. His eyes had been closed, his head propped up on a pouch, and his hands folded upon his chest. Why had he received such different treatment from that meted out to the others? . . .

And then that bareheaded man. It was he—a very handsome fellow too—who had given me my first shock and brought it home to my wondering mind that the men who watched me were all dead.

You see, all but he had their faces in the deep shade of the big peaks of their *képis*—whilst he, bareheaded and shot through the centre of the forehead, was dead obviously—even to short-sighted me, looking up from below against the strong sunlight; even to me, deceived at first by his lifelike attitude.

And, as I glanced at their two *képis* lying there, I noticed something peculiar.

One had been wrenched and torn from within. The lining, newly ripped, was protruding, and the inner leather band was turned down and outward. It was as though something had recently been torn violently out of the cap—something concealed in the lining perhaps? . . .

No, it was not the freak of a ricochetting bullet. The standing man had been hit just above the nose and under the cap, the recumbent man was hit in the chest.

'Now what is this?' thought I. 'A man shot through the brain does not remove his cap and tear the lining out. He gives a galvanic start, possibly spins round, and quietly he falls backwards. His limbs stretch once and quiver, and he is still for ever. His tight-fitting cap may, or may not, fall off as he goes down—but there is no tearing out of the lining, no turning down of the leather band.'

Bullets play funny tricks, I know, but not upon things they do not touch. This bullet had been fired, I should say, from a palm tree, and almost on a level with the roof:

anyhow, it had entered the head below the cap. There was no hole in *that* whatsoever. To which of these two men did the cap belong? . . .

Had all been normal in that terrible place, all lying dead as they had fallen, I might never have noticed this torn cap. As it was—where everything was extraordinary, and the mind of the beholder filled with suspicion and a thousand questions, it was most interesting and remark· able. It became portentous. It was one more phenom· enon in that focus of phenomena!

And from that cap and its recently torn and still protruding lining—oh yes, most obviously torn quite recently, with its edging of unsoiled threads, frayed but clean— from that cap, I looked quite instinctively at the paper crushed in the left hand of the dead officer. I know not why I connected these two things in my mind. They connected themselves perhaps—and I was about to take the paper from the rigid fist, when I thought, 'No! Everything shall be done in order and with correctness. I will touch nothing, do nothing, until the Sergeant-Major returns and I have a witness.'

If I was to be *procureur, juge d'instruction,* judge and jury, coroner, and perhaps, avenger—everything should be done in due form—and my report upon the impossible affair be of some value, too.

But without touching the paper, I could see, and I saw with surprise—though the *bon Dieu* knows I had not much capacity for surprise left in my stunned mind— that the writing was in English!

Why should *that* be added to my conundrums? . . . A paper with English writing on it, in the hand of a dead French officer in a block-house in the heart of the *Terri- toire Militaire* of the Sahara!"

"Perhaps the bloke was English," suggested Lawrence "I have heard that there are some in the Legion."

"No," was the immediate reply. "That he most certainly was not. A typical Frenchman of the Midi—a stoutish, florid, blue-jowled fellow of full habit. Perhaps a Provençal—thousands like him in Marseilles, Arles,

Nimes, Avignon, Carcassonne, Tarascon. Might have been
the good Tartarin himself. Conceivably a Belgian; *possibly* a Spaniard or Italian, but most certainly not an
Englishman. . . . Still less was the standing man, an olive-
cheeked Italian or Sicilian.''

"And the recumbent bareheaded chap?" said Lawrence.

"Ah—quite another affair, that! He might very well
have been English. In fact, had I been asked to guess
at his nationality, I should have said, 'A Northerner
certainly. English most probably.' He would have been
well in the picture in the Officers' Mess of one of your
regiments. Just the type turned out by your Public
Schools and Universities by the thousand.

What you are thinking is exactly what occurred to
me. English writing on the paper; an English-looking
legionary; his cap lying near the man who held the paper
crushed in his hand; the lining just torn out of the cap;
. . . Ha! Here was a little glimmer of light, a possible
clue. I was just reconstructing the scene when I heard
the Sergeant-Major ascending the stair. . . .

Had this Englishman killed the *sous-officier* while the
latter tore some document from the lining of the man's
cap? Obviously not. The poor fellow's bayonet was in
its sheath at his side, and if he *had* done it—how had he
got himself put into position?''

"Might have been shot afterwards," said Lawrence.

"No. He was *arranged*, I tell you," was the reply,
"and he most assuredly had not arranged himself. Besides, he was bareheaded. Does a man go about bear-
headed in the afternoon sun of the Sahara? But to my
mind the question doesn't arise—in view of the fact of
that inexplicable bayonet.

One bayonet more than there were soldiers and rifles!

No—I ceased reconstructing the scene with *that* one as
the slayer, and I had no reason to select anyone else for the
rôle. . . . Then I heard the bull voice of Sergeant Lebaudy,
down in the oasis, roar '*Formez les faisceaux*' and '*Sac
à terre*,' and came back to facts as the Sergeant-Major
approached and saluted.

'All in order, *mon Commandant*,' reported he, and fell to eyeing the corpses.

'Even to half-smoked cigarettes in their mouths!' he whispered. *'The fallen who were not allowed to fall—the dead forbidden to die.'* Then—'But where in the name of God is Jean the Trumpeter?'

'Tell me that, *Chef,* and I will fill your *képi* with twenty-franc pieces—and give you the Grand Cross of the Legion of Honour,' said I.

The Sergeant-Major blasphemed, crossed himself, and then said, 'Let us get out of here while we can.'

'Are you a Sergeant-Major or a young lady?' I enquired—and as one does, in such circumstances, rated him soundly for feeling exactly as I did myself; and the more I said, the more angry and unreasonable I grew. You know how one's head and one's nerves get, in that accursed desert, George.''

''I know, old son,'' agreed Lawrence. ''I have found myself half-ready to murder a *piccin*, for dropping a plate.''

''Yes—the best of us get really insane at times, in that hellish heat and unnatural life. . . . But I got a hold upon myself and felt ashamed—for the good fellow took it well.

'Did Your Excellency make a thorough search?' he asked, rebukingly polite.

'But, my dear *Chef,* what need to make a thorough search for a living man, a hale and hearty, healthy soldier, in a small place into which he had been sent to open a gate? *Mon Dieu!* he has legs! He has a tongue in his head! If he were here, wouldn't he *be* here?' I asked.

'Murdered perhaps,' was the reply.

'By whom? Beetles? Lizards?' I sneered.

He shrugged his shoulders, and pointed to the *sous-officier* with a dramatic gesture.

That one had not been murdered by beetles or lizards!

'Yes,' said I. 'Now we'll reconstruct this crime, first reading what is on this paper,' and I opened the stiffened fingers and took it. There was a dirty crumpled torn envelope there, too. Now *Georges, mon vieux,* prepare yourself. You are going to show a little emotion, my frozen Englishman!''

Lawrence smiled faintly.

"It was a most extraordinary document," continued de Beaujolais. "I'll show it to you when we get on board the ship. It was something like this: On the envelope was, *'To the Chief of Police of Scotland Yard and all whom it may concern.'* And on the paper, *'Confession. Important. Urgent. Please publish.*

For fear that any innocent person may be suspected, I hereby fully and freely confess that it was I, and I alone, who stole the great sapphire known as "Blue Water."' '' ...

"What!" shouted George Lawrence, jumping up. "What? *What* are you saying, de Beaujolais?"

"Aha! my little George," smiled the Frenchman, gloating. "And where is the *phlegme Britannique* now, may I ask? That made you sit up, quite literally, didn't it? We do not yawn now, my little George, do we?"

George Lawrence stared at his friend, incredulous, open-mouthed.

"But that is Lady Brandon's jewel! ... What on earth ..." stammered Lawrence, sitting down heavily. "Are you romancing, de Beaujolais? Being funny?"

"I am telling you what was written on this paper—which I will show you when I can get at my dispatch-case, my friend," was the reply.

"Good God, man! *Lady Brandon!* ... Do you mean to say that the 'Blue Water' has been pinched—and that the thief took refuge in the Foreign Legion, or drifted there somehow?" asked Lawrence, lying back on his roll of bedding.

"I don't mean to say anything—except to tell my little tale, the dull little tale that has bored you so, my George,'" replied de Beaujolais, with a malicious grin.

George Lawrence swung his feet to the ground and stood up again. Never had his friend seen this reserved, taciturn, and unemotional man so affected.

"I don't get you. I don't take it in," he said. "Lady Brandon's stone! *Our* Lady Brandon? The 'Blue Water'

that we used to be allowed to look at sometimes? Stolen!
. . . And you have found it?" . . .

"I have found nothing, my friend, but a crumpled and
bloodstained piece of paper in a dead man's hand," was
the reply.

"With Lady Brandon's name on it! It's absurd, man.
. . . In the middle of the Sahara! And *you* found it. . . .
With her name on it! . . . Well, I'm absolutely damned!"
ejaculated Lawrence.

"Yes, my friend. And perhaps you begin to realise how
'absolutely damned' I was, when I read that paper—sticky
with blood. But probably I was not as surprised as you
are now. Even that could not have surprised me very
much then, I think," said de Beaujolais.

Lawrence sat down.

"Go on, old chap," he begged. "I sincerely apologise
for my recent manners. Please tell me everything, and
then let us thrash it out. . . . Lady Brandon! . . . The
'Blue Water' stolen!" . . .

"No need for apologies, my dear George," smiled his
friend. "If you seemed a little unimpressed and bored at
times, it only gave me the greater zest for the *dénouement*,
when you should hear your . . . our . . . friend's name
come into this extraordinary story."

"You're a wily and patient old devil, Jolly," said the
astounded Lawrence. "I salute you, Sir. A logical old
cuss, too! Fancy keeping *that* back until now, and telling
the yarn neatly, in proper sequence and due order, until
the right point in the story was reached, and then . . ."

"Aha! the *phlegme Britannique*, eh, George!" chuckled
de Beaujolais. "Wonderful how the volatile and impetuous
Frenchman could do it, wasn't it? And there is something
else to come, my friend. All in 'logical proper sequence
and due order' there comes another little surprise."

"Then, for God's sake, get on with it, old chap! . . .
More about Lady Brandon, is it?" replied Lawrence, now
all animation and interest.

"Indirectly, *mon cher Georges*. For that paper was
signed—*by whom?*" asked the Frenchman, leaning forward,

tapping his friend's knee, staring impressively with narrowed eyes into those of that bewildered gentleman.

And into the ensuing silence he slowly and deliberately dropped the words, *"By Michael Geste!"*

Lawrence raised himself on his elbow and stared at his friend incredulous.

"By *Michael Geste!* Her nephew! You don't mean to tell me that *Michael Geste* stole her sapphire and slunk off to the Legion? 'Beau' Geste! *Get* out . . ." he said, and fell back.

"I don't mean to tell you anything, my friend, except that the paper was signed 'Michael Geste.'"

"Was the bareheaded man he? Look here, *are* you pulling my leg?"

"I do not know who the man was, George. And I am not pulling your leg. I saw two or three boys and two so beautiful girls, once, at Brandon Abbas, years ago. This man might have been one of them. The age would be about right. And then, again, this man may have had nothing on earth to do with the paper. Nor any other man on that roof, except the *sous-officier*—and he most certainly was not Michael Geste. He was a man of forty or forty-five years, and as I have said, no Englishman."

"Michael would be about twenty or so," said Lawrence. "He was the oldest of the nephews. . . . But, my dear Jolly, the Gestes don't *steal!* They are her nephews. . . . I am going to put some ice on my head."

"I have wanted a lot of ice to the head, the last few weeks, George. What, too, of the murdered *sous-officier* and the utterly vanished trumpeter?"

"Oh, damn your trumpeter and *sous-officier*," was the explosive reply. "Michael Geste! . . . Lady Brandon. . . . Forgive me, old chap, and finish the story . . ." and George Lawrence lay back on his couch and stared at the roof of the carriage.

Lady Brandon! The only woman in the world.

§ 7.

And as the train rumbled on through the sweltering coastlands toward Lagos, Major de Beaujolais, highly pleased with the success of his neat and clever little *coup,* continued his story.

"Well, my George, figure me there, with this new astoundment, this extraordinary accompaniment to the sinister and bewildering mystery of an inexplicable murder and an inexplicable disappearance. . . .

And then, 'What is in the paper, might one respectfully enquire, *mon Commandant,*' asked the Sergeant-Major.

'The confession of a thief—that he stole a famous jewel,' I replied.

'Which was the thief?' said he.

'Oh, ask me some questions, my good imbecile!' said I. 'Ask me where the trumpeter is, and whose is this bayonet, and who disposed these dead men as defenders, and who fired two shots, and whether I am mad or dreaming,' I answered—and then pulled myself together. 'Now come with me,' I bade him. 'We will make one more search below, and then *déjeuner,* and a quiet, sensible, reasonable discussion of the facts, before we bury these brave fellows, detail an *escouade* of our men as garrison, and return to Tokotu. I shall leave you in command here until we get orders and reliefs.'

The Sergeant-Major looked distinctly dubious at this. '*Here*—for weeks!' he said softly.

We made our tour below, and, as before, nothing unusual met the eye, and there was no sign of the trumpeter, alive or dead. We had seen him climb on to that parapet and apparently no living eye had beheld him again.

I was past wonder. I accepted things.

Very well, this was a place where Commandants are murdered by non-existent people; soldiers vanish like a whiff of smoke; and English letters concerning one's friends are found in the hands of dead Frenchmen. Very good. Be it so. We would 'carry on' as you say, and do our duty.

'Think hard—and be prepared to pick holes in the theories I shall propound an hour hence,' said I to the Sergeant-Major, as we passed out of the gate, and I proceeded to the oasis where my excellent Achmet had prepared my soup and coffee. . . .

You do not want to hear my theories, George, and there was no need for the Sergeant-Major to point out the impossibilities and absurdities in them. They leapt to the eye immediately.

It all came back to the bald facts that there must be a soldier of the garrison missing, that he must have taken his rifle and left his bayonet in the *sous-officier,* instead of shooting him and awaiting praise and reward; that my trumpeter had vanished; that the dead *sous-officier* had been in possession of a confession, real or bogus, to the effect that Michael Geste had stolen his aunt's famous sapphire.

There it was—and nothing but lunacy could result from theory-making about the *sous-officier's* murder, the trumpeter's disappearance, or Michael Geste's confession and how it got there.

No—you do not want to hear those perfectly futile theories—those explanations that explained nothing. But it may interest you to hear that I was faced that evening, on top of the rest of my little pleasures, with a military mutiny."

"Good Lord!" ejaculated Lawrence, turning to the speaker.

"Yes. At four o'clock I ordered the Sergeant-Major to fall the men in, and I would tell off the new garrison for Zinderneuf.

In a most unusual manner the Sergeant-Major hung fire, so to speak, instead of stepping smartly off about his duty.

'Well?' said I sharply.

'There is going to be trouble, *mon Commandant,*' he faltered.

'*Mon Dieu,* there is!' I snapped, 'and *I* am going to make it, if I have any nonsense. What do you mean?'

'Sergeant Lebaudy says that Corporal Brille says that the men say . . .'

'Name of the Name of the Name of Ten Thousand Thundering Tin Devils,' I shouted. . . . 'You say that he says that they say that she says,' I mocked. '*Va t'en, grand babbilard!*' I roared at him. 'I'll be on parade outside those gates in ten seconds, and if you and your gibbering chatterboxes are not awaiting me there at attention . . .' and my poor Sergeant-Major fled.

I was the more angry at his news, for I had subconsciously expected something of the sort.

What else, with these ignorant, superstitious clods, who were the bravest of the brave against human foes? None like them. Every man a hero in battle. . . . But what of that House of Death with its Watchers? That place into which their comrade had boldly climbed—and never come forth again.

Rastignac had begun it. And they had seen him face instant death rather than enter it—Rastignac, the fearless reckless devil, whose bravery alone had prevented his escapades from bringing him to a court-martial and the Zephyrs. He, of all men, was afraid of the place. There is nothing so infectious as *that* sort of panic. . . .

Well! One more fact to accept.

If the men would not enter the fort of Zinderneuf, they would not enter the fort of Zinderneuf—and that was that.

But if the will of these scoundrels was coming into conflict with the will of Henri de Beaujolais, there were exciting times ahead. Since they sought sorrow they should certainly find it—and as I put on my belt and boots again, I felt a certain elation.

'Action is always action, *mon Henri*,' said I to myself, 'and it will be a change from these thrice-accursed theories and attempts to explain the inexplicable and reconcile the irreconcilable.'

Bah! I would teach my little dogs to show their teeth, and I rode, on a mule, over to the fort. There I bade Dufour and Lebaudy select an *escouade* of the worst men, all *mauvais sujets* of that Company. They should garrison either Zinderneuf fort, or else the grave that had been dug for those brave 'fallen who had not been allowed to fall.' . . .

As I rode up, the Sergeant-Major Dufour called the men to attention, and they stood like graven images, the selected *escouade* on the right, while I made an eloquent speech, the funeral oration of that brave band to whom we were about to give a military funeral with all the last honours that France could render to the worthy defenders of her honour and her Flag.

Tears stood in my eyes and my voice broke as I concluded by quoting:—

> *'Soldats de la Légion,*
> *De la Légion Étrangère,*
> *N'ayant pas de nation,*
> *La France est votre mère.'*

Then, when the selected new garrison got the order, *'Par files de quatre. En avant. Marche,'* that they might march into the fort and begin their new duties by bringing the dead out for burial—they did something quite otherwise.

Taking the time from the right, with smartness and precision they stooped as one man, laid their rifles on the ground, rose as one man and stood at attention!

The right-hand man, a grizzled veteran of Madagascar, Tonquin, and Dahomey, took a pace forward, saluted, and with wooden face, said, 'We prefer to die with Rastignac.'

This was flat disobedience and rank mutiny. I had hardly expected quite this.

'But Rastignac is not going to die. He is going to live —long years, I hope—in the *Joyeux*. You, however, who are but cowardly sheep, led astray by him, shall have the better fate. You shall die now, or enter Zinderneuf fort and do your duty. . . . Sergeant-Major, have those rifles collected. Let the remainder of the Company right form, and on the order *'Attention pour les feux de salve,'* the front rank will kneel, and on the order, *"Feu,"* every man will do his duty.'

But I knew better, George. That was precisely what they *wouldn't* do; and I felt that this was my last parade. That accursed fort was still exerting its horrible influence. These fools feared that it would kill them if they entered it, and I feared it would kill them if they did not. For let me but handle them wrongly now, and they would shoot me and the non-commissioned officers and march off into the desert to certain death, as they weakened from thirst and starvation. They would be harried and hunted and herded along by the Arabs, and daily reduced in numbers until a sudden rush swept over them and nothing remained for the survivors but horrible tortures.

Mutinous dogs they might be, and fools they were—but no less would the responsibility for their sufferings and deaths be mine if I mishandled the situation. I thought of other desert-mutinies in the Legion.

It was an awkward dilemma, George. If I ordered the Company to fire upon the squad, they would refuse and would thereby become mutineers themselves. They would then feel that they might as well be hung for a sheep as a lamb, and, having shot me, take their chance of escape and freedom.

If, on the other hand, I condoned this refusal of the *escouade*—what of military discipline? Duty to my country came before my duty to these fellows, and I must not allow any pity for their probable fate to come between me and my duty as a French officer.

I decided that if they *would* die, then die they must—but I at least could do my best to save them. Without deviating from the path of duty, I would hold out a hand to them.

If the *escouade* would not enter the fort they must expiate their military crime. If the Company would not carry out my orders and fire on the mutineers, they must expiate *their* crime.

If I were to be shot, I should at least be saved the unpleasantness of reporting that my men had mutinied, and I should die in the knowledge that I had done my duty.

Yes—I would make it clear that disobedience to my orders would be death. Swift and sudden for some, lingering and horrible for many, sure and certain for all. Then I would 'carry on' as you say. Was I right, George?"

"I think you were quite right, Jolly," agreed Lawrence.

"As I was deciding thus, all in the space of a few seconds, with every eye upon me and a terrible tension drawing every face," continued de Beaujolais, "the Sergeant-Major

approached and saluted. I eyed him coldly. With his
back to the men, he whispered:

'They won't do it, *mon Commandant*. For God's sake
do not give the order. They are rotten with *cafard* and
over-fatigue. That Rastignac is their hero and leader.
They will shoot you and desert *en masse*. . . . A night's
rest will work wonders. . . . Besides, Lieutenant St. André
and the Senegalese will be here by midnight. It is full
moon to-night.'

'And shall we sit and wait for the Senegalese, Dufour?'
I whispered back. 'Would you like to ask these fellows to
spare us till they come?'

And looking from him to the men I said loudly:

'You are too merciful, Sergeant-Major. We don't do
things thus in the Spahis. But these are not Spahis. However, in consideration of the most excellent march the men
have made, I will do as you beg and give these *cafard*-
stricken fools till moon-rise. It gives me no pleasure to
inflict punishment, and I hope no man will insist on being
punished. We are all tired, and since you intercede for
your men I grant a four-hour holiday. At moon-rise, our
motto is "*Work or die*." Till then, all may rest. After
then, the dead will be buried and the fort garrisoned. I
hope there will be no *more* dead to be buried to-night.'

And I rode back to the oasis, hearing as I did so the voice
of the Sergeant-Major, exhorting the men and concluding
with the order, '*Rompez*.'

He joined me a few minutes later.

'They'll never do it, *mon Commandant*,' said he.
'They'll fear the place worse than ever by moonlight. In
the morning we could call for volunteers to accompany us.
And then the Senegalese . . .'

'That will do, Dufour,' said I. 'They will render
instant obedience at moon-rise, or take the consequences. I
have strained my military conscience already to satisfy my
private conscience. If, after four hours' rest and reflection,
they still decide to mutiny—on their heads be it! No responsibility rests on me. If they mutiny, they do it in cold
blood. If they obey orders before the Senegalese arrive,

no great harm has been done, and discipline has been maintained. That is the very utmost length to which I can go in my desire to save them.'

'To save *them, mon Commandant!* It is *you* I am trying to save,' stammered the good fellow.

Patting him on the shoulder as he turned to go, I bade him send me a couple of the most influential men of the *escouade* and two or three of the best of the remainder— leaders of different cliques, if there were any.

I would point out to them the inevitable and awful results to the men themselves, of disobedience and mutiny. I would speak of the heroism, discipline, and dutifulness of the dead. I would point out to them that in the event of mutiny, they themselves would either be loyal and die at the hands of the mutineers, or become deserters and die at the hands of the Arabs. I would then send them back among their fellows—and abide the issue. . . .

It was while I awaited their arrival that I wished our army more resembled yours in one particular—the relationship between officers and men. Our fellows get too much non-commissioned officer and too little officer. We are too remote from them. We do not play games with them, get to know them, interest ourselves in them as fellow human beings, in the way that your officers do. Too often it is a case with us of hated non-coms. and stranger-officers. Particularly is this so in the Legion. The non-coms. are all-powerful and tyrannical; the officers are utterly uninterested in the men as individuals, and do not even know their names.

And I was not one of their own officers of the Legion. I was a Spahi officer, superintending the organising of mule-cavalry out of infantry; or rather, making ordinary infantry into mounted infantry, that the Legion might hope to compete with the Touaregs in mobility. We wanted mounted riflemen down there just as you did in the Boer War, or else the Arabs served us as the Boers did you at first.

I certainly had not been unduly harsh or oppressive during the time I had been with this particular lot; but, on the

other hand, I certainly had no *personal* influence with them.
I did not know them, nor they me, and all our lives seemed
likely to be forfeit in consequence. . . .

However, I talked to the men whom Dufour brought, and
did my best under the heavy handicap of not so much as
knowing their names. Finally, I dismissed them with the
words:

'For your lives, influence your friends wisely and well,
and get it into their heads that at moon-rise we will have
obedience with honour and safety, or disobedience with dishonour, misery, and death. For at moon-rise, the chosen
escouade will enter the fort and bring out the dead, or the
company will fire upon them. . . . *Au 'voir, mes enfants.'*

Of course, I knew the danger of making any reference to
what would happen if the company refused to fire on the
escouade—but it was foolish to pretend to ignore the possibility of such a thing. But I made no allusion to the Senegalese, and the coercion or punishment of white men by
black.

It *might* be that the company would obey orders, if the
escouade remained mutinous, and it *might* be that all would
reflect upon the coming of the Senegalese.

Anyhow, I was on a knife-edge, and all depended upon
the effect on these rascals of a four-hour rest and the words
of the men to whom I had talked. There was just a chance
that St. André and his Senegalese might arrive in time to
influence the course of affairs—but I most certainly could
not bring myself to postpone the issue until his arrival, and
then take shelter behind the blacks. With the full moon
well up in the sky—by its beautiful soft light—we should
see what we should see . . .

And then, just as the men turned to go, I had an idea.
Suppose some of them would volunteer to go over the fort
with me; see for themselves that there was nothing to be
afraid of; and then report to their fellows that all was well.

Their statement and the inevitable airs of superiority
which they would give themselves, might well counteract
Rastignac's influence and their superstitious fears. If some
of these men, selected for character and influence, went back

in the spirit of, 'Well, cowards, *we* have been in there and
it is much the same as any other such cursed hole—except
that somebody had a great idea for diddling the Arabs,'
the others would probably take the line, 'Well, where you
can go, we can. Who are *you* to swagger?'

Yes—I would try it. Not as though I were really per-
suading or beseeching, and anxious to prove that the
escouade had nothing to fear if sent to garrison the place.
No—merely as offering them, superior soldiers, an opportunity of seeing the fort before its remarkable dispositions
were disturbed.

'Wait a moment,' said I, as they saluted and turned to
go. 'Is there a man of courage among you—a man, *par
exemple* such as the trumpeter, brave enough to enter an
empty fort with me?'

They looked sheepish for a moment. Someone murmured,
"And where *is* Jean the Trumpeter?" and then I heard a
curious whispered remark:

'*Gee! I sure would like to see a ghost, Buddy,*' and the
whispered reply:

'*Sure thing, Hank, and I'd like to see ole Brown some
more.*'

Two men stepped forward as one, and saluted.

They were in extraordinary contrast in body, and some
similarity in face, for one was a giant and the other not
more than five feet in height, while both had clean-shaven
leathery countenances, somewhat of the bold Red Indian
type.

You know what I mean—lean hatchet faces, biggish
noses, mouths like a straight gash, and big chins. By their
grey eyes they were Northerners, and by their speech Americans.

'You would like to see the fort and how it was manned
to the last by heroes—victorious in death?' I asked.

'*Oui, mon Commandant,*' they replied together.

'Isn't there a *Frenchman* among you?' I asked the rest.

Another man, a big sturdy Gascon he looked, saluted and
joined the Americans. Then what they now call 'the herd
instinct' and 'mob-psychology' came into play, and the
others did the same.

Good! I had got the lot. I would take them round the fort as though doing honour to the dead and showing them as an example—and then I suddenly remembered . . .''

"The murdered *sous-officier*," said George Lawrence.

"Exactly, George! These fellows must not see him lying there with a French bayonet through him! I must go in first, alone, and give myself the pleasant task of removing the bayonet. I would cover his face, and it would be assumed that he had been shot and had fallen where he lay. Yes, that was it. . . .

'Good! You shall come with me then,' said I, 'and have the privilege of treading holy ground and seeing a sight of which to talk to your grandchildren when you are old men. You can also tell your comrades of what you have seen, and give them a fresh pride in their glorious Regiment,' and I bade the Sergeant-Major march them over to the fort.

Mounting my mule, which had not been unsaddled, I rode quickly across to the gate. The sentry had been withdrawn.

Dismounting, I hurried up to the roof, to perform the distasteful duty I could not very well have delegated to the Sergeant-Major. I emerged from the darkness of the staircase on to the roof.

And there I stood and stared and stared and rubbed my eyes—and then for a moment felt just a little faint and just a little in sympathy with those poor superstitious fools of the *escouade*. . . . For, my dear George, *the body of the sous-officier was no longer there!* Nor was that of the bareheaded recumbent man!''

"Good God!" ejaculated Lawrence, raising himself on his elbow and turning to de Beaujolais.

"Yes, that is what I said," continued the other. "What else was there to say? *Were* there djinns, afrites, evil spirits in this cursed desert, even as the inhabitants declared? Was the whole thing a nightmare? Had I dreamt that the body of a French *sous-officier* had lain here, with a French bayonet through it? Or was I dreaming now?

And then I think my temperature went up two or three degrees from the mere hundred and two that one disregards; for I remember entertaining the wild idea that perhaps a living man was shamming dead among these corpses. Moreover, I remember going round from corpse to corpse and questioning them. One or two that seemed extra life-like I took by the arm, and as I shouted at them, I shook them and pulled at them until they fell to the ground, their rifles clattering down with them.

Suddenly I heard the feet of men upon the stair, and pulled myself together. The Sergeant-Major and the half-dozen or so of legionaries came out on to the roof.

I managed to make my little speech as they stared round in amazement, the most amazed of all being the Sergeant-Major, who gazed at the smeared pool of blood where the body of the *sous-officier* had lain.

The two Americans seemed particularly interested, and appeared to be looking for comrades among the dead.

When would one of the men salute and ask respectfully the first of the hundred questions that must be puzzling them: *'Where is their officer?'*

And what should I reply? They could see for themselves that the Arabs had not entered and carried him off. Perhaps their minds were too full of the question: *'Where is Jean the Trumpeter?'* for the other question to formulate itself.

I had made no reference to the disappearance of the trumpeter; but I knew that they had seen him enter the fort and had waited, as I did, for an astounding quarter of an hour, to see him come out again. They had watched me go in alone, at the end of that time, and had seen me emerge alone. What could I say?

It seemed to me to be best to say nothing on that subject, so I said it.

After a few minutes that seemed like a few hours, I bade Dufour take the men round the outbuildings, and then march them back to the oasis.

As he disappeared, last, down the stair, I called him back and we were alone together. Simultaneously we said the same words: *'Did you move it?'*—and each of us knew that the other knew nothing about it!

I laughed loudly, if not merrily, and the Sergeant-Major

produced the oath of a lifetime; in length and originality, remarkable even for the Legion.

'Quite so, *Chef*,' said I. . . . 'Life grows a little complicated.'

'I'll give a complicated death to this *farceur*, when I find . . .' growled he as I motioned him to be off. 'Blood of the devil, I will!'

He clattered down the stairs, and, soon after, I heard his voice below, as he led the group of men across the courtyard.

'Not much here to terrify the great Rastignac, *hein?*' he jeered.

'But there is certainly something here to terrify *me*, my friend,' I observed to myself, and made my way back to my mule and the oasis. . . . In fact, I fled. . . .

Well, George, *mon vieux*, what do you think happened? Did the *escouade* obey and enter the fort like lambs, or did they refuse and successfully defy me, secure in the knowledge that the others would not fire on them?"

"You are alive to tell the tale, Jolly," was the reply. "That's the main thing."

"On account of the importance of a part of it to you, my George, eh?" smiled the Frenchman.

"Oh, not at all, old chap," Lawrence hastened to say, with a somewhat guilty smile. "Simply on account of the fact that you are spared to France and to your friends."

"I thank you, my little George. Almost might you be a Frenchman," said de Beaujolais, with an ironical bow. "But tell me, what do you think happened? Did they obey and enter, or did they refuse?"

"Give it up, Jolly. I can only feel sure that one of the two happened," replied Lawrence.

"And that is where you are wrong, my friend, for neither happened," continued de Beaujolais. "They neither obeyed and entered, nor disobeyed and stayed out!"

"Good Lord!" ejaculated Lawrence. "What then?"

And this time it was the Frenchman who suggested a little refreshment.

§ 8.

"Well, this is the last 'event' on that remarkable programme, *mon cher Georges*," resumed de Beaujolais a little later. "A very appropriate and suitable one too. . . . '*A delightful open-air entertainment concluded with fireworks*,' as the reporters of *fêtes champêtres* say."

"Fireworks? Rifle-fire works do you mean?" asked Lawrence.

"No, my George, nothing to speak of. Just fireworks. Works of fire. . . . I will tell you. . . .

I let the moon get well up, and then sent my servant, Achmet, for the Sergeant-Major, and bade that good fellow to parade the men as before, with the fort a hundred paces in their rear, the garrison *escouade* on the right of the line.

This party would either march into the fort or not. If *not*—then the remainder would be ordered to right-form and shoot them where they stood, for disobedience in the field, practically in the presence of the enemy.

The remainder would either obey or not. If *not*—then I would at once give the order to 'pile arms.' If they did this, as they might, from force of habit, they would immediately be marched off to the oasis and would be 'arrested' by the non-commissioned officers and marched back to Tokotu, under escort of the Senegalese, to await court-martial. If they did not pile arms, the non-commissioned officers were to come at once to me, and we would prepare to sell our lives dearly—for the men would mutiny and desert. Possibly a few of the men would join us, and there was a ghost of a chance that we might fight our way into the fort and hold it, but it was infinitely more probable that we should be riddled where we stood.

'*Bien, mon Commandant*,' said Dufour, as he saluted, and then, hesitatingly, 'Might I presume to make a request and a suggestion. May I stand by you, and Rastignac stand by me—with the muzzle of my revolver against his liver—it being clear that, at the slightest threat to you, Rastignac's digestion is impaired? If he knows that just this will happen, he also may give good advice to his friends. . . .'

'Nothing of the sort, Dufour,' I replied. 'Everything will proceed normally and properly, until the men themselves behave abnormally and improperly. We shall lead and command soldiers of France until we have to fight and kill, or be killed by, mutineers against the officers of France in the execution of their duty. Proceed.'

Would you have said the same, George? It seemed to me that this idea of the Sergeant-Major's was not much better than that of waiting for the Senegalese. Would you have done the same in my place?"

"I can only *hope* I should have had the courage to act as bravely and as wisely as you did, Jolly," was the reply.

"Oh, I am no hero, my friend," smiled de Beaujolais, "but it seemed the right thing to do. I had not in any way provoked a mutiny—indeed, I had stretched a point to avert it—and it was my business to go straight ahead, do my duty, and abide the result.

But it was with an anxious heart that I mounted the mule again and cantered over to the fort.

I had thought of going on a camel, for, it is a strange psychological fact, that if your hearers have to look up to you physically, they also have to look up to you metaphysically as it were. If a leader speaks with more authority from a mule than from the ground, and with more weight and power from a horse than from a mule, would he not speak with still more from a camel?

Perhaps—but I felt that I could *do* more, somehow, in case of trouble, if I could dash at assailants with sword and revolver. I am a cavalry man and the *arme blanche* is my weapon. Cold steel and cut and thrust, for me, if I had to go down fighting. You can't charge and use your sword on a camel, so I compromised on the mule—but how I longed for my Arab charger and a few of my Spahis behind me! It would be a fight then, instead of a murder. . . .

It was a weird and not unimpressive scene. That sinister fort, silver and black; the frozen waves of the ocean of sand, an illimitable silver sea; the oasis a big, dark island upon it; the men, statues, inscrutable and still.

What would they do? Would my next words be my last?

Would a double line of rifles rise and level themselves at my breast, or would that *escouade,* upon whom everything depended, move off like a machine and enter the fort?

As I faced the men, I was acutely interested, and yet felt like a spectator, impersonal and unafraid. I was about to witness a thrilling drama, depicting the fate of one Henri de Beaujolais, quite probably his death. I hoped he would play a worthy part on this moonlit stage. I hoped that, even more than I hoped to see him survive the play. I was calm. I was detached. . . ."

George Lawrence sighed and struck a match.

"I cast one more look at the glorious moon and took a deep breath. If this was my last order on parade, it should be worthily given, in a voice deep, clear, and firm. Above all firm. And as my mouth opened, and my lower jaw moved in the act of speech—I believe it dropped, George, and my mouth remained open.

For, from that enigmatical, brooding, fatal fort—there shot up a tongue of flame!

'Mon Dieu! Regardez!' cried the Sergeant-Major, and pointed. I believe every head turned, and in the perfect silence I heard him whisper, *'Spirits, ghosts, devils!'*

That brought me to myself sharply. 'Yes, imbecile!' I said. 'They carry matches and indulge in arson! Quite noted incendiaries! Where is Rastignac?'

I asked that because it was perfectly obvious that someone was in the fort and had set fire to something highly inflammable. I had been in the place an hour or two before. There was certainly no sign of fire then, and this was a sudden rush of flame.

As I watched, another column of smoke and fire burst forth in a different place.

'He is tied up back there, *mon Commandant,'* replied Dufour.

'The forbidden *crapaudine?'* I asked.

'I *told* Corporal Brille to tie him to a tree,' was the reply.

Anyhow it could not be Rastignac's work, for he would not have entered the place, even had he been left at liberty and had an opportunity to do so.

'Send and see if he is still there—and make sure that everyone else is accounted for,' I ordered.

It was useless to detail a *pompier* squad to put the fire out. We don't have hose and hydrants in the desert, as you know. When a place burns, it burns. And, *mon Dieu, how* it burns in the dry heat of that rainless desert! The place would be gone, even if the men would enter it, by the time we had got our teaspoonfuls of water from the oasis. And, to tell you the truth, I did not care how soon, or how completely it *did* go!

This fire would be the funeral pyre of those brave men. It would keep my fools from their suicidal mutiny. It would purge the place of mystery. Incidentally it would save my life and military reputation, and the new fort that would arise in its place would not be the haunted, hated prison that this place would henceforth have been for those who had to garrison it.

I gave the order to face about, and then to stand at ease. The men should watch it burn, since nothing could be done to save it. Perhaps even they would realise that human agency is required for setting a building on fire—and, moreover, whoever was in there had got to come out or be cremated. They should see him come. . . . But who? Who? The words *Who?* and *Why?* filled my mind. . . .

All stood absolutely silent, spellbound.

Suddenly the spell was broken and back we came to earth, at an old familiar sound.

A rifle cracked, again and again. From the sound the firing was towards us.

The Arabs were upon us!

Far to the right and to the left, more shots were fired.

The fort blazing and the Arabs upon us!

Bullets whistled overhead and I saw one or two flashes from a distant sand-hill.

No one was hit, the fort being between us and the enemy. In less time that it takes to tell I had the men turned about and making for the oasis—*au pas gymnastique*—'at the double,' as you call it. There we should have cover and water, and if we could only hold the devils until they were nicely between us and St. André's Senegalese, we would avenge the garrison of that blazing fort.

They are grand soldiers, those Légionnaires, George. No better troops in our army. They are to other infantry what my Spahis are to other cavalry. It warmed one's heart to see them double, steady as on parade, back to the darkness of the oasis, every man select his cover and go to ground, his rifle loaded and levelled as he did so.

Our camel vedettes rode in soon after. Two of them had had a desperate fight, and two of them had seen rifle-flashes and fired at them, before returning to the oasis, thinking the Arabs had rushed the fort and burnt it.

In a few minutes from the first burst of fire, the whole place was still, silent, and apparently deserted. Nothing for an enemy to see but a burning fort, and a black brooding oasis, where nothing moved.

How I hoped they would swarm yelling round the fort, thinking to get us like bolted rabbits as we rushed out of it! It is not like the Arabs to make a night attack, but doubtless they had been hovering near, and the fire had brought them down on us.

Had they seen us outside the fort? If so, they would attack the oasis in the morning. If they had not seen us, anything might happen, and the oasis prove a *guet-apens*, with the burning or burnt-out fort as the bait of the trap.

What were they doing now? The firing had ceased entirely. Probably making their dispositions to rush us suddenly at dawn, from behind the nearest sand-hills. Their game would be to lull us into a sense of security throughout a peaceful night and come down upon us at daybreak, like a whirlwind, as we slept.

And what if our waiting rifles caught them at fifty yards, and the survivors turned to flee—on to the muzzles of those of the Senegalese? . . .

It was another impressive scene in that weird drama, George. A big fire, by moonlight, in the heart of the Sahara, a fire watched by silent, motionless men, breathlessly awaiting the arrival of other players on the stage.

After gazing into the moonlit distance until my eyes

ached, expecting to see a great band of the blue-veiled
mysterious Silent Ones suddenly swarm over a range of
sand-hills, I bethought me of getting into communication
with St. André.

I had ordered him to follow by a forced march, leaving a
suitable garrison at Tokotu, when I dashed off with the
'always ready' emergency-detachment on camels, preceding
by an hour or so the 'support' emergency-detachment on
mules, with water, rations, and ammunition.

These two detachments are more than twice as fast as the
best infantry, but I reckoned that St. André would soon be
drawing near.

It was quite possible that he might run into the Arabs,
while the latter were watching the oasis—if they had seen
us enter it, or their skirmishers established the fact of our
presence.

So far, we had not fired a shot from the oasis, and it was
possible that our presence was unsuspected.

This might, or might not, be the same band that had
attacked the place. If they were the same, they might be
hanging about in the hope of ambushing a relieving force.
If St. André arrived while the fort was burning, they would
have no chance of catching him unawares. If he came after
the flames had died down, he might march straight into a
trap. There would certainly be a Targui scout or two out
in the direction of Tokotu, while the main body did business
at Zinderneuf.

Anyhow, I must communicate with St. André if possible.
It would be a good man that would undertake the job
successfully—for both skill and courage would be required.
There was the track to find and follow, and there were the
Arabs to face.

To lose the former was to die of thirst and starvation; to
find the latter was to die of tortures indescribable.

On the whole it might be better to send two. Twice the
chance of my message reaching St. André. Possibly more
than twice the chance, really, as two men are braver than
one, because they hearten each other.

I went round the oasis until I found the Sergeant-Major,

who was going from man to man, prohibiting any firing without orders, any smoking or the making of any noise. This was quite sound and I commended him, and then asked for a couple of men of the right stamp for my job.

I was not surprised when he suggested two of the men who had been into the fort with me, and passed the word for the two Americans. He recommended them as men who could use the stars, good scouts, brave, resourceful, and very determined.

They would, at any rate, stand a chance of getting through the Arabs and giving St. André the information that would turn him from their victim into their scourge, if we had any luck.

When the big slow giant and the little quick man appeared and silently saluted, I asked them if they would like to undertake this duty. They were more than ready, and as I explained my plans for trapping the Arabs between two fires, I found them of quick intelligence. Both were able to repeat to me, with perfect lucidity, what I wanted them to say to St. André, that he might be able to attack the attackers at dawn, just when they were attacking me.

The two left the oasis on camels, from the side opposite to the fort, and after they had disappeared over a sand-hill, you may imagine with what anxiety I listened for firing. But all was silent, and the silence of the grave prevailed until morning.

After two or three hours of this unbroken, soundless stillness, the fire having died down in the fort, I felt perfectly certain there would be no attack until dawn.

All who were not on the duty of outposts-by-night slept, and I strolled silently round and round the oasis, waiting for the first hint of sunrise and thinking over the incredible events of that marvellous day—certainly unique in my fairly wide experience of hectic days.

I went over it all again from the moment when I first sighted the accursed fort with its flag flying over its unscaled walls and their dead defenders, to the moment when my eyes refused to believe that the place was on fire and blazing merrily.

At length, leaning against the trunk of a palm tree and longing for a cigarette and some hot coffee to help me keep awake, I faced the east and watched for the paling of the stars. As I did so, my mind grew clearer as my body grew weaker, and I decided to decide that all this was the work of a madman, concealed in the fort, and now burnt to death.

He had, for some reason, murdered the *sous-officier* with a bayonet (certainly he must be mad or he would have shot him) ; and he had, for some reason, silently killed the trumpeter and hidden his body—all in the few minutes that elapsed before I followed the trumpeter in. (Had the murderer used *another* bayonet for this silent job?) He had for some reason removed the *sous-officier's,* and the other man's, body and concealed those too, and, finally, he had set fire to the fort and perished in the flames.

But where was he while I searched the place, and why had he not killed me also when I entered the fort alone?

The lunacy theory must account for these hopelessly lunatic proceedings—but it hardly accounts for the murdered *sous-officier* having in his hand a confession signed, 'Michael Geste,' to the effect that he had stolen a jewel, does it, my old one?''

"It does *not,* my son, and that, to me, is the most interesting and remarkable fact in your most interesting and remarkable story," replied Lawrence.

"Well, I decided, as I say, to leave it at that—just the mad doings of a madman, garnished by the weird coincidence of the paper,'' continued de Beaujolais, "and soon afterwards the sky grew grey in the east.

Before a rosy streak could herald the dawn we silently stood to arms, and when the sun peeped over the horizon we beheld St. André's Senegalese skirmishing beautifully towards us!

There wasn't so much as the smell of an Arab for miles.
. . . No, St. André had not seen a living thing—not even the two scouts I had sent out to meet him. Nor did anyone else ever see those two brave fellows. I have often wondered what their fate was—Arabs or thirst. . . .

I soon learnt that one of St. André's mule-scouts had

ridden back to him, early in the night, to say that he had
heard rifle-shots in the direction of Zinderneuf. St. André
had increased his pace, alternating the quick march and the
pas gymnastique until he knew he must be near his goal.
All being then perfectly silent he decided to beware of an
ambush, to halt for the rest of the night, and to feel his way
forward, in attack formation, at dawn.

He had done well, and my one regret was that the Arabs
who had caused the destruction of Zinderneuf were not
between me and him as he closed upon the oasis.

While the weary troops rested, I told St. André all that
had happened, and asked for a theory—reserving mine
about the madman. He is a man with a brain, this St.
André, ambitious and a real soldier. Although he has private means, he serves France where duty is hardest, and life
least attractive. A little dark pocket-Hercules of energy
and force.

'What about this, Major?' said he, when I had finished
my account, and, having fed, we were sitting, leaning our
weary backs against a fallen palm trunk, with coffee and
cigarettes at hand.

'Suppose your trumpeter killed the *sous-officier* himself
and deserted there and then?'

'*Mon Dieu!*' said I; 'that never occurred to me. But
why should he, and why use his bayonet and leave it in the
body?'

'Well—as to why he *should*,' replied St. André, 'it might
have been revenge. This may have been the first time he
had ever been alone with the *sous-officier*, whom he may
have sworn to kill at the first opportunity. . . . Some
fancied or real injustice, when he was under this man at
Sidi-bel-Abbès or elsewhere. The sight of his enemy, the
sole survivor, alone, rejoicing in his hour of victory and
triumph, may have further maddened a brain already mad
with *cafard*, brooding, lust of vengeance, I know not what
of desperation.'

'Possible,' I said, and thought over this idea. 'But no,
impossible, my friend. Why had not the *sous-officier* rushed
to the wall, or up to the look-out platform when I ap-

proached? I fired my revolver six times to attract attention
and let them know that relief had come, and two answering
rifle-shots were fired! Why was he not waving his *képi*
and shouting for joy? Why did he not rush down to the
gates and throw them open?'

'Wounded and lying down,' suggested St. André.

'He was not wounded, my friend,' said I. 'He was
killed. That bayonet, and nothing else, had done his business.'

'Asleep,' suggested the Lieutenant, 'absolutely worn out.
Sleeping like the dead—and thus his enemy, the trumpeter,
found him, and drove the bayonet through his heart as he
slept. He was going to blow the sleeper's brains out, when
he remembered that the shot would be heard and would
have to be explained. Therefore he used the bayonet, drove
it through the man, and then, and not till then, he realised
that the bayonet would betray him. It would leap to the
eye, instantly, that *murder* had been committed—and not
by one of the garrison. So he fled.'

'And the revolver, with *one* chamber fired?' I asked.

'Oh—fired during the battle, at some daring Arab who
rode round the fort, reconnoitring, and came suddenly into
view.'

'And the paper in the left hand?'

'I do not know.'

'And who fired the two welcoming shots?'

'I do not know.'

'And how did the trumpeter vanish across the desert—
as conspicuous as a negro's head on a pillow—before the
eyes of my Company?'

'I do not know.'

'Nor do I,' I said.

And then St. André sat up suddenly.

'*Mon Commandant*,' said he, 'the trumpeter did not
escape, of course. He murdered the *sous-officier* and then
hid himself. It was he who removed the two bodies when
he again found himself alone in the fort. He may have had
some idea of removing the bayonet and turning the stab
into a bullet-wound. He then meant to return to the Com-

pany with some tale of cock and bull. But remembering that you had already seen the body, and might have noticed the bayonet, he determined to set fire to the fort, burn all evidence, and rejoin in the confusion caused by the fire.

He could swear that he had been knocked on the head from behind, and only recovered consciousness in time to escape from the flames kindled by whoever it was who clubbed him. This is all feasible—and if improbable it is no more improbable than the actual facts of the case, is it?'

'Quite so, *mon Lieutenant*,' I agreed. 'And why did he not rejoin in the confusion, with his tale of cock and bull?'

'Well—here's a theory. Suppose the *sous-officier* did shoot at him with the revolver and wounded him so severely that by the time he had completed his little job of arson he was too weak to walk. He fainted from loss of blood and perished miserably in the flames that he himself had kindled. Truly a splendid example of poetic justice.'

'Magnificent,' I agreed. 'The Greek Irony, in effect. Hoist by his own petard. Victim of the mocking Fates, and so forth. The only flaw in the beautiful theory is that *we should have heard the shot*—just as we should have heard a rifle-shot had the trumpeter used his rifle for the murder. In that brooding heavy silence a revolver fired on that open roof would have sounded like a seventy-five.'

'True,' agreed St. André, a little crestfallen. 'The man was mad then. He did everything that was done, and then committed suicide or was burnt alive.'

'Ah, my friend,' said I, 'you have come to the madman theory, eh? So had I. It is the only one. But now I will tell you something. The trumpeter did *not* do all this. He did *not* murder the *sous-officier*, for that unfortunate had been dead *for hours*, and the trumpeter had not been in the place ten *minutes!*'

'And that's that,' said St. André. 'Let's try again.' And he tried again—very ingeniously too. But he could put forward no theory that he himself did not at once ridicule.

We were both, of course, weary to death and more in need of twenty-four hours' sleep than twenty-four conun-

drums—but I do not know that I have done much better
since.

And as I rode back to Tokotu, with my record go of
fever, my head opened with a tearing wrench and closed
with a shattering bang, at every stride of my camel, to the
tune of, '*Who killed the Commandant, and why, why,
why?*' till I found I was saying it aloud.

I am saying it still, George." . . .

§ 9.

Passengers by the *Appam*, from Lagos to Birkenhead,
were interested in two friends who sat side by side in
Madeira chairs, or walked the promenade deck in close
and constant company.

The one, a tall, bronzed, lean Englishman, taciturn, forbidding, and grim, who never used two words where one
would suffice; his cold grey eye looking through, or over,
those who surrounded him; his iron-grey hair and moustache, his iron-firm chin and mouth, suggesting the iron
that had entered into his soul and made him the hard, cold,
bitter person that he was, lonely, aloof, and self-sufficing.
(Perhaps Lady Brandon of Brandon Abbas, alone of
women, knew the real man and what he might have been;
and perhaps half a dozen men liked him as greatly as all
men respected him.)

The other, a shorter, stouter, more genial person, socially
inclined, a fine type of French soldier, suave, courtly, and
polished, ruddy of face and brown of eye and hair, and
vastly improved by the removal, before Madeira, of a three
years' desert beard. He was obviously much attached to
the Englishman. . . .

It appeared these two had something on their minds, for
day by day, and night by night, save for brief intervals
for eating, sleeping, and playing bridge, they interminably
discussed, or rather the Frenchman interminably discussed,
and the Englishman intently listened, interjecting mono-
syllabic replies.

When the Englishman contributed to the one-sided dia-
logue, a listener would have noted that he spoke most often

of a bareheaded man and of a paper, speculating as to the identity of the former and the authorship of the latter.

The Frenchman, on the other hand, talked more of a murder, a disappearance, and a fire. . . .

"How long is it since you heard from Lady Brandon, Jolly?" enquired George Lawrence, one glorious and invigorating morning, as the *Appam* ploughed her steady way across a blue and smiling Bay of Biscay.

"Oh, years and years," was the reply. "I was at Brandon Abbas for a week of my leave before last. That would be six or seven years ago. I haven't written a line since the letter of thanks after the visit. . . . Do you correspond with her at all regularly?"

"Er—no. I shouldn't call it regular correspondence exactly," answered George Lawrence. "Are you going to Brandon Abbas this leave?" he continued, with a simulated yawn.

"Well—I feel I ought to go, *mon vieux*, and take that incredible document, but it doesn't fit in with my plans at all. I could post it to her, of course, but it would mean a devil of a long letter of explanation, and I loathe letter-writing 'fatigues' more than anything."

"I'll take it if you like," said Lawrence. "I shall be near Brandon Abbas next week. And knowing Michael Geste, I confess I am curious."

Major de Beaujolais was conscious of the fact that "curious" was not exactly the word he would have used. His self-repressed, taciturn, and unemotional friend had been stirred to the depths of his soul, and had given an exhibition of interest and emotion such as he had never displayed before in all de Beaujolais' experience of him.

What touched Lady Brandon evidently touched him—to an extent that rendered "curious" a curious word to use. He smiled to himself as he gravely replied:

"But excellent, *mon vieux!* That would be splendid. It will save me from writing a letter a mile long, and Lady Brandon cannot feel that I have treated the *affaire* casually, and as if of no importance. I explain the whole matter to you, her old friend, give you the document, and ask you to lay it before her. You could say that while supposing the document to be merely a *canard,* interesting only by reason of how and where it was found, I nevertheless think that she ought to have it, just in case there is anything I can do in the matter."

"Just that," agreed Lawrence. "Of course 'Beau' Geste never stole the sapphire, or anything else; but I suppose, as you say, a document like that ought to go to her and Geste, as their names are mentioned."

"Certainly, *mon ami.* And if the stone *has* been stolen, the paper might be an invaluable clue to its recovery, Hand-writing, for example, a splendid clue. She could please herself as to whether she put it in the hands of your Criminal Investigation Department at Scotland Yard and asked them to get in touch with our police. . . . Assure her of my anxiety to do absolutely anything I can in the matter—if either the jewel or Michael Geste should be missing."

"Righto, Jolly," was the reply. "I'll drop in there one day. Probably the first person I shall see will be 'Beau' Geste himself, and probably I shall see the 'Blue Water' the same evening."

"No doubt, George," agreed de Beaujolais, and added, "Do you know Michael Geste's handwriting?"

"No. Never saw it to my knowledge," was the reply. "Why do you ask? You don't suppose that Beau Geste wrote that, do you?"

"I have given up supposing, my friend," said de Beaujolais. "But I shall open my next letter from you with some alacrity. Either this 'Blue Water' is stolen or it is not. In either case that paper, in a dead man's hand, at Zinderneuf, is uniquely interesting. But if it *has* been stolen, it will be of practical as well as unique interest; whereas if it has not been stolen, the unique interest will be merely theoretical."

"Not very practical from the point of view of recovery, I am afraid. It looks as though the thief and the jewel and the story all ended together in the burning of Zinderneuf fort," mused Lawrence.

"*Mon Dieu!* I never thought of it before. The biggest and finest sapphire in the world, valued at three-quarters of a million francs, may be lying at this moment among the rubble and rubbish of the burnt-out ruins of Zinderneuf fort!" said de Beaujolais.

"By Jove! So it may!" agreed Lawrence. "Suppose it has been stolen. . . . If I wired to you, could anything be done about making a search there, do you think?"

For a moment George Lawrence had visions of devoting his leave to jewel-hunting, and returning to Brandon Abbas with three-quarters of a million francs' worth of crystallised alumina in his pocket.

"That will require prompt and careful consideration, directly we learn that the stone has gone, George," said de Beaujolais, and added: "This grows more and more interesting. . . . A treasure hunt at Zinderneuf! Fancy the Arabs if the information got about! Fancy the builders of the new fort, and the garrison! Zinderneuf would become the most popular outpost in Africa, instead of the least—until the sapphire was found. If it *is* there, I suppose the surest way to lose it for ever would be to hint at the fact . . . No, we should have to keep it very quiet and do all the searching ourselves, if possible. . . . Good heavens above us! More complications!" He smiled whimsically.

George Lawrence pursued his vision and the two fell silent for a space.

"Supposing that stone had actually been in the pocket of a man on that roof, when it collapsed into the furnace below," said de Beaujolais as he sat up and felt for his cigarette case, "would the jewel be destroyed when the body of the man was cremated? Does fire affect precious stones?"

"Don't know," replied Lawrence. "We could find that out from any jeweller, I suppose. I rather think not. Aren't they, in fact, formed in the earth by a heat greater than any furnace can produce?"

"Of course," agreed de Beaujolais. "You could make as many diamonds as you wanted if you could get sufficient heat and pressure. They are only crystallised carbon. Fire

certainly wouldn't hurt a diamond, and I don't suppose it
would hurt any other precious stone."

"No," he mused on. "If the Blue Water has been
stolen, it is probably safe and sound at this moment in
Zinderneuf, adorning the charred remains of a skeleton"
. . . and George Lawrence day-dreamed awhile, of himself,
Lady Brandon, and the sacrifice of his leave to the making
of a great restoration. Of his leave? Nay, if necessary, of
his career, his whole life.

("Describe me a man's day-dreams and I will describe
you the man," said the Philosopher. He might have described George Lawrence as a romantic and quixotic fool-
errant, which he was not, or perhaps merely as a man in
love, which he was. Possibly the Philosopher might have
added that the descriptions are synonymous, and that therefore George Lawrence was both.)

He was awakened from his reverie by the voice of de
Beaujolais.

"Queer, that it never got into the papers, George," mused
that gentleman.

"Yes. It is," agreed Lawrence. "I should certainly
have seen it if it had. I read my *Telegraph* and *Observer*
religiously. . . . No, I certainly should never have missed
it. . . . Probably the damned thing was never stolen at all."

"Looks like it," said his friend. "Every English paper
would have had an account of the theft of a famous jewel
like that. . . . Though it is just possible that Lady Brandon hushed it up for some reason. . . . What about an
aperitif, my old one?"

And, his old one agreeing, they once more dropped the
subject of Beau Geste, the "Blue Water," Zinderneuf, and
its secret.

On parting in London, Major de Beaujolais handed a
document to George Lawrence, who promised to deliver it,
and also to keep his friend informed as to any developments of the story.

The Major felt that he had the middle of it, and he
particularly desired to discover its beginning, and to follow
it to the end.

CHAPTER II

GEORGE LAWRENCE TAKES THE STORY TO LADY
BRANDON AT BRANDON ABBAS

AS his hireling car sped along the country road that led
to the park gates of Brandon Abbas, George Lawrence's heart beat like that of a boy going to his first love-
tryst.

Had she married him, a quarter of a century ago, when
she was plain (but very beautiful) Patricia Rivers, he
probably would still have loved her, though he would not
have been in love with her.

As it was he had never been anything but in love with
her from the time when he had taken her refusal like the
man he was, and had sought an outlet and an anodyne in
work and Central Africa.

As the car entered the gates and swept up the long, winding avenue of Norman oaks, he actually trembled, and his
bronzed face was drawn and changed in tint. He drew off
a glove and put it on again, fingered his tie, and tugged
at his moustache.

The car swept round a shrubbery-enclosed square at the
back of the house, and stopped at a big porch and a hos-
pitably open door. Standing at this, Lawrence looked into
a well-remembered panelled hall and ran his eye over its
gleaming floor and walls, almost nodding to the two suits
of armour that stood one on each side of a big, doorless
doorway. This led into another hall, from, and round, which
ran a wide staircase and galleries right up to the top of the
house, for, from the floor of that hall one could look up
to a glass roof three stories above. He pictured it and past
scenes enacted in it, and a woman with slow and stately
grace, ascending and descending.

Nothing seemed to have changed in those two and a half

decades since she had come here, a bride, and he had visited her after seven years of exile. He had come, half in the hope that the sight of her in her own home, the wife of another man, would cure him of the foolish love that kept him a lonely bachelor, half in the hope that it would do the opposite, and be but a renewal of love.

He had been perversely glad to find that he loved the woman, if possible, more than he had loved the girl; that a callow boy's calf-love for a maiden had changed to a young man's devotion to a glorious woman; that she was to be a second Dante's Beatrice.

Again and again, at intervals of years, he had visited the shrine, not so much renewing the ever-burning fire at her altar, as watching it flame up brightly in her presence. Nor did the fact that she regarded him so much as friend that he could never be more, nor less, in any way affect this undeviating unprofitable sentiment.

At thirty, at thirty-five, at forty, at forty-five, he found that his love, if not unchanged, was not diminished, and that she remained, what she had been since their first meeting, the central fact of his life—not so much an obsession, an *idée fixe*, as his reason for existence, his sovereign, and the audience of the play in the theatre of his life.

And, each time he saw her, she was, to his prejudiced eye, more desirable, more beautiful, more wonderful. . . .

Yes—there was the fifteenth-century chest in which reposed croquet mallets, tennis rackets, and the other paraphernalia of those games. She had once sat on that old chest, beside him, while they waited for the dog-cart to take him to the station and back to Africa, and her hand had rested so kindly in his, as he had tried to find something to say—something other than what he might not say. . . .

Opposite to it was the muniment-box, into which many an abbot and holy friar had put many a lead-sealed parchment. It would be full of garden rugs and cushions. On that, she had sat beside him, after his dance with her, one New Year's Eve. . . .

Same pictures of horse and hound, and bird and beast; same antlers and foxes' masks and brushes; same trophies he had sent from Nigeria, specially good heads of lion, buffalo, gwambaza, and gazelle.

From these his eye travelled to the great fire-place, on each side of which stood a mounted Lake Tchad elephant's foot, doing menial service, while above its stone mantel, a fine trophy of African weapons gleamed. One of his greatest satisfactions had always been to acquire something worthy to be sent to Brandon Abbas—to give her pleasure and to keep him in mind.

And now, perhaps, was his real chance of giving her pleasure and keeping himself, for a space, very much in her mind. He pulled the quaint old handle of a chain, and a distant bell clanged.

A footman approached, a stranger.

He would enquire as to whether her ladyship were at home. But as he turned to go, the butler appeared in the doorway from the inner hall.

"Hallo, Burdon! How are you?" said Lawrence

"Why, Mr. George, sir!" replied the old man, who had known Lawrence for thirty years, coming forward and looking unwontedly human.

"This is a real pleasure, sir."

It was—a real five-pound note too, when the visitor, a perfect gent, departed. Quite a source of income Mr. Lawrence had been, ever since Henry Burdon had been underfootman in the service of her ladyship's father.

"Her Ladyship is at the Bower, sir, if you'd like to come straight out," he continued, knowing that the visitor was a very old friend indeed, and always welcome. "I will announce you."

Burdon led the way.

"How is Lady Brandon?" enquired Lawrence, impelled to unwonted loquacity by his nervousness.

"She enjoys very good health, sir—considering," replied the butler.

"Considering what?" asked Lawrence.

"Everything, sir," was the non-committal reply.

The visitor smiled to himself. A good servant, this.

"And how is his Reverence?" he continued.

"Queer, sir, very. And gets queerer, poor gentleman," was the answer.

Lawrence expressed regret at this bad news concerning the chaplain, as the Reverend Maurice Ffolliot was always called in that house.

"Is Mr. Michael here?" he asked.

"No, sir, he ain't. Nor none of the other young gentlemen," was the reply. Was there anything unusual in the old man's tone? . . .

Emerging from the shrubbery, crossing a rose-garden, some lawn-tennis courts, and a daisy-pied stretch of cedar-studded sward, the pair entered a wood, followed a path beneath enormous elms and beeches, and came out on to a square of velvet turf.

On two sides, the left and rear, rose the great old trees of a thickly forested hill; on the right, the grey old house; and from the front of this open space the hillside fell away to the famous view.

By wicker table and hammock-stand, a lady reclined in a *chaise longue*. She was reading a book and her back was towards Lawrence, whose heart missed a beat and hastened to make up for the omission by a redoubled speed.

The butler coughed at the right distance and upon the right note, and, as Lady Brandon turned, announced the visitor, hovered, placed a wicker chair, and faded from the scene.

"*George!*" said Lady Brandon, in her soft deep contralto, with a pleased brightening of her wide grey eyes and flash of beautiful teeth. But she did not flush nor pale, and there was no quickening of her breathing. It was upon the man that these symptoms were produced by the meeting, although it was a meeting anticipated by him, unexpected by her.

"*Patricia!*" he said, and extended both hands. She took them frankly and Lawrence kissed them both, with a curiously gentle and reverent manner, an exhibition of a George Lawrence unknown to other people.

"Well, my dear!" he said, and looked long at the unlined, if mature, determined, clever face before him—that of a woman of forty years, of strong character and of aristocratic breeding.

"Yes," he continued.

"Yes, 'what,' George?" asked Lady Brandon.

"Yes. You are positively as young and as beautiful as ever," he replied—but with no air of gallantry and compliment, and rather as a sober statement of ascertained fact.

"And you as foolish, George. . . . Sit down—and tell me why you have disobeyed me and come here before your wedding. . . . Or—or—are you married, George?" was the smiling reply.

"No, Patricia, I am not married," said Lawrence, relinquishing her hands slowly. "And I have disobeyed you, and come here again without bringing a wife, because I hoped you might be in need of my help. . . . I mean, I feared you might be in trouble and in need of help, and hoped that I might be able to give it."

Lady Brandon fixed a penetrating gaze on Lawrence's face—neither startled nor alarmed, he felt, but keen and, possibly, to be described as wary, or at least watchful.

"Trouble? In need of help, George? How?" she asked, and whatever of weariness or watchfulness had peeped from her eyes retired, and her face became a beautiful mask, showing no more than reposeful and faintly-amused interest.

"Well—it is a longish story," said Lawrence. "But I need not inflict it on you if you'll tell me if Beau Geste is all right and—er—the 'Blue Water'—er—safe and sound and—er—all that, you know."

"What?" ejaculated his hearer sharply.

There was no possible doubt now, as to the significance of the look on Lady Brandon's face. It certainly could be called one of alarm, and her direct gaze was distinctly watchful and wary. Had not she also paled very slightly? Undoubtedly she frowned faintly as she asked:

"What are you talking about, George?"

"Beau Geste, and the 'Blue Water,' Patricia," replied

Lawrence. "If I appear to be talking through my hat, I am not really, and will produce reason for my wild-but-not-wicked words," he laughed. "There is method in my madness, dear."

"There's madness in your method," replied Lady Brandon a trifle tartly, and added: "Have you seen Michael, then? Or what? Tell me!"

"No. I have not seen him—but . . ."

"Then *what* are you talking about? What do you know?" she interrupted, speaking hurriedly, a very sure sign that she was greatly perturbed.

"I don't *know* anything, Patricia, and I'm asking *you*, because I have, most extraordinarily, come into possession of a document that purports to be a confession by Beau that he stole the 'Blue Water,'" began Lawrence.

"Then it *was* . . ." whispered Lady Brandon.

"Was what, Patricia?" asked Lawrence.

"Go on, dear," she replied hastily. "How and where did you get this confession? Tell me quickly."

"As I said, it's a long story," replied Lawrence. "It was found by de Beaujolais at a place called Zinderneuf in the French Soudan, in the hand of a dead man . . ."

"Not *Michael!*" interrupted Lady Brandon.

"No—a Frenchman. An *adjudant* in charge of a fort that had been attacked by Arabs . . ."

"*Our* Henri de Beaujolais?" interrupted Lady Brandon, again. "Who was at school with you? . . . Rose Cary's son?"

"Yes. He found it in this dead officer's hand . . ." replied Lawrence.

"Er—*has* the sapphire been stolen, Patricia, and—er—excuse the silly question—*is* this Beau's writing?" and he thrust his hand into the inner pocket of his jacket.

"But of course it isn't," he continued as he produced an envelope and extracted a stained and dirty piece of paper.

Lady Brandon took the latter and looked at it, her face hard, enigmatical, a puzzled frown marring the smoothness of her forehead, her firm shapely mouth more tightly compressed than usual.

She read the document and then looked out into the distance, down the coombe, and across the green and smiling plain, as though communing with herself and deciding how to answer.

"Tell me the whole story from beginning to end, George," she said at length, "if it takes you the weekend. But tell me this quickly. *Do* you know anything more than you have told me, about either Michael or the 'Blue Water'?"

"I know nothing whatever, my dear," was the reply, and the speaker thought he saw a look of relief, or a lessening of the look of alarm on his hearer's face, "but what I have told you. You know as much as I do now—except the details, of course."

George Lawrence noted that Lady Brandon had neither admitted nor denied that the sapphire had been stolen, had neither admitted nor denied that the handwriting was that of her nephew.

Obviously and undoubtedly there was something wrong, something queer, and in connection with Beau Geste too.

For one thing, he was missing and she did not know where he was.

But since all questions as to him, his handwriting, and the safety of the jewel had remained unanswered, he could only refrain from repeating them, and do nothing but tell his story, and, at the end of it, say: "If the 'Blue Water' is not in this house, Patricia, I am going straight to Zinderneuf to find it for you."

She would then, naturally, give him all the information she could, and every assistance in her power—if the sapphire had been stolen.

If it had not, she would, of course, say so.

But he wished she would be a little less guarded, a little more communicative. It would be so very easy to say: "My dear George, the 'Blue Water' is in the safe in the Priests' Hole as usual, and Michael is in excellent health

and spirits," or, on the other hand, to admit at once:
"The 'Blue Water' has vanished and so has Michael."

However, what Patricia Brandon did was right. For
whatever course of action she pursued, she had some excellent reason, and he had no earthly cause to feel a little
hurt at her reticence in the matter.

For example, if the impossible had come to pass, and
Beau Geste had stolen the sapphire and bolted, would
it not be perfectly natural for her to feel most reluctant
to have it known that her nephew was a thief—a despicable
creature that robbed his benefactress?

Of course. She would even shield him, very probably—
to such an extent as was compatible with the recovery of
the jewel.

Or if she were so angry, contemptuous, disgusted, as
to feel no inclination to shield him, she would at any rate
regard the affair as a disgraceful family scandal, about
which the less said the better. Quite so.

But to *him*, who had unswervingly loved her from his
boyhood, and whom she frequently called her best friend,
the man to whom she would always turn for help, since
the pleasure of helping her was the greatest pleasure he
could have? Why be reticent, guarded, and uncommuni-
cative to him?

But—her pleasure was her pleasure, and his was to
serve it in any way she deigned to indicate. . . .

"Well, we'll have the details, dear, and tea as well," said
Lady Brandon more lightly and easily than she had spoken
since he had mentioned the sapphire.

"We'll have it in my boudoir, and I'll be at home to
nobody whomsoever. You shall just talk until it is time
to dress for dinner, and tell me every least detail as you
go along. Everything you think, too; everything that
Henri de Beaujolais thought;—and everything you think
he thought, as well."

As they strolled back to the house, Lady Brandon slipped
her hand through Lawrence's arm, and it was quickly
imprisoned.

He glowed with the delightful feeling that this brave and strong woman (whose devoted love for another man was, now, at any rate, almost maternal in its protecting care), was glad to turn to him as others turned to her.

How he yearned to hear her say, when his tale was told: "Help me, George. I have no one but you, and you are a tower of strength. I am in great trouble."

"You aren't looking too well, George, my dear," she said, as they entered the wood.

"Lot of fever lately," he replied, and added: "I feel as fit as six people *now*," and pressed the hand that he had seized.

"Give it up and come home, George," said Lady Brandon, and he turned quickly toward her, his eyes opening widely. "And let me find you a wife," she continued.

Lawrence sighed and ignored the suggestion.

"How is Ffolliot?" he asked instead.

"Perfectly well, thank you. Why shouldn't he be?" was the reply—in the tone of which a careful listener, such as George Lawrence, might have detected a note of defensiveness, almost of annoyance, of repudiation of an unwarrantable implication.

If Lawrence did detect it, he ignored this also.

"Where is the good Sir Hector Brandon?" he asked, with casual politeness.

"Oh, in Thibet, or Paris, or East Africa, or Monte Carlo, or the South Sea Islands, or Homburg. Actually Kashmir, I believe, thank you, George," replied Lady Brandon, and added: "Have you brought a suit-case or must you wire?"

"I—er—am staying at the Brandon Arms, and have one there," admitted Lawrence.

"And how long have you been at the Brandon Arms, George?" she enquired.

"Five minutes," he answered.

"You must be tired of it then, dear," commented Lady Brandon, and added: "I'll send Robert down for your things."

§ 2.

That evening, George Lawrence told Lady Brandon all that Major de Beaujolais had told him, adding his own ideas, suggestions, and theories. But whereas the soldier had been concerned with the inexplicable events of the day, Lawrence was concerned with the inexplicable paper and the means by which it had reached the hand of a dead man, on the roof of a desert outpost in the Sahara.

Throughout his telling of the tale, Lady Brandon maintained an unbroken silence, but her eyes scarcely left his face.

At the end she asked a few questions, but offered no opinion, propounded no theory.

"We'll talk about it after dinner, George," she said.

And after a poignantly delightful dinner à deux—it being explained that the Reverend Maurice Ffolliot was dining in his room to-night, owing to a headache—George Lawrence found that the talking was again to be done by him. All that Lady Brandon contributed to the conversation was questions. Again she offered no opinion, propounded no theory.

Nor, as Lawrence reluctantly admitted to himself, when he lay awake in bed that night, did she once admit, nor even imply, that the "Blue Water" had been stolen. His scrupulous care to avoid questioning her on the subject of the whereabouts of the sapphire and of her nephew, Michael Geste, made this easy for her, and she had availed herself of it to the full. The slightly painful realisation, that she now knew all that he did whereas he knew nothing from her, could not be denied.

Again and again it entered his mind and roused the question, "*Why* cannot she confide in me, and at least say whether the sapphire has been stolen or not?"

Again and again he silenced it with the loyal reply, "For some excellent reason. . . . Whatever she does is right."

After breakfast next day, Lady Brandon took him for a long drive. That the subject which now obsessed him (as it had, in a different way and for a different reason, obsessed de Beaujolais) was also occupying her mind, was demonstrated by the fact that, from time to time, and à propos of nothing in particular, she would suddenly ask him some fresh question bearing on the secret of the tragedy of Zinderneuf.

How he restrained himself from saying, "Where is Michael? *Has* anything happened? *Is* the 'Blue Water' stolen?" he did not know. A hundred times, one or the other of these questions had leapt from his brain to the tip of his tongue, since the moment when, at their first interview, he had seen that she wished to make no communication or statement whatever.

As the carriage turned in at the park gates on their return, he laid his hand on hers and said:

"My dear—I think everything has now been said, except one thing—your instructions to me. All I want now is to be told exactly what you want me to do."

"I will tell you that, George, when you go. . . . And *thank* you, my dear," replied Lady Brandon.

So he possessed his soul in patience until the hour struck.

§ 3.

"Come and rest on this chest a moment, Patricia," he said, on taking his departure next day, when she had telephoned to the garage, "to give me my orders. You are going to make me happier than I have been since you told me that you liked me too much to love me."

Lady Brandon seated herself beside Lawrence and all but loved him for his chivalrous devotion, his unselfishness, his gentle strength, and utter trustworthiness.

"We have sat here before, George," she said, smiling, and, as he took her hand:

"Listen, my dear. This is what I want you to do for me. Just *nothing* at all. The 'Blue Water' is not at Zinderneuf, nor anywhere else in Africa. Where Michael is I do not know. What that paper means, I cannot tell. And thank you so much for wanting to help me, and for asking no questions. And now, good-bye, my dear, dear friend. . . ."

"Good-bye, my dearest dear," said George Lawrence, most sorely puzzled, and went out to the door a sadder but not a wiser man.

§ 4.

As the car drove away, Lady Brandon stood in deep thought, pinching her lip.

"To think of that now!" she said. . . . " 'Be sure your sins.' . . . The world *is* a very small place . . . " and went in search of the Reverend Maurice Ffolliot.

§ 5.

In regard to this same gentleman, George Lawrence entertained feelings which were undeniably mixed.

As a just and honest man, he recognised that the Reverend Maurice Ffolliot was a gentle-souled, sweet-natured, lovable creature, a finished scholar, a polished and cultured gentleman who had never intentionally harmed a living creature.

As the jealous, lifelong admirer and devotee of Lady Brandon, the rejected but undiminished lover, he knew that he hated not so much Ffolliot himself, as the fact of his existence.

Irrationally, George Lawrence felt that Lady Brandon would long outlive that notorious evil-liver, her husband. But for Ffolliot, he believed, his unswerving faithful devotion would then get its reward. Not wholly selfishly, he considered that a truer helpmeet, a sturdier prop, a stouter shield and buckler for this lady of many responsibilities, would be the world-worn and experienced George Lawrence, rather than this poor frail recluse of a chaplain.

Concerning the man's history, all he knew was, that he had been the curate, well-born but penniless, to whom Lady Brandon's father had presented the living which was in his gift. With the beautiful Patricia Rivers, Ffolliot had fallen disastrously and hopelessly in love.

Toward the young man, Patricia Rivers had entertained a sentiment of affection, compounded more of pity than of love.

Under parental pressure, assisted by training and comparative poverty, ambition had triumphed over affection, and the girl, after some refusals, had married wealthy Sir Hector Brandon.

Later, and too late, she had realised the abysmal gulf that must lie between life with a selfish, heartless, gross roué, and that with such a man as the companion of her youth, with whom she had worked and played and whose cleverness, learning, sweet nature, and noble unselfishness she now realised.

Lawrence was aware that Lady Brandon fully believed that the almost fatal nervous breakdown which utterly changed Ffolliot in body and mind, was the direct result of her worldly and loveless marriage with a mean and vicious man. In this belief she had swooped down upon the poor lodgings where Ffolliot lay at death's door, wrecked in body and unhinged of mind, and brought him back with her to Brandon Abbas as soon as he could be moved. From there he had never gone—not for a single day, nor a single hour.

When he recovered, he was installed as chaplain, and as "the Chaplain" he had been known ever since.

Almost reluctantly, George Lawrence admitted that most of what was good, simple, kind, and happy in that house emanated from this gentle presence. . . .

Pacing the little platform of the wayside station, it occurred to George Lawrence to wonder if he might have more to tell the puzzled de Beaujolais had his visit to Brandon Abbas included the privilege, if not the pleasure, of a conversation with the Reverend Maurice Ffolliot.

PART II

THE MYSTERY OF THE "BLUE WATER"

CHAPTER I

BEAU GESTE AND HIS BAND

"**I** THINK, perhaps, that if Very Small Geste were allowed to live, he might retrieve his character and find a hero's grave," said the Lieutenant.

"And what would he do if he found a hero's grave?" enquired the Captain.

"Pinch the flowers off it and sell them, I suppose. As for retrieving his character, it is better not retrieved. Better left where it is—if it is not near inhabited houses, or water used for drinking purposes . . ."

"Oh, *please* let him live," interrupted Faithful Hound. "He is very useful at times, if only to try things on."

I was very grateful to Faithful Hound for daring to intercede for me, but felt that she was rating my general usefulness somewhat low.

"Well, we'll try bread and water on him, then," said the Captain after a pause, during which I suffered many things. "We'll also try a flogging," he added, on seeing my face brighten, "and the name of Feeble Geste. . . . Remove it."

And I was removed by the Lieutenant, Ghastly Gustus, and Queen Claudia, that the law might take its course. It took it, while Faithful Hound wept apart and Queen Claudia watched with deep interest.

I used to dislike the slice of bread and the water, always provided for these occasions, even more than the "six of the best," which was the flogging administered, more in sorrow than in anger, by the Captain himself.

The opprobrious name only lasted for the day upon which it was awarded, but was perhaps the worst feature of a punishment. The others passed and were gone, but the name kept one in the state of unblessedness, disgraced and outcast. Nor was one allowed in any way to retaliate

upon the user of the injurious epithet, awarded in punishment after formal trial, however inferior and despicable he
might be. One had to answer to it promptly, if not cheerfully, or far worse would befall.

This was part of the Law as laid down by the Captain,
and beneath his Law we lived, and strove to live worthily,
for we desired his praise and rewards more than we feared
his blame and punishments.

The Captain was my brother, Michael Geste, later and
generally known as "Beau" Geste, by reason of his remarkable physical beauty, mental brilliance, and general
distinction. He was a very unusual person, of irresistible
charm, and his charm was enhanced, to me at any rate, by
the fact that he was as enigmatic, incalculable, and incomprehensible as he was forceful. He was incurably romantic, and to this trait added the unexpected quality of a bull-
dog tenacity. If Michael suddenly and quixotically did
some ridiculously romantic thing, he did it thoroughly and
completely, and he stuck to it until it was done.

Aunt Patricia, whose great favourite he was, said that he
combined the inconsequent romanticism and reckless courage of a youthful d'Artagnan with the staunch tenacity and
stubborn determination of a wise old Scotchman!

Little wonder that he exercised an extraordinary fascina-
tion over those who lived with him.

The Lieutenant, my brother Digby, was his twin, a quarter of an hour his junior, and his devoted and worshipping
shadow. Digby had all Michael's qualities, but to a less
marked degree, and he was "easier," both upon himself and
other people, than Michael was. He loved fun and laughter, jokes and jollity, and, above all, he loved doing what
Michael did.

I was a year younger than these twins, and very much
their obedient servant. At preparatory school we were
known as Geste, Small Geste, and Very Small Geste, and I
was, indeed, Very Small in all things, compared with my
brilliant brothers, to please whom was my chief aim in life.

Probably I transferred to them the affection, obedience,
and love-hunger that would have been given to my parents

in the ordinary course of events; but we were orphans, remembered not our mother nor our father, and lived our youthful lives between school and Brandon Abbas, as soon as we emerged from the Chaplain's tutelage.

Our maternal aunt, Lady Brandon, did more than her duty by us, but certainly concealed any love she may have felt for any of us but Michael.

Childless herself, I think all the maternal love she had to spare was given to him and Claudia, an extraordinarily beautiful girl whose origin was, so far as we were concerned, mysterious, but who was vaguely referred to as a cousin. She and a niece of Aunt Patricia, named Isobel Rivers, also spent a good deal of their childhood at Brandon Abbas, Isobel being, I think, imported as a playmate and companion for Claudia when we were at school. She proved an excellent playmate and companion for us also, and, at an early date, earned and adorned the honorary degree and honourable title of Faithful Hound.

A frequent visitor, Augustus Brandon, nephew of Sir Hector Brandon, often came during our holidays, in spite of the discouragement of the permanent name of Ghastly Gustus and our united and undisguised disapproval.

One could not love Augustus; he was far too like Uncle Hector for one thing, and, for another, he was too certain he was the heir and too disposed to presume upon it. However, Michael dealt with him faithfully, neither sparing the rod nor spoiling the child. . . .

§ 2.

I do not remember the precise crime that had led to my trial and sentence, but I recollect the incident clearly enough, for two reasons.

One was that, on this very day of my fall from grace, I achieved the permanent and inalienable title and status of Stout Fella, when, inverting the usual order of precedence, Pride came after the Fall. The other reason was that, on that evening, we had the exciting privilege of seeing and handling the "Blue Water," as it is called, the great sapphire which Uncle Hector had given to Aunt Patricia as a wedding gift. I believe his great-grandfather, "Wicked Brandon," had "acquired" it when soldiering against Dupleix in India.

It is about the loveliest and most fascinating thing I have ever seen, and it always affected me strangely. I could look at it for hours, and it always gave me a curious longing to put it in my mouth, or crush it to my breast, to hold it to my nose like a flower, or to rub it against my ear.

To look at it was, at one and the same time, most satisfying and most tantalising, for one always longed to do more than merely look—and, moreover, more than merely touch, as well. So wonderful and beautiful an object seemed to demand the exercise of all five senses, instead of one or two, for the full appreciation of all the joy it could offer.

When I first heard the charitable remark, "Sir Hector Brandon bought Patricia Rivers with the 'Blue Water' and now owns the pair," I felt that both statements were true.

For what other reason could a woman like Aunt Patricia have married Uncle Hector, and did not he still own the "Blue Water"—and so retain his sole claim to distinction?

Certainly his wife did not own it, for she could not wear it, nor do anything else with it. She could merely look at it occasionally, like anybody else. That was something anyhow, if it affected her as it did me. . . .

My degree of S.F. (Stout Fella) I earned in this wise. One of Michael's favourite and most thrilling pastimes was "Naval Engagements." When this delightful pursuit was in being, two stately ships, with sails set and rudders fixed, were simultaneously shoved forth from the concrete edge of the lily-pond, by the Captain and the Lieutenant respectively.

They were crowded with lead soldiers, bore each a battery of three brass cannon, and were, at the outset, about a yard apart. But to each loaded brass cannon was attached a fuse, and, at the Captain's word, the fuses were lighted as the ships were launched from their harbours.

The Captain presided over the destinies of the ship that flew the White Ensign and Union Jack, and the Lieutenant over those of the one that carried the Tri-couleur of France.

There was a glorious uncertainty of result. Each ship might receive a broadside from the other, one alone might suffer, or both might blaze ineffectually into the blue, by reason of a deviation of their courses. After the broadsides had been exchanged, we all sat and gloated upon the attractive scene, as the ships glided on, wreathed in battle-smoke, perhaps with riddled sails and splintered hulls (on one memorable and delightful occasion with the French ship dismasted and the Tri-couleur trailing in the water).

I was then privileged to wade, like Gulliver at Lilliput, into the deep, and bring the ships to harbour where their guns were reloaded by Michael and Digby, and the voyage repeated. . . .

On this great day, the first combat was ideal. The ships converged, the guns of both fired almost simultaneously, splinters flew, soldiers fell or were sent flying overboard, the ships rocked to the explosions and concussion of the shot, and then drifted together and remained locked in a death-grapple to the shouts of "Boarders ready" and "Prepare to receive boarders," from the Captain and Lieutenant.

"Fetch 'em in, Feeble Geste," said Michael, imagination sated, and tucking up my trousers, I waded in, reversed the ships, and sent them to port.

The next round was more one-sided, for only one of the French ship's guns fired, and that, the feeblest. Neither the big gun amidships, that carried either a buckshot or half a dozen number-sixes, nor the stern-chaser swivel-gun was properly fused.

I waded in again, turned the French ship, and, with a mighty bang, her big gun went off, and I took the charge in my leg. Luckily for me it was a single buckshot. I nearly sat down.

"I'm shot," I yelped.

"Hanging would be more appropriate," said the Captain. "Come here."

Blood oozed from a neat blue hole, and Faithful Hound uttered a dog-like howl of woe and horror.

Claudia asked to be informed exactly how it felt.

"Just like being shot," I replied, and added: "I am going to be sick."

"Do it in the pond then," requested the Captain, producing his pocket-knife and a box of matches.

"Going to cauterise the wound and prevent its turning sceptic?" enquired the Lieutenant, as the Captain struck a match, and held the point of the small blade in the flame.

"No," replied the Captain. "Naval surgery without æsthetics. . . . Cut out the cannon-ball."

"Now," continued he, turning to me as I sat wondering whether I should shortly have a wooden leg, "will you be gagged or chew on a bullet? I don't want to be disturbed by your beastly yells."

"I shall not yell, Captain," I replied with dignity, and a faint hope that I spoke the truth.

"Sit on his head, Dig," said Michael to the Lieutenant; but waving Digby away, I turned on my side, shut my eyes, and offered up my limb.

"Hold his hoof then," ordered the Captain. . . .

It was painful beyond words; but I contrived to hold my peace, by biting the clenched knuckle of my forefinger, and to refrain from kicking by realising that it was impossible, with Digby sitting on my leg and Claudia standing on my foot.

After what seemed a much longer time than it was, I heard Michael say, apparently from a long way off: "Here it comes," and then, a cheer from the Band and a dispersal of my torturers, announced the recovery of the buckshot.

"Shove it back in the gun, Dig," said the Captain; "and you, Isobel, sneak up to the cupboard outside our bathroom and bring me the scratch-muck."

The Faithful Hound, mopping her tear-bedewed face, sped away and soon returned with the scratch-muck (the bottle of antiseptic lotion, packet of boric lint, and roll of bandage, which figured as the *sequelæ* to all our minor casualties).

I believe Michael made a really excellent job of digging out the bullet and dressing the wound. Of course, the ball had not penetrated very deeply, or a penknife would hardly have been the appropriate surgical tool; but, as things were, a doctor could not have been very much quicker, nor the healing of the wound more clean and rapid.

And when the bandage was fastened, the Captain, in the presence of the whole Band and some temporary members, visitors, raised me to the seventh heaven of joy and pride by solemnly conferring upon me in perpetuity, the rank and title of Stout Fella, in that I had shed no tear and uttered no sound during a major operation of "naval surgery without æsthetics."

Further, he awarded me the signal and high honour of a full-dress "*Viking's funeral.*"

Now a Viking's funeral cannot be solemnised every day in the week, for it involves, among other things, the destruction of a long-ship.

The dead Viking is laid upon a funeral pyre in the centre of his ship, his spear and shield are laid beside him, his horse and hound are slaughtered and their bodies placed in attendance, the pyre is lighted, and the ship sent out to sea with all sail set.

On this occasion, the offending French ship was dedicated to these ocean obsequies.

A specially selected lead soldier was solemnly endowed with the name and attributes of *The Viking Eorl, John Geste,* laid upon a matchbox filled with explosives, a pyre of matches built round him on the deck of the ship (the ship drenched with paraffin), his horse laid at the head of his pyre, and a small (china) dog at his feet.

All being ready, we bared our heads, Michael, with raised hand, solemnly uttered the beautiful words, "*Ashes to ashes and dust to dust, if God won't have you the devil must,*" and, applying a match to the pyre, shoved the long-ship (late French battleship) well out into the middle of the lily-pond.

Here it burned gloriously, the leaping flames consuming the mast and sail so that the charred wreckage went by the board, and we stood silent, envisaging the horrors of a burning ship at sea.

As the vessel burned down to the water's edge, and then disappeared with hissings and smoking, Michael broke the ensuing silence with words that I was to remember many years later in a very different place. (Apparently Digby remembered them too.)

"*That's* what I call a funeral!" said Michael. "Compare that with being stuck ten feet down in the mud and clay of a beastly cemetery for worms to eat and maggots to wriggle about in you. . . . Cripes! I'd give something to have one like that when my turn comes. . . . Good idea! I'll write it down in my will, and none of you dirty little dogs will get anything from me, unless you see it properly done."

"Righto, Beau," said Digby. "I'll give you one, old chap, whenever you like."

"So will I you, Dig, if you die first," replied Michael to his twin, and they solemnly shook hands upon it. . . .

My gratification for these honours was the greater in that nothing had been further from my thoughts than such promotion and reward. Frequently had I striven in the past to win one of the Band's recognised Orders of Merit —Faithful Hound, Good Egg, Stout Fella, or even Order of Michael (For Valour)—but had never hitherto won any decoration or recognition beyond some such cryptic remark from the Captain as, "We shall have to make John, Chaplain to the Band, if he does many more of these Good Deeds. . . ."

That evening when we were variously employed in the schoolroom, old Burdon, the butler, came and told us that we could go into the drawing-room.

Claudia and Isobel were there, the former talking in a very self-possessed and grown-up way to a jolly-looking foreign person, to whom we were presented. He turned out to be a French cavalry officer, and we were thrilled to discover that he was on leave from Morocco where he had been fighting.

"Bags I we get him up to the schoolroom to-morrow," whispered Michael, as we gathered round a glass dome, like a clock-cover, inverted over a white velvet cushion on which lay the "Blue Water" sapphire.

We looked at it in silence, and, to me, it seemed to grow bigger and bigger until I felt as though I could plunge head first into it.

Young as I was, I distinctly had the feeling that it would not be a good thing to stare too long at that wonderful concentration of living colour. It seemed alive and, though inexpressibly beautiful, a little sinister.

"May we handle it, Aunt Patricia?" asked Claudia, and, as usual, she got her way.

Aunt Patricia lifted off the glass cover and handed the jewel to the Frenchman, who quickly gave it to Claudia.

"That has caused we know not what of strife and sorrow and bloodshed," he said. "What a tale it could tell!"

"Can you tell tales of strife and bloodshed, please?" asked Michael, and as Claudia said, "Why, of course! He leads charges of Arab cavalry like *Under Two Flags*," as though she had known him for years, we all begged him to tell us about his fighting, and he ranked second only to the "Blue Water" as a centre of attraction.

On the following afternoon, the Captain deputed Claudia to get the Frenchman to tell us some tales.

"Decoy yon handsome stranger to our lair," quoth he. "I would wring his secrets from him."

Nothing loth, Claudia exercised her fascinations upon him after lunch, and brought him to our camp in the Bower, a clearing in the woods near the house.

Here he sat on a log and absolutely thrilled us to the marrow of our bones by tales, most graphically and realistically told, of the Spahis, the French Foreign Legion, the Chasseurs d'Afrique, Zouaves, Turcos, and other romantically named regiments.

He told us of desert warfare, of Arab cruelties and chivalries, of hand-to-hand combats wherein swordsman met swordsman on horseback as in days of old, of brave deeds, of veiled Touaregs, veiled women, secret Moorish cities, oases, mirages, sand-storms, and the wonders of Africa.

Then he showed us fencing-tricks and feats of swords-

manship, until, when he left us, after shaking our hands
and kissing Claudia, we were his, body and soul. . . .

"I'm going to join the French Foreign Legion when I
leave Eton," announced Michael suddenly. "Get a commission and then join his regiment."

"So am I," said Digby, of course.

"And I," I agreed.

Augustus Brandon looked thoughtful.

"Could I be a *vivandière* and come too?" asked Isobel.

"You shall all visit me in your officers' uniforms," promised Claudia. "French officers always wear them in
France. Very nice too." . . .

Next day we went back to our preparatory school at
Slough.

§ 3.

The next time I saw the "Blue Water" was during the
holidays before our last half at Eton.

The occasion was the visit of General Sir Basil Malcolmson, an authority on gems, who was, at the time, Keeper of
the Jewel House at the Tower of London, and had, I think,
something to do with the British Museum. He had written
a "popular" history of the well-known jewels of the world,
under the title of *Famous Gems,* and was now writing a second volume dealing with less-known stones of smaller value.

He had written to ask if he might include an account
of the "Blue Water" sapphire and its history.

I gathered from what Claudia had heard her say, that
Aunt Patricia was not extraordinarily delighted about it,
and that she had replied that she would be very pleased to
show Sir Basil the stone; but that very little was known of
its history beyond the fact that it had been "acquired"
(kindly word) by the seventh Sir Hector Brandon in India
in the eighteenth century, when he was a soldier of fortune
in the service of one of the Nawabs or Rajahs of the
Deccan, probably Nunjeraj, Sultan of Mysore.

The General was a very interesting talker, and at dinner
that night he told us about such stones as the Timour
Ruby, the Hope Diamond, and the Stuart Sapphire (which

ís in the King's crown), until the conversation at times
became a monologue, which I, personally, greatly enjoyed.

I remember his telling us that it was he who discovered
that the Nadirshah Uncut Emerald was not, as had been
supposed, a lump of glass set in cheap and crude Oriental
gold-work. It had been brought to this country after the
Mutiny as an ordinary example of mediæval Indian jewel-
setting, and was shown as such at the Exhibition at the
Crystal Palace. Sir Basil Malcolmson had examined it and
found that the "scratches" on it were actually the names
of the Moghul Emperors who had owned it and had worn
it in their turbans. This had established, once and for
all, the fact that it is one of the world's greatest historic
gems, was formerly in the Peacock Throne at Delhi, and
literally priceless in value. I think he added that it was
now in the Regalia at the Tower of London.

I wondered whether the "Blue Water" and the "Nadirshah Emerald" had ever met in India, and whether the
blue stone had seen as much of human misery and villainy
as the great green one. Quite possibly, the sapphire had
faced the emerald, the one in the turban of Shivaji, the
Maratha soldier of fortune, and the other in that of Akh-
bar, the Moghul Emperor.

And I remember wondering whether the stones, the one
in the possession of a country gentleman, the other in that
of the King of England, had reached the ends of their
respective histories of theft, bloodshed, and human suffering.

Certainly it seemed impossible that the "Blue Water"
should again "see life" (and death)—until one remembered that such stones are indestructible and immortal, and
may be, thousands of years hence, the cause of any crime
that greed and covetousness can father. . . .

Anyhow, I should be glad to see the big sapphire again,
and hear anything that Sir Basil might have to say about it.

I remember that Augustus distinguished himself that
evening.

"I wonder how much you'd give Aunt for the 'Blue
Water,' " he remarked to Sir Basil.

"I am not a dealer," replied that gentleman.

And when Claudia asked Aunt Patricia if she were going to show Sir Basil the Priests' Hole and the hiding-place of the safe in which the sapphire reposed, the interesting youth observed:

"Better not, Aunt. He might come back and pinch it one dark night—the sapphire I mean, not the Hole."

Ignoring him, Aunt Patricia said that she would take Sir Basil and the other guest, a man named Lawrence, a Nigerian official who was an old friend, and show them the Priests' Hole.

The conversation then turned upon the marvellous history of the Hope Diamond, and the incredible but true tale of the misfortune which invariably befell its possessor; upon Priests' Holes and the varying tide of religious persecution which led to the fact that the same hiding-place had sheltered Roman Catholic priests and Protestant pastors in turn; and upon the day when Elizabethan troopers, searching for Father Campion, did damage to our floors, pictures, panelling, and doors (traces of which are still discernible), without discovering the wonderfully-contrived Priests' Hole at all.

It was near the end of this very interesting dinner that our beloved and reverend old friend, the Chaplain, made it more memorable than it otherwise would have been.

He had sat throughout dinner behaving beautifully, talking beautifully, and looking beautiful (with his ivory face and silver hair, which made him look twenty years older than he was), and then, just as Burdon put the decanters in front of him, he suddenly did what he had never done before—"broke out" in Aunt Patricia's presence. We had often known him to be queer, and it was an open secret in the house that he was to be humoured when queer (but if open, it was still a secret nevertheless), though he was always perfectly normal in Aunt Patricia's presence.

And now it happened!

"Burdon," said he, in the quiet voice in which one speaks "aside" to a servant, "could you get me a very beautiful white rabbit with *large* pink eyes, and, if possible, a nice pink ribbon round its neck? A mauve would do. . . . But on no account pale blue ribbon, Burdon.''

It was a bad break and we all did our best to cover it up by talking fast—but Burdon and Michael were splendid.

"Certainly, your Reverence,'' said Burdon without turning a hair, and marched straight to the screen by the service-door, as one expecting to find a white rabbit on the table behind it.

"That's a novel idea, sir,'' said Michael. "I suppose it's a modern equivalent of the roast peacock brought to table in its feathers, looking as though it were alive? Great idea . . .''

"Yes,'' Digby took him up. "Boar's head, with glass eyes and all that. Never heard of a rabbit served in its jacket though, I think. Good idea, anyhow.''

The Chaplain smiled vacantly, and Augustus Brandon giggled and remarked:

"I knew a man who jugged his last hair, though.''

I hastened to join in, and Isobel began to question the Chaplain as to the progress of his book on Old Glass, a book which he had been writing for years, the subject being his pet hobby.

I wondered whether my aunt, at the head of the table, had noticed anything. Glancing at her, I saw that she looked ten years older than she had done before it happened.

As I held the door open, when the ladies retired after dinner, she whispered to me in passing, "Tell Michael to look after the Chaplain this evening. He has been suffering from insomnia and is not himself.''

But later, in the drawing-room, when the "Blue Water'' was smiling, beguiling, and alluring from its white velvet cushion beneath the glass dome, and we stood round the table on which it lay, the Chaplain certainly was himself, and, if possible, even more learned and interesting on the subject of gems than the great Sir Basil.

I was very thankful indeed, for my heart ached for Aunt Patricia as she watched him; watched him just as a mother would watch an only child of doubtful sanity, bal-

anced between her hope and her fear, her passionate denial
of its idiocy, her passionate joy in signs of its normality.

§ 4.

Poor Aunt Patricia! She had contracted an alliance
with Sir Hector Brandon as one might contract a disease.
The one alleviation of this particular affliction being its
intermittence; for this monument of selfishness was generally anywhere but at home, he being a mighty hunter
before the Lord (or the Devil) and usually in pursuit of
prey, biped or quadruped, in distant places. It is a good
thing to have a fixed purpose, an aim, and an ambition in
life, and Sir Hector boasted one. It was to be able to say
that he had killed one of every species of beast and bird
and fish in the world, and had courted a woman of every
nationality in the world! A great soul fired with a noble
ambition.

As children, we did not, of course, realise what Aunt
Patricia suffered at the hands of this violent and bad man
when he was at home, nor what his tenants and labourers
suffered when he was absent.

As we grew older, however, it was impossible to avoid
knowing that he was universally hated, and that he bled
the estate shamefully and shamelessly, that he might enjoy
himself abroad.

Children might die of diphtheria through faulty drains
or lack of drains; old people might die of chills and rheu-
matism through leaking roofs and damply rotting cottages;
every farmer might have a cankering grievance; the estate-
agent might have the position and task of a flint-skinning
slave-owner; but Sir Hector's yacht and Sir Hector's lady-
friends would lack for nothing, nor his path through life
be paved with anything less than gold.

And Lady Brandon might remain at home to face the
music—whether angry growls of wrath, or feeble cries of
pain.

But we boys and girls were exceedingly fortunate, a
happy band who followed our leader Michael, care-free and
joyous. . . .

§ 5.

I think that the feat of Michael's that impressed us most, was his sustaining the rôle of a Man in Armour successfully for what seemed an appallingly long time. (It was nearly long enough to cause my death, anyhow!)

We were in the outer hall one wet afternoon, and the brilliant idea of dressing up in one of the suits of armour occurred to the Captain of the Band.

Nothing loth, we, his henchmen, quickly became Squires of, more or less, High Degree, and with much ingenuity and more string, more or less correctly cased the knight in his armour.

He was just striking an attitude and bidding a caitiff to die, when the sound of a motor-horn anachronistically intruded and the Band dispersed as do rabbits at the report of a gun.

Michael stepped up on to the pedestal and stood at ease (Ease!) Digby fled up the stairs, the girls dashed into the drawing-room, Augustus and another visitor rushed down a corridor to the service-staircase, and I, like Ginevra, dived into a great old chest on the other side of the hall.

There I lay as though screwed down in a coffin and pride forbade me ignominiously to crawl forth. I realised that I was suffering horribly—and the next thing that I knew was that I was lying on my bed and Michael was smiting my face with a wet sponge while Digby dealt kindly blows upon my chest and stomach.

When sufficiently recovered and sufficiently rebuked for being such an ass, I was informed that Aunt Patricia had driven up with a "black man"—mystery of mysteries!—and had confabulated with him right in front of the Man in Armour, afterwards speeding the "black man" on his way again in her car.

We were much intrigued, and indulged in much speculation—the more, in that Michael would not say a word beyond that such a person *had* come and had gone again, and that he himself had contrived to remain so absolutely still in that heavy armour that not a creak, rustle, clank, or

other sound had betrayed the fact that there actually was
a Man in the Armour!

In the universal and deserved admiration for this feat,
my own poor performance in preferring death to discovery
and dishonour passed unpraised.

I must do Michael the justice, however, to state that directly Aunt Patricia had left the hall, he had hurried to
raise the lid of the chest in which I was entombed, and
had himself carried me upstairs as soon as his armour was
removed and restored to its place.

Digby, who, from long and painful practice, was an expert bugler, took down his old coach-horn from its place
on the wall and blew what he said was an "honorific fan-
fare of heralds' trumpets," in recognition of the *tenacity*
displayed both by Michael and myself.

I must confess, however, that in spite of Michael's reticence concerning the visit of the "black man," we others
discussed the strange event in all its bearings.

We, however, arrived at no conclusion, and were driven
to content ourselves with a foolish theory that the strange
visitor was in some way connected with a queer boy, now
a very distinguished and enlightened ruler in India. He
was the oldest son and heir of the Maharajah, his father,
and had been at the College for the sons of Ruling Princes
in India, I think the Rajkumar College at Ajmir, before
coming to Eton.

He was a splendid athlete and sportsman, and devoted
to Michael to the point of worship.

Aunt Patricia welcomed him to Brandon Abbas at
Michael's request, and when he saw the "Blue Water"
he actually and literally and completely fainted.

I suppose the sight of the sapphire was the occasion
rather than the cause, but the fact remains. It was queer
and uncanny beyond words, the more so because he never
uttered a sound, and neither then nor subsequently ever
said one syllable on the subject of the great jewel!

And so we lived our happy lives at Brandon Abbas,
when not at our prep. school, at Eton, or later, at Oxford.

CHAPTER II

THE DISAPPEARANCE OF THE "BLUE WATER"

AND then, one autumn evening, the face of life changed as utterly and suddenly as unexpectedly. The act of one person altered the lives of all of us, and brought suffering, exile, and death in its train.

I am neither a student nor a philosopher, but I would like some convinced exponent of the doctrine of Free Will to explain how we are anything but the helpless victims of the consequences of the acts of other people. How I envy the grasp and logic of those great minds that can easily reconcile *"unto the third and fourth generation,"* for example, with this comfortable doctrine!

On this fine autumn evening, so ordinary, so secure and comfortable, so fateful and momentous, we sat in the great drawing-room of Brandon Abbas, after dinner, all together for what proved to be the last time. There were present Aunt Patricia, the Chaplain, Claudia, Isobel, Michael, Digby, Augustus Brandon, and myself.

Aunt Patricia asked Claudia to sing, and that young lady excused herself on the score of being out of sorts and not feeling like it. She certainly looked pale and somewhat below her usual sparkling standard of health and spirits. I had thought for some days that she had seemed preoccupied and worried, and I had wondered if her bridge-debts and dressmakers' bills were the cause of it.

With her wonted desire to be helpful and obliging, Isobel went to the piano, and for some time we sat listening to her sweet and sympathetic voice, while my aunt knitted, the Chaplain twiddled his thumbs, Claudia wrestled with some unpleasant problem in frowning abstraction, Augustus shuffled and tapped his cigarette-case with a cigarette he dared not light, Digby turned over the leaves of a magazine, and Michael watched Claudia.

Presently Isobel rose and closed the piano.

"What about a game of pills?" said Augustus, and before anyone replied, Claudia said:

"Oh, Aunt, *do* let's have the 'Blue Water' down for a little while. I haven't seen it for ages."

"Rather!" agreed Michael. "Let's do a gloat, Aunt," and the Chaplain supported him and said he'd be delighted to get it, if Lady Brandon would give permission.

Only he and Aunt Patricia knew the *secret* of the Priests' Hole (excepting Sir Hector, of course), and I believe it would have taken an extraordinarily ingenious burglar to have discovered it, even given unlimited opportunity, before tackling the safe in which the "Blue Water," with other valuables, reposed. (I know that Michael, Digby, and I had spent countless hours, with the knowledge and consent of our aunt, in trying to find, without the slightest success, the trick of this hiding-place of more than one hunted divine. It became an obsession with Michael.) . . .

Aunt Patricia agreed at once, and the Chaplain disappeared. He had a key which gave access to the hiding-place of the keys of the safe which the Priests' Hole guarded.

"What *is* the 'Blue Water' worth, Aunt Patricia?" asked Claudia.

"To whom, dear?" was the reply.

"Well—what would a Hatton Garden person give for it?"

"About a half what he thought his principal would be willing to offer, perhaps."

"And what would that be, about, do you suppose?"

"I don't know, Claudia. If some American millionaire were very anxious to buy it, I suppose he'd try to find out the lowest sum that would be considered," was the reply.

"What *would* you ask, supposing you *were* going to sell it?" persisted Claudia.

"I certainly am not going to sell it," said Aunt Patricia, in a voice that should have closed the conversation. She had that day received a letter from her husband announcing his early return from India, and it had not cheered her at all.

"I did hear someone say once that Uncle Hector was offered thirty thousand pounds for it," said Augustus.

"Did you?" replied Aunt Patricia, and at that moment the Chaplain returned, carrying the sapphire on its white velvet cushion, under its glass dome. He placed it on a table under the big hanging chandelier, with its countless cut-glass pendants and circle of electric bulbs.

There it lay, its incredible, ineffable, glowing blue fascinating us as we gazed upon it.

"It *is* a wonderful thing," said Isobel, and I wondered how often those very words had been said of it.

"Oh, let me kiss it," cried Claudia, and with one hand the Chaplain raised the glass dome, and with the other handed the sapphire to Aunt Patricia, who examined it as though she had not handled it a thousand times. She looked through it at the light. She then passed it to Claudia, who fondled it awhile.

We all took it in turn, Augustus throwing it up and catching it as he murmured, "Thirty thousand pounds for a bit of glass!"

When Michael got it, I thought he was never going to pass it on. He weighed and rubbed and examined it, more in the manner of a dealer than an admirer of the beautiful.

Finally, the Chaplain put it back on its cushion and replaced the glass cover.

We sat and stood around for a few minutes, while the Chaplain said something about Indian Rajahs and their marvellous hereditary and historical jewels.

I was standing close to the table, bending over and peering into the depths of the sapphire again; Augustus was reiterating, "Who says a game of pills, pills, pills?" when, suddenly, as occasionally happened, the electric light failed, and we were plunged in complete darkness.

"What's Fergusson up to now?" said Digby, alluding to the head chauffeur, who was responsible for the engine.

"It'll come on again in a minute," said Aunt Patricia, and added, "Burdon will bring candles if it doesn't. . . . Don't wander about, anybody, and knock things over."

Somebody brushed lightly against me as I stood by the table.

"Ghosts and goblins!" said Isobel in a sepulchral voice. "Who's got a match? A skeleton hand is about to clutch my throat. I can see . . ."

"Everybody," I remarked, as the light came on again, and we blinked at each other in the dazzling glare, so suddenly succeeding the velvet darkness.

"Saved!" said Isobel, with an exaggerated sigh of relief, and then, as I looked at her, she stared wide-eyed and open-mouthed, and then pointed speechless. . . .

The "Blue Water" had vanished. The white velvet cushion was bare, and the glass cover covered nothing but the cushion.

§ 2.

We must have looked a foolish band as we stood and stared, for a second or two, at that extraordinarily empty-looking abode of the great sapphire. I never saw anything look so empty in my life. Aunt Patricia broke the silence and the spell.

"*Your* joke, Augustus?" she enquired, in that rarely-used tone of hers that would have made an elephant feel small.

"Eh? *Me?* No, Aunt! Really! I swear! *I* never touched it," declared the youth, colouring warmly.

"Well—there's someone with a sense of humour all his own," she observed, and I was glad that I was not the misguided humorist. Also I was glad that she had regarded the joke as more probably Augustan than otherwise.

"You were standing by the table, John," she continued, turning to me. "Are you the jester?"

"No, Aunt," I replied with feeble wit, "only the Geste."

As Digby and Michael both flatly denied any part in this poor practical joke, Aunt Patricia turned to the girls.

"Surely not?" she said, raising her fine eyebrows.

"No, Aunt, I was too busy with ghosts and goblins and the skeleton hand, to use my own hand for sticking and peeling—I mean picking and stealing," said Isobel.

"*I* haven't got it," said Claudia.

Lady Brandon and the Reverend Maurice Ffolliot eyed the six of us with cold severity.

"Let us say nothing of the good taste displayed, either in the act or in the denial," said the former, "but agree that the brilliant joke has been carried far enough, shall we?"

"Put the brilliant joke back, John," said Augustus. "You were the only one near it when the light went out."

"I have said that I didn't touch the sapphire," I replied.

"Suppose *you* put it back, Ghastly," said Digby, and his voice had an edge on it.

"And suppose *you* do!" blustered Augustus angrily.

Digby, who was standing behind him, suddenly raised his right knee with sufficient force to propel the speaker in the direction of the table—an exhibition of ill manners and violence that passed unrebuked by Aunt Patricia.

"I haven't *got* the beastly thing, I tell you," shouted the smitten one, turning ferociously upon Digby. "It's one of you three rotters."

It was an absurd situation, rapidly degenerating into an unpleasant one, and my aunt's lips were growing thinner, and her eyebrows beginning to contract toward her high-bridged nose.

"Look here, sillies!" said Isobel, as we brothers glared at Augustus and he glared at us. "I am going to turn all the lights out again for two minutes. Whoever played the trick, and told the fib, is to put the 'Blue Water' back. Then no one will know who did it. See?" and she walked away to the door, by which were the electric-light switches.

"Now!" she said. "Everybody keep still except the villain, and when I switch the lights on again, there will be the 'Blue Water' laughing at us."

"Oh, rot," said Augustus, and out went the lights before Aunt Patricia or the Chaplain made any comment.

Now it occurred to me that it would be very interesting to know who had played this silly practical joke and told a silly lie after it. I therefore promptly stepped towards the table, felt the edge of it with my right hand and then, with a couple of tentative dabs, laid my left hand on top of the glass dome. Whoever came to return the sapphire must touch me, and him I would promptly seize. I might not have felt so interested in the matter had it not been twice pointed out that it was I who stood against the table when the light failed.

Isobel's device for securing the prompt return of the sapphire was an excellent one, but I saw no reason why I should linger under the suspicion of having been an ass and a liar, for the benefit of Augustus.

So there I stood and waited.

While doing so, it occurred to me to wonder what would happen if the joker did not have the good sense to take advantage of the opportunity provided by Isobel. . . .

Perfect silence reigned in the big room.

"I can't do it, my boots creak," said Digby suddenly.

"I can't find the cover," said Michael.

"Another minute, villain," said Isobel. "Hurry up."

And then I was conscious that someone was breathing very near me. I felt a faint touch on my elbow. A hand came down lightly against my wrist—and I grabbed.

My left hand was round a coat-sleeve, beneath which was the stiff cuff of a dress shirt, and my right grasped a wrist. I was very glad that it was a man's arm. Had it been a girl's I should have let go. Ghastly Gustus, of course. . . . It was just the silly sort of thing he would do, and it was just like him to take advantage of the darkness, when he found the joke had fallen remarkably flat. I did not envy him the look that would appear on Aunt Patricia's face when the light went up and he was discovered in my grip.

I would have let him go, I think, had he not endeavoured to put the blame on me, and insisted on my nearness to the table when the light failed.

I was a little surprised that he did not struggle, and I was prepared for a sudden violent twist and a swift evasion in the dark.

He kept perfectly still.

"I am going to count ten, and then up goes the light. Are you ready, villain?" came the voice of Isobel from the door.

"Yes, I've put it back," said Digby.

"So have I," said Michael, close to me.

"And I," echoed Claudia.

Then Isobel switched on the light, and I found that my hands were clenched on the right arm of—my brother Michael!

I was more surprised than I can say.

It was only a small matter, of course; a pointless practical joke and a pointless lie, but it was so utterly unlike Michael. It was unlike him to do it, and more unlike him flatly to deny having done it. And my surprise increased when Michael, looking at me queerly, actually remarked:

"So it was *me*, John, was it? Oh, *Feeble* Geste!"

I felt absurdly hurt, and turning to Augustus said, "I apologise, Gussie. I admit I thought it was you."

"Oh, don't add insult to injury," he replied. "Put the beastly thing back, and stop being a funny ass. Enough of you is too much."

Put the beastly thing back! I turned and looked at the cushion. It was empty still. I looked at Michael and Michael looked at me.

"Oh, shove it back, Beau," I said. "It's all been most extraordinarily clever and amusing, I'm sure. But I'm inclined to agree with Gussie."

Michael gave me one of his long, thoughtful, penetrating looks. "H'm," said he.

Isobel came over from the door.

"I *do* think you might have played up, sillies," said she. "Put it back, Beau, and let's have a dance. May we, Aunt?"

"Certainly," said Aunt Patricia, "as soon as ever the great humorist in our midst has received our felicitations," and I really pitied the said humorist, when he should make his avowal, annoyed with him as I felt.

The Chaplain looked from face to face of the six of us and said nothing. Aunt Patricia did the same.

We all stood silent.

"Now stop this fooling," said she. "Unless the 'Blue Water' is produced at once, I shall be very seriously annoyed."

"Come on, somebody," said Digby.

Another minute's silence.

It began to grow unbearable.

"I am waiting," said Lady Brandon at last, and her foot began to tap.

From that moment the matter became anything but a joke, swiftly growing unpleasant and increasingly so.

§ 3.

I shall not forget the succeeding hours in a hurry, and their horrible atmosphere of suspicion—seven people suspecting one of the other seven, and the eighth person pretending to do so.

My capable and incisive aunt quickly brought things to a clear issue, upon getting no reply to her "I am waiting," and her deliberate look from face to face of the angry and uncomfortable group around her.

"Maurice," said she to the Chaplain, laying her hand upon his sleeve, her face softening and sweetening incredibly, "come and sit by me until I have asked each of these young people a question. Then I want you to go to bed, for it's getting late," and she led him to a big and deep chesterfield that stood on a low dais in a big window recess.

Seating herself with the air and presence of a queen on a throne, she said, quietly and very coldly:

"This is getting serious, and unless it ends at once, the consequences will be serious too. For the last time I ask the boy, or girl, who moved the 'Blue Water,' to give it to me, and we will end the silly business now and here, and make no further reference to it. If not . . . Come, this is absurd and ridiculous. . . ."

"Oh, come off it, John," said Augustus, "for God's sake."

Nobody else spoke.

"Very well," said my aunt, "since the fool won't leave his folly. . . . Come here, Claudia. . . . Have you touched the 'Blue Water' since the Chaplain restored it to its place?" She laid her hand on Claudia's arm, drew her close, and looked into her eyes.

"No, Aunt. . . ."

"No, Aunt," said Claudia again.

"Of course not," said Aunt Patricia. "Go to bed, dear. Good night."

And Claudia departed, not without an indignant glance at me.

"Come here, Isobel," continued my aunt. "Have you touched the 'Blue Water' since the Chaplain put it back in its place?"

"No, Aunt, I have not," replied Isobel.

"I am sure you have not. Go to bed. Good night," said Lady Brandon.

Isobel turned to go and then stopped.

"But I might have done, Aunt, if the idea had occurred to me," she said. "It is just a joke, of course."

"Bed," rejoined her aunt, and Isobel departed with a kind glance at me.

Aunt Patricia turned to Augustus.

"Come here," she said coldly, and with a hard stare into his somewhat shifty eyes. "Please answer absolutely truthfully—for your own sake. If you have got the 'Blue Water' and give it to me now, I shall not say another word about the matter. Have you?"

"I swear to God, Aunt . . ." broke out Augustus.

"You need not swear to God, nor to me, Augustus," was the cold reply. "Yes or No. Have you got it?"

"*No*, Aunt! I take my solemn oath I . . ." the unhappy youth replied vehemently, when the cold voice interrupted:

"Have you touched the sapphire since the Chaplain put it under its cover?"

"No, Aunt. *Really*, I haven't! I assure you I . . ." began Augustus, to be again interrupted by the cold question:

"Do you know where the 'Blue Water' is now?"

"No, Aunt," promptly replied he, "upon my soul I don't. If I did, I'd jolly well . . ."

"John," said my aunt, without further notice of Augustus, "do you know where the stone is?"

"No, Aunt," I replied, and added, "nor have I touched it since the Chaplain did."

She favoured me with a long, long look, which I was able to meet quite calmly, and I hope not at all rudely. As I looked away, my eyes met Michael's. He was watching me queerly.

Then came Digby's turn. He said quite simply and plainly that he knew nothing about the jewel's disappearance and had not touched it since it was passed to him by Claudia, and handed on by him to Isobel.

There remained Michael. He was the culprit, or else one of us had told a most deliberate, calculated, and circumstantial lie, inexcusable and disgraceful.

I felt angrier with Michael than I had ever done in my life, yet I was angry rather *for* him than with him. It was so utterly unlike him to do such a stupid thing, and to allow all this unpleasant and undignified inquisition to go on, when a word from him would have ended it.

Why must my idol act as though he had feet of clay—or, at any rate, smear clay upon his feet? The joke was unworthy, but the lie was really painfully so.

I have no objection to the good thumping lie that is "a very present help in time of trouble," told at the right time and in the right cause (such as to save the other fellow's bacon). But I have the strongest distaste for a silly lie that merely gives annoyance to other people, and puts blame upon an innocent person.

From the moment I had caught him in the act of trying to return the jewel secretly, I had felt sick with indignation, and literally and physically sick when, his effort frustrated by me, he had pretended innocence and held on for another opportunity of returning the thing unseen.

Had I not myself caught him in the very act, he was, of all of us, the last person whom I should have suspected. He and Isobel, that is to say. I should have strongly suspected Augustus, and, his innocence established, I should have supposed that Digby had fallen a victim to his incurable love of joking—though I should have been greatly surprised.

Had Digby then been proved innocent, I am afraid I should have suspected Claudia of wishing to turn the limelight on herself by an innocently naughty escapade—before I should ever have entertained the idea of Michael doing it and denying it.

Now that all had firmly and categorically declared their absolute innocence and ignorance in the matter, I had no option (especially in view of my catching him at the spot) but to conclude that Michael had been what I had never known him to be before—a fool, a cad, and a liar.

I could have struck him for hurting himself so.

"Michael," said Aunt Patricia very gravely, very coldly, and very sadly, "I'm sorry. More so than I can tell you, Michael. Please put the 'Blue Water' back, and I will say no more. But I doubt whether I shall feel like calling you 'Beau' for some time."

"I *can't* put it back, Aunt, for I haven't got it," said Michael quietly, and my heart bounded.

"Do you know where it is, Michael?" asked my aunt.

"I do not, Aunt," was the immediate reply.

"Have you touched the sapphire since the Chaplain did, Michael?" was the next question.

"I have not, Aunt," was the quiet answer.

"Do you know anything about its disappearance, Michael?" asked the hard level voice.

"I only know that *I* have had nothing whatever to do with its disappearance, Aunt," answered my brother, and I was aghast.

"Do you declare that all you have just said is the absolute truth, Michael?" was the final question.

"I declare it to be the whole truth, and nothing but the truth," was the final answer.

§ 4.

What was I to think? Certainly I could not think that Michael was lying. Equally certainly I could not forget that I had caught his hand on the glass cover.

On the whole, if I had to doubt either Michael or the evidence of my senses, I preferred to do the latter. When we got out of that terrible room, I would go to him when he was alone, and say, "Beau, old chap, just tell *me* you didn't touch the thing—and if you say you didn't, there's an absolute end of it." And so there would be as far as I was concerned. . . .

On hearing his last words, my aunt sat and stared at Michael. The silence grew horrible. At length she began to speak in a low frozen voice.

"This is inexpressibly vulgar and disgusting," she began. "One of half a dozen boys and girls, who have practically grown up here, is a despicable liar and, apparently, a common thief—or an uncommon one. I am still unable to think the latter. . . . Listen. . . . I shall leave the cover where it is and I shall lock the doors of this room at midnight and keep the keys, except the key of that one. Bring it to me, Digby. . . . Thank you.

"This key I shall put in the old brass box on the ledge above the fire-place in the outer hall. The servants will have gone to bed and will know nothing of its whereabouts. I ask the liar, who is present, to take the opportunity of returning the sapphire during the night, relocking the door, and replacing the key in the brass box. If this is *not* done by the time I come down to-morrow, I shall have to conclude that the liar *is* also a thief, and act accordingly. For form's sake I shall tell Claudia and Isobel."

"Come, Maurice," she added, rising and taking the Chaplain's arm. "I do hope you won't let this worry you, and give you a sleepless night."

The poor Chaplain looked too unhappy, bewildered, and bemused to speak.

Having locked two of the doors, Lady Brandon, followed by the Chaplain, swept from the room without a "Good night" to any of us.

I think we each heaved a sigh of relief as the door shut. I certainly did.

And now, what?

Digby turned upon Augustus.

"Oh, you unutterable cheese-mite," he said, apparently more in sorrow than in anger. "I think de-bagging is indicated. . . . And a leather belt," he added, "unless anyone's pumps are nice and swishy."

I said nothing. It was not the hand of Augustus that I had caught feeling for the cover.

He glared from one to the other of us like a trapped rat, and almost shrieked as Digby seized him.

"You lying swine," he shouted. "Who was by the table when the light failed and came on again? Who was grabbing who, when Isobel turned it on?"

I looked at Michael, and Michael looked at me.

"Yes," screamed Augustus seeing the look, and wriggling free.

"By Jove!" said Digby, "if he pinched it, he's *got* it. . . . Come to my arms, Gus!" and in a moment he was sitting upon the prostrate form of the hysterically indignant youth, and feeling the pockets of his dinner-jacket from the outside.

"Not in his breast-pockets . . . side . . . waistcoat . . . trousers . . . no—the beggar hasn't got it unless he has swallowed it," announced Digby. Then . . . "Might have shoved it behind a cushion or dropped it somewhere. . . . Come on, out with it, Gus, and let's get to bed."

"You filthy, lying, beastly cad," blubbered Augustus in reply, showing the courage of the cornered rat.

I don't think he had ever defied or insulted either of my brothers before in his life.

I expected to see him promptly suffer grief and pain at their hands, but Michael did the unexpected, as usual.

"Why, I believe the little man's innocent after all," he said quite kindly.

"You *know* I am, you damned hypocrite," shouted Augustus. "Weren't you and John fumbling at the cover when she turned the light on—you cowardly blackguards."

Digby's hand closed on the scruff of the boy's neck.

"If I have accused you wrongly, Gussie, I'll humbly apologise and make it up to you," said he. "But if we find you *did* do it—oh, my little Gussie . . .!"

"And if you find it was Michael, or John, or yourself?" sneered the dishevelled and shaking Augustus.

Michael looked hard at me and I looked hard at him.

"Look here," said Digby, "presumably the thing is in

the room. Aunt wouldn't pinch her own jewel. The Chaplain has no use for it nor for thirty thousand pounds. No one supposes Isobel did it—nor Claudia. That leaves us four, and we haven't been out of the room. Come on, find it. Find it, Gussie, and I'll swear that *I* put it there," and Digby began throwing cushions from sofas and chairs, moving footstools, turning up rugs, and generally hunting about, the while he encouraged himself, and presumably Augustus, with cries of "Good dog! . . . Fetch 'em, boy! . . . Seize 'em, Gussie! . . . Sick 'em, pup! . . . Worry 'im, Gus!" and joyful barks.

Michael and I searched methodically and minutely, until it was perfectly clear that the "Blue Water" was not in the room, unless far more skilfully concealed than would have been possible in the dark and in the few minutes at the disposal of anyone who wished to hide it.

"Well, that's that," said Digby at last. "We'd better push off before Aunt comes down to lock the door. I don't want to see her again to-night. Damned if I don't feel guilty as soon as she looks at me."

"Perhaps you are!" snarled Augustus.

"You never know, do you?" grinned Digby.

"Better tidy up a bit before we go," suggested Michael. "Servants'll smell a rat if it's like this to-morrow."

"Smell a herd of elephants, I should think," answered Digby, and we three straightened the disordered room, while Augustus sullenly watched us, with an angry, bitter sneer, and an occasional snarl of "Beastly humbugs," or, "Lying hypocrites."

"Come to the smoking-room, you two?" said Digby to Michael and me, when we had finished.

"Yes—go and fix it up, cads," urged Augustus.

"Go to bed, Ghastly," replied Digby, "and don't forget the key will be in the brass box on the ledge over the fireplace in the outer hall. Bung off."

"For two damns I'd sit in the hall all night, and see who comes for it," was the reply, and the speaker glanced at me.

"Don't let *me* find you there, or I shall slap you," said Digby.

"No, I shouldn't be popular if I went there now and refused to budge, should I?" was the angry retort.

"Lord! It's a long worm that has no turning," cryptically remarked Digby, as Augustus took what was meant to be a dignified departure. "And a long lane that has no public-house," he added.

"Either that lad's innocent or he's a really accomplished young actor," I observed, looking after the retreating Augustus as we crossed the hall, where we said "Good night" to a yawning footman, and made our way down a corridor to the smoking-room.

§ 5.

"Well, my sons, what about it?" said Michael, poking up the fire, as we threw ourselves into deep leather arm-chairs and produced pipes.

"Pretty go if the damned thing isn't there in the morning," said Digby.

"I wonder if she'd send to Scotland Yard?" he added, blowing a long cloud of smoke towards the ceiling.

"Filthy business," said Michael. "Fancy a fat mystery-merchant prowling about here and questioning everybody!"

"What a lark!" chuckled Digby. "Jolly glad the servants are out of it all right, poor beggars."

"Beastly vulgar business, as Aunt said," observed Michael.

"And a bit rough on her too—apart from any question of thirty thousand pounds," said I.

"Shake her faith a bit in human nature, what?" said Digby. "But, damn it—the beastly thing will be there all right in the morning."

"I hope to God it will," said I from the bottom of my heart, and found that Michael and I were staring at each other again.

"Reconstruct the dreadful crime," suggested Digby. "Wash out Aunt and the Chaplain."

"And the girls," said Michael. "If anyone even glanced at the possibility of Claudia stealing, I'd wring his beastly neck until he could see all down his beastly back."

"I'd wring the neck of anyone who even glanced at the possibility of Isobel stealing—until he hadn't a head to see with," added Digby.

"Wouldn't it be too silly to be worth noticing at all?" I asked. I was thinking more particularly of Isobel.

"Let's go and *beat* young Gussie," said Digby.

"Gussie doesn't know a thing about it," said Michael. "Nothing but genuine injured innocence would have given him the pluck to call us 'Filthy liars,' and 'Damned hypocrites.' You know, if he'd been guilty, he'd have been conciliatory, voluble, and tearful—oh, altogether different. A much more humble parishioner."

"Believe you're right, Beau," agreed Digby. "Nothing like a sense of injustice to put you up on the bough. . . . 'Sides, young Gus hasn't the guts to pinch anything really valuable. . . . And if he'd taken it for a lark and hadn't been able to put it back, he'd have hidden it behind a cushion till he could. I quite expected to find it in some such place. That's why I gave him the chance. . . . If he *has* got it, he'll shove it back to-night," he added.

"He hasn't," said Michael—and again Michael and I found ourselves looking at each other.

"Well—that leave us three then," said I.

"It does," said Michael.

"You can count me out, old son," grinned Digby. "Search me."

"Which reminds one, by the way, that we didn't search ourselves, or each other, when we searched Gussie," said I. "It would have been fairer . . ."

"Most undignified and unnecessary," put in Michael.

"So Gussie seemed to find," chuckled Digby.

"Then that leaves you and me, John," said Michael.

"Yes, it leaves me and you, Beau," I agreed, and again we stared at each other.

"I did not take the 'Blue Water,' Beau," I said.

"*Nor did I*, John," said Michael.

"Then there's a mis-deal somewhere," remarked Digby, "and Gussie *must* have done it. Anyhow—it'll be put back in the night. Must be."

"What do you say to our sitting here until we hear somebody come down to the hall? That door always makes a frightful row," I suggested.

"Certainly not," said Michael sharply.

"Why not?" I asked, eyeing him.

"Why, you ass, it might not be . . . I mean we might . . . Anyhow, we've no right to interfere with Aunt's arrangements. She has given the person a chance . . ."

Michael was by no means fluent. He turned to Digby.

"Don't you think so, Dig?" he asked.

"Any ass can sit up who wants to," was the prompt reply. "I have had enough of to-day, myself. Who's coming up?" He rose and yawned.

"I say," he chuckled, "what a lark to pinch the key and hide it."

"Don't be a fool," said Michael. "Let's go to bed," and we went with our usual curt "Good nights." . . .

But it was easier, for me at least, to go to bed than to go to sleep, although my brain seemed somewhat numbed and dulled. I lay and tossed and turned, refusing to believe that Michael had done this disgusting thing, and unable, somehow, to believe that Augustus had. It did not occur to me to doubt Digby—and, as I have said, I should never have dreamt of doubting Michael, had I not caught him.

Leaving out Aunt Patricia, the Chaplain, Digby, and Augustus, there remained Isobel, Claudia, Michael, and I. Eliminating Isobel, there remained Claudia, Michael, and I. It could not be Claudia. How *could* it be Michael?

Had *I* done it myself?

Such was my mental condition by this time that I actually entertained the idea. I had read a book not so long before, in which, after a most tremendous mystery and bother, it turned out that the innocent hero had committed the crime while in a somnambulistic condition.

That could not apply in my case, of course. . . . There was no question or possibility of sleep-walking or trance about it—but might I not, absolutely unconsciously or subconsciously, have put the thing in my pocket without knowing it? People undoubtedly did do absurd things in fits of absent-mindedness, to their subsequent incredulous astonishment. I had never done such things myself—but might I not have begun doing them now? It was certainly as possible as it was utterly improbable. I actually got up and searched my clothes.

Of course I found nothing, and hour after hour of cogitation and reiterated argument brought me nearer and nearer to the conclusion that either Augustus or Michael was the culprit.

Having repeatedly arrived at this inevitable point, I delivered myself of the unhelpful verdict, *"Augustus or Michael—guilty. And I believe Augustus isn't, and Michael couldn't be!"*

Anyhow, daylight would find the wretched stone back in its place, and the whole business would be merely a very unsatisfactory and annoying puzzle, until it faded from the memories of the eight people who knew of it.

I turned over and made another resolute effort to go to sleep—a foolish thing to do, as it is one of the best ways of ensuring wakefulness.

My mind went off on a new tack. Suppose the "Blue Water" were not put back during the night? What exactly would happen?

One thing would be clear at any rate—that a determined effort was being made to steal the jewel, by somebody who intended to convert it into money.

Certainly Lady Brandon, that *maîtresse femme*, was not the person to accept that "lying down," and she would surely take precisely the same steps for its recovery that she would have taken had it been stolen by burglars or a servant. She would communicate with the police, and see that no one left the house until the matter was in official hands.

It would be inexpressibly unpleasant and degrading. I imagined the questioning, the searching, the loathsome sense of being under suspicion—even Isobel and Claudia. At four o'clock in the morning the whole affair looked unutterably beastly.

And then I pulled myself together. *Of course* it would be all right. The idiot who had played the fool trick, and been too feeble to own up, would have replaced the jewel. Probably it was there now. The said idiot would have been only too anxious to get rid of it as soon as Aunt Patricia had put the key in the brass box. . . . Why not go and make sure?

Of course—and then one could put the silly business out of one's mind and get some sleep.

I got out of bed, pulled on my dressing-gown, and put my feet into bedroom slippers. Lighting one of the emergency candles which stood on the mantelpiece, I made my way down the corridor to the upper of the two galleries that ran round the four sides of the central hall, and descended the stairs that led to the gallery below, and thence to the hall. Crossing this, I entered the outer hall, avoided the protruding hand and sword-hilt of a figure in armour, and made my silent way to the big stone fire-place.

On the broad shelf or mantelpiece, some six feet from the ground, was the ancient brass box, dating from the days of pack-horse travel, in which my aunt had placed the key.

Only she hadn't—or someone had removed it—for the box was quite empty!

Was this a trap, a trick of Lady Brandon's to catch the guilty one? Justly or unjustly, I thought she was quite capable of it.

If so, presumably I was caught again in this indiscriminating trap that another should have adorned. I was reminded of the occasion many years before, when she suddenly entered the schoolroom and said, "The naughty child that has been in the still-room has got jam on its chin," and my innocent and foolish hand promptly went up to my face to see if, by some wild mischance, it were jammy.

Well—the best thing to do now was to fade swiftly and silently away ere the trap closed; and I turned, wondering whether Aunt Patricia were watching.

That was an absurd idea, of course.

Then I wondered if the box contained some scent of

indelible odour, which would betray the guilty hand that had come in contact with it.

Equally absurd.

As I crossed the hall, I also thought of finger-prints.

Had she polished the lid and front of the box with the intention of having it examined by experts for the identification of the owner of the fingers that touched it during the night? Less absurd, perhaps, but utterly improbable. Such an idea might have occurred to her had it been certain that the "Blue Water" was really stolen by a thief who had meant to get away with it.

And supposing that were really the case, and the jewel were not replaced during the night?

There were my finger-prints, anyhow, if she had really thought of this plan! And there they were if it occurred to her later, in the event of the sapphire not being restored. I re-entered the central hall—not more than half a minute later than I had left it—and saw someone coming toward me. He, or she, carried no light, and, of course, could identify me, the candle being just in front of my face.

"Well, Gussie," said I. "Cold morning."

"Well, John. Looking for the key?" said the voice of my brother Michael.

"Yes, Beau," I answered. "It's not there."

"No, John," said Michael quietly. "It's here," and he held it out towards me.

"*Beau!*" I said miserably.

"*John!*" he mocked me.

A wave of sick disgust passed over me. What *had* come over my splendid brother?

"Good night," I said, turning away.

"Or morning," replied Michael, and, with a short laugh, he went into the outer hall.

I heard him strike a match and there followed the rattle of the key and the clang of a falling lid. He had evidently thrown the key carelessly into the box, and dropped the lid without any attempt at avoiding noise.

I went back to bed and, the affair being over and the mystery solved, fell into a broken sleep.

§ 6.

I was awakened at the usual time by David, the under-footman, with my hot water.

"Half-past seven, sir," said he; "a fine morning when the mist clears."

"Thank you, David," I replied, and sat up.

What was wrong? Of course—that idiotic affair of last night, and Michael's heavy fall from his pedestal. Well, there are spots on the sun, and no man is always himself. Why dwell on one fault rather than on a hundred virtues? But it *was* unlike Michael to tell such silly pointless lies to cover a silly pointless trick.

I dressed and went downstairs, taking a mashie and a ball from the glory-hole, a small room or large cupboard off the corridor that leads to the smoking-room. I would do a few approach shots from the tennis-courts to the paddock and back, before the breakfast-gong went at half-past eight.

Crossing the rose-garden I ran into Claudia. This surprised me, for she was more noted for being the last arrival at breakfast than for early rising. It struck me that she looked seedy and worried, and she was certainly deep in some unpleasant slough of thought when she saw me.

As she did so, her face cleared and brightened, rather too suddenly and artificially, I thought.

"Hullo, early worm," said she.

"Hullo, early bird," I replied. "What's up?"

"What do you mean?" asked Claudia.

"I thought you looked a bit off colour and bothered," replied I, with masculine tactlessness.

"Rubbish," said Claudia, and passed on.

I dropped my ball at the back of the tennis-courts, and strove in vain to smite it. I scooped generous areas of turf from the lawn, topped my ball, sliced it into a holly bush, threw my club after it, and slouched off, my hands deep in my pockets and anger (with Michael) deep in my soul.

Returning to the house I saw Burdon crossing the hall, the gong-stick in his hand. The brass box leered at me cynically as I passed.

Having washed my hands in the lavatory by the glory-hole, I went into the dining-room.

The fire was blazing merrily, a silver kettle was simmering on its spirit-stand on the table, a delicious smell came from the sideboard, where three or four covered silver dishes sat on their metal platform, beneath which burnt spirit-lamps. The huge room—with its long windows, looking on two sides to the loveliest view in Devon; its great warm-tinted Turkey carpet hiding most of the ancient oak floor; its beautifully appointed table, flooded with sunshine; its panelled walls and arched ceiling—was a picture of solid, settled comfort, established and secure.

Digby was wandering about the room, a plate of porridge in one hand, and a busy spoon in the other. Augustus was at the sideboard removing cover after cover, and adding sausages to eggs and rashers of bacon.

"Good effort, Gus," said Digby, eyeing the piled mass as he passed him with his empty porridge plate. "Shove some kedgeree on top."

"Had it," said Augustus. "This is going on top of the kedgeree."

"Stout citizen," approved Digby, getting himself a clean plate.

Isobel was sitting in her place, and I went to see what I could get for her.

As I stood by her chair she put her left hand up to mine and gave it a squeeze.

"I'll wait for Aunt Patricia, John," she said.

Michael came in.

"Aunt come down?" he asked, and added a belated "'Morning, everybody."

"No," replied Digby. "Watch me gobble and go. I'm not meeting Aunt till the day's been aired a bit."

"Claudia down yet?" enquired Michael, ignoring him.

"I saw her in the garden," I said.

"I'll tell her breakfast's ready," he observed, rising and going out.

"Take her a kidney on a fork," shouted Digby, as the door closed.

We sat down, and conversation was in abeyance for a few minutes in favour of the business of breakfast.

"I suppose the Crown Jewels are all present and correct by now?" said Digby suddenly, voicing what was uppermost in all our thoughts. "Door's still locked. I tried it."

"Of course it's all right," I said.

"Seen it?" asked Augustus.

"Or was it too dark?" he added, with a sneer.

"No—I haven't seen it," I replied. "But of course, it's there all right."

"You should know, of course," said Augustus.

"Shut it, Ghastly," said Digby, "or I'll have your breakfast back."

"You're a coarse lout, Digby," remarked Augustus calmly.

" 'Streuth!" murmured Digby to the world in general. "Isn't the gentleman's courage coming on?"

It struck me that it was. I had never known Augustus so daring, assured, and insolent before. I felt more and more convinced that, as Michael had said, nothing but genuine injured innocence and a sense of injustice could have wrought this change.

The door opened, and Claudia, followed by Michael, entered. She looked very white and Michael very wooden and *boutonné*. I saw Isobel give her a sharp glance as she sat down and said :

" 'Morning . . . Aunt not been down yet?"

"No, no. Gobble and go. If asked about sapphires, say you don't know," chanted Digby, beating time with a spoon on his cup.

Michael foraged at the sideboard for Claudia, and then went to the coffee-table. I watched his face as he took the coffee-pot and milk-jug from their tray and held them poised one in each hand, over the cup. His face was perfectly inscrutable and his hands absolutely steady—but 1 knew there was something very wrong.

He looked up and saw me watching him.

" 'Morning, bun-face," quoth he. "Sleep well?"

"Except for one unpleasant dream, Beau," I replied.

"H'm," said Michael, and I tried to analyse the sound, but found it as non-committal as his face.

He returned to his place beside Claudia, and as he seated himself, Aunt Patricia entered the room.

We rose, and I drew back her chair, and then we stood petrified in a complete silence.

One look at her face was sufficient, as she stopped half-way from the door. I knew before she spoke almost the words she was going to say.

"I have come to request that none of you—*none* of you —leave the house to-day," she said. "Unless, that is, one of you cares to say, even now at the eleventh hour, 'A fool and a liar I am, but a criminal I am not!'"

No one spoke or moved. I looked at Michael and he at me.

"No?" continued Lady Brandon. "Very well. But please understand that if I go out of this room without the 'Blue Water,' I will have no mercy. The thief shall pay a thief's penalty—*whoever* it may be."

She paused and fixed her coldly angry gaze on me, on Augustus, on Michael, on Digby, on Isobel, on Claudia.

No one spoke or moved, and for a full minute Lady Brandon waited.

"Ah!" said she at last, and then, "One other thing please note very carefully. The servants know *nothing* of this, and they are to know nothing. We will keep it to ourselves —as long as possible, of course—that one of you six is a treacherous, ungrateful lying thief."

And then Michael spoke:

"Say one of us four, please, Aunt Patricia."

"Thank you, Michael," she replied cuttingly. "You four are among the six. And I will apply to you when I need the help of your wisdom in choosing my words."

"I think you might say '*one of you three brothers,*'" Augustus had the audacity to remark.

"Hold your miserable tongue," was Lady Brandon's discouraging reply.

"As I was saying," she continued, "the servants are to know nothing—and neither is anybody else. Until, of course, the police-court reporters have the story, and the newspapers are adorned with the portrait of one of your faces."

Once again her scornful glance swept us in turn, this time beginning with Michael and going on to Augustus.

"Very well, then," she went on. "No one leaves the house, and no one breathes a word of this to anyone but the eight people who already know of it . . ."

"Except to a detective or the police, of course," she added, with an ominous note and a disdainful edge to her voice. "The Chaplain is ill," she concluded, "and I don't wonder at it."

She turned and walked to the door. Before opening it, she faced us once again.

"Have you anything to say—Michael?" she asked.

"Leave the girls out of it—and Augustus," he replied.

"Have you anything to say, Digby?"

"No, Aunt. Awful sorry, and all that," replied Digby, and I seemed to see his lips forming the words, "No, no. Gobble and go. . . ."

"John?" and she looked even more disdainful, I thought.

"No, Aunt—except that I agree with Michael, *very* strongly," I answered.

"Augustus?"

"It's a damned shame . . ." blustered Augustus.

"Very helpful," Lady Brandon cut him short with cruel contempt.

"Claudia?"

"No, Aunt."

"Isobel?"

"No, Aunt," answered Isobel. "But please, please wait another day and . . ."

". . . And give the thief time to dispose of it, were you going to say?" interrupted Aunt Patricia.

She opened the door.

"Then that is all, is it?" she asked. "No one has anything to say? . . . *Very well!*" and she went out, closing the door quietly behind her.

§ 7.

"I hate skilly and loathe picking oakum, don't you, Ghastly?" remarked Digby conversationally, as we stared at each other in utter consternation.

"You foul, filthy, utter cads," spluttered Augustus, looking from Digby to me and then to Michael.

"Cuts no ice, Gus. Shut it," said Michael, in a perfectly friendly voice, and added, "Run along and play if you can't be serious. . . . Come with me, John," and turning to the girls, said, "Do me a favour, Queen Claudia and Faithful Hound."

"Of course," said Isobel.

"What is it?" asked Claudia.

"Put this wretched business out of both your minds, by means of my absolute assurance and solemn promise that it will be settled and cleared up to-day."

"How?" asked Claudia.

"Oh, *Michael*, dear!" said Isobel, and glanced at me.

"Never mind how, for the minute, Claudia," replied Michael. "Just believe and rest assured. Before you go to bed to-night, everything will be as clear as crystal."

"Or as blue as sapphire," said Digby, and added, "By Jove! I've got an idea! A theory! . . . My dog Joss got alarmed at the sudden darkness, jumped on a chair to avoid the crush, wagged his tail to show faith and hope, knocked over the cover, reversed his engine, and smelt round to see what he'd done, found nothing and yawned in boredom—and inhaled the 'Blue Water.' "

"Perhaps he was thirsty and *drank* the 'Blue Water'?" amended Isobel.

"Both very sound theories. Sounder still if Joss had been in the room," said Michael. "Come, John."

I followed my brother out into the hall. He led the way to his room.

"Take a pew, Johnny. I would hold converse with thee on certain dark matters," he said as we entered.

Having locked the door, he put his tobacco-jar on the low table beside the low arm-chair in which I was sitting.

"You leave the carbon cake too long in your pipes," he said. "That's what cracks them. Unequal expansion of the carbon and the wood, I suppose. You ought to scrape it out once a month or so."

He seated himself opposite to me and sprawled in the low chair, with his knees higher than his head.

"Oh, I like a well-caked pipe," I replied. "Nuttier and cooler."

"Ah, well! So long as you can afford to crack your pipes," he said lazily, and sat silent for a minute or two.

I was quite under his spell again, and had to keep whipping my feelings up into a state of resentment and disgust to maintain them in the condition that common justice demanded. If he were going to restore the sapphire that evening as he had hinted, why on earth couldn't he have done it just now? For the matter of that, why on earth couldn't he have returned it last night when he went to the drawing-room? Why had he ever denied taking the thing at all?

"Well, son, what about it?" he said suddenly.

"Yes, what about it, Beau?" I replied.

He looked at me quizzically.

"What's the game, should you think, Johnny?" he asked.

"That's what I want to know," I answered. "It seems a damned silly one, anyhow."

"Quite," agreed Michael. "Quite very. *Very* quite. *And* a little rough on the girls and our good Augustus."

"Exactly," said I. "And on Aunt Patricia."

An uncomfortable silence followed.

"Well?" said Michael, at length.

"Oh, put it back, Beau," I implored. "God alone knows what you're playing at! Do *you?*"

Michael sat up and stared at me.

"Oh? You say '*Put it back,*' do you, John?" he said slowly and thoughtfully.

"I do," I replied. "Or look here, Beau. Aunt thinks a lot of you, and devilish little of me. It would be doing her a real kindness not to let her know it was you after all. Give it here, and I'll . . ." I coloured and felt a fool.

"*Eric, or Little by Little. A Story of School Life.* . . . *The Boy with the Marble Brow,*" murmured Michael, smiling. But his voice was very kind. . . .

"This grows interesting, Johnny," he went on. "If I go and fetch the 'Blue Water' now, will you take it to Aunt Patricia and say, '*Alone I did it. I cannot tell a lie. It is a far, far better thing I do* . . .' ?"

"Those very words, Beau," I grinned. "On condition you tell me what the game was, and why you did such a damned silly thing."

Thank God the wretched business was going to end—and yet, and yet . . . I felt quite sure that Michael would not let me take the blame—much as I would have preferred that to the wretched feeling of our Michael being the object of Aunt Patricia's scorn and contempt. The more she liked him and approved him now, the more would she dislike and despise him then. She might forbid him the house.

Michael rose.

"You really will?" he asked. "If I go and get it now, you'll take it straight to Aunt Patricia and say you pinched it for a lark?"

"Only too glad of the chance, Beau," I answered. "To get the beastly business over and done with and forgotten—and the girls and Gussie and Digby out of the silly mess."

"H'm," said Michael, sitting down. "You would, eh?"

"And might I ask you a question or two, John?" he went on.

"What were you doing with your hand on the glass cover when I put my hand on it last night?"

"Waiting to catch the ass that was returning the 'Blue Water,'" I replied.

"H'm! Why did you want to catch him?"

"Because I had twice been accused of the fool trick—just because I was standing close to the table when the light failed."

"So you were, too. . . . And what were you doing downstairs last night when I found you in the hall?"

"Looking for the key, Beau, as I told you," I answered.

"And what did you want the key for?"

"To see whether the sapphire had been put back—and to get some peace of mind and sleep, if it had."

"Did you go into the drawing-room?"

"No," I answered.

"Why not?"

"What need? I took it for granted that you had returned it," replied I.

"H'm," said Michael. "Suppose a vote were taken among the eight of us, as to who is likeliest to be the thief, who do you suppose would top the poll?"

"Augustus," I stated promptly.

"Do you think he is the culprit?" asked my brother.

"No, I do *not*," I replied significantly.

"Nor I," answered the enigmatic Michael. "In fact, I know he's not."

He sat silent, smoking reflectively for a few minutes.

"Go through the list," he said suddenly. "Would Aunt pinch her own jewel?"

"Hardly," said I.

"Would the Chaplain?"

"Still less," said I.

"Would Claudia?" he asked next—almost anxiously, I fancied (absurdly, no doubt).

"Don't be a fool," I replied.

"Would Isobel?"

"Don't be a cad," I said.

"Would Digby?"

"Utterly preposterous and absurd," I answered.

"Would Augustus?"

"I feel certain that he *didn't*, anyhow," I answered.

"Would you?"

"I didn't, as it happens," I assured him.

"Would I?"

"I should have thought you almost the last person in the world, Beau," I assured him.

"Looks as though I did it then, doesn't it?" he asked. "Because if Augustus and Digby and you didn't do it—who the devil did, if I didn't? Yes—it looks as though I am the thief."

"It does—to me only, though. Nobody else knows that I found you downstairs," I said. "Why *didn't* you put it back then, Beau?" I asked.

"*Wish I had,*" he said.

There came a bang at the door.

"Who's there?" cried Michael.

"Me," bawled the ungrammatical Digby.

Michael unlocked the door.

"What's up?" he asked.

"Isobel wants to speak to us three. She's been looking for you two. A thought has struck her. Blow severe but not fatal. All about the Painful Event. . . ."

"Where is she?" asked Michael.

"I said I'd lead you by the ear to the smoking-room at an early date—unless either of you had done a bunk with the loot," replied Digby.

"Well—I haven't fled yet, but I shall want a Bradshaw after lunch," said Michael, adding, "Let's go and hear Isobel's great thought. Generally worth hearing."

We went downstairs and made our way to the smoking-room. The brass box caught my eye, and an idea also struck *me* with some violence, as I noticed that the lid and front seemed brighter than the rest of it.

"Don't expose me yet, John," said Michael as we crossed the hall.

"John been catching you out?" asked Digby.

"Caught me last night, didn't you, John?" replied Michael.

"Red-handed," said I.

"It's blue-handed that Aunt wants to cop someone," said Digby, opening the door of the smoking-room. "Sapphire-blue."

Isobel was sitting by the fire looking tearful and depressed. It was at me that she looked as we entered.

"Caught them both in the act of bolting, Isobel," said Digby. "They've each got a half of the 'Blue Water'—about a pint apiece. But they are willing to hear your words if you are quick."

"Oh, I *am* so miserable," moaned Isobel. "I have been

such a wicked, *wicked* beast. But I can't bear it any longer."

"Leave it with us, dear," said Digby, "and forget it. We'll smuggle it back, and share Aunt's few well-chosen words among us, won't we, Beau?"

"What's the trouble, child?" asked Michael.

"I've let Augustus take the blame all this time," she sobbed.

"Didn't notice him taking any," observed Digby. "Must be a secret blame-taker, I suppose."

"Augustus is perfectly innocent and I could have proved it, the moment Aunt began to question us last night. A word from me would have saved him from all suspicion— and I never said it," she went on.

"Why, dear?" I asked her.

"Oh, I don't know. . . . Yes, I do. It would have looked like exculpating myself too," she replied. "Besides, I didn't know *who* had done it. And it was more or less of a silly practical joke last night. . . . And, of course, I thought the person who had taken it would say so, or at least put it back. But now—it's awful. And I can't keep quiet any longer. I thought I'd tell you three before I told Aunt."

"Well—what is it, Faithful Hound?" asked Michael.

"Why, when the light went out—you know I said, '*Ghosts and goblins and skeleton hands,*' or something? Well, I half frightened myself and half pretended, and I clutched somebody's arm. When the light went up I found it was Augustus I was hugging—and let go so quickly that nobody noticed, I suppose."

"That settles it," said Digby. "It wasn't poor Gussie. Couldn't have been," he added, "unless those two were one and did it together."

"Don't be an ass, Dig," I said, for poor Isobel was really upset about it.

"Oh, never!" said Digby. "Absolutely never!"

"Well—I like our Augustus all the better for not having adduced this bit of evidence himself," said I.

"Bless the dear boy," said Digby, "and I searched all his little pockets. I must find him and forgive him."

"Have you told Claudia this?" asked Michael.

"Yes," replied Isobel. "But she seems to think that I may have been mistaken."

"Which is absurd, of course," she added.

"Well—friend Gussie ought to be much obliged to you, both for hanging on to him in the dark, and for remembering it, Isobel," said Michael.

"Tell her at once and get it off your conscientious chest, Isobel," said I.

She looked at me long and miserably, almost apologetically I thought, and went out of the room.

"Say, citizens," said Digby as the door closed, "what I want to know is this. Who pinched this here gem we're being bothered about? Officious and offensive fella, I consider—but Gussie now being out of it, it must be one of us three. . . . Excuse my mentioning it then, but me being out of it, it must be one of you *two*. Now unless you really want the damned thing, I say, *'Put it back.'*"

Michael and I once again looked at each other, Michael's face being perfectly expressionless.

"I think of bolting with it, as I told Isobel just now," said Michael.

"John going with his half too?" asked Digby.

"No," replied Michael for me. "I'm taking it all."

"Well, old horse," said Digby, looking at his watch, "could you go soon after lunch? I want to run up to town to see a man about a dog, and Aunt seems to have other views for us—until the matter is cleared up."

"Do my best to oblige," said Michael, as I quietly slipped from the room to carry out the idea which had occurred to me as I crossed the hall.

I went to the brass box. Finger-prints were very faintly discernible on its highly-polished lid and front. Going to the wash-basin in the room opening off the neighbouring corridor, I damped my handkerchief, and rubbed soap, hard, on the wet surface. The hall was still empty when I returned, and I promptly began scouring the lid and front of the box.

It was easier, however, to remove the finger-marks than

to remove the signs of their removal. I did not wish it to be obvious that someone had been doing—what I was doing.

Under a heavy curtain, in a recess in the panelling, hung overcoats, caps, mufflers, and such outdoor garments. A silk scarf of Digby's struck me as being just the thing I wanted.

I had restored to the box the brilliance which had been its before I soaped it, and was giving it a final wipe with the silk, when the door from the corridor swung open, Michael entered, and I was caught in the act.

And then I saw that in his hand was a piece of wash-leather and a silver-duster, presumably purloined from the butler's pantry!

"Ah!" he said. "Removing all traces of the crime?"

"All—I hope, Beau," I replied.

"Sound plan too," he observed. "Just going to do it myself," and he passed on.

Having finished my task, I placed the fingers of my right hand on top of the box, my thumb on the front, and left as fair and clear a set of finger-prints as I could contrive.

How could it possibly matter to me if a detective identi-fied them as mine? I hadn't taken the "Blue Water," and nobody could prove that I had.

And why was Michael so anxious that his finger-marks should not be found there as a piece of evidence to be coupled with the fact that I had been seen holding his wrist, above the glass cover, when the lights were turned on?

I went up to my room despairing, and trying to recall what I had read, somewhere, about the method of examin-ing finger-prints. I believe they blow a fine powder on to them and then apply carbon-paper or tissue-paper, and take a photograph of the result.

Anyhow, if Aunt had been wily enough to polish the box, just where we would touch it, so that she could get the finger-prints of the person who opened it, she'd get mine all right and those of nobody else, when the detectives came.

§ 8.

Aunt Patricia did not appear at lunch, nor did Claudia. The Chaplain was still ill in bed.

As Burdon and a footman always waited at that meal, there was no general conversation on the one subject of interest to us all.

It was a painful meal, to me at any rate, though Digby seemed perfectly happy, and Michael unconcerned. The only reference to the theft was during a brief absence of the servants.

"Did you tell Aunt what you proposed to tell her? What did she say?" asked Michael of Isobel.

"Yes. . . . She said, somewhat cryptically, '*Virtue is its own reward,*' and nothing else," replied Isobel.

"Gussie," said Digby, "Isobel has—one cannot say 'bearded' of a lady—let us say faced—Aunt Patricia in her wrath, in order to tell her that you must be absolutely innocent of sin, and quite above or beneath suspicion."

"What do you mean?" snarled Augustus.

"She very kindly went to the lioness's den," continued Digby, "to say that she seized you and hung on to you last night while the lights were out—and that, therefore, you could not possibly have gone to the table and pinched the sapphire, as she was hanging on to your arm. I sincerely apologise to you, Gussie, and hope you'll forgive me."

"*My* arm?" said Augustus, in deep and genuine surprise, ignoring the apology, and quickly adding, "Oh—yes—er—of course. Thanks, Isobel."

We all looked at him. I had been watching him when he spoke, and to me his surprise was perfectly obvious.

"Then Aunt knows *I* didn't do it?" he said.

"Yes, Gussie," Isobel assured him, "and I'm *awfully* sorry I didn't say it, at once, last night."

"Yes—I thought you *might* have done so," replied our Augustus.

"Isobel is not so keen on exculpating herself too, you see," said I, glaring at the creature. "*If* she were holding your arm, she could not have gone to the table herself. Proving your innocence proves her own."

"Well—she might have thought of me," he grumbled.

"She has, Gussie," said Michael; "we shall all think of

you, I'm sure. . . . Anyhow, we are all sorry we were unkind and suspicious."

"Suspicious! *You!*" said Augustus. "Huh!"

"Yes—and I'm sorry I searched you, Ghastly," put in Digby. . . . "I'll unsearch you by and by, if you're not careful," he added.

And then David and Burdon came in with the next course.

After lunch, feeling disgruntled and miserable, I went along to the billiard-room to knock the balls about, as one could not very well leave the house in face of Lady Brandon's request.

Augustus was before me and I turned to retreat. I was in no mood to suffer Augustus gladly.

"Police come yet?" he jeered.

"No—you're safe for the present," I replied.

"You heard what Isobel said at lunch," he squealed.

"Yes," said I, going out, "you could hardly believe your ears, could you?" and I am afraid that the anger that I felt was almost entirely due to my conviction that he was absolutely innocent. Isobel could not very well be mistaken. I suppose that Augustus must have quite forgotten the incident until Isobel mentioned it, or else had never noticed it at all. Certainly that was far more probable, than that Isobel had made a mistake as to whom she had clutched in the darkness, especially as she did not leave go until the lights came on and started us all blinking at each other.

I went up to my bedroom, feeling deadly tired after my wakeful night and all the worry, and threw myself on my bed.

I was awakened from a heavy sleep by the entrance of Digby, a couple of hours later. He held a letter in his hand.

"Hi, hog," quoth he, "wake up and listen. . . . Latest edition," and he sat himself down heavily on the foot of the bed.

"What's up now?" I yawned, rubbing my eyes.

"We've got to use our wits and do something to help Beau. Show the mettle of our pastures and all that. . . . Beau's done a bunk. Left this note with David. Says he pinched the 'Blue Water,' and isn't going to face the police."

"*What?*" I cried.

"Read it," said Digby, and passed the letter to me.

"*My dear Dig,*" it ran, "*I have told David to give you this at four o'clock, by which time I shall be well on my way to—where I am going. Will you please tell Aunt that there is no further need to chivvy any of you about the 'Blue Water.' If the police come or a mystery-merchant from Scotland Yard, tell them that you knew that I was in sore straights—or is it straits (or crookeds?) for money, but that you think that this is my first offence and I must have been led away by bad companions (you and John, of course).* KEEP *an eye on young John, and tell him I hope he'll be a good boy. If I send you an address later, it will be in absolute confidence, and relying wholly on your utterly refusing to give it to* ANYBODY, *for any reason whatsoever. I do hope that things will settle down quickly and quietly, now that the criminal is known. Sad, sad, sad! Give my love to Claudia.*

Ever thine,

Michael."

"It *can't* be true," I said. "It's impossible."

"Of course it is, fat-head," replied Digby. "He's off on the romantic tack. Taking the blame and all that. . . . Shielding his little brother. . . ."

"Which?" I asked. "You?"

"No," said Digby.

"Me?" I asked.

"Subtle mathematician," observed Digby.

"But I didn't do it," I said.

"Nor did I," said Digby, and added, "Let's say 'Taking the blame and *thinking* he's shielding his little brother' then."

"But, Dig," I expostulated, "do you think Beau seriously supposes for one moment that you or I would steal a valuable jewel—and from Aunt Patricia of all people?"

"Somebody has stolen it, haven't they?" said Digby. "And I tell you what, my lad," he added; "you say that Beau would never seriously suppose that you or I would steal it—but you yourself seriously supposed that Beau had!"

"How do you know?" I asked, aghast.

"By the way you looked at him—oh, half a dozen times."

"I had reason to suspect him," I said.

"What reason—except that you caught hold of his wrist in the dark, when he was probably doing just what you were doing, trying to catch Gussie in the act of putting it back?" asked Digby.

"I'd rather not say any more about it, Dig," I replied. "It's Beau's business after all, and . . ."

"Don't be a colossal ass," interrupted Digby. "Of course it's Beau's business, and that's what we are talking about. The more we both know, the more we can both help him—either to get away, or to come back. . . . If we knew he is guilty, which, of course, he isn't, we could draw red herrings across his trail; and if we knew he is innocent, which he is, we could lay for the real thief and catch him out."

"Beau doesn't want him caught out, evidently," said I.

"What—not if it's the miserable Gussie?" asked my brother indignantly.

"It isn't," said I. "And Beau knows it."

"Well—let's have those reasons, and we'll get to work," said Digby. "You needn't feel as though you were giving Beau away. There is no more harm in my knowing than in your knowing, and there may be some good. I am not asking you to tell Aunt, or the police, am I, bun-head?"

This was true enough. No harm could result from Digby's knowing all that I knew.

Moreover, if, as Digby assumed, Michael were shielding somebody else, presumably he would welcome any evidence that strengthened the case against himself.

"Well," said I reluctantly, "it's like this, Dig. . . . Beau went down to the drawing-room last night. I met him with the key in his hand . . ."

"And what were *you* doing, if one might ask?" interrupted my brother.

"Going to see if the 'Blue Water' had been returned," I replied.

"Anyhow, *Beau* hadn't returned it, had he?" grinned Digby.

"No—but at the time I, naturally enough, thought he had," said I, "and I suppose that fixed the idea in my mind. I first got the idea—naturally enough, again—when I caught his hand hovering over the glass cover in the darkness."

"Anything else?" asked Digby.

"Yes, the third reason I had for suspecting Beau—though I put my faith in him before all reason—was that I found him going to the brass box with a leather and duster to rub out the finger-prints he had made in taking and returning the key."

Digby whistled.

"Ingenious," he murmured. "As artful as our Auntie, if she had the idea. . . . Detectives would have the idea anyhow."

"I think she did have the idea," I said. "I believe she went straight from the drawing-room and polished all the finger-marks from the lid and front of the damned thing."

"And how do you know that Beau was on to the dodge?" asked Digby.

"He said so. He came into the hall with the cleaning-things in his hand, just as I was doing it myself."

Digby stared.

"Doing it yourself?" he said. *"Why?"*

"Oh, can't you see?" I groaned. *"If* Beau had been playing the wild ass, I didn't want his finger-prints to be found there, on top of the fact that I had been seen clutching his fist in the drawing-room."

"Yours were there as well as his," observed Digby, "if you went to the box for the key."

"Yes—they were," said I, "and they are there, alone, now."

"Stout fella," approved Digby. "I'll go and shove mine

on too, and fog the Sherlocks. . . . But you really are a goat," he went on. "Don't you see that Beau was probably going to do precisely what *you* were doing? He was going to polish the beastly thing clean of all foot-marks, and then jab his own on."

"Why?" I asked.

"To shield the real culprit, of course," said Digby patiently.

"Yes—but *why?*" I repeated. "Why should Beau be a gratuitous ass and take the blame instead of—Gussie, for example? He'd have been more likely to nose him out and then slipper him well."

"Because he knew it wasn't Gussie," replied my brother solemnly.

"Who then?" I asked.

"He didn't know," answered Digby. "But isn't it as clear as mud, that since it wasn't Gussie or Isobel, it was you or me—or else *Claudia?*"

I was silent.

"Now look here, John," went on Digby. " 'Nuff said, and time to do something instead. But first of all, do you still suspect Beau?"

"I have never suspected him," I replied. "I have only realised that I caught his hand, met him with the drawing-room key, and know he was going to rub finger-prints off the brass box."

"Plain yes or no," said Digby. "Do you suspect Beau?"

"Absolutely not," I said promptly. "No. No. *No!*"

"Very good then. Now—Did *you* do it?"

"I did not," said I.

"Nor did I. Very well! Since Isobel and Augustus mutually prove each other innocent, as she was holding his arm, yards from the table all the time—who is left?"

"*Claudia?*" said I unhappily.

"*Now* d'you get it?" smiled Digby, leaning back against the bottom of the bed, and clasping his hands round his knee.

"Good God, man," I cried, starting up. "You don't mean to tell me you suspect *Claudia* of jewel-stealing?"

"Keep calm," he replied. "I am not talking about whom I suspect. I am asking you who remains if you eliminate me and yourself as admittedly innocent, and Isobel and Augustus as proven innocent."

"Michael and Claudia!" I murmured. "Which idea is the more ridiculous?" I said aloud.

"Equally impossible," answered Digby. "Also the fact remains that it was one of those two—*if* it wasn't you. Furthermore, the fact remains that Michael has bolted for one of two reasons—because he is a frightened thief, or because he wished to shield the guilty person—you or Claudia."

A silence fell between us.

"I'm going dotty," said I at last.

"I've gone," said Digby, and we sat staring at each other.

After a time he rose.

"Got to get a move on," he said.

"What are you going to do?" I asked.

"Dunno," he replied.

As he was leaving the room I said, "Do you think Michael suspects either me or you, Digby?"

"No," he replied. "He *knows* we didn't do it."

"Do you think he suspects Claudia, then?"

"Er—*no*—of course not," he answered.

"Then?"

"He only *knows* that one of us three *did* do it," he replied and went out, leaving me staring at the door.

I lay down again to think.

§ 9.

Dinner that night was an extraordinary meal, at which only Isobel, Claudia, Augustus, and I appeared.

Lady Brandon, said Burdon, was dining in her own room; his Reverence the Chaplain was, by Dr. Warrender's orders, remaining in bed; Mr. Michael was not in his room when David took up his hot water; and Mr. Digby had been seen going down the drive soon after tea.

"Shocking bad form, I call it—Michael and Digby going

out like this—after what Aunt said," remarked Augustus as the service-door swung to, when the servants went out for the coffee.

"You're an authority on good form, of course," I said.

"Where has Beau gone?" asked Claudia.

"He didn't tell me," I replied.

"Don't suppose he told anybody," sneered Augustus.

"Come into the drawing-room soon," said Isobel, as I held the dining-room door open for the girls to go out.

"I'm coming now," I replied. "As soon as I have had some coffee."

I did not want a *tête-à-tête* with Augustus, and I was more than a little disturbed in mind as to the meaning of Digby's absence.

What could be the reason of his defiance of Aunt Patricia's prohibition of our leaving the house? Was it possible that he knew more than he had told me?

Perhaps he had gone to the village telegraph-office to try to get into communication with Michael at one of the several places to which he might have gone.

It would be something important that would make him risk giving Aunt Patricia cause to think that he had been guilty of an ungentlemanly disobedience to her request.

I drank my coffee in silence, and in silence departed from the room. I could not forgive Gussie for being innocent and forcing Michael to suspect Claudia, Digby, or me; me to suspect Claudia, Digby, or Michael; and Digby to suspect Claudia, Michael, or me.

Most unjust of me, but most human, I fear.

In the drawing-room Isobel was at the piano, playing softly to herself, and Claudia sat staring into the fire.

I strolled over to the huge piano and sat down near it.

"Where *can* Michael be?" said Claudia.

"And Digby," added Isobel.

"I don't know," said I.

"Really and truly?" asked Claudia.

"Yes," said I. "I honestly have not the faintest idea as to where either of them is."

"I wish they'd come in," said Isobel.

"Oh, I can't bear this room," cried Claudia suddenly, and springing up, went out. As I opened the door for her, I fancied I caught a glimpse of tears on her half-averted face, though I was not prying.

As I closed the door, Isobel rose from the piano and came towards me. She looked very lovely, I thought, with her misty blue eyes, misty golden hair, as fine as floss-silk, and her sweet expression. How gentle and dear she was!

"Johnny," she said, laying her hands on my chest and looking up into my eyes, "may I ask you a silly question? Just once and for all? I know the answer, but I want to hear you say it."

"Certainly, dear," said I.

"You won't be angry, Johnny?"

"Have I ever been angry with you, Isobel? Could I be?" I asked.

She looked into my eyes steadily for a few moments.

"Did you take the 'Blue Water,' John?" she asked.

"No, my dear, I did not," I replied, and drew her to me. And then Isobel threw her arms round my neck and I kissed her on the lips.

She burst into tears, and lifting her up in my arms, I carried her to a sofa and sat hugging her to my breast and covering her face with kisses. It had suddenly come upon me that I loved her—that I had always loved her. But hitherto it had been as a charming darling playmate and companion, and now it was as a woman.

If this knowledge between us were a result of the theft of the "Blue Water," I was glad it had been stolen.

"Darling! Darling! Darling!" I whispered as I kissed her. "Do you love me, darling Isobel?" I asked, and, for reply, she smiled starrily through her tears, put her arms round me, and pressed her lips to mine.

I thought my heart was stopping.

"Love you, dearest?" she asked. "You are just my life. I have loved everything you have said or done, since I was a baby!"

"Don't cry," I said, ashamed of my inarticulate inadequacy.

"I'm crying for joy," she sobbed. "Now you have told *me* you didn't do it, I know you didn't."

"What made you think I did?" I asked.

"I *didn't* think so," she replied with feminine logic; "only it was you who were against the table, John; it was you whom Michael caught; and I saw you go down in the night—to put it back, as I thought."

"Saw me?" I asked, in surprise.

"Yes, dear. I was awake and saw a light go by my door. It shone underneath it. And I came out and looked over the banisters."

"I went to see if the wretched thing had come back," I said. "And it was rather I who caught Michael than Michael who caught me, when you turned the lights out. We were both expecting to catch Gussie, and caught each other."

"And, oh, I have been so wretchedly unhappy," she went on, "thinking appearances were so against you, and yet knowing I was allowing Gussie to remain under suspicion when I knew it wasn't he. . . . But when it seemed the thing was actually stolen, I couldn't keep quiet any longer. It was bad enough when it was only a practical joke, as we thought. . . . And then I seemed to be helping to bring suspicion towards you when I cleared Gussie. . . ."

She wiped away a tear.

"I don't care now," she smiled. "Nothing on earth matters. So long as you love me—I don't see how I can have a care in the world. . . . You're *sure*, darling?"

I endeavoured to express myself without the use of halting and unfluent speech.

"When did you first love me?" asked my sweet and beautiful darling, when I released her.

"I don't know," I said. "I have always loved you, and now I worship you, and I always shall," and again she gave me a long embrace that seemed to stop the beating of my heart and lift me up and up to an incredible heaven of ecstasy and joy almost unbearable.

The sound of footsteps and a hand on the door brought us back to earth. We sprang to our feet, and when David entered, Isobel was putting away her music, and I was consulting a small pocket-book with terrific abstraction from my surroundings.

"Excuse me, sir," said David, halting before me. "Might I speak to you, sir?"

"You're doing it, David," said I.

"In private, sir, a moment," he explained.

I went to the door with him, and having closed it, he produced a note and gave it to me.

"Mr. Digby, sir. He very specially instructed me to give you this in private at ten o'clock this evening, sir, thank you, sir."

"Thank you, David," said I, and went along to the smoking-room, opening the letter as I went.

Although I felt that I ought to be filled with apprehension, anxiety, and trouble, my heart sang for glee, and I could have danced down the long corridor, to the surprise and disapproval of the various stiff and stately Brandons, male and female, who looked down from its walls.

"This is most selfish and wrong," said I, and repressed a desire to sing, whistle, and whoop, and literally jump for joy.

"Isobel! Isobel! Isobel!" sang my heart. "Isobel loves me and I love Isobel. . . ."

The smoking-room was empty, and I could hear the click of balls from the neighbouring billiard-room, showing why. Gussie was evidently at his favourite, somewhat aimless, evening employment.

I turned up the lights, poked up the fire, pulled up the biggest and deepest chair, and filled my pipe and lit it.

Had I come straight here from the dining-room, and here received Digby's letter, I should have snatched it, and opened it with sinking heart and trembling fingers.

Now, nothing seemed of much importance, compared with the great fact of which my heart was chanting its pæan of praise and thanks to God.

Love is very selfish I fear—but then it *is* the very selves of two people becoming one self. . . .

And then I read poor Digby's letter. It was as follows:—

"My dear John,

I now take up my pen to write you these few lines, hoping they find you as they won't find me. After terrific thought and mental wrestling, which cost me a trouser-button, I have come to the conclusion that I can no longer deceive you all and let the innocent suffer for my guilty sin or sinny guilt.

I go to find my noble-hearted twin, to kneel at his feet and say, 'Brother, I have sinned in thy sight' (but it was in the dark really), 'and am no more worthy to be called anything but what I am.'

No one knows the shame I feel, not even me; and, by the time you get this, I shall be well on my way to—where I am going.

Will you please tell Aunt that Michael's noble and beautiful action has wrung my heart, and I wish he had wrung my neck. I cannot let him take the blame for me, like this. I shall write to her from Town.

When you find yourself in the witness-dock or prisoner's-box tell the Beak that you have always known me to be weak but not vicious, and that my downfall has been due to smoking cigarettes and going in for newspaper competitions. Also that you are sure that, if given time, I shall redeem myself by hard work, earn thirty shillings a week at least, and return the thirty thousand pounds out of my savings.

Write and let me know how things go on, as soon as I send you an address—which you will, of course, keep to yourself. Give my love to Isobel.

Play up and don't forget you've GOT *to stand by me and make people realise the truth that I actually am the thief—or suspicion still rests on Claudia (since Isobel and Gussie are out of it), if we three do not provide the criminal amongst us. And, of course, I can't let Beau suffer for me.*

Directly you hear from him, let him know by wire that I have confessed and bolted, and that he can return to Brandon Abbas and admit that he was shielding the real culprit (whom he knew to be ME *or* YOU *or* CLAUDIA*!). Give my love to Isobel.* Ever thine, Digby."*

For a moment this drove even Isobel from my mind.

It had never occurred to me for one moment that Digby had actually fled, as Michael had done. Could it be possible that he was speaking the truth in the letter?

Could he have stolen the "Blue Water" as he said, and had Michael's flight and shouldering of the blame forced his hand and compelled him, in very shame, to confess? . . .

Or did he, in his heart of hearts, think that Michael was really guilty and had fled rather than allow three innocent people to lie under suspicion with himself? Had Digby, thinking this, fled to divert suspicion from the guilty Michael, to confuse the issue and divide the pursuit, thus giving him a better chance to get clear away? . . .

Probably neither. It was much more likely that his idea was to help to shield the person whom Michael thought he was shielding, and at the same time to share with Michael the suspicion thus diverted from the guilty person.

The moment it was known that Michael had fled, the world and his wife would say, "The vile young thief!"

Directly Digby followed him they would say, "Which of them *is* the thief?" and no eye would be turned enquiringly upon those who, in their conscious innocence, had remained at home.

And whom *did* Michael and Digby suspect, if they were both innocent?

Obviously either Claudia or me.

And if they could no more suspect me than I could suspect them . . . ?

It dawned on me, or rather it was stabbed into my heart suddenly, as with a knife, that it was quite as much *my* affair to help in preventing suspicion, just or unjust, from falling upon Claudia; and that if they could face obloquy, poverty, hardship, and general wrecking of their lives for Claudia and for me and for each other—why, so could I for them, and that it was my duty to go too.

Moreover, when detectives and criminal-experts got to work on the case, they would be quite capable of saying that there was nothing to prevent Isobel and Augustus from being in collusion to prove each other innocent, and would suspect one or both of them the more.

To us, who knew her, it was completely proven that Augustus was innocent, because she said so.

To a detective, it would more probably be a clue to the guilty person—the girl who produced this piece of "evidence" which incidentally proclaimed her own innocence.

Moreover, the wretched Augustus had most undoubtedly been *surprised* when Isobel said he must be innocent as she had been holding on to him all the time the light was out. If this came out, it would certainly fix the suspicion on Isobel, and if it did not, there was a strong probability that her declaration concerning Augustus would, as I have said, suggest collusion between them.

The more reason then for me to strengthen the obvious solution—that the thief was one of the Gestes.

If three people fled confessing their guilt, that was where the collusion would be—among the three rascally brothers who had plotted to rob their relative and share the spoil.

That the oldest had weakened and fled first, was to his credit, or not, according to whether you more admired courage or confession; but obviously and incontestably, the blame must lie upon these three, and not among those who remained at home and faced the music.

"*But*," said the voices of prudence, cowardice, and common sense, as well as the voice of love, "*two are enough to take the blame, surely? Let people say it was one of those two, or perhaps the two in partnership.*"

"*And why*," replied the voices of self-respect and pride, "*should those two share the blame (or the honour)? Why should they shield Isobel and* YOU, *as well as Claudia, from suspicion?*" and to the latter voice I listened.

I could not possibly sit at home and enjoy life while the Captain and the Lieutenant were in trouble, disgrace, and danger—my whole life-training, as well as instincts, forbade.

I think that within two minutes of reading Digby's letter, the question of my going was quite definitely answered, and only the minor questions of where I should go, and

whether I should say anything to Isobel, remained to be
settled. And one of these two problems was subconsciously
solved, though I had not intentionally considered it and
come to a decision.

From the moment that I had learnt of Michael's flight,
I had had somewhere, just below the level of consciousness,
a vague remembrance of the existence of a romantic-sound-
ing, adventurous corps of soldiers of fortune, called the
French Foreign Legion.

When thinking of Michael, and seeing mental pictures
of him in the setting of Brandon Abbas, our "Prep." school,
Eton and Oxford, one of the clearest of these dissolving
views had been of a group of us in the Bower, at the feet of
a smart and debonair young French officer, who had thrilled
us with dramatic tales of Algeria, Morocco, and the Sahara;
tales of Spahis, Turcos, Zouaves, Chasseurs d'Afrique, and
the French Foreign Legion of Mercenaries; tales of hot life
and brave death, of battle and of bivouac. At the end,
Michael had said:

"I shall join the French Foreign Legion when I leave
Eton. . . . Get a commission and go into his regiment,"
and Digby and I had applauded the plan.

Had Michael remembered this, and was he, even now, on
his way to this life of adventure and glory, determined to
win his way to soldierly renown under a *nom de guerre?*
. . . It would be so like Michael.

And Digby? Had he had the same idea and followed
him? It would be so like Digby.

And I? Should I follow my brothers' lead, asking nothing better than to do as they did, and win their approval?
. . . It would be so like me.

Three romantic young asses! I can smile at them now.
Asses without doubt; wild asses of the wildest; but still,
with the imagination and the soul to be romantic asses,
thank God!

§ 10.

As compensation for a smaller share of the gifts of courage, cleverness, and general distinction possessed by my

brilliant brothers, I have been vouchsafed a larger measure of prudence and caution—though some may think that still does not amount to much.

I have met few men to equal Michael and Digby in beauty, physical strength, courage, and intelligence; but I was, in spite of being an equally incurably romantic, "longer-headed" than they, and even more muscular and powerful. This is tremendous praise to award myself, but facts are facts.

Having decided to join them in disgrace and blame, as well as to join them in the flesh if I could—going to the Legion to look for them in the first place—I settled down to consider details, ways, and means.

I can think better in the dark, so I knocked out my pipe, burnt Digby's letter, and went up to bed.

The first fact to face, and it loomed largest and most discouraging of all, was separation from Isobel in the very moment of finding her. Paradoxically, however, the very exaltation and excitement of this wonderful thing that had happened, this finding of her, carried me along and gave me the power to leave her.

I was *tête-montée*, beside myself, and above myself, abnormal.

I would show my love that I, too, could do a fine thing, and could make a personal sacrifice to ward off from women, one of whom was mine, "the slings and arrows of outrageous fortune," outrageous suspicion and annoyance.

To leave her would be misery unspeakable—but what a beautiful misery and poignantly delightful sorrow for the heart of romantic youth to hug to itself!

Also I knew that it was quite useless for such children as ourselves—she nineteen and I twenty—at present penniless and dependent, to think of formal engagements and early marriages. Love was all and love was enough, until I should return, bronzed and decorated, successful and established, a distinguished Soldier of Fortune, to claim her hand.

I would then take my bride to be the admired and beloved Pride of the Regiment, a soldier's star and stay and queen. . . . (Twenty is a great age at which to be—with love in your heart and life before you. . . .)

Should I tell her what I was going to do and have one last beautifully-terrible hour, with her in my arms, or should I write her a letter to be given to her after I had gone?

I am glad to say that I had the grace to look at it from her point of view, and to decide according to what I thought would be better for her.

In the letter I could give the impression that this was only a short separation, and that I was writing to say *"Au revoir"* rather than "Good-bye."

If I told her in an interview, my obvious wretchedness and woebegone countenance would contradict my words. I knew I should kiss and embrace her as if for the last time on earth, and look as though I were going to the scaffold rather than into hiding for a while, until the missing jewel turned up, or the thief was caught.

Yes—I had better write, being careful to avoid the suggestion that this was any more a "separation" than my going back to Oxford for the next term would have been.

That question was settled.

The next thing to consider was the problem of procedure.

I should want sufficient money and kit to enable me to get to France and subsist for a few days, probably in Paris.

Ten pounds or so, a change of underclothing, and a toothbrush, would be the sort of thing. With a very small suit-case one would be quite comfortable.

My watch, links, studs, cigarette-case, and a good gold pencil which I possessed would provide ample funds. I had more than sufficient ready money for my fare to London, and could there raise enough to carry me on to Paris and keep me for a few days.

I would breakfast with the others, and quietly walk off to catch the ten-forty to Exeter, and take the eleven-forty-five thence to London, arriving about three o'clock. I would cross to France the next day, getting there in the evening; sleep at an hotel, and, as soon as possible, become a soldier of France.

Whatever my brothers had done, I should at least have

followed their example worthily, and have given a realistic and convincing imitation of the conduct of a frightened and desperate thief, fleeing from the consequences of his crime and the shame of facing his relatives and former friends.

And if Michael and Digby were actually there when I arrived—why, I should regret nothing but the separation from Isobel—a separation, albeit, during which I would qualify, in age, position, and income, for the honour of becoming her husband.

I think I had arrived at the position of Commander-in-Chief in Algeria and Grand Commander of the Legion of Honour when I fell asleep. . . .

I awoke in the morning in a very different frame of mind from that of the morning before. My heart was full of pride that Isobel loved me and was mine. My brain was full of schemes and plans, and my whole being tingled gloriously with a sense of high adventure.

"If youth but knew . . ."

When David brought my hot water, with his inevitable, "Half-past seven, sir, and a fine morning" (when the rain stops, or the fog clears, as the case might be), I told him I should give him a letter, after breakfast, which he was to give privately to Miss Rivers at the first convenient opportunity after eleven o'clock.

I thought it better to give it to David than to a maid. He had obeyed instructions in the case of Michael's letter to Digby, and Digby's letter to me, and a maid would be more likely to chatter in the servants' hall.

I did not think that there was the slightest suspicion in that quarter, and, as Aunt Patricia had said, there was no reason why there should be any, provided the mystery of the "Blue Water" was solved without the aid of the police.

I could have posted my letter to her of course, but that would have involved delay, and an anxious night for her. It would also mean a post-mark, and I thought it would be better for her to be able to say, with perfect truth, that she had not the vaguest idea as to where I had gone.

When I had dressed, I put my brushes and shaving-tackle into an attaché-case, and crammed in a shirt, collars, and socks, and then went down to the smoking-room, and, after some unsatisfactory efforts, wrote to Isobel:

> "*My darling beautiful Sweetheart,*
>
> *I had a letter from Digby last night. He has bolted because he thinks that Michael has shouldered the blame and disgrace of this theft in order to protect the innocent and shield the guilty person (who must appear to him to be Claudia, Digby, or myself, as it is not you nor Gussie). Digby told me that it was not he, and he refuses to believe that it is Michael. I don't think he suspects me either.*
>
> *Now, you'll be the first to agree that I can't sit at home and let them do this, believing them to be innocent. And if either of them were guilty, I'd want, all the more, to do anything I could to help. Were it not for leaving you, for a little while, just when I have found you, I should be rather enjoying it, I am afraid.*
>
> *Anyhow, I should have had to leave you in a little while, when I went up to Oxford again, and that would have been an eight weeks' separation. As it is, we are only going to be parted until this silly wretched business is cleared up. I expect the thief will return the thing anonymously as soon as he or she finds that we three are all pretending we did it, and that we will not resume our ordinary lives until restitution is made.*
>
> *You know that I didn't do it, and I know that you didn't, and that's all that really matters; but you wouldn't have me hold back when the Captain and Lieutenant of the Band are out to divert suspicion from the innocent and to shame the guilty into returning Aunt's property!*
>
> *I'll send you an address later on, so that you can tell me what happens—but, just at first, I want you to have no idea where I am, and to say so.*
>
> *You'd despise me, really, in your heart, if I stayed at home, though I know you'll miss me and want me back. I shall come, of course, the moment you let me know that the affair is cleared up. Meanwhile, no ass of a detective will be suspecting you or Claudia, or poor innocent Gussie, since obviously one of the absconding three (or all of them)*

must be the thief. Aunt will go to the police about it of course, and they will soon be on our track, and trouble no one at Brandon Abbas.

And now, darling Isobel, darling Faithful Hound, I am not going to try to tell you how much I love you—I am going to do it before you get this. But everything is different since last night. The world is a perfectly glorious place, and life is a perfectly glorious thing. Nothing matters, because Isobel loves me and I love Isobel—for ever and ever. I want to sing all the time, and to tell everybody.

Isn't love absolutely WONDERFUL?

> *Always and always,*
> *Your devoted, adoring, grateful*
> *Sweetheart."*

This honest, if boyish, effusion I gave to David, and repeated my instructions.

He contrived to keep his face correctly expressionless, though he must have wondered how many more of us were going to give him epistles to be privately delivered after their departure to other members of the household.

Leaving the smoking-room, I met Burdon in the corridor.

"Can you tell me where Mr. Michael is, sir?" he asked. "Her ladyship wishes to see him."

"No, I can't, Burdon," I replied, "for the excellent reason that I don't know."

"Mr. Digby's bed have not been slep' in either, sir," he went on. "I did not know the gentlemen were going away. . . . Nothing packed nor nothing."

"They didn't tell me they were going, Burdon," I said, putting on an owlish look of wonder and speculation. "They're off on some jaunt or other, I suppose. . . . I hope they ask me to join them."

"Racing, p'r'aps, sir?" suggested Burdon sadly.

"Shocking," said I, and left him, looking waggish to the best of my ability. . . .

There were only the four of us at breakfast again.

Isobel's face lit up radiantly as our glances met, and we telegraphed our love to each other.

"Anyone heard how the Chaplain is?" asked Claudia.

"I went to see him last night," replied Isobel, "but the nurse said he was asleep."

"Nurse?" asked Augustus.

"Yes," said Isobel. "Dr. Warrender thought he ought to have a night-nurse, and Aunt Patricia telegraphed for one. He's going to get up to-day though, the nurse told me."

"Where's Digby?" asked Augustus.

"Why?" I said elliptically.

"Burdon asked me if I'd seen him, and said he wasn't in last night."

"I know no more than you do where he is," I honestly assured him.

"Funny—isn't it?" he sneered.

"Most humorous," I agreed.

"Perhaps Aunt will think so," countered Augustus unpleasantly. . . . "First Michael and then Digby, after what she said about not leaving the house!"

"Ought to have consulted you first, Gussie," said Claudia.

"Looks as though they didn't want to consult the police, if you ask me," he snarled.

"We didn't ask you, Gussie," said Isobel, and so the miserable meal dragged through.

Towards the end of it, Burdon came in.

"Her ladyship wishes to see Mr. Digby," he said to the circumambient air.

"Want a bit of doing, I should say," remarked Augustus, with a snigger.

"He's not here, Burdon," said I, looking under the table.

"No, sir," replied Burdon gravely, and departed.

"You next, my lad," Augustus stated, eyeing me severely. "I wonder if the detectives have come."

Burdon returned.

"Her ladyship would like to see you in her boudoir, after breakfast, sir," said he to me.

"Told you so," remarked Augustus, as the door closed behind the butler.

"Where do you think the others have gone?" asked

Claudia, turning to me. "They can't have *run away* surely? Not both of them?"

"Doesn't look like it, does it?" put in Augustus.

"If they have gone away it's for an excellent reason," said Isobel.

"Best of reasons," agreed Augustus.

"Quite the best, Claudia," said I, looking at her. "*If* they have 'run away,' as you said, it is to turn suspicion away from the house and everybody in it, of course."

"Oh, of course," agreed Augustus again.

"Just what they would do," said Isobel quietly.

"It would be like Michael," said Claudia in a low voice, and getting up, went quickly out of the room.

"And Digby," added I, as she did so.

Augustus departed soon after, with a malicious "Up you go" to me, and a jerk of his thumb in the direction of Aunt Patricia's room. Our recent roughness and suspicion evidently rankled in his gentle breast.

As soon as we were alone, I turned to Isobel, who sat beside me, put my arms round her and gave and received a long kiss.

"Come out to the Bower a minute, darling," said I, and we scuttled off together.

There I crushed her to my breast and kissed her lips, her cheeks, and eyes, and hair, as though I could never have enough, and never stop.

"Will you love me for ever, darling?" I asked. "Whatever may happen to us, or wherever we may be?"

She did not reply in words, but her answer was very satisfying.

"Aunt wants me," then said I, and bolted back to the house. But I had no intention of seeing Aunt Patricia.

Mine should be the more convincing rôle of the uneasy, trembling criminal, who, suddenly sent for, finds he has not the courage to face the ordeal, and flees before the ominous sound of the summons.

I was very glad this had happened, as it would appear to have given me the cue for flight.

When first sent for, I was found peacefully eating my

breakfast in fancied security. When again sent for, I should be missing—obviously terrified of the command and guiltily afraid to obey it.

Going to my room, I took my attaché-case from the wardrobe, pocketed a photograph of Isobel, and went quietly down the service staircase that debouched by the luggage-lift in a passage opening into the outer hall. In a minute I was across the shrubbery and into the drive at a bend which hid it from the house.

Twenty minutes' walking brought me to the station, where I booked to Exeter. That would not tell anybody very much, for though I was perfectly well known to everybody at our local station, it would be extremely unlikely that I should be traced from so busy a junction as Exeter, in the crowd that would be booking for the morning train to Waterloo.

As I waited on our platform, I was conscious of an almost unbearable longing to go back to Brandon Abbas and Isobel. How *could* I leave her like this, now, the very day after I had found her?

I felt a bigger lump in my throat than I had ever known since I was a child. It was utterly horrible.

But for the excitement and adventure of the business, I think I should have succumbed to the longing to return. But when two loving people part, one going on a journey, it is always the departing one who suffers the less.

It is inevitable that the distractions of travel, movement, change, shall drug the pain to which the other is equally exposed without the amelioration of mental and bodily occupation.

So, between my mind and the agony of separation from Isobel came the deadening and protecting cloak of action and of the competing thoughts of other matters—journey's end, the future, money, Paris, Algeria, the probabilies of finding Michael and Digby. . . .

Anyhow, I conquered the yearning to go back to her, and when the local train loafed in I got into it, with a stiff upper lip and a bleeding heart, and set out on as eventful and strange a journey as ever a man took.

CHAPTER III

THE GAY ROMANTICS

"Curs'd from the cradle and awry they come
Masking their torment from a world at ease;
On eyes of dark entreaty, vague and dumb,
They bear the stigma of their souls' disease."

I REMEMBER nothing of that horrible journey from Exeter to Waterloo. It passed as a bad dream passes, and I awoke from it in London.

As has happened to others in the history of that city, I found that, in such circumstances, London was a very large place, and myself a very small and lonely atom of human dust therein.

Walking out from Waterloo Station into the unpleasing purlieus thereof, I was tempted to go to the quiet and exclusive hotel that the Brandons had patronised for very many years, and where I was well known and should feel a sense of being at home among friends.

For this very reason I resisted the temptation, and was aided to do so by the question of finance. Whatever I did, I must leave myself sufficient money for my journey to Paris and subsistence there until I should become a soldier of France, to be lodged, boarded, clothed, and paid by Madame la République.

The first thing to do was to convert my disposable property into cash, a distasteful undertaking, but essential to further progress along the path I had elected to follow. If I had to do nothing more unpleasant than that, I told myself, as I walked along down a mean street toward Westminster Bridge, the said path would be no thorny one.

And, at that moment, my eye fell upon what I took to be the very place I wanted—a pawnbroker's shop, stuffed to bursting with a most heterogeneous collection of second-hand merchandise. ranging from clothing and jewellery

by way of boxing-gloves, guns, knives, meerschaum pipes
and cigar-holders, cameras, umbrellas and walking-sticks,
field-glasses, portmanteaux, to concertinas, cornets, and
musical instruments of every description.

I entered and found a young gentleman, of markedly
Hebraic appearance, behind the counter. I expected to
hear him say:

"Vat d'ye vant, Mithter?" and waggle his hands, palms
upwards, near his shoulders, as I remembered a song, last
heard at Oxford, anent one Solomon Levi and his store
at Chatham Street.

For some reason, best known to himself, he wore a
bowler hat of proportions so generous that it rested upon
the nape of his neck and his ears, depressing the latter
well-developed organs, so that they drooped forward as
droops the tired lily—though in no other way did they
suggest that flower.

To compensate for the indoor wearing of this outdoor
garment, he had discarded his coat, exposing shirt-sleeves
that again did not suggest the lily. A very large watch-
chain adorned a fancy waistcoat that was certainly worn
by him at meal-times also, and his diamond tie-pin bore
testimony to his financial solidity and to his taste.

I fear I looked at him for a few seconds longer than
good manners could approve—but then he looked at me
for precisely the same length of time, though with a
difference. For I was looking with a wondering admiration, whereas he was regarding me with little of wonder
and less of admiration.

It was perfectly clear that he did not regard me as
a buyer, though by what instinct or experience he could
tell, I know not.

"Surely," thought I, "even if I have not the appearance
of one who comes to buy, I still do not look like a needy,
seedy seller?"

But he knew! He knew; and his silence was eloquent.

As his bold brown eyes regarded me, his curved nostril
curved a little more, and his large ripe lips, beneath the
pendulous nose, ripened while I watched.

He said no word, and this fact somewhat disconcerted me, for I had hitherto regarded the Children of Israel as a decidedly chatty race.

I broke the heavy silence of the dark mysterious shop, and added strange sounds to the strange sights and stranger smells.

"I want to sell my watch and one or two things," said I to this silent son of Abraham's seed.

He did not triumph in the manifest rightness of his judgment that I was a contemptible seller and not an admirable buyer. He did not do anything at all, in fact. He did not even speak.

No word nor sigh nor sound escaped him.

I produced my watch and laid it at his feet, or rather at his stomach. It was gold and good, and it had cost twenty-five pounds. (I allude to the watch.)

" 'Ow much?" said the child of the Children of Israel.

"Er—well—isn't that rather for you to say?" I replied. "I know it cost twenty-five pounds and is an excellent . . ."

" 'Ow much?" interrupted the swarthy Child.

"How much will you give me?" I replied. . . . "Suppose we split the difference and you . . ."

" 'Ow much?" interrupted the Child again.

"Ten pounds?" I suggested, feeling that I was being reasonable and, indeed, generous. I did not wish my necessitous condition to weigh with him and lead him to decrease his just profits.

"Two quid," said the Child promptly.

"Not a tenth of what it cost?" said I, on a note of remonstrance. "Surely that is hardly a fair and . . ."

"Two quid," interrupted the Child, whose manners seemed less rich than his attire.

I was tempted to take up the watch and depart, but I felt I could not go through all this again. Perhaps two pounds was the recognised selling price of all gold watches?

Producing my cigarette-case, gold pencil, and a tiny jeweller's box containing my dress studs, I laid them before this spoiler of Egyptians, and then detached my links from my shirt-cuffs.

" 'Ow much?" enquired the Child once more.

"Well," replied I, "the pencil is pretty heavy, and the studs are good. So are the links. They're all eighteen carat and the . . ."

" 'Ow much?" repeated the voice, which I was beginning to dislike.

"Ten pounds for the watch, pencil, and . . ."

"Four quid," the Child replied, in the voice of Fate and Destiny and Doom, and seeking a toothpick in the pocket of his "gent.'s fancy vest," he guided it about its lawful occasions.

This would not do. I felt I must add at least five pounds to what I already had. I was a little vague as to the absolutely necessary minimum, but another five pounds seemed to me to be very desirable.

"Oh, come—make it seven," said I, in the bright tone of encouragement and optimism.

The Child regarded the point of his toothpick. It appeared to interest him far more than I, or my poor affairs, could ever do.

"Six," said I, with falsely cheerful hopefulness.

The toothpick returned to duty, and a brooding silence fell upon us.

"Five, then," I suggested, with a falsely firm finality.

The Child yawned. For some reason I thought of onions, beer, and garlic, things very well in their way and their place, and quite pleasing to those who like them.

"Then I'm afraid I've wasted your valuable time," said I, with deep wiliness, making as though to gather up my despised property.

The Child did not trouble to deny my statement. He removed his bowler hat and looked patiently into its interior, as good men do in church. The hair of the head of the Child was most copiously abundant, and wonderfully curly. I thought of oil-presses, anointed bulls of Bashan, and, with bewildered awe, of the strange preferences of Providence.

However, I would walk to the door and see whether, rather than let me go, he would offer five pounds for what had cost at least fifty.

As I did so, this representative of the Chosen People cocked an eye at my dispatch-case.

"Wotcher got there?" he growled.

Imitating his excellent economy of words, I opened the case without reply, and removing a silk shirt, vest, and socks, displayed three collars, a pair of silver-backed hair-brushes, a comb, a silver-handled shaving-brush, a razor, an ivory nail-brush, a tooth-brush, and a silver box containg soap.

"Five quid the lot and chance if you've pinched 'em," said the Child.

"You'll give me five pounds for a gold watch, links, studs, and pencil-case; a silver cigarette-case, hair-brushes, and shaving-brush; a razor, shirt, vest, socks, collars, and a leather dispatch-case?" I enquired politely.

"Yus," said the Child succinctly.

Well, I could get shaved for a few pence, and in a couple of days I should probably be in uniform.

"I'll keep the tooth-brush and a collar," I remarked, putting them in my pocket.

"Then chuck in the walkin' stick and gloves, or it's four-fifteen," was the prompt reply.

I gazed upon the Child in pained astonishment.

"I gotter *live*, ain't I?" he replied, in a piteous voice, to my cruel look.

Forbearing to observe *"Je ne vois pas la nécessité,"* I laid my stick and gloves on the counter, realising that, in any case, I should shortly have no further need of them.

The Child produced a purse, handed me five pounds, and swept my late property into a big drawer.

"Thank you," said I, departing. "Good evening."

But the Child apparently did not think it was a good evening, for he vouchsafed no reply.

One should not judge a race by single specimens, of course, but—racial antipathy is a curious thing. . . .

Crossing Westminster Bridge, with about ten pounds in my pocket, misery in my heart, and nothing in my hand, I made my way along Whitehall to Trafalgar Square, sorely tempted by the sight and smell of food as I passed various places devoted to the provision of meals, but not of beds.

It had occurred to me that it would be cheaper to dine, sleep, and breakfast at the same place, than to have dinner somewhere, and then go in search of a bedroom for the night and breakfast in the morning.

As I walked, I thought of the hotels of which I knew —the Ritz, the Savoy, the Carlton, Claridge's, the Grosvenor, the Langham, and certain more discreet and exclusive ones in the neighbourhood of the Albany (where Uncle Hector kept a *pied-à-terre* for his use when in England).

But both their cost and their risks were almost as much against them as were those of our own family hotel. Even if I could afford to go to such hotels as these, it was quite likely that the first person I should run against, in the one I selected, would be some friend or acquaintance.

I decided to approach one of those mines of information, or towers of strength and refuge, a London policeman.

"Take a bus to Bloomsbury, and you'll find what you want. Russell Square, Bedford Square, British Museum. All round that neighbourhood," was the reply of the stalwart to whom I applied for advice, as to a cheap, quiet, and decent hotel.

I obeyed his words, and had an edible dinner, a clean and comfortable bed, and a satisfying breakfast, for a surprisingly small sum, in an hotel that looked on to the British Museum and seemed to be the favoured of the clergy—it being almost full of men of religion and their women-folk of even more religion.

The "young lady" at the bureau of this chaste hostelry did something to enhance the diminished self-respect that my Israelite had left to me, by making no comment upon the fact that I was devoid of luggage, and by refraining from asking me to produce money in advance of hospitality. Perhaps she had a more discerning eye, or perhaps merely a softer heart, than had the child of Abraham, Isaac, and Jacob; or perhaps she was merely more of a fool.

Nevertheless I was glad to get away in the morning and to seek the shop of a hairdresser, after sleeping, for the first time in my life, without pyjamas, and bathing without a sponge. I was also glad to feel that the tips which I had given, with apologies for their modesty, to the waiter and chamber-maid had seemed quite adequate in their sight, and to cover my known deficiencies both of evening wear and night-gear.

It was extraordinary how naked I felt without my links, and how dishevelled without having used a brush and comb.

Finding a desirable barber's in Oxford Street, I was shaven and shampooed and went on my way, if not rejoicing, at any rate in better case, and feeling more my own man.

§ 2.

My journey to Paris was uneventful and uncomfortable, confirming me in my opinion that economy in travelling is one of the dearest economies of all.

Personally, I would always rather travel first class and miss my meals, than travel third and enjoy three good ones, on a day's journey. Nor is this in the least due to paltry exclusiveness and despicable snobbishness. It is merely that I would rather spend the money on a comfortable seat, a pleasant compartment, and freedom from crowding, than on food with cramped circumstance. Let him who, in his wisdom, would rather spend his money on good food and have the discomfort, do so by all means.

De gustibus non disputandum, as the learned say, and likewise, *Chacun à son goût.*

Anyhow, the third-class journey was by no means to my *goût* at the time, though the day quickly came when it would have seemed the height of luxury.

From Charing Cross (where I turned my pounds into

francs and felt much richer) to Dover I contrasted the
beautiful county of Kent with my own Devon, in favour
of the latter; and, at Dover, I went on board the cross-
Channel steamer, deeply and appreciatively inhaling the
glorious air, after that of the dusty, stuffy, crowded compartment in which I had travelled down.

Mentally I was in a curious condition, for while one
half of myself ached unbearably for Isobel, the other
half rejoiced wildly at the thought of adventure, travel,
novelty, spacious life, mysterious Africa, the desert, fighting, and all that appeals to the heart of romantic youth.

At Calais, the sight of a French soldier, a sentry near
the Custom House, gave me a real thrill.

Was I actually going to wear that uniform myself in
a day or two? A _képi_, baggy red breeches, and a long
overcoat, buttoned back from the legs? How much more
attractive and romantic than the familiar British uniform that seemed to suggest Hyde Park and nurse-maids,
rather than palms, oases, Moorish cities, and desert warfare.

So is the unknown always better than the known, and
the thing we have not, better than that we have. . . .

At the Gare du Nord I experienced, in an intensified
form, that sense of loneliness and utter insignificance that
had assailed me at Waterloo; and I went out into the
bright uproar of gay Paris, feeling anything but bright,
uproarious, or gay myself. I was once more faced with
the problem of hotels, for I had not the least idea as to
how one set about offering one's services to France as a
mercenary soldier, and the first thing to do, therefore,
was to find a roof and a bed to serve me while I set about
the quest.

My knowledge of Paris hotels was confined to the
Meurice, Crillon, the Bristol, and the Ambassadors, but
I knew these to be expensive, and, moreover, places at
which I might meet acquaintances. There was no great
likelihood of my meeting anyone who knew me well; but
there was a chance, and I wanted to behave precisely as
a guilty fugitive would do.

If I were traced, and it were found that I had gone, in London and Paris, to places where I might meet friends, it would hardly look as though I were a genuine jewel-thief, anxious to cover his tracks as he fled the country.

On the other hand, I did not want to blunder into an obscure cheap hotel, without luggage, an obvious foreigner, and run the risk of a visit from a polite but inquisitive *agent de police,* as seemed to me quite possible, if I and my explanations struck the proprietor as peculiar. . . .

A whimsical idea struck me. Why not go to the police themselves for advice on the subject of avoiding such trouble?

Sauntering along the noisy busy thoroughfare that passes the Gare du Nord, I looked out for a gendarme.

Presently I saw one standing on an island in the middle of the road, silent, inscrutable, immobile, heavily caped, oppressed by great responsibilities. Crossing to him, I raised my hat, and in my best and politest French (which is not bad, thanks to a French governess in our youth, and the Chaplain's wisdom and care), asked him if he could direct me to a good quiet hotel.

Moving his eyes, but not his head, nor any other portion of his majestic person, he examined me from top to toe and back again.

"Monsieur is English," he pronounced.

I acknowledged the truth of his statement, wondering how he knew I was not German, Swiss, Danish, Swedish, Norwegian, nor Dutch.

"Hôtel Normandie, Rue de l'Échelle," he announced without hesitation.

"And how do I get there, *Monsieur l'Officier?*" I asked.

"*Fiacre,*" was the prompt, terse reply, and the all-seeing official eye left me and sought among the traffic. A white-gloved hand was suddenly raised, and an open cab, driven by a many-caped gentleman, who did not look like a teetotaller, approached.

"Normandie, Rue de l'Échelle," said my gendarme to the *cocher,* and gave me a military salute, as I thanked him, raised my hat, and stepped into the carriage.

I enjoyed the drive through beautiful Paris in the mingled glow of late sunset and the myriad lights of the shops and streets; but my heart sank a little as the cab drew up before a fashionable-looking hotel that stood at a busy corner, close to the Rue de Rivoli and to the Rue de la Paix.

It looked as expensive as the best. However, Fate had sent me here, and here I would stay.

Trying to look as unconcerned as a luggageless traveller may, I entered the hall, received the bow of an imposing hall-porter, and marched straight ahead, past the grand staircase and the dining-room, to where I could see the bureau, and beyond it, the palm-decked *fumoir*.

At the bureau, a very pretty girl was talking to an American in American.

This was good luck. I could make a much more con-vincing show in English than in my pedantic and careful French.

Standing near, and trying to look like an eccentric for-eigner who habitually went about without stick or gloves in order that he might keep his hands in his pockets, I waited for the American to go.

Meanwhile, it was quite impossible to avoid hearing what was said by the keen-faced, square-shouldered, lumpy-toed, baggy-trousered, large-hatted gentleman to the lady, what time she chewed a cud of sweet recollection and Mangle's Magnificent Masticating Gum or similar enduring comestible.

When at length he took his key and went, I turned to the girl.

"So you was raised in Baltimore!" said I rapturously. "Fancy that being your home town now! Isn't it just the cutest place? Peachiest gals and bulliest cakes in America! . . . Say, I reckon this gay Paree hasn't got anything on little old New York!" . . .

"My!" said the young lady. "Do'you know Baltimore? You don't say!" and she smiled sweetly upon me.

"*Know Baltimore!*" said I, and left it at that. . . .
"Lots of Americans and English here, I suppose," I went

on, "since the hotel folk are wise (and lucky) enough to have you in the bureau? And I suppose you speak French as well as any Parisian?"

"My, yes," she smiled. "Most as well as I speak good old U. S. . . . Why, yes—lots of home people and Britishers here. . . . Most of our waiters can help 'em out too, when they're stuck for the French of *'Yes, I'll have a high-ball, Bo,'* " and she tinkled a pretty little laugh.

"Guess that's fine," said I. "I want to turn in here for a day or two. All upset at my place." (Very true, indeed.) "Just to sleep and breakfast. Got a vacant location?"

"Sure," said my fair friend, and glanced at an indicator. *"Troisième.* Eighteen francs. No—breakfast only —fourteen. Going up now?" And she unhooked a key and passed it to me with a brief *"Deux cent vingt deux.* The bell-hop will show you."

"Not bringing any stuff in," I said, and drew my entire fortune from my pocket, as one who would pay whatever was desired in advance, and the more the merrier.

"Shucks," said my friendly damsel, and I gathered that I was deemed trustworthy.

In the big book that she pushed to me I wrote myself down as Smith, but clung to the "John," that there might be something remnant and stable in a whirling and dissolving universe.

"Guess I'll hike up and take possession now," said I thereafter, and with my best smile and bow I turned to the lift before she could send to the hall-porter to dispatch a supposititious suit-case to the spot.

The lift-boy piloted me to number two hundred and twenty-two, where, safe inside, I bolted the door and drew breath.

"J'y suis, j'y reste," said I, in tribute to my very French surroundings . . . . "and the less they see of me below, the less they'll notice my lack of luggage and evening kit."

It occurred to me that it might be worth the money to

buy a pair of pyjamas and have them sent to Monsieur
Smith, No. 222 Hôtel Normandie. If I laid them out on
the flat square pillow that crowned the lace-covered bed,
the chambermaid would not be so likely to comment on
the paucity of my possessions, particularly if I locked the
wardrobe and pocketed the key as though to safeguard
a valuable dressing-case.

If I also avoided the dining-room, where, in my lounge-
suit, I should be extremely conspicuous among the fashionable evening throng, I might well hope to dwell in peaceful obscurity without rousing unwelcome interest and attention, in spite of the inadequacy of my equipment.

I decided to sally forth, buy some pyjamas, order them
to be sent in at once, and then fortify myself with a two-
franc dinner and a glass of *vin ordinaire*—probably *très
ordinaire*—in some restaurant.

After an uncomfortable wash in the *lavabo,* I strolled
nonchalantly forth, made my purchases, and enjoyed a
good and satisfying meal in a cheerful place situated in
a somewhat ignobler part of the Rue de Rivoli, at a little
distance from the fashionable centre of Paris.

Returning to my over-furnished unhomely room, I spread
out the gay pyjamas which awaited me, and wondered
when the chamber-maid would come to turn down the
bed. And then I realised that I need have felt no anxiety,
for I had only to bolt the door and shout something when
she came, and she would depart in ignorance of my complete lack of luggage and possessions.

However, I should not be able to keep her out in the
morning, when I went in search of breakfast and the
recruiting-office, and then the pyjamas and the locked
wardrobe ould play their part.

Even as I stood revolving these important trifles in my
youthful breast, the door opened and in burst a hard-
featured middle-aged woman. Anything less like the
French chamber-maid of fiction and the drama could not
well be imagined; for she was fair-haired, grey-eyed, un-
prepossessing, and arrayed in a shapeless black frock, plain
apron, and ugly cap.

With a curt apology she flicked down a corner of the
bed-clothes, slapped the pyjamas down (in what is presumably the only place whence a self-respecting hotel guest
can take them up), glanced at the unused washstand, and
scurried from the room.

As I heard her unlock the door of the next apartment,
almost before she had closed mine, I realised that she was
far too busy to concern herself with my deficiencies, and
ceased to worry myself on the subject.

Feeling that sleep was yet far from me, and that if
I sat long in that unfriendly room I should go mad, I
descended to the *fumoir*, sought a big chair in a retired
nook, and, from behind a deplorable copy of *La Vie
Parisienne*, watched the frequenters of this apparently popular lounge.

Here I thought long thoughts of Isobel, my brothers,
and Brandon Abbas; and occasionally wondered what
would happen on the morrow.

Nothing at all would happen until I had discovered the
procedure for enlisting in the Foreign Legion, and the
discovery of that procedure must be to-morrow's business.

Were I a romancer as well as a romantic, now would
be the moment for me to announce the dramatic entry
of the French officer who had fired our young imaginations,
years before, and sown the seeds now bearing fruit.

As I sat there in the lounge of the Paris hotel, he would
enter and call for coffee and a cognac. I should go up
to him and say, '*Monsieur le Capitaine* does not remember
me, perhaps?'' He would rise, take my hand, and say,
"*Mon Dieu!* The young Englishman of Brandon Abbas!"
I should tell him of my ambition to be a soldier of France,
to tread in his footsteps, to rise to rank and fame in the
service of his great country, and he would say, "Come with
me—and all will be well. . . .''

Unfortunately he did not enter, and presently, finding
myself the last occupant of the lounge and inclined to
yawn, I crept unwillingly to bed. I fell asleep, trying to
remember his name.

§ 3.

The next day was Sunday, and I spent it miserably between the lounge and my bedroom.

On Monday morning, after a spongeless bath and an unsatisfying *petit déjeuner,* I sallied forth and put myself in the hands of an excellent barber, and, while enjoying his deft ministrations, had a bright idea. I would pump this chatty person.

"You don't know Algeria, I suppose?" I asked the man.

"But no, Monsieur," he replied. "Is Monsieur going there?"

"I hope to," I said. "A magnificent colony of your great country, that."

Ah, it was, indeed. Monsieur might well say so. A wonderful achievement and the world's model colony. Growing too, always growing. . . . This excellent *pénétration pacifique* to the South and towards Morocco. . . .

"They do the pacific penetration by means of the bayonets of the Foreign Legion mostly, don't they?" I asked.

The Frenchman smiled and shrugged.

"A set of German rascals," he said. "But they have their uses. . . ."

"How do you get them?" I asked.

Oh, they just enlisted. Made their *engagements volontaires,* like anybody else, at the head recruiting-office of the French army in the Rue St. Dominique. Simply enlisted there and were packed off to Africa. . . .

"But I thought service was wholly compulsory in this country?" said I. "How then do you have recruiting-offices for a conscript army?"

The worthy soul explained at length, and so far as I could follow his swift idiomatic talk, that any Frenchman could, if he liked, volunteer for service before the time came when he *must* serve, whether he liked it or not. Sometimes, for business reasons, it was very convenient to get it over and done with, instead of having it to do later, when one was established. Hence the recruiting-office for the French army. But no Frenchman could volunteer for the Legion until he had done his compulsory service. . . .

I let him talk on, keeping the words *Rue St. Dominique* clearly in my mind the while. I had got what I wanted, and the sooner I found this recruiting-office the better, for funds would soon be running low.

On leaving the shop I hailed a *fiacre*, said, "Rue St. Dominique," and jumped in, excusing my extravagance by my absolute ignorance of the route, and the need for haste.

Again I enjoyed the drive, feeling excited and buoyant, and filled with the sense of adventure. After a time, I found we were in what appeared to be the military quarter of Paris, and I saw the *École Militaire* and some cavalry-barracks. The streets were thronged with men in uniform, and my heart beat higher and higher as the cab turned from the Esplanade des Invalides into the Rue St. Dominique.

As the *cocher* looked round enquiringly at me, I thought it would be as well to pay him off here at the corner.

Perhaps it might not be good form to drive up, in style, to a recruiting-office, and, in any case, there was no need to let the man know where I was going. . . .

I found the Rue St. Dominique to be a wholly uninspiring thoroughfare, narrow, gloomy, and dingy in the extreme.

Walking along it and glancing from side to side, I soon found the building of which I was in search.

Over the door of a dirty little house was a blue-lettered notice testifying that the place was the BUREAU DE RECRUTEMENT. Below the label was the bald, laconic observation, ENGAGEMENTS VOLONTAIRES.

Well, here then was my bureau of recruitment and here would I make my "voluntary engagement," and if the Path of Glory led but to the grave, its beginning was quite in keeping with its end, for a more sepulchral-looking abode of gloom than this ugly little government-office I have never seen.

Crossing the road, I pushed open a rusty iron gate, undeterred by its agonised or warning shriek, crossed the neglected cemetery garden of this gay place, thrust back a swing door, and entered a long dark passage.

I could see no notice recommending all to abandon hope who entered here, but my drooping spirits were unraised by a strangling odour of carbolic, coal-gas, and damp.

On the wall was a big placard which, in the sacred names of Liberty, Equality, and Fraternity, offered to accept for five years the services of any applicant for admission to *La Legion Étrangère* (provided he was between the ages of eighteen and forty), and to give him a wage of a halfpenny a day.

There seemed to me to be little of Liberty about this proposal, less of Equality, and least of Fraternity.

On the other hand, it was an *engagement volontaire,* and anyone who didn't like the offer could leave it. No one was compelled to accept it, and there was no deception —on the placard at any rate.

I read the notice through again, half hoping that while I did so, someone would come and ask my business, some sound break the heavy smelly silence of Glory's cradle.

But none did, and "with well-feigned hopefulness I pushed forth into the gloom."

Venturing on, I came to a kind of booking-office ticket-window, above which were repeated the words *Engagements Volontaires.*

I looked in, and in a severe office or orderly-room, beheld an austere person in uniform, seated at a table and writing busily. The two gold stripes above his cuff inclined me to suppose that he was a non-commissioned officer, though of what rank and eminence I knew not.

He ignored me and all other insects.

How to attract his attention?

I coughed gently and apologetically. I coughed appealingly. I coughed upbraidingly, sorrowfully, suggestively, authoritatively, meekly, imperiously, agreeably, hopefully, hopelessly, despairingly, and quite vainly. Evidently I should not cough my way to glory.

"*Monsieur le Capitaine,*" I murmured ingratiatingly.

The man looked up. I liked him better when looking down.

"Monsieur would appear to have a throat-trouble," he observed.

"And Monsieur an ear-trouble," I replied, in my young ignorance and folly.

"What is Monsieur's business?" he enquired sharply.

"I wish to join the *Légion Étrangère*," I said.

The man smiled, a little unpleasantly, I thought.

"*Eh, bien,*" he remarked, "doubtless Monsieur will have much innocent amusement at the expense of the Sergeant-Major there too," and I was quite sure that his smile was unpleasant this time.

"Is Monsieur only a Sergeant-Major then?" I enquired innocently.

"I am a Sergeant-Major," was the reply, "and let me tell Monsieur, it is the most important rank in the French army."

"No?" said I, and lived to learn that this piece of information was very little short of the simple truth.

"Wait by that door, please," requested the Sergeant-Major, indicating one marked *Commandant de Recrutement,* and I felt that he had also said, "Wait, just wait, my friend, until you have enlisted."

I waited.

I should think I waited an hour.

Just as I was contemplating another visit to the buttery-hatch or ticket-office window, the door opened and my friend, or enemy, appeared.

"Be pleased to enter, Monsieur," said he suavely, and I, for some reason, or for no reason, bethought me of a poem of childhood's happy days, entitled, "The Spider and the Fly," as I entered a large, bare orderly-room.

But it was no spider that I encountered within, but a courtly and charming gentleman of the finest French type. I know nothing of his history, but I am very sure that he was of those who are "born," as the French say, and that if, in the Terror, his great-grandfather did not perish on the guillotine, it was not because he wasn't an aristocrat.

He was a white-haired, white-moustached, handsome man, dressed in a close-fitting black tunic and baggy red over-alls with a broad black stripe. His cuffs were adorned with bands of gold and of silver braid, and his sleeves with the five *galons* of a Colonel.

"A recruit for the Legion, *mon Commandant,*" said the Sergeant-Major, and stood stiffly at attention.

The Colonel looked up from the desk at which he was writing, as, entering, I bared my head and bowed; he rose and extended his hand, with a friendly and charming smile.

Not thus, thought I, do British colonels welcome recruits to the ranks of their regiments.

"And you, too, wish to enlist in our Foreign Legion, do you?" he said as we shook hands. "Has England started an export trade in the best of her young men? I don't see many Englishmen here from year's end to year's end, but you, *mon enfant,* are the third this week!"

My heart gave a bound of hopeful joy. . . .

"Anything like me, sir?" I asked.

"*Au bout des ongles,*" was the reply. "Were they your brothers by any chance? . . . But I will ask no indiscreet questions."

I felt happier than I had done since I had kissed Isobel.

"Yes, *mon Commandant,*" I replied. "I wish to become a soldier of France if you will have me."

"And do you understand what you are doing. Monsieur?" asked the Colonel.

"I have read the placard outside," said I.

"It is not quite all set forth there," he smiled. "The life is a very hard one. I would urge no one to adopt it, unless he were a born soldier and actually desirous of a life of discipline, adventure, and genuine hardship."

No, this certainly was not a case of the spider and the fly—or it was an entirely new one, wherein the spider discouraged flies from entering the web.

"I wish to join, sir," I said. "I have heard something of the life in the Sahara from an officer of Spahis, whom I once knew."

The Colonel smiled again.

"Ah, *mon enfant*," said he, "but you won't be an officer of Spahis, you see. . . . Nor an officer of the Legion either, except after some very long and lean years in the ranks and as a non-commissioned officer."

"One realises that one must begin at the bottom, *mon Commandant*," I replied.

"Well—listen then," said the Colonel, and he recited what he evidently knew by heart from frequent repetition.

"The *engagement volontaire* for *La Légion Étrangère* is for five years, in Algiers, or any other French colony, and the pay is a *sou* a day. A *légionnaire* can re-enlist at the end of the five years, and again at the end of ten years. At the end of fifteen years he is eligible for a pension varying according to his rank. A foreigner, on completion of five years' service, can claim to be naturalised as a French subject. . . . You understand all that, *mon enfant?*"

"Yes, I thank you, *mon Commandant*," I replied.

"Mind," continued the Colonel, "I say nothing of what is understood by the term 'service' in the Legion. It is not all pure soldiering at times.

"Nor do I say anything as to the number of men who survive to claim the pension. . . ."

"I am not thinking of the pension, *mon Commandant*," I replied; "nor of the alleged 'pay,' so much as of a soldier's life, fighting, adventure, experience. . . ."

"Ah, there is plenty of that," said the Colonel. "Plenty of that. It is a real military school and offers the good soldier great and frequent chances of distinction, glory, decoration, and promotion. Some of our most famous generals have been in the Legion, and several of the highest and most distinguished officers of the Legion began their career in its ranks. . . . Also, if you can show that you have been an officer in the army of your own country, you can begin as a probationary-corporal, and avoid the ranks altogether."

"Please accept me as a recruit, *mon Commandant*," said I.

"Ah, we'll see first what the doctor has to say about

you—though there is little doubt about *that*, I should think," smiled the Colonel, and pulled a form towards him.

"What is your name?"

"John Smith," said I.

"Age?"

"Twenty-one years" (to be on the safe side).

"Nationality English?"

"Yes, *mon Commandant*."

"Very well. If you pass the doctor I shall see you again. *Au 'voir, Monsieur*," and with a curt nod to the Sergeant-Major, the Colonel resumed his writing.

The Seregant-Major opened the door with a still suave "This way, if you please, Monsieur," and led me across the passage into a room already tenated by half a dozen civilians, whom I rightly supposed to be fellow-recruits for the Foreign Legion.

I got a fleeting impression of seedy, poorer-class people, two being brush-haired, fair, fattish, and undoubtedly German, before the Sergeant-Major, opening another door in this waiting-room, motioned me to enter a small closet, from which another door led elsewhere.

"Remove *all* clothing, please," said the Sergeant-Major, and shut me in.

This was unpleasant but presumably unavoidable, and I obeyed. Before I had begun to shiver, the second door opened and I was invited to submit myself to the close and searching investigations of an undergrown but over-nourished gentleman, from beneath whose white surgical smock appeared the baggy red trousers of the French army.

This official, presumably an army-surgeon, was easily able to establish the belief in my mind that *his* ancestors had not perished on the guillotine. (Certainly not during the Terror, anyhow.) More probably they danced round it, or possibly operated it.

When he had quite finished with my vile body, he bade me replace it in the closet, clothe it, and remove it with all speed. This, nothing loth, I did, and was re-conducted by the Sergeant-Major to the Colonel's office.

"Well, *mon enfant*," smiled the old officer, "you are accepted."

"And can I enlist at once, sir?" I enquired eagerly.

"Not until you have slept on it," was the reply. "Come here again to-morrow morning, if you are still of the same mind, and I will enrol you. But think well—think well. And remember that, until you sign your name on the form which I shall give you to-morrow, you are absolutely free, and have committed yourself in no way whatsoever. Think well—think well. . . ."

And thanking him gratefully, I went from the room, hoping that all French officers were of this stamp, as kindly and as truly gentlemanly. My hope was not fulfilled.

In the corridor, the Sergeant-Major observed, "I sincerely hope Monsieur will return," and as I assured him, with thanks, that I should do so, I fancied, rightly or wrongly, that his smile was a little mocking.

§ 4.

Emerging from the stuffy gloom, I walked down the Rue St. Dominique with a light, gay step. I could have danced along, whistling and singing, for I felt practically certain that Michael and Digby were but a day or two ahead of me upon this romantic road, and that I might overtake them at any moment. Probably they were both still in France, possibly in Paris. Once I rejoined them, I should no longer feel this deadly loneliness, and should have someone to whom to talk about Isobel.

Journeys end in lovers' meetings—and but for this separation from her, there would not be the immeasurable joy of our reunion.

Really I ought to be very thankful and very happy. I was about to rejoin Michael and Digby, and to live with them again; Isobel loved me and was awaiting my return; and I was on the threshold of a great adventure in an unknown foreign land.

Knowing that I should, after to-morrow morning, live at the charges of *Madame la République* (albeit she seemed of a careful and economical turn of mind), my funds were ample, and I would take a *fiacre* back to the fashionable quarter and spend the rest of my last day of freedom in sight-seeing and idleness.

I would sit in the Tuileries Gardens, visit the Louvre, look in the shops, have an outdoor meal in the Bois, and generally behave as does the tourist who has a few hours and a few francs to spend.

I carried out my programme, whiled away the day, and crept up to my bedroom at night, too tired for anything but the blessed dreamless sleep of healthy youth.

In the morning I paid my bill and departed from the Hôtel Normandie with a curious sense of escape. I did not in the least mind becoming a halfpenny soldier and herding with all sorts and conditions of men; but I did dislike being in a first-class hotel without my dinner-kit, a change of clothes, and the small necessities of the toilet.

I again drove to the Rue St. Dominique, and, on the way, endeavoured to talk to myself as though a person of wisdom and experience were talking to another of sense and discretion. But I greatly fear that this is not what happens when I address myself.

"You have only to stop this *fiacre,* turn about, and go back," said I to me, "and there is no harm done. You will still be a free man, and can go back to Brandon Abbas as soon as you like."

But the only reply was, "Beau . . . Digby. . . . Stand by your pals through thick and thin. Adventure: Romance: Success: Fame and Fortune: and then England, Home, and Isobel . . ." and much similar youthful nonsense.

At the *Bureau de Recrutement* I was shown into a waiting-room by the Sergeant-Major, who observed:

"Ah, Monsieur has come back then! Good!" and smiled unattractively. Again I was reminded of a poem of early childhood, this time of a Lady of Riga who indulged in an unorthodox joy-ride.

In the waiting-room were some of the men I had seen on the previous day in the doctor's ante-chamber.

Among them were the Teutonic-looking pair, and I

thought it probable that if I suddenly called out *"Waiter!"* or *"Garçon!"* they would both spring eagerly forward. They looked very harmless, insignificant, and unattractive —also terribly poor.

The rest were a mixed lot, Latins of sorts, apparently with nothing in common but dire poverty. They did not seem in the least ruffianly nor criminal, but just ordinary workingmen, desperately poor, and as anxious and worried as hungry, homeless people always are.

It was rather curious to feel that whereas, a few minutes ago, I had been a little uncomfortable by reason of my sartorial deficiencies, I now felt uncomfortable at being so obviously a fashionably-clad and well-nourished member of a wholly different class.

My well-cut and fairly-new clothing seemed to mock the rags and general seediness of these poor fellows, my future comrades—all of whom would very probably prove much tougher soldiers than I should.

Before long, the Sergeant-Major returned and bade me follow him to the Colonel's office.

"Ah, *mon enfant*," said the old soldier, as I entered and bowed, "so you have not thought better of it, eh? Well, well, you must now do as you please."

"I wish to enlist, *mon Commandant*," I replied.

"Then read this form and sign it," he said, with a distinct sigh. "Remember though, that as soon as you have done so, you will be a soldier of France, entirely amenable to martial law, and without any appeal whatsoever. Your friends cannot possibly buy you out, and your Consul cannot help you, for five years. Nothing but death can remove you from the Legion."

I glanced over the grey printed form, a contract by which the signatory undertook to serve the French Republic for five years, as a soldier in the *Légion Étrangère*.

Five years was a long time—but Isobel would only be twenty-three at the end of it, and if Michael and Digby had done this, I could do the same. . . . It would be nice to return, a Colonel at twenty-five, and take Isobel to my regiment. . . . I signed my name.

"A little error, *mon enfant?*" smiled the Colonel, on reading my signature. "Or you prefer this *nom-de-guerre,* doubtless?"

I had written "J. Geste"!

Blushing and looking a fool, I asked to be allowed to change my mind and put my own name, and the kindly old gentleman, tearing up the form, gave me another which I signed "John Smith."

"Now, my boy, listen to me," said the Colonel. "You are a duly enlisted soldier of France and must join your regiment at once. If you do not do so, you will be treated as a deserter. You are to catch the Marseilles train from the Gare de Lyon this evening—nine-fifteen—and report yourself to the non-commissioned officer whom you will see waiting at the Marseilles terminus. Should you fail to find him, ask any *gendarme* to direct you to Fort St. Jean, and report yourself there. Don't forget. Fort St. Jean, the military depôt," and he rose and extended his hand. "I wish you good luck and quick promotion, *mon enfant,*" he added. "Is there anything else I can tell you?"

"Do you always advise applicants to think better of it, sir?" I asked.

He looked at me a little sharply.

"I am not here to deter people from joining the Foreign Legion," he said. . . . "But some strike me as better suited to the life than others," he added, with a kindly shake of the hand. "Good-bye and good luck."

I thanked him and turned to commence my "ride on the Tiger" (along the Path of Glory).

"Come with me, recruit," said the Sergeant-Major, as he closed the door, "and move smartly."

In his office, he made out a railway-warrant for Marseilles, and a form that proclaimed the bearer to be John Smith, a soldier of the Legion, proceeding to the depôt in Algeria. He then unlocked a drawer, produced a cash-box, and doled out three francs on to the table.

"Subsistence-money, recruit," said he. "A squandering of public funds. Three *sous* would be ample."

I added two francs to them.

"Let us part friends, Sergeant-Major," said I, for I hate leaving ill-feeling behind me if I can avoid it.

"Recruit," replied he, pocketing the money, "you will get on. . . . *If* you respect and please all Sergeant-Majors. Good-bye."

And once more I found myself in the Rue St. Dominique, but no longer a free man. I had, with my own hand, padlocked about my ankle a chain unbreakable, the other end of which was somewhere in the desert of Sahara.

Having burnt my boats, I was quite anxious to push on, and I found myself deciding to go by the next train, instead of waiting till the evening. Had I realised that I was to sit for eighteen hours on an uncushioned wooden seat, I might have felt less eager. Eighteen hours the journey did last, however, and each hour more wearisome than the one before. I think the train must have visited every town and village in France, and the entire population have clattered noisily into my ancient, uncomfortable, unclean compartment, throughout the night. Certainly I reached Marseilles feeling ancient, uncomfortable, and unclean myself; and, unlike the compartment, very empty.

It was a wretched journey, rendered no pleasanter by the attentions of the guard, who, having seen from my railway-warrant that I was going to the Legion, behaved somewhat in the manner of a clever captor and skilful goaler.

He was of a type of Frenchman that I do not like (there are several of them), and though he refrained from actual reproaches and abuse, he made it clear to me that I could not escape him, and to my fellow-travellers that they had a possible danger in their midst. Not precisely a convict; nor, so far as he actually *knew*, an ex-convict; but still, one who was going to join the Foreign Legion.

On arrival at the terminus, this worthy soul saved me the trouble of finding my non-commissioned officer, by himself finding the man and handing me over to him, with the air of one who has deserved well of his country and of his kind.

"There!" said he to the Sergeant. "There he is! Another little bird for your cage," and so depressed was I by hunger, sleeplessness, and aching bones that I so far departed from good manners and the equal mind as to say:

"Oh, for God's sake don't be such a funny little fat ass," but as I spoke in English he may have thought that I did but offer felicitations and regards.

I rather liked the look of the Sergeant. He was a dapper, alert person, and his bronzed face, though hard as iron, was not brutal nor vicious. He struck me as looking uncommonly like a man. He wore the usual uniform of the French infantry, but with a broad blue woollen sash round the waist, green epaulettes instead of red, and Zouave trousers.

Looking me over with a cold official stare, he asked me if I spoke French, and demanded my name, papers, and nationality.

"Another Englishman," he remarked to my intense joy. "Well—it might have been worse."

"Are you alone?" he enquired, and finding that I was, so far as I knew, bade me follow him.

Surely Michael and Digby were here, and I should see them in the next few minutes. I cheered up tremendously.

He led the way out of the station and down into the busy street and the exhilarating air and sunshine of Marseilles.

By the side of the taciturn Sergeant I walked, longing to ask him about the "other Englishmen," whose recent arrival he had implied by his exclamation, on hearing my nationality.

But his manner did not encourage polite converse, and, truth to tell, I had an even deeper longing at the moment—for the appeasement of a very healthy appetite.

I waxed diplomatic.

"A Sergeant would not share a bottle of wine with a recruit, I suppose, Monsieur?" I asked as we passed an attractive-looking café, from beneath whose gay striped awnings marble-topped tables and comfortable cane chairs shrieked an invitation to rest and refreshment.

"He would not, *bleu*," was the reply. "Not only from

a natural sense of superiority, but also because it would be against the regulations.   Neither is he addressed as 'Monsieur.'   He has a military rank, and he is saluted by those who address him. . . . Some Sergeants, properly approached, might refresh themselves, perhaps, while a deserving *bleu* did the same. . . .''

I halted and saluted as though he were an officer.   (Correct procedure in the French army, I found.)

"Monsieur le Sergent," said I, "will you honour me by drinking a glass of wine at this restaurant while I get some food?   I am very hungry,'' and I produced a five-franc piece.

"Be here in quarter of an hour, *bleu*,'' was the reply, and taking the coin the Sergeant crossed the road to a wine-shop, as I promptly dived into the café and hungrily devoured my last civilian meal—an excellent one in every detail, down to the crisp rolls, fresh butter, and coffee worthy of the name.

I rose, feeling what Digby would call ''a better and a wider man.''

Sauntering out under the awning, and seeing nothing of my Sergeant, I sat me down, filled and lighted my pipe, and gazed about me.   Fortified and refreshed, I felt by no means unhappy.

I had not long feasted my eyes upon the novel and interesting scene provided by the thronged thoroughfare, when the Sergeant, crossing the road, approached.   I rose promptly, saluted smartly, and fell in beside him.

He eyed my clothes.

"Have you any more money, *bleu?*'' he asked.

"Yes, Sergeant,'' I replied, feeling a little disappointed in him.

"Because if you have not, I shall return you three francs,'' quoth he.

I assured him that this was wholly unnecessary, though a very kindly thought—and regretted my suspicions.

"Well, I will give you some good advice instead then,'' said the worthy man.

I thanked him sincerely.

"Beware the Algerian wine then," he began. "The blessing and the curse of the army of Africa. I have just drunk two bottles of it. Excellent. . . . Beware of women, the blessing and the curse of all men. I have married three of them. Terrible. . . ."

I gave my solemn promise to beware, to be very ware, and neither to drink nor to marry to excess.

"Secondly, *bleu*," he went on, "when things are bad, do not make them worse, for they will be quite bad enough."

This also seemed sound advice, and I said so.

"And, thirdly—resist the decrees of Heaven if you will, but not those of your Corporal. . . . Of course, no one would dream of resisting the will of a Sergeant."

I agreed that no sane person would do this.

"Of course! . . . But it is when you are insane that you must be careful," warned my mentor.

"Insane?" I asked.

"Yes, *bleu*," was the reply. "All good *légionnaires* go insane at times. Then they are apt to do one of *the* three horrible things. Kill themselves, kill their comrades, or defy a Sergeant."

"Why should they go insane?" I enquired in some alarm.

"They shouldn't, but they do," said my mentor. "We call it *le cafard*. The cockroach. It crawls round and round in the brain, and the greater the heat, the monotony, the hardship, the overwork, the over-marching, and the drink—the faster goes the beetle and the more it tickles. . . . Then the man says, '*J'ai le cafard*,' and runs amok, or commits suicide, or deserts, or defies a Sergeant. . . . Terrible. . . . And do you know what is the egg of this beetle? No? It is absinthe. Absinthe is the uncle and aunt of the grandparents of *cafard*. It is the vilest poison. Avoid it. I know what I am saying. I was brought up on it. . . . Terrible. . . . I had some just now, after my wine. . . ."

I promised never to look on the absinthe when it was green, nor, indeed, when it was any other colour.

"Then you will not get real *cafard*," continued the

worthy man, "and you will not kill a comrade nor defy
a Sergeant. You will only commit suicide, or desert and
'die in the desert."

"Did you ever do any of these terrible things, *Monsieur
le Sergent?*" I asked.

"No, *bleu.* I did not even commit suicide," was the
reply. "I merely shaved my head, painted it red, white,
and blue, and was thus esteemed as a true patriot."

I began to think that two bottles of wine and an unspecified quantity of absinthe had stimulated the Sergeant's imagination, but learnt later that what he told
me was absolutely true. (When engaged in repainting
one of the striped sentry boxes of the barracks or the
outpost where he was stationed, he had painted one side
of his shaven head red and the other side blue, and separated these colours with a broad white stripe. This had
drawn attention to him, and he had riveted that attention
by desperate courage and resource during the operations
and battle of Cinq Palmiers.)

"And what can one do to escape *le cafard?*" I asked.

"Nothing," was the discouraging reply. "Mental occupation is good, and promotion is better. But in the desert,
while the Arab finds two things, the European finds three.
They are there, and, therefore, there they are. . . ."

I tried to look intelligent and enquiring.

"The Arab inevitably finds sun and sand—too much of
both. The European inevitably finds sun, sand, and madness—too much of all three," he went on. "This madness
is in the air, I suppose, or in the sun's rays. I do not
know, even, I, although I know so much. And now you
have talked more than is seemly. Silence, *bleu.* . . ."

And I was silent, though inclined to ask why he addressed me as "*bleu.*" I did not feel particularly blue,
and I was quite sure I did not look blue in the slightest
degree. (Later I learnt that it is French army-slang
for a recruit, and has as much or little meaning as the
English name of "rookie" for the same class of soldier.)
The use of my tongue being now prohibited, I used my
eyes instead, and enjoyed the marvellous panorama of

the Marseilles waterside, where Arabs, Negroes, Levantines, Chinese, Moors, Annamese, Indians, and the lascars and seamen of the ships of all nations, seemed as numerous as the French themselves.

I was reminded of the story of the Tower of Babel as we made our way through the throng and round the boxes, bales, sacks, barrels, trucks, carts, trolleys, and waggons over which the gesticulating crowds swarmed and howled.

Among the sailing-ships, tramps, Oriental-looking barques, yachts, brigs, schooners, cargo-boats, and liners, moored along the quays, I kept looking for the English flag, flying at the stern; and was delighted as often as my eye fell upon it.

I had thought, at first, that all the ships must be French, as each flew the Tri-couleur at the mast, until I realised that this was complimentary to France, while the national flag flew at the stern.

My head was beginning to ache with the noise, heat, hustle, and eye-strain, when we arrived at our destination, a mediæval fort on the water's edge, obsolete, and dilapidated, with an ancient lighthouse tower, and a drawbridge, leading over a moat to a great door.

One half expected to see that the sentries were halberdiers in breastplate and jerkin, trunk hose, and peaked morion. . . .

"Here we are, and hence—we are here," observed my Sergeant. . . . "Good-bye, *bleu,* and may the devil admire you."

"The same to you, Sergeant, and very many thanks," I replied.

To the Sergeant of the Guard at the gate he merely remarked, "Recruit. Legion. Poor devil!" and turning, departed, and I saw him no more.

"Follow me, you," said the Sergeant of the Guard, and led the way along prison-like stone corridors, damp, mouldering, echoing, and very depressing.

Halting at a door, he opened it, jerked his thumb in the direction of the interior, and shut the door behind me as I entered.

I was in my first French barrack-room.

Round the walls stood a score or so of cots and a number of benches, the remaining furniture of the room being a big table and a stove. Round the latter, at the table, on cots and on benches, lounged a varied assortment of men in civilian clothes—clothes ranging from well-cut lounge-suits to corduroy and rags.

Michael and Digby were not among these men, and I was sensible of a deep feeling of bitter disappointment as I realised the fact.

All these recruits looked at me, but though conscious of their regard, I was much more conscious of the poisonous foulness of the atmosphere of the room. It was horrible.

Every window was tightly shut, and every man (and the charcoal stove) was smoking, so far as I could determine with a rapid glance round the reeking place.

Presumably the men were smoking tobacco, but it was no tobacco with which I was familiar. I was reminded of gardeners' bonfires and smouldering rubbish.

Without thinking of what I was doing, I naturally and instinctively turned to the nearest window, manfully wrestled with it, and succeeded in throwing it open.

I am not in a position categorically to affirm that this was positively the first time that a window had ever been opened in Fort St. Jean, but it might well have been, to judge by the interest, not to say consternation, evoked by my simple action. What would have happened to me had a corporal or old soldier been present, I do not know.

At the table a group of three or four men who were playing cards, seemed to take unbrage at my action or my audacity. Their ejaculations sounded like those of great surprise mingled with resentment. One of them rose and turned towards me.

"You do not like the atmosphere of our little nest, perhaps?" he said, unpleasantly, and with a threatening and bullying note in his voice.

"No," I replied, and looking him carefully up and down, added, "Nor you, either. What are you going to do about it?"

This was ill-mannered of me. I admit it. I was bringing my style to the level of this unpleasant-looking individual. But it seemed to me to be the best level on which to meet him. I thought it a sound plan to begin as I meant to go on, and I had not the least intention of allowing that going-on to include any undue Christian meekness. I was the last person in the world to bully anybody, and I intended to be the last person to be bullied.

I did not wish to begin by making an enemy, but still less did I wish to begin by allowing the establishment of any sort of ascendancy on the part of a fellow-recruit.

"Oho! You don't like the look of me, don't you?" said the fellow, advancing.

"Not a bit," said I, looking him over appraisingly, and then "staring him out" as we used to say in the nursery.

I could not quite "place" the individual. He certainly was not a workman and he was not a prince in disguise. A clerk, or shopman, probably, I thought, and learned later that he was a French petty official named Vogué, "rehabilitating" himself—recovering his papers and civic rights by five years' Legion service, after conviction of defalcation, and a light sentence.

"You want that window open?" he said, changing the subject.

"Monsieur is intelligent," said I.

"Suppose I want it shut?" he enquired.

"Come and shut it," said I, with disgraceful truculence.

"Suppose we all want it shut?" he hedged.

"Then there is an end of the matter," I replied. "If the majority prefer to poison themselves, they have a perfect right to do so."

"Come back and be quiet, Nosey," called one of the card-players, and he returned, grumbling.

I seated myself on the cot nearest to the open window, and put my hat on the dirty straw-stuffed pillow. . . . What next?

"Like the ceiling raised any?" enquired a quiet drawling voice behind me, in English.

Turning, I regarded the ceiling.

"No," I said, "it will do," and studied the speaker.

He was lying at full length on the next cot, a very small, clean-shaven man with a prominent nose and chin, a steel-trap mouth, and a look of great determination and resolution. His eyes were a very light grey, hard and penetrating, his hair straw-coloured and stubbly, his face sallow, lantern-jawed, and tanned. He looked a hard case and proved to be what he looked.

"How did you know I was English?" I asked as he stared thoughtfully at me.

"What else?" he replied, deliberately. "Pink and white. . . . Own the earth. . . . *'Haw! Who's this low fellah? Don't know him, do I? . . .* Dude. . . . *'Open all the windahs now I've come!' . . .* British!"

I laughed.

"Are you an American?" I enquired.

"Why?" he replied.

"What else?" I drawled. *" 'Sure thing, Stranger.'* . . . Don't care who owns the earth. . . . Great contempt for the effete English. . . . Tar and feathers. . . . Stars and Stripes. . . . *'I come from God's Own Country and I guess it licks Creation.' . . .* Uneasy self-assertion. . . ."

The American smiled. (I never heard him laugh.)

"Bo," said he, turning to the next cot, "here's a Britisher insulting of our pore country. . . . Handin' out the rough stuff. . . . Fierce, ain't it?"

A huge man slowly turned from contemplation of the ceiling, raised his head, ceased chewing, and regarded me solemnly. He then fainted with a heartrending groan.

"Killed my pard, you hev," said the little man. "He's got a weak heart. . . . Damn sight weaker head though, haven't you, Bo?" he added, turning to his friend, who had recovered sufficiently to continue his patient mastication either of tobacco or chewing-gum.

Lying there, Bo appeared to be some seven feet in length, four in breadth, and two in depth.

In face he greatly resembled the small man, having the same jutting chin, prominent nose, tight mouth, and hard leathery face. His eyes were of a darker grey, however, and his hair black and silky.

He also looked a hard case and a very bad enemy. Con-versely, though, I gained the impression that he might be a very good friend. Indeed, I liked the look of both of them, in spite of the fact that I seemed to fill them with a sort of amused contempt.

"Ses you suffers from oneasy self-insertion, Hank," went on the little man.

"Ain't inserted nawthen to-day, Buddy," replied the giant mildly. "Nary a insert. I'm oneasy in me innards, but it ain't from what you ses, Stranger. Nope. I could insert a whole hog right now, and never notice it."

"Don't go fer ter rile the Britisher, Hank, with yer silly contradicshusness," implored the other. "He don' like it, an' he don' like us. You don't want ter go gittin' inter no trouble. So shet up and go on sufferin' from oneasy self-insertion."

"Means well," continued the speaker, turning to me, "but he ain't et nawthen excep' cigarette-ends for three or four days, an' he ain't at his best."

I stared. Was it possible that they were really hungry? Certainly they looked lean and haggard enough to be starving.

I had felt quite bad enough an hour or two ago, after missing a single meal. . . . I should have to go carefully if I wanted to give food, and not offence.

"Would you gentlemen lunch with me?" I asked, diffi-dently. "Brothers-in-arms and all that. . . ."

Two solemn faces turned and regarded me.

"He's calling you a gentleman, Hank," said the little man at length. "He don' mean no real harm though. He's talkin' English to you. . . . Hark! . . . You listen and improve your mind."

I made another effort. "Say," quoth I, "I gotta hunch I wanta grub-stake you two hoboes to a blow-out. Guess I can cough up the dough, if yew ain't too all-fired proud to be pards with a dod-gasted Britisher." A good effort, I thought.

"Gee!" said Hank, and they rose as one man.

"Put it right there, son," said the big man, extending the largest hand I have ever seen.

I took it, and in the crushing-match that ensued, endeavoured to hold my own. It was a painful business, and when I limply took the horny fist of Buddy in turn, I was handicapped in the squeezing competition. However, I was able to give him a worthy grip, though his hand was stronger than mine.

"Where can we get something?" I asked, and Buddy said there was certain to be a canteen about. He had never yet heard of a case where a thirsty soldier, with money, was not given every encouragement to get rid of it.

"I can't drink till I've et, pard," said Hank to me. " 'Twouldn't be right. If I drinks on an empty stummick, I gets onreasonable if interfered with by the bulls. . . . Bash a sheriff or somethin'. . . . When I ain't starvin', lickker on'y makes me more and more lovin' to all mankind. Yep, I gotta eat first."

"They'll have eats in the canteen," opined Buddy. "even in this God-fersaken section."

At that moment, the door of the room was thrown open by a soldier, and he entered carrying one end of a long board on which stood a row of tin bowls. Another soldier appeared at the other end, and together they bawled, *"Soupe!"*

It was invitation enough, and both the long arms of Hank shot out, and, in a moment, he was on his bed, a bowl in either hand.

Buddy followed his example.

I looked round. There appeared to me to be more bowls than there were people in the room. I snatched two, before the rush of hungry men from other parts of the room arrived with outstretched hands.

This disgusting exhibition of greed on my part cannot be excused, but may be condoned as it was not made in my own interests. I was not hungry, and the look of the stuff was not sufficiently tempting for me to eat for eating's sake. By the time I reached my cot, Hank had emptied one bowl, and was rapidly emptying the other.

"Gee! That's what I come to the Legion for," he said, with a sigh of content. When he had finished, I offered him one of my two.

"Fergit it," said he.

"I want to," said I.

He stared hard at me.

"Not hungry," I assured him.

"Honest Injun?" he asked doubtfully, but extending his hand.

"Had a big breakfast an hour ago," said I. "I never take soup in the middle of the morning. I got this for you and Mr.——er . . ."

"Buddy," said the little man and took the other bowl. Hank swallowed his third portion.

"You're shore white, pard," he said.

"Blowed-in-the-glass," agreed Buddy, and I felt I had two friends.

A large German lumbered up gesticulating, and assailed Hank.

"You eat dree!" he shouted in guttural English. "I only eat vun! Himmel! You damn dirdy tief!"

"Sure thing, Dutchy," said Buddy. "Don't yew stand fer it! You beat him up. You make him put it back."

The German shook a useful-looking fist under Hank's nose.

"I cain't put it back, Dutch," said he mildly. " 'Twouldn't be manners," and, as the angry German waxed more aggressive, he laid his huge and soupy hand upon the fat angry face, and pushed.

The German staggered back and fell heavily, and sat looking infinitely surprised.

"*Now*, pard," said Hank to me, "I could shore look upon the wine without no evil effecks to nobody," and we trooped out in search of the canteen.

The big gloomy quadrangle of Fort St. Jean was now crowded with soldiers of every regiment of the army of Africa, the famous Nineteenth Army Corps, and, for the first time, I saw the Spahis of whom the French officer had talked to us at Brandon Abbas.

Their trousers were voluminous enough to be called skirts, in fact one leg would have provided the material for an ample frock. Above these garments they wore sashes that appeared to be yards in length and feet in width. In these they rolled each other up, one man holding and manipulating the end, while the other spun round and round towards him, winding the sash tightly about himself as he did so.

Gaudy waistcoats, zouave jackets, fez caps, and vast scarlet cloaks completed their picturesquely barbaric costumes.

Besides the Spahis were blue-and-yellow Tirailleurs, pale blue Chasseurs d'Afrique, and red-and-blue Zouaves, blue Colonial Infantry, as well as artillerymen, sappers, and soldiers of the line, in their respective gay uniforms.

There was a babel of noise and a confusing turmoil as these leave-men rushed about in search of pay-corporals, *fourrier-sergents,* kit, papers, food, and the canteen. The place was evidently the clearing-house and military hotel for all soldiers coming from, or returning to, the army of Africa.

Following the current that flowed through this seething whirlpool, in the direction of a suggestive-looking squad of huge wine-casks that stood arrayed outside an open door, we found ourselves in the canteen and the presence of the national drink, good red wine.

"No rye-whiskey at a dollar a drink here, Bo," observed Buddy, as we made our way to a zinc-covered counter, and found that everybody was drinking claret at three-halfpence the bottle. "Drinks are on you, pard. Set 'em up."

"Gee! It's what they call 'wine,' " sighed Hank. "Gotta get used to it with the other crool de*priv*ations and hardships," and he drained the tumbler that I filled.

"It *is* lickker, Bo," replied Buddy tolerantly, and drained another.

It was, and very good liquor too. It struck me as far better wine than one paid a good deal for at Oxford, and good enough to set before one's guests anywhere.

Personally I am a poor performer with the bottle, and regard wine as something to taste and appreciate, rather than as a thirst-quenching beverage.

Also I freely confess that the sensation produced by more than enough, or by mixing drinks, is, to me, most distasteful.

I would as soon experience the giddiness caused by spin-

ning round and round, as the giddiness caused by alcohol.
More than a little makes me feel sick, silly, depressed, and
uncomfortable, and I have never been able to understand
the attraction that intoxication undoubtedly has for some
people.

It is therefore in no way to my credit that I am a strictly
sober person, and as little disposed to exceed in wine as in
cheese, pancakes, or dry toast.

"Quite good wine," said I to the two Americans, "but
I can't say I like it as a drink between meals."

I found that my companions were of one mind with me,
though perhaps for a different reason.

"Yep," agreed Buddy. "Guess they don't allow no in-
toxicatin' hard lickkers in these furrin canteens."

"Nope," remarked Hank. "We gotta swaller this an'
be thankful. P'r'aps we kin go out an' have a drink when
we git weary-like. . . . Set 'em up again, Bo," and I procured them each his third bottle.

"You ain't drinkin', pard," said Buddy, eyeing my half-
emptied first glass.

"Not thirsty," I replied.

"Thirsty?" said Hank. "Don' s'pose there's any water
here if you was," and feeling I had said the wrong thing,
covered my confusion by turning away and observing the
noisy, merry throng, drinking and chattering around me.
They were a devil-may-care, hard-bitten, tough-looking
crowd, and I found myself positively looking forward to
being in uniform and one of them.

As I watched, I saw a civilian coming from the door
towards us. I had noticed him in the barrack-room. Although dressed in an ill-fitting, shoddy, shabby blue suit, a
velvet tam-o'-shanter, burst shoes, and apparently nothing
else, he looked like a soldier. Not that he had by any means
the carriage of an English guardsman—far from it—but
his face was a soldier's, bronzed, hard, disciplined, and of
a family likeness to those around.

Coming straight to us, he said pleasantly, and with only
the slightest foreign accent:

"Recruits for the Legion?"

"Yes," I replied.

"Would you care to exchange information for a bottle?" he asked politely, with an ingratiating smile which did not extend to his eyes.

"I should be delighted if you will drink with us," I replied, and put a two-franc piece on the counter.

He chose to think that the money was for him to accept, and not for the fat little man behind the bar to change.

"You are a true comrade," said the new-comer, "and will make a fine *légionnaire*. There are a dozen bottles here," and he spun the coin. "Now ask me anything you want to know," and he included the two stolid Americans in the graceful bow with which he concluded. He was evidently an educated and cultured person and not English.

"Sure," said Hank. "I wants ter know when we gits our next eats."

"An' if we can go out and git a drink," added Buddy.

"You'll get *soupe,* bread, and coffee at about four o'clock, and you won't be allowed to leave here for any purpose whatever until you are marched down to the boat for Oran," was the prompt reply.

His hearers pursed their lips in stolid silence.

"When will that be?" I asked.

"To-morrow by the steam-packet, unless there is a troopship going the day after," answered the new-comer. "They ship the Legion recruits in—ah—dribbles? dribblings? driblets? Yes, driblets—by every boat that goes."

"Suppose a friend of mine joined a day or two before me," I asked, "where would he be now, do you suppose?"

"He is at Fort St. Thérèse at Oran now," was the reply. "And may go on to Saida or Sidi-bel-Abbès to-morrow or the next day. Sidi, probably, if he is a strong fellow."

"Say, you're a walking encyclopedestrian," remarked Buddy, eyeing the man speculatively, and perhaps with more criticism than approval.

"I can tell you anything about the Legion," replied the man in his excellent refined English—about which there was no accent such as that of a Londoner, north-country-man, or yokel, but only a slight foreign suggestion—"I am an old *légionnaire*, rejoining after five years' service and my discharge.''

"Speaks well for the Legion,'' I remarked cheerfully.

"Or ill for the chance of an ex-*légionnaire* to get a crust of bread,'' he observed, less cheerfully.

"Been up against it, son?'' asked Hank.

"Starved. Tramped my feet off. Slept in the mud. Begged myself hoarse—for work. . . . Driven at last to choose between gaol and the Legion. . . . I chose the Legion, for some reason. . . . Better the devils that you know than flee to the devils that you know not of. . . .''

"Guy seems depressed,'' said Hank.

"May I finish your wine?'' went on the man. "It would be a sin to waste it.''

"Pray do,'' said I, surprised; and reminded myself that I was no longer at Oxford.

"You speak wonderful English,'' I remarked.

"I do,'' was the reply; "but better Italian, Hindustani, and French. Legion French, that is.''

"An' how's that, ole hoss?'' enquired Buddy.

"Father an Italian pastry-cook in Bombay. Went to an English school there, run by the Jesuit Fathers. Talked Hindustani to my ayah. Mother really talked it better than anything else, being what they call a country-bred. Daughter of an English soldier and an Eurasian girl. Got my French in the Legion, of course,'' explained the stranger.

And then I was unfortunate, in that I partly blundered and partly was misunderstood. What I meant to say, for the sake of being conversational, was:

"And how did you come to find yourself in Africa, so very far from home?'' or something chatty like that. What I actually did say was:

"Why did you join the Legion?'' which sounded very bald.

"For the same reason that *you* did. For my health,'' was the sharp reply, accompanied by a cold stare.

I had done that which is not done.

"And did you find it—healthy?'' enquired Buddy.

"Not exactly so much heal*thy* as hel*lish*,'' replied the

Italian in brief and uncompromising style, as he drained his glass (or perhaps mine).

We all three plied him with questions, and learned much that was useful and more that was disturbing. We also gathered that the gentleman was known as Francesco Boldini to his friends, though he did not say by what name the police knew him.

I came to the conclusion that I did not like him extraor. dinarily much; but that in view of his previous experience he would be an exceedingly useful guide, philosopher, and friend, whose knowledge of the ropes would be well worth purchasing.

I wished I could send him on ahead for the benefit of my brothers, who had, I felt certain, come this way two or three days before me. Indeed, I refused to believe other-wise or to face the fact of my crushing disappointment and horrible position if they had not done so. I was aroused from thoughts of what might, and might not, be before me by a tremendous uproar as the artillerymen pres-ent united in roaring their regimental song:

> "*Si vous voulez jouir des plaisirs de la vie,*
> *Engagez vous ici, et dans l'artillerie.*
> *Quand l'artilleur de Metz change de garnison,*
> *Toutes les femmes de Metz se mettent au balcon.*
> *Artilleur, mon vieux frère,*
> *A ta santé vidons nos verres;*
> *Et répétons ce gai refrain:*
> *Vivent les Artilleurs; à bas les fantassins . . ."*

and much more.

When they had finished and cheered themselves hoarse, a little scoundrelly-looking fellow sprang on a barrel and sang a remarkably seditious and disloyal ditty, of which the chorus, apparently known to all, was:

> "*Et quand il faut servir ce bon Dieu de République,*
> *Où tout le monde est soldat malgré son consentement,*
> *On nous envoi grossir les Bataillons d'Afrique,*
> *A cause que les Joyeux s'aiment pas le gouvernement,*
> *C'est nous les Joyeux,*
> *Les petits Joyeux,*
> *Les petits marlous Joyeux qui n'ont pas froid aux yeux. . ."*

At the conclusion of this song of the battalion of convicted criminals (known as the *Bataillon d'Infanterie
Légère d'Afrique,* or, more familiarly, as the *"Bat d'
Af"*), the men of the Colonial Infantry, known as *Mar-
souins,* lifted up their voices in their regimental song.
These were followed by others, until I think I heard all the
famous marching-songs of the French army—including that
of the Legion, sung by Boldini. It was all very interesting
indeed, but in time I had had enough of it. . . .

When we returned to the barrack-room, on the advice of
Boldini, to be in time for the evening meal, I formally re-
tained that experienced and acquisitive gentleman as guide,
courier, and mentor, with the gift of ten francs and the
promise of such future financial assistance as I could give
and he should deserve.

"I am sorry I cannot spare more just at present," said
I, in unnecessary apology for the smallness of the retaining fee; and his reply was illuminating.

"Ten francs, my dear sir," he said, "is precisely two
hundred days' pay to a *légionnaire.* . . . Seven months'
income. Think of it!" . . .

And I thought of it.

Decidedly I should need considerable promotion before
being in a position to marry and live in comfort on my
pay. . . .

§ 5.

"Dinner," that evening, at about five o'clock, consisted
of similar *"soupe,"* good greyish bread, and unsweetened,
milkless coffee. The first came, as before, in tin basins,
called *"gamelles"*; the second was thrown to us from a
basket; and the coffee was dipped from a pail, in tin mugs.

The *soupe* was a kind of stew, quite good and nourishing, but a little difficult to manipulate without spoon or
fork. I found that my education was, in this respect, inferior to that of my comrades. After this meal—during
which the German eyed our party malevolently, and Vogué,
the gentleman who had objected to my opening the window,
alluded to me as a "sacred *nicodème,*" whatever that may

be—there was nothing to do but to adjourn once more to the canteen.

Here it was my privilege to entertain the whole band from the barrack-room, and I was interested to discover that both the German, whose name proved to be Glock, and the unpleasing Vogué, were both charmed to accept my hospitality, and to drown resentment, with everything else, in wine.

It is quite easy to be lavishly hospitable with wine at about a penny a pint.

Fun grew fast and furious, and I soon found that I was entertaining a considerable section of the French army, as well as the Legion's recruits.

I thoroughly enjoyed the evening, and was smitten upon the back, poked in the ribs, wrung by the hand, embraced about the neck, and, alas, kissed upon both cheeks by Turco, Zouave, Tirailleur, Artilleur, Marsouin, and Spahi, even before the battalion of bottles had been routed by the company of men.

I noticed that Boldini waxed more foreign, more voluble, and more unlovable, the more he drank.

If he could do anything else like a gentleman, he certainly could not carry his wine like one.

"Sah!" he hiccupped to me, with a strident laugh, "farmerly arlso there were a gross of bahtles and few men, and now arlso there are only gross men and a few bahtles!" and he smote me on the back to assist me to understand the jest. The more he went to pieces under the influence of liquor, the more inclined was I to think he had a larger proportion of Oriental strain than he pretended.

I liked him less and less as the evening wore on, and I liked him least when he climbed on the zinc-covered counter and sang an absolutely vile song, wholly devoid of humour or of anything else but offence. I am bound to admit, however, that it was very well received by the audience.

"What you t'ink of *thatt*, sah?" he enquired, when he had finished.

I replied that I preferred not to think of it, and proposed to address him in future as Cloaca Maxima.

Meanwhile, Hank and Buddy, those taciturn, observant, non-committal, and austerely-tolerant Americans, made hay while the sun of prosperity shone, drank more than any two of the others, said nothing, and seemed to wonder what all the excitement was about, and what made the "pore furriners" noisy.

"Ennbody 'ud think the boobs hed bin drinkin'," observed Buddy at last, breaking a long silence (his own silence, that is, of course). To which remark Hank replied:

"They gotta pretend thisyer wine-stuff is a hard drink, an' act like they got a whiskey-jag an' was off the water-waggon. Only way to keep their sperrits up. . . . Wise guys too. You'd shore think some of 'em had bin drinkin' lickker. . . .

"Gee! . . . There's 'Taps!'" he added, as the "Lights out" bugle blew in the courtyard, and the company broke up, "an' we gotta go to bed perishin' o' thirst, fer want of a drink. . . ."

Back to our barrack-room we reeled, singing joyously.

As I sat on my cot undressing, a little later, Buddy came over to me and said, in a low voice:

"Got 'ny money left, pard?"

"Why, yes. Certainly," I replied. "You're most welcome to . . ."

"Welcome nix," was the reply. "If you got 'ny money left, shove it inside yer piller an' tie the end up—or put it inside yer little vest an' lie on it. . . ."

"Hardly necessary, surely?" said I. "Looks rather unkind and suspicious, you know. . . ."

"Please yerself, pard, o' course," replied Buddy, "and let Mister Oompara Tarara Cascara Sagrada get it," and he glanced meaningly at Boldini, who was lying, fully dressed, on his cot.

"Oh, nonsense," said I, "he's not as bad as all that. . . ."

Buddy shrugged his shoulders and departed.

"I gotta evil mind," he remarked as he did so.

I finished undressing, got into the dirty sheetless bed, put my money under my pillow, and then lay awake for a long time, dreaming of Isobel, of Brandon Abbas, and, with

a sense of utter mystification, of the wretched "Blue
Water" and its mysterious fate. . . .

Only last Wednesday. . . . Only eight people—one of
whom it obviously must be. . . . A wretched vulgar thief.
. . . And where were Michael and Digby now? Were they
together, and only forty-eight hours ahead of me on the
Path of Glory, which, according to Boldini, led to the grave
with a certainty and a regularity bordering upon monotony? . . . I fell asleep. . . .

I was awakened in the morning by the shrilling of bugles.

A corporal entered the room, bawled:

"*Levez-vous donc! Levez-vous donc!*" at the top of his
voice, and departed.

I partly dressed, and then felt beneath my pillow for
my money.

It was not there.

I felt savage and sick. . . . Robbed! . . . The beastly
curs. . . .

"Here it is," said the voice of Buddy behind me.
"Thought I'd better mind it when I aheered yore nose-
sighs. . . . Shore enuff, about four a.m. this morning, over
comes Mister Cascara Sagrada to see how youse agettin'
on. . . . '*All right, Bo,*' ses I, speakin' innercent in me
slumbers, '*I'm amindin' of it,*' I ses. . . ."

"No?" said I, "not really?"

"You betcha," replied Buddy, "an' Mister Cascara
Sagrada says, '*Oh, I thought somebody might try to rob
him,*' he says. . . . '*So did I,*' I says, '*And I was right
too,*' I says, an' the skunk scoots back to his hole."

"Thanks, Buddy," I said, feeling foolish, as I took the
notes and coins.

"I tried to put you wise, Bo," he replied, "and now you
know."

Curiously enough, it did not enter my mind to doubt the
truth of what he had told me.

After a breakfast-lunch of *soupe* and bread, we were ordered by a sergeant to assemble in the courtyard.

Here he called the roll of our names, and those of a
freshly-arrived draft of recruits; formed us in fours, and

marched us to the *bassin*, where a steamer of the *Messageries Maritimes* line, the *Général Negrier*, awaited us.

We were herded to the fo'c'sle of this aged packet, and bidden by the corporal, who was going in charge of us, to use the ocean freely if we should chance to feel unwell, as it was entirely at our disposal.

" 'We have fed our seas for a thousand years,' " thought I, and was grateful that, on this glorious day, the sea did not look at all hungry.

But if the sea were not, we soldiers of misfortune undoubtedly were. Very hungry, indeed, and as the hours passed, we grew still hungrier. Towards evening, the Château d'If and the tall lighthouse having been left far behind, murmurs on the subject of dinner began to be heard. We loafed moodily about the well-deck, between the fo'c'sle and the high midship bridge structure, talking both in sorrow and in anger, on the subject of food.

Personally I thought very regretfully of the dining-room at Brandon Abbas, and of the dinner that was even then being served therein. Tantalising odours were wafted to us from the saloon below the bridge, and our ears were not unaware of the stimulating rattle of plates and cutlery.

"When shall we get something to eat?" I asked Boldini, as he emerged from the fo'c'sle hatch.

"By regulations we should have had *soupe,* bread, and half a litre of wine at five o'clock," he replied. "Quite likely the cook is going to make a bit out of us, for these swine often do. . . ."

However, there was activity, I observed, in the cook's galley, near the fo'c'sle—the cook-house in which the sailors' food was prepared—so we hoped for the best while fearing the worst.

An hour later, when we were an hour hungrier and angrier, Hank's usually monumental patience had dwindled to imperceptibility.

"Here, you, Cascara," quoth he, pushing into the knot of men in the centre of which Boldini harangued them on their rights and the cause of their present wrongs, "you know the rules of this yer game. Why ain't we got no eats yet?"

"Because this thieving swine of a son of a sea-cook is going to make a bit out of us," replied Boldini.

"Thet so, now?" observed Hank mildly. "Then I allow he ain't agoin' ter live to enjy it. Nary a enjy. So he can tell himself Good-bye, for he ain't goin' to see himself no more, if I don't get no dinner. Nope. . . . ."

I gathered from Boldini that it would be quite impossible for me to get at the corporal, as I proposed to do, since he was away in the second-class quarters, and I should be prevented from leaving the fo'c'sle if I tried to do so.

"But I can let you have a roll," he said, "if it is worth a franc to you. I don't want to starve, you know," and his pleasant smile was a little reminiscent of the Wicked Uncle in my nursery-tale book of the Babes in the Wood.

It appeared that, anticipating just what had happened, he had secreted four rolls when breakfast was served at Fort St. Jean that morning. I gave him three francs, and a roll each to Hank and Buddy.

"You have a great soul, Boldini," I remarked, on purchasing the bread, and was distressed at the unkindly guffaw emitted by Buddy at my words. An hour or so later, all signs of activity having ceased to render the cookhouse attractive, it seemed but too true that food was not for us. The mob of recruits grumbled, complained, and cursed in half a dozen languages. Darkness fell, and Hank arose.

A huge greasy creature, grossly fat, filthily dirty in clothes and person, and with a face that was his misfortune, emerged from the cooking-house. He eyed us with sourest contempt.

I suggested to Boldini that the scoundrel might sell us what he ought to have given us. Boldini replied that this was precisely what would happen, on the morrow, when we were *really* hungry—provided we had money and chose to pay his prices.

Hank strode forward.

"Thet Slushy?" he enquired softly.

"That's the swine," replied Boldini.

"Come and interpretate then," requested Hank, and marched up to the cook, closely followed by Buddy.

"When do we get our doo an' lawful eats, Slush?" he asked mildly.

The cook ignored him utterly and turned to go in lofty silence, but a huge hand shot out and sank with the grip of a vice into the fat of his bulging neck, another seized his wrist, and he was run as a perambulator is run by a child, straight to the side of the ship.

"Ask the pore gink if he can swim any," requested Hank, holding the man's head over the side.

Boldini did so.

The gink kicked out viciously, but made no other reply.

"Up with it, Bud—*attaboy!*" whooped Hank, and Buddy diving at the agitated legs, gathered them in, and raised them on to the taffrail.

The crowd of recruits cheered joyously.

I thought the man was really going overboard, and begged them not to waste a perfectly good cook.

"Sure," said Hank. "He's gotta get us some grub first," and they threw the cook on the deck un-gently.

The man lumbered to his feet, and, again seizing him, Hank ran him to the galley and threw him through the door.

"*Cookez-vous, pronto!*" quoth he, and the cook seized a heavy iron saucepan and rushed out again.

But alas, it was as a weapon and not as a utensil that he wished to use it. Swinging it up with all his strength—he found it wrenched from his hand and placed ringingly upon his head.

"He's contumelious," said Hank. "He's onobedient to my signs," and became earnest. Taking the man by the throat he started to choke him.

"Tell him I'm hungry, Bo," he said to Boldini. "Tell him he can eat outer my hand when I ain't riz by hunger. . . . I gotta eat outer his pots first though."

Boldini assured the cook that Hank would tear him limb from limb, and the angry crowd of recruits would see that nobody rescued him either.

The fellow ceased to struggle, and Hank hurled him into the galley.

A sort of ship's quartermaster, followed by a sailor, came

up, and I feared trouble. Visions of us all in irons, awaiting a court-martial at Oran, floated before my eyes.

"Assaulting the cook?" quoth the man in uniform.
"Good! Kill the thrice-accursed thieving food-spoiler, and
may *le bon Dieu* assist you."

I gathered that he was not very fond of Slushy.

"His assistance will not be required, *Monsieur le Contre-
maître*," said the smiling Boldini, and with horrible oaths
and grimaces and the worst possible grace, the cook produced a number of loaves of bread, a pail of cold stew, and
some macaroni.

"We'll have that hot," announced Boldini, pointing to
the stew.

With very violent curses the cook said we would not—
and the crowd snarled.

On understanding this reply, Hank instructed Boldini
to inform the cook that unless he did precisely as he was
told, there would be great sorrow for him when we had fed.
If he were obedient he would be forgiven.

The stew was put over the galley-fire in a great pan.

"Can't he rustle a few onions and sech?" enquired
Buddy, pushing into the galley.

Seeing that he was a very small man, the cook gave him
a violent shove in the chest, and sent him staggering.

"I'll talk to you posthumorously, Cookie," said Buddy,
with ominous calm. "We wants you whole and hearty
like, for the present."

"Out, little dog! Out, you indescribable pollution,"
snarled the cook in French.

Under Boldini's instruction and Hank's compulsion, the
cook produced a string of onions and added them to the
soupe.

"Watch him well, or he'll poison us," advised Glock, the
German, who, but yesterday, had called Hank a "dirdy
tief" and now appeared to love him as a brother.

He watched, very well, and gave every encouragement we
could think of.

Before long, we were squatting on the deck, each man
with a well-filled *gamelle* of excellent stew and a loaf of

bread, feeding heartily and calling blessing on Hank, the hero of the hour. Vogué tried to kiss him.

Again the fat cook emerged from the galley in search of relaxation and repose, and with a curse turned to go

"He ought by rights to give us each a litre of wine," said Boldini. "He's got it and means to sell it."

"Say, Bo," shouted Hank thereupon. "Don' desert us! Did you say it was wine or cawfee you was keeping fer us?"

Boldini translated.

" '*Cré bon sang!*" roared the cook, raising his hands above his head, and then shaking his big dirty fist at Boldini. "To hell with you starving gutter-scrapings! You foul swine of the slums of Europe! You . . ."

"Sounds good!" remarked Buddy.

"I guess he's saying '*No*,' " opined Hank. "I'll make signs to him agin," and he rose and strode towards the gesticulating ruffian.

The cook retreated into the galley, one hand to his throat.

"Look out for a knife," called Boldini.

But the cook was cowed, and reappeared with a wooden bucket containing three or four quarts of wine. This he handed to Hank, with a wish that it might choke him first and corrode his interior after.

He then requested Boldini to inform us that we were a cowardly gang of apaches and wolves, who were brave enough in a band, and slinking curs individually. He would fight and destroy every one of us—except the big one—and glad of the chance.

Boldini did so.

"I'm the smallest," remarked Buddy, and left it at that, while he finished his bread and wine.

I am a law-abiding person by nature and by training (or I was at that time), and regretted all this unseemliness. But what a loathsome blackguard a man must be to swindle hungry bewildered men (whose pay was a halfpenny a day and who had joined the army to get it!), to rob them of their meagre allowance of food in order that he might sell it to them for their last coppers, when they could hold out no longer.

According to Boldini it was this scoundrel's regular
custom to pretend to each draft of ignorant browbeaten
foreigners that the Government made no provision for
them, and that what they wanted they must buy from him.
If they were absolutely penniless they got precisely nothing
at all for forty-eight hours, and the cook sold their wine
and rations to other steerage passengers or to the sailors.

When they understood this, Hank and Buddy discussed
the advisability of "sure eradicating" the man—its desirability being self-evident. They decided they must leave
this duty, with so many others, unperformed, as the *Messageries Maritimes* Company might behave officiously and
prefer French law to lynch law.

"But I'll expostulate some with the all-fired skunk—
when we finished with him as a cook," observed Buddy....

We lay on the deck propped against the hatch far into
the glorious night, Hank and Buddy rolling cigarettes with
my tobacco, and leaves from my pocket-book, while I enjoyed my dear old briar, as we listened to Boldini's wonderful tales of the Legion. . . .

The moon rose and flooded the sea with silver light. . . .
By this time to-morrow, I might be with Michael and
Digby. . . . I began to nod, fell asleep, woke cold and stiff,
and retired to a very unpleasant hole in the fo'c'sle, where
there were tiers of bunks and many sorrows.

I slept for about ten hours and woke feeling as fit as a
fiddle and ready for anything—particularly breakfast.

§ 6.

According to Boldini, this should be provided at eleven
o'clock, and should consist of stew and bread. At ten-
thirty, by his advice, we appointed Hank as spokesman and
sergeant, with Boldini as interpreter, "fell in" in front
of the galley, and awaited events like a squad on parade.

"Eats at eleven, hot and plentiful, Slushy," said Hank,
as the cook came to the galley-door in obvious surprise at
the orderly disciplined assembly.

The cook snarled and swore.

"Do he want me to make signs to him?" asked Hank of the interpreter.

Boldini informed the cook that the draft knew precisely what its rights were, and that it was going to have them. If there was delay or shortage, or if anybody suffered any ill-effects from the food, the big man was going to beat him to a jelly.

Then, lest the cook should complain, and there be trouble at Oran, the big man was coming with a few staunch friends to see that the cook disappeared overboard, during the night! Oh, yes, we were a desperate gang, old soldiers who wouldn't be swindled, and the big man was ex-Champion Heavy Weight of America. Also, if we were well and plentifully fed, we might refrain from reporting the cook's robberies and swindles in the proper quarter....

The cook affected immense amusement, but I thought his laughter a trifle forced, as Hank's grim leathern face creased and broke into a dental smile that held no love.

"Squad'll parade right here at eleven, *pronto,* for the hand-out, Slushy," said Hank. "Be on time—and stay healthy. . . . Squad—dismiss."

"*Rompez!*" shouted Boldini, and then made all clear to the cook.

At eleven, Hank's sergeant-like crisp bawl, "Recruits—*fall in,*" could be heard all over the ship; Buddy appointed himself bugler and whistled an obvious dinner-call, and Boldini roared, "*Rangez-vous, légionnaires!*"

The way in which the order was obeyed, made it clear to me that I was about the only recruit who was not an old soldier. There was nothing to be surprised at in this, however, since most continental armies are conscript, and every man is a soldier. Certainly Hank and Buddy had been in the army. Later I learned that they had together adorned the ranks of that fine and famous corps, the Texas Rangers.

Without a word, the cook filled the *gamelles* with hot stew, and Hank passed one to each man, together with a loaf. He then gave the order to dismiss, and we sat us down and fed in contentment and good-humour.

At eventide the scene was repeated, and again we ate, and

then we sat and smoked and listened to the Munchause-nesque tales of Boldini, who had certainly "seen life" as he said.

He was boastful and he was proud of escapades that did him little credit. If he spoke the truth, he was a brave man and a very dishonest one. He plainly revealed himself as extremely cunning, tricky, avaricious, and grasping. And yet, with all his cleverness and greed, here he was, glad to accept a *sou* a day again, to keep himself from starving.

Buddy did not like him.

"A crook," opined he. "Crooked as a snake with the belly-ache. . . ."

Early on the third day we sighted the African coast.

After breakfast—*soupe* and bread again—Buddy requested Boldini to ask the cook to step outside.

"What for?" asked the cook contemptuously.

Buddy requested that the man should be informed that he was a coyote, a skunk, a low-lifer, a way down ornery bindle-stiff, a plate-licking dime-pinching hobo, a dodgasted greaser, a gol-durned sneak-thief, and a gosh-dinged slush-slinging poke-out-pinching piker."

Boldini merely said:

"The little man calls you a mean lying thief and a cowardly mangy cur. . . . He spits on you and he wants to fight you. He is a *very* little man, *chef.*"

He was, and the cook rushed out to his doom. I fancy myself as an amateur boxer. Buddy was no amateur and the cook was no boxer. I thought of a fat sluggish snake and an angry mongoose, of which Uncle Hector had once told us.

It was not a fight so much as an execution. Buddy was a dynamic ferocity, and the thieving scoundrel was very badly damaged.

When he could, or would, rise no more, Hank dragged the carcase into the galley, reverently bared his head, and softly closed the door, as one leaving a death-chamber.

"He's restin'. Hush!" he murmured.

Hank and Buddy never held official rank in the muster-roll of the Legion, but they held high rank in the hearts of the *légionnaires* who knew them. That recruit-squad would certainly have followed them anywhere, and have obeyed them blindly.

Sandstone cliffs appeared, opened out to a tiny harbour, and we approached a pier.

We were at Oran, and the Corporal who was supposed to be in charge of us made his first appearance on our fore-deck, formed us up, and handed the squad over to a Sergeant, who came on board for the purpose.

The Sergeant called the roll of our names, ascertained that we could "form fours," "form two deep," and turn left and right correctly, and then marched us ashore.

"I am in Africa!" said I to myself, as we tramped through the wide clean streets of the European-looking little town.

Down a street of flat-roofed houses we marched, and across the broad *place*, stared at by half-naked negroes, burnous-clad Arabs, French soldiers, ordinary European civilians, and promenading ladies and officers.

On through more wide streets to narrow slums and alleys we went, till at length the town was behind us and the desert in front.

For an hour or more we marched by a fine road across the desert, up the sandstone hills on to the cliff-top, until we came in sight of an old and ugly building, another obsolete Fort St. Jean, which Boldini said was Fort St. Thérèse and our present destination.

Into the courtyard of this barrack-hostelry we marched, and here the roll of our names was again called, this time by a *sous-officier*. All were present and correct, the goods were delivered, and we were directed to break off and follow our Sergeant to a barrack-room.

As I went in behind him, with Boldini and the German, Glock, behind me, a well-known voice remarked:

"Enter the Third Robber." *It was Digby's.*

Michael and Digby were sitting side by side on a bench, their hands in their pockets, their pipes in their mouths, and consternation upon their faces!

"Good God!" exclaimed Michael. "You unutterable young fool! God help us! . . ."

I fell upon them. While I shook Michael's hand, Digby shook my other one, and while I shook Digby's hand, Michael shook my head. They then threw me upon the common "bed" (about twenty feet long and six broad) and shook my feet, finally pulling me on to the ground. I arose and closed with Digby, and Michael pushed us both over. We rose and both closed with Michael, until all three fell in a heap.

We then felt better, and realised that we were objects of interest and concern, alike to our acquaintances and to the strangers within our gates.

"Gee!" said Buddy. "Fightin' already! Beat 'em up, Bo."

"Dorg-fight," observed Hank. "Chew their ears, son."

"Mad English," shrugged Vogué, the French embezzler. "They fight when civilised people embrace."

Boldoni was deeply interested.

"Third *robber!*" he said on a note of mingled comment and enquiry to Glock.

"Beau and Dig," said I, "let me introduce two shore-enough blowed-in-the-glass, dyed-in-the-wool, whole-piece White Men from God's Own Country—Hank and Buddy. . . . My brothers, Michael and Digby."

They laughed and held out their hands.

"Americans possibly," said Digby.

"Shake," said Hank and Buddy as one man, and the four shook gravely.

"Mr. Francesco Boldini," said I. "My brothers," and neither Michael nor Digby offered his hand to the Italian, until that gentleman reached for it effusively.

"I think wine is indicated, gentlemen," he said, and eyeing us in turn, added, " *'when we three robbers meet again,'* so to speak." Michael invited Hank and Buddy to join us, and Boldini led the way and did the honours of Fort St. Thérèse.

In this canteen the wine was as good as, and even cheaper than, the wine at Fort St. Jean—cheaper than ordinary draught-beer in England.

We three sat, drinking little, and watching the others drink a good deal, for which Michael insisted on paying.

We were soon joined by some old *légionnaires,* who appeared to be stationed permanently at the place, and, from them and Boldini, heard innumerable lurid stories of the Legion, for the truth of all of which they vouched, with earnest protestations and strange oaths. I noticed that the earnestness and strangeness of the latter were in inverse proportion to the probability of the former.

"I perceive we are not about to enter *'an academy for the sons of gentlemen where religious and moral training, character-forming and development of the intelligence, are placed before examination-cramming,'* my son," observed Digby to me, quoting from the syllabus of our preparatory school, as we left the canteen.

"No," said I, "but it sounds an uncommonly good school for mercenary soldiers" (and we found that it was certainly that).

"One hopes that this is not a fair sample of our future home-life and domestic surroundings," remarked Michael as we entered the barrack-room.

It was an utterly beastly place, dark, dirty, and depressing, its sole furniture being the great wooden guard-bed before mentioned (which was simply a huge shelf, innocent of mattress or covering, on which a score or so of men could lie side by side), a heap of evil-looking brown blankets in a corner, and a couple of benches. The place would have disgraced a prison if used as a common cell.

However, Boldini assured us that things would be quite different at the depôt at Saida or Sidi-bel-Abbès—and I assumed that to be different they must be better, for they couldn't be worse.

Our evening meal was the now familiar *soupe* and bread, and Boldini told us that the unvarying African daily ration was half a pound of meat and three *sous* worth of vegetables served as stew, a pound and a half of bread, half an ounce of coffee, and half an ounce of sugar. He said it was nourishing and sufficient but deadly monotonous, and, as to the latter, I was prepared to believe him. The

prospect of two meals a day, and those eternally and un-
deviatingly similar, seemed unexhilarating and I said so.

"One gets used to it," said Boldini, "just as one gets
used to 'eternally' washing with soap and water. If you
are content to wash daily with soap and water you can be
content to feed daily on *soupe* and bread. . . . Or do you
occasionally wash with champagne and a slice of cake—or
hot tea and a lump of coal—as a change from the 'eternal'
water and soap? . . ."

"Of course," he added impudently, "if you are going
to come the fine gentleman and swell mobsman . . ."

"Don't be an ass, Boldini," said I, with a cold stare.
"Or at any rate, try not to be an ass."

He eyed me speculatively and complied. Master Boldini
struck me as a gentleman who would need keeping in his
place. Whatever that might be, it was not going to be one
of the offensive familiarity that breeds contempt. I was
not quite certain, but I was under the impression that
"swell mobsman" was a thieve's-kitchen term for a well-
dressed and "gentlemanly" swindler, burglar, and general
criminal, in a superior way of business.

After *soupe*, there was nothing to do but to return to the
canteen, as we were not allowed to leave the Fort. We
spent the evening there, and I was glad to see that Beau
and Digby seemed to like Hank and Buddy as much as I
did, and that the two Americans, so far as one could judge
of the feelings of such taciturn people, reciprocated.

Digby constituted himself host, and everybody was quite
happy and well-behaved.

With one or two exceptions, none of the recruits, whether
of my own draft, or of that with which my brothers had
come, struck me as interesting.

They were just a fairly representative collection of very
poor men from France, Belgium, Germany (chiefly Alsace
and Lorraine), Spain, Austria, and Switzerland.

They looked like labourers, artisans, soldiers in mufti,
newspaper-sellers, shop-boys, clerks, and the usual sort of
men of all ages whom one would see in the poorer streets
of any town, or in a Rowton House.

They certainly did not look like rogues and criminals.

Two or three, out of the couple of dozen or so, were well-dressed and well-spoken, and one of them, I felt sure, was an ex-officer of the French or Belgian army.

At any rate, he had "soldier" stamped all over him, was well-dressed, smart, dapper, and *soigné;* was well-educated and had charming manners. He called himself Jean St. André, but I suspected a third name, with a *de* in front of it. He had rather attached himself to us three, and we all liked him.

It struck me that community of habits, tastes, customs, and outlook form a stronger bond of sympathy than community of race; and that men of the same social caste and different nationality were much more attracted to each other than men of the same nationality and different caste. . . .

When the canteen closed, Beau proposed that we should shorten the night as much as possible, and spend the minimum of time in that loathsome cell, lying packed like sardines on the bare boards of the guard-bed shelf, with a score of men and a million insects.

Digby observed that the sandy ground of the courtyard would be no harder and much cleaner; and the air, if colder, infinitely preferable to the fug of the Black Hole of St. Thérèse.

We selected an eligible corner, seated ourselves in a row propped against the wall, still warm from the day's sunshine, and prepared for a night under the wonderful African stars.

"Well, my poor, dear, idiotic, mad pup—and what the devil do you think you're doing here?" began Michael, as soon as we were settled and our pipes alight.

"Fleeing from justice, Beau," said I. "What are you?"

"Same thing," replied Michael.

"And you, Dig?" I asked.

"Who, me?" answered Digby. "Well, to tell you the truth, I, personally, am, as it were, what you might call —er—fleeing from justice. . . .

"*Three* fleas," he observed, breaking a long silence.

"Did you bring the 'Blue Water' with you, John?" asked Digby.

"No," I said. "No, I didn't bring it with me."

"Careless," remarked Digby.

"Did you bring it, Beau?" I asked.

"Yes," answered Michael.

"Careful," commented Digby.

"Did you bring it with you too, Dig?" I enquired.

"Never travel without it," was the reply.

"I suppose one of us three has got it," I said wearily.

"Two of us," corrected Digby.

"Oh, yes, it's here all right," said Michael. "What would be the good of our being here if it were not?

"Bring us up to date about things," he added. "How's everybody bearing up?"

I told them the details of my evasion; of how I had declined an interview with Aunt Patricia; of how the shock of somebody's disgraceful behavior had been too much for the Chaplain's health; of the respective attitudes of Augustus, Claudia, and Isobel.

"It *is* rough on Claudia," said Michael, "and, in a different way, on the poor old Chaplain."

"And in a different way, again, on Aunt Patricia," I observed.

"Thirty thousand pounds," mused Digby. "What price dear Uncle Hector, when she breaks it to him? He'll go mad and bite her."

"Doesn't bear thinking of," said I.

"Deuced lucky for young Gussie that Isobel was able to clear him," mused Digby.

"That's what makes it so hard on Claudia—or would have done, if we hadn't bolted," said Michael. "Gussie and Isobel being out of it—it was she or one of us. . . ."

In the silence that followed, I was aware of a sound, close beside us, where a buttress of the wall projected. Probably a rat or some nocturnal bird; possibly a dog.

"Well—it *was* one of us," said Michael, "and we have demonstrated the fact. We've overdone it a bit, though.

"Why couldn't you have enjoyed your ill-gotten gains

in peace, at home, John?'' he went on. ''Or left me to enjoy mine abroad? Why this wholesale emigration?''

''Yes,'' agreed Digby, ''absolute mob. They won't be able to decide whether we were all in the job together, or whether we're chasing each other to get a share of the loot.''

''No,'' said Michael. ''Problem'll worry them like anything.''

''When are we to let them know we're in the Legion, Beau?'' I asked.

''We're not there yet,'' was the reply.

''When we are,'' I pursued.

''Dunno. . . . Think about it,'' said Michael.

''Don't see why we should let 'em know we're all there together,'' said Digby. ''Better if one was at, or up, the North Pole, the other up the South Pole, and the third sitting on the Equator. More mystery about it—and they wouldn't know which to chase first.''

''Something in that,'' agreed Michael. ''If we are all together (since you two have come), we are obviously all implicated—all three thieves. If we are scattered, two of us must be innocent. There is a doubt on each of us, but not a stain on any particular one of us. . . . Why write at all, in fact? We are just runaway criminals. They don't write home. . . .''

''*My* strength is as the strength of ten, because my heart is puah,'' bleated Digby.

''*My* strength will be as the strength of eleven if you don't shut up,'' warned Michael.

''I don't see the point really, Beau,'' I objected. ''We prove nothing at all by being scattered. We might still all be criminals. We could easily have planned to pinch the sapphire, to bolt in different directions, and to share the loot by meeting later on. . . . Or we could share without meeting. One of us could dispose of it in Amsterdam or somewhere, bank the money, and send a third of it to each of the others by draft or cheque, or something. . . .''

''Hark at the young criminal!'' said Digby. . . . ''Hasn't he got a mind?'' . . .

"What I mean is," I explained, "it's a bit rough on—
er—those that are left at home, not to let them know where
we are—alive or dead and all that. . . ."

"Thinking of Gussie?" asked Digby.

"Besides," I went on, "how are they to let us know if
the damned thing turns up? . . . And how are we to
know how they are getting on? . . ."

"True," agreed Michael. "We ought to let Aunt
Patricia know that we are hale and hearty, and she ought
to be in a position to let us know if anything happens or
turns up. What we *don't* want to do meanwhile, is to
spoil the impression that one of us is the thief. . . . I
still think it would help to keep suspicion on us, and to
deepen the mystery, if we don't let it be known that we
are all together. . . . We don't want some fool saying that
we three agreed to take the blame and share it, and so
cleared out together to the same place . . . while the thief
is still at Brandon Abbas. . . ."

"Who *did* pinch the filthy thing?" said Digby, voicing
once more the question that I had asked myself a thousand
times.

"I did," said Michael.

"Then why the devil don't you put it back?" asked
Digby.

"Too late now," answered Michael. "Besides, I want
to lie low and then sell it for thirty thousand pounds,
five years hence; invest the money in various sound things,
and have the income (of fifteen hundred to two thousand
a year) for life. . . . Live like Uncle Hector—sport, hunting, travel, big-game shooting, flat in town, clubs. . . ."

"On Uncle Hector's money?" I said.

"Doubles the joy of it, what?" replied Michael.

"Funny thing that," put in Digby. "It's just what I'm
going to do—except that I find one can't get more than
about twenty thousand, and I'm going to put it into a
South Sea Island plantation and an Island trading concern.
. . . Have the best schooner in the Islands, and be my own
supercargo. . . . Every third year, come home and live
the gay life on my twenty-per-cent profits. I reckon to

make about four thousand a year. Yes. . . . Marquesas, Apia, Honolulu, Tahiti, Papeete, Kanakas, copra, ukuleles, lava-lavas, surf-riding, Robert Louis Stevenson. . . .''

"What are you going to do with the 'Blue Water' meanwhile?" I asked, humouring the humorists.

"Always carry it about with me," said Digby. "If I get an eye knocked out I shall wear it in the empty socket. . . . Blue-eyed boy. . . . Good idea, that. . . .''

"Or you might put it where the monkey put the nuts—develop a pouch in your cheek. Very simple for you, I should think," I suggested.

"Both rotten ideas," objected Michael. "Marsupial is the tip. Kangaroo's custom. They carry about their young and their money and things in a sort of bag, you know . . . in front . . . accessible. I keep it on me, night and day—wash-leather pouch in a money-belt. I thought it all out beforehand, and bought the thing in London. . . . Got to kill the man before you can rob him. Hatton Garden diamond-merchants wear them when they travel. Round their little tummies under their little vests. . . .''

"What makes them all look so paunchy," corroborated Digby.

"You haven't told us what *you* are going to do, John," he went on. "Are you going to lie low for the five years and then sell it? . . . What are you going to do with the money?"

"Divide it with you and Beau," I replied.

"Oh, stout fella," approved Digby. "He puts us to shame, Beau, doesn't he? Let's put him to death in return, and keep his share.''

"Quite," agreed Michael. "We've got to find out what he's done with it first, though. . . .''

And so we ragged and chatted, sitting there, three of the most incredibly foolish young fools in their folly, but perfectly care-free and leaving to the morrow what the morrow might bring forth. . . .

Towards morning we dozed, and the dawn found us cold, stiff, and aching, but quite happy. We were together; life, the world, and adventure were before us.

§ 7.

A third draft of recruits arrived after morning *soupe*, and we learnt that all were to be evacuated that day, one half going to Saida, the depôt of the Second Regiment of the Foreign Legion, and the remainder to Sidi-bel-Abbès, the depôt of the First Regiment.

The question that at once agitated our breasts was as to whether we could keep together.

We rather preferred the idea of the First Regiment to that of the Second, simply because it was the First; but we did not much care either way, provided we were not separated. To that we simply would not agree.

I was distinctly pleased to find that the two Americans wished to come with us.

They had no more intention of parting from each other than we three had, but provided that they could keep together they wanted to go where we went.

To us came Boldini as we strolled round the courtyard.

"Let's stick together, we four," quoth he. "I'm going to the First, and you'd better come too. I know all the ropes there, and can put you up to everything. Get you in right with the corporals. . . . Sergeant Lejaune's a friend of mine. . . ."

"We three are certainly going together," said Michael, "and we want the two Americans to come with us, and we prefer the First, on the whole. Have we any say in the matter?"

"Ten francs would have a say," replied Boldini. "They'd talk louder than six men. Put up the ten francs, and I can work it that we six go to the First. . . . But why bother about the Americans? They are uncultivated people."

"We're going to cultivate them," punned Michael.

We produced the ten francs and Boldini departed to "arrange" the matter, as he said.

Whether we owed anything to his efforts or not, I never knew. He may have "squared" a corporal, or he may merely have notified our wish to go together to the *Premier*

Étranger. Or, again, it may merely have been by chance that we found ourselves in the half detailed for Sidi-bel-Abbès.

As we "fell in" to march to the station, I and St. André stood behind Michael and Digby, while Boldini and an English-speaking Swiss, named Maris, stood behind Hank and Buddy, who were next to Michael and Digby. Thus, when we "formed fours," my brothers and I and St. André made one "four," and Hank, Buddy, Boldini, and Maris the "four" behind us.

This Maris seemed an excellent person. He had been a travelling valet and courier, and had all the experience, address, linguistic knowledge, and general ability to be expected of a person who could earn his living in that capacity. He attached himself to us because he liked the English, and was, as he naïvely observed, "fond of gentlemen." He was a smiling, pleasant fellow of agreeable manners and attractive appearance.

At Oran station we entrained in about the poorest and slowest conveyance ever drawn by steam. This specimen of the West Algerian Railway Company's rolling-stock made its way from Oran to Sidi-bel-Abbès at an average rate of ten miles an hour, and in spite of the novelty of the scenery and of the population of the wayside stations, we grew very weary of it.

Our two "fours" and a couple of Germans filled one compartment, and we whiled away the time by questioning Boldini concerning life in the Legion, and by listening to his innumerable stories.

It seemed somewhat dream-like to me, to be sitting in a tiny bare third-class railway-carriage, somnolently rolling across Africa in company with my brothers, two Americans, an ex-officer of a continental army, an Anglo-Indian Italian, a Swiss courier, and a pair of German workmen, listening to tales of a life as far removed from that of Europe as are the Arabian Nights.

Watching the slowly-passing scenery of the country-side, I was surprised at its difference from what one might have expected in Africa, it being neither of desert nor jungle,

but a cultivated country of fields, farms, orchards, and
gardens. It was not until we were approcahing our destination that sand-hills and desert encroached and a note of
wildness and savagery prevailed.

Negro and Arab boys and men brought fruit to our
window at every station, and very fine grapes, oranges,
melons, and figs could be bought extremely cheaply.

"This is all right," remarked Digby, who was always
very fond of fruit, "if one can get fruit at this price in
Sidi-bel-Abbès."

"Yes," said Boldini drily, "if you devote your entire
income entirely to fruit, you'll be able to get a little every
day of your life."

A halfpenny a day for fruit does not sound much, but
the devotion of one's total income to it seems excessive.

"No income tax?" asked Digby, and we were relieved,
if surprised, to hear that there was none.

We reached Sidi-bel-Abbès Station in the evening, and
were received by a sergeant and corporals, were lined up
and marched off, in fours, along a broad road. At the
station gate I noticed a picket of non-commissioned officers,
who sharply scrutinised all who passed it.

As we marched along, I got a somewhat Spanish impression of the town, probably because I heard the tinkling of a
guitar and saw some women with high combs and mantillas,
among the nondescript Europeans who were strolling between the yellow houses. Entering the town itself, through
a great gate in the huge ramparts, we were in a curiously
hybrid Oriental-European atmosphere in which moved
stately Arabs, smart French ladies, omnibuses, camels, half-
naked negroes, dapper officers, crowds of poor Jewish-look-
ing working-folk, soldiers by the hundred, negroes, grisettes,
black newspaper boys selling the *Écho d'Oran*, pig-tailed
European girls, Spaniards, Frenchmen, Algerian Jews,
Levantines, men and women straight from the Bible, and
others straight from the Boulevards, Arab policemen,
Spahis, Turcos, Zouaves, and Chasseurs d'Afrique.

No less hybrid was the architecture, and the eye passed
from white gleaming mosque with glorious minaret to

gaudy café with garish lights; from showy shops to shut-
tered Oriental houses; from carved balconies and coloured
tiles to municipal clock-towers and enamel advertisements;
from Moorish domes and arches to French newspaper kiosks
and lampposts; from Eastern bazaars to Western hotels and
clubs and Government offices and secretariats.

And almost everywhere were beautiful avenues of palms
and groves of olives, ably seconding the efforts of Moorish
mosque and Arab architecture in the unequal struggle between artistic Oriental romance and vulgar Occidental
utilitarianism. Hybridism insisted through other senses
too, for the ear caught now the *"Allah Akbar! Lah illah
il Allah! Ya Saidna Mohammed rais ul Allah!"* of the
muezzin on the minaret; the shouting of an angry Spanish
woman; the warning cries in *sabir* of a negro driver;
snatches of French conversation from passing soldiers; the
loud wrangling in Arabic of a police *goumier* and some
camelmen; and a strange haunting chorus from behind a
wall, of:

> *"Travaja la muqueir*
> *Travaja bono*
> *Bono bezef la muqueir*
> *Travaja bono."*

And to the nostrils were wafted scents of Eastern food
and Western drink, camel-dung fires and Parisian patch-
ouli; Eastern spices and Western cooking; now the odour
of unwashen Eastern men, now of perfumed Western
women.

"Kind of 'Algeria at Olympia,' this," observed Digby.
"Good spot. Reminds one of Widdicombe."

Turning from a main thoroughfare we entered a lane that
ran between the barracks of the Spahi cavalry and those of
the Foreign Legion.

Through the railings of great iron gates we could see a
colossal three-story yellow building, at the far side of a
vast expanse of parade ground.

"Our College," remarked Digby.

On either side of the gates were guard-house and prison.

A small door was opened beside the gates, and we filed through.

The guard, seated on a long bench outside the guard-house, observed us without enthusiasm. The Sergeant of the Guard emerged and looked us over, and then closed his eyes, while he slowly shook his head.

A knot of men, clad in white uniform with wide blue sashes round their waists, gathered and regarded us.

"*Mon Dieu!*" said one, "there's that blackguard Boldini back again. As big a fool as he is a knave, evidently!"

Boldini affected deafness.

And then appeared upon the scene the only man I have ever met who seemed to me to be bad, wholly bad, evil all through, without a single redeeming virtue save courage.

He came from the regimental offices, a fierce-looking, thick-set, dark man, with the face and figure of a prize-fighter; glaring and staring of eye, swarthily handsome, with the neck and jowl of a bull-dog. He also had the curious teeth-baring, chin-protruding jaw-thrust of a bull-dog, and there were two deep lines between the heavy beetling brows.

A digression: This was Colour-Sergeant Lejaune, a terrible and terrifying man, who had made his way in the Legion (and who made it further still) by distinguishing himself among distinguished martinets as a relentlessly harsh and meticulous disciplinarian, a savagely violent taskmaster, and a punishing non-com. of tremendous energy, ability, and courage.

To his admiring superiors he was invaluable; to his despairing subordinates he was unspeakable. He was a reincarnation and lineal descendant of the overseers who lashed the dying galley-slaves of the Roman triremes, and as different from the officers as were the overseers from the Roman centurions.

He would have made a splendid wild-beast tamer, for he had all the courage, strength, forceful personality, hardy over-bearing consciousness of superiority, and contemptuous, callous brutality required in that bold, ignoble profession. And it pleased him to regard himself as one, and to treat his legionaires as wild beasts; as dangerous, evil, savage, criminal brutes, instead of as what they were—fairly representative specimens of the average population of the countries from which they came.

Nor should it be supposed that Colour-Sergeant Lejaune was himself a typical representative specimen of his class, the Legion non-com. Though these men are usually harsh and somewhat tyrannical martinets, they are not villainous brutes.

Lejaune was. He took an actual delight in punishing, and nothing angered him more than to be unable to find a reason for doing it.

Probably he began by punishing (to the fullest extent of his powers and opportunity), in order to secure the most perfect discipline and to display his zeal, efficiency, and worth as a strong non-com.; and, from that, came to punish as a habit, until the habit became a taste, and then a lust and an obsession.

And later, through the coming to the Legion of a deserter from the Belgian army, we learnt a sinister, significant, and explanatory fact.

Lejaune had been dismissed from the Belgian Congo service for brutalities and atrocities exceeding even the limit fixed by good King Leopold's merry men.

There had been an exposure engineered by foreign missionaries, a world-wide scandal, and some white-washing—in the course of which Lejaune had been washed out.

From being a sergeant of the Belgian army, and a Congo rubber-station factor, autocratic, well-paid, and with absolute power, he had become a legionary, and by forcefulness, energy, and courage had made good.

Once more he had scope for the brutality, violence, and ferocious arrogance that had been his assets in the Belgian Congo, of terrible memory.

At times he was undoubtedly mad, and his madness took the form of sadistic savagery.

Upon this man, Boldini certainly had some claim, or between them there was some bond, for Lejaune never punished Boldini, and they were at times seen in private

confabulation, though, of course, no non-commissioned
officer ever walked out, nor drank, with a private soldier.

The Belgian deserter, one Vaerren, declared that Boldini
had been a civilian subordinate in the Congo, and in Lejaune's district, and had been imprisoned for peculation
and falsifying his trade returns.   Of the truth of this I
know nothing, but I do know that Lejaune favoured the
man and procured his promotion to Corporal, when he
himself became Sergeant-Major.

And it was into the hands of this Lejaune that we were
now delivered.

To resume: Colour-Sergeant Lejaune called the roll of
our names and looked us over.

Noting the insignificant stature of Buddy, a pocket Her-
cules, his face set in a contemptuous sneer.

"An undersized cur," he remarked to the Sergeant of
the Guard.

"Guess I've seen better things than you dead on a sticky
fly-paper, anyhow," replied Buddy promptly.

Mercifully Lejaune knew no English—but he knew that
a wretched recruit had dared to open his miserable mouth.

"Silence, dog!" he roared. "Open your foul lips again,
and I'll close them for a month with my boot. . . . Speak
again, you hound, and I'll kick your teeth down your
throat."

Buddy had not understood a word. He had seen a sneer,
and heard contemptuous words; and he had dared to presume upon being an ignorant recruit, not even in uniform.
Now he heard an angry roar, and was too old a soldier to
do anything but stiffen to attention.

It was borne in upon him that there was *some* pep to
Legion sergeants, and they were *some* roosters, on their own
dung-hill. Better argue with a New York cop on Broadway
at midnight, than to donate back-chat to the rough-neck.

But the mischief was done, and Buddy was a marked
man. More, any friend of Buddy was a marked man, and
any friend of his friend's, unto the third and fourth generation.

When the bloodshot eye of Colour-Sergeant Lejaune fell

upon Boldini, it halted, and a long look passed between the two men. Neither spoke.

Upon us three Gestes he looked with disfavour.

"Runaway pimps," he said. "Show me your hands."

We held them out.

"Going to tell our fortunes. . . . Beware of a dark ugly man," whispered Digby to me.

The Colour-Sergeant regarded our decently kept hands and snorted:

"I'll harden those for you, by God. . . . Never done a stroke of work in your lives. . . . I'll manicure you before you die. . . . I'll make you wish you had gone to gaol instead."

He looked Hank over.

"A lazy hulk, I'll take my oath," he observed. "I'll teach you to move quickly, in a way that'll surprise you," he promised.

"Shore, Bo," replied Hank mildly, wishing to be polite, though ignorant of what had been said to him. "Spill another mouthful," he added encouragingly.

"Silence, you chattering ape from the trees!" roared Lejaune. "Speak again and I'll tie your wrists to your ankles in the small of your back for a week. By God, I'll cripple you for life, you two-legged talking camel."

And Hank also grasped that silence is frequently more than gold and speech much less than silver.

Having duly impressed the draft, Colour-Sergeant Lejaune announced that the Seventh Company would be afflicted with the lot of us, and serve it right. He then suddenly roared:

"*Garde à vous! Pour defiler! Par files de quatre, à droit,*" and looked eagerly and anxiously for a victim. His face clouded with chagrin and disappointment. The draft had moved like guardsmen. Those who understood French had sprung to attention and turned like machines, and those who did not understand the actual words had moved with them.

"*En avant. . . . Marche!*" he concluded, and we stepped off like the old soldiers most of us were.

Across the drill-ground we marched to the storeroom of the *fourrier-sergent* of the Seventh Company, and received our kit which, in addition to two cloth uniforms, included white fatigue uniforms, linen spats, underclothing, the blue woollen sash or cummerbund, cleaning materials, soap and towels, but no socks, for the Legion does not wear them.

We were then inspected by the *adjudant-major*, who corresponds to the English adjutant (whereas the *adjudant* is a non-commissioned officer), and marched by a corporal to our *casernes*, or barrack-rooms.

Going up staircases and along corridors, a squad of ten of us, including Boldini, St. André, Vogué, Maris, Glock, Buddy, Hank, my brothers, and myself, were directed to our room—a huge, clean, well-ventilated bare chamber, in which were thirty beds. Here we were handed over to some *légionnaires*, who were polishing their belts, cartridge-pouches, and accoutrements.

"*Bleus,*" said Corporal Dupré to these men. "Show them what to do, Schwartz, Colonna, Brandt, Haff, and Delarey. . . . Kit, bedding, *paquetage, astiquage,* everything. Don't go *en promenade* before they know their boots from their *képis.*"

"All right, Corporal," said one of the men, and when the Corporal had gone out, changed his tone as he went on:

"The devil damn all *bleus.* Why couldn't you go to hell, instead of coming here to waste our time? . . . However, you shall repay us in the canteen. Come on, get to work now, and the sooner we can get to the bottles . . ."

But Boldini had a word to say.

"Wriggle back into the cheese you crawled out of, you one-year, half-baked imitation of a soldier," he snapped. "I was a legionary and fought in Madagascar, Morocco, and the Soudan when you were in the foundling orphanage."

"Name of a name of a name of a name!" gabbled one of the men, "if it isn't old Boldini come back!" and he roared with laughter and threw himself on a bed.

"Wait till I'm a corporal, friend Brandt," said Boldini. "I'll make you laugh louder than that."

He did not have to wait, however, as the man redoubled his yells of laughter.

The return of Boldini, for some reason, struck him as a most priceless joke.

"Here, you Colonna, Schwartz, and Haff, take those five and I'll attend to these," said Boldini; and proceeded to direct us to appropriate beds and put our kit on them.

He then gave us a clever exhibition of clothes-folding, and built up a secure and neat little *paquetage* of uniform and kit on the shelf above his bed.

"There you are—do that first," said he. "Everything in elbow-to-finger-tip lengths, piled so," and we set about folding coats, trousers, overcoats, and kit, as he had done, and putting the pile on the shelf at the head of the bed as there was no kit-bag or box of any sort.

Having done this, we had our first lesson in *astiquage,* the polishing of belts, and cartridge-pouches, with wax and rags; and then in rifle-cleaning.

We were next conducted downstairs and out to the concrete open-air *lavabo,* and shown where to wash our white canvas fatigue-uniforms. We were then hurried to the canteen, that we might do our duty to our comrades of the *escouade* and pay our footing.

The scene here resembled that in the canteens of Forts St. Jean and St. Thérèse, save that the men were all *légionnaires,* of course, and the person behind the bar was a woman, a veritable French *vivandière* and *fille du regiment.*

Here again, a few francs procured an incredible quantity of wine and all was harmony, noise, and hectic gaiety of the kind induced by alcohol. Returning to our barrack-room at the call of the "Lights out" bugle, we completed our preparations for the morrow by the meagre light of the *caserne* night-lamp.

We gathered that we should be aroused by the *garde-chambre* at five-fifteen in the morning, and should have to be on recruit-parade at five-thirty in white uniform and sash, with knapsack, rifle, belts, and bayonet, and that everything must be immaculate and shining. Also that, before quitting the room, the blankets and mattresses of the bed must be folded and piled, and arranged to a hair breadth accuracy, and the floor beneath the bed swept clean.

Apparently this cleanliness need not extend to the person, for there were no washing facilities of any sort in the room, nor on the whole of that floor of the barracks, nor on the one below. An eccentric, in search of a morning wash, had to make his way down four flights of stairs to a rude and crude kind of lavatory on the ground-floor.

As the *garde-chambre* saw no reason to arouse himself more than a quarter of an hour before he was himself due for parade, and then had to fetch the coffee-pail before arousing the others, this was apt to be a crowded quarter of an hour of inglorious life.

So, with the conscientious fears of the ignorant novice, at least one recruit endeavoured to have everything right and ready before he went to bed, and secretly determined to wake himself at half-past four next morning, to make a good beginning.

Michael's bed was in the corner by the huge window, Boldini's was next, Digby's next, and then that of an Italian calling himself Colonna. Mine came next, then Brandt's, then Buddy's, then Haff's, and then Hank's— always an old *légionnaire* next to a recruit, and so on throughout the room.

In the corner by the door, was the bed of Corporal Dupré, who was in command of the *escouade* and in charge of the room.

He was an active, noisy, bustling person, humorous and not unkindly when sober; when overfull of canteen wine he was sullen, suspicious, and dangerous. Being very fond of wine he was easily approachable by anyone who chose to provide it—or rather the means of purchasing it.

While we three and the Americans were gathered in a group, putting the last touches to our kit and extracting information and advice from Boldini, he came into the room, undressed and went to bed.

As he lay down he bawled:

"Silence! If any man makes a sound. between now and

sunrise, he'll make the next sound in hospital," and **fell** asleep.

We got into our beds in a silence that could be felt.

I remained awake, because I was anxious to go to sleep; and lay thinking of Isobel, of what was happening at Brandon Abbas, of our strange position, and of the "Blue Water."

When I thought of what now lay before me, I was unutterably thankful that my guess, or instinct, had been right, and that I was with Michael and Digby.

It would have been rather terrible to find myself in this galley alone. With Beau and Digby here, it would be just adventure—hard, rough, and dangerous, no doubt—but no easy flowery path leads to any place worth arriving at.

And what of Michael and Digby? They each still pretended to be the culprit, which was doubly as absurd an idea as that either one of them should be.

Michael's look had been one of sheer horror and consternation when he had caught sight of me at Fort St. Thérèse, and he had seemed to feel that my flight was a complication and a catastrophe on which he had never reckoned.

Had he felt the same about Digby, or had Digby known more than he told me? I must try to find out. . . .

I fell asleep and was awakened, apparently a minute later, by the *garde-chambre* shouting something as he lit a big central lamp that hung from the ceiling.

Men sat up in bed; each took a tin mug from a hook below the shelf above his head, and held it out to the *garde-chambre*, who went round with a great jug, giving everybody about half a pint of coffee. It was hot, strong, and good.

The Corporal shouted:

"*Levez-vous! Levez-vous!*" and then, as on the Eve of Waterloo, "there was hurrying to and fro—and sudden partings," if not "tremblings of distress and cheeks all pale. . . ."

Michael, Digby, and I rushed to the far-off lavatory, dashed our heads into water and fled back towelling.

I found my bed "made," my kit laid out neatly, my boots brushed, everything put ready as by a valet, and Brandt sweeping under my bed.

I stared in astonishment.

"A couple of *sous, comrade!*" said Brandt, and I understood. An income of a halfpenny a day is one that will stand a good deal of augmenting.

Turning to see if I could do anything for Michael or Digby, I found that Boldini and Colonna were before me, each earning in a few minutes, as a valet, what it took them two days to earn as a soldier.

In a surprisingly short time, all were dressed and ready, the *garde-chambre* had swept up the dust and dirt that the men had brushed out from under the beds, and Corporal Dupré had been round to see that the beds were properly made and everything tidy. Then, following upon a shout of *"Garde à vous,"* the Colour-Sergeant of the Company entered and inspected the room and the men.

All prayed that he might find no fault, for if he did, he would punish the Corporal, and the Corporal would punish the offenders tenfold.

In the French army, non-commissioned officers can, like prefects in our public schools, award punishments without reference to officers. They give the punishment, enter it in the *livre de punitions,* and there is an end of the matter —unless the officer, inspecting the book, increases the punishment by way of punishing the offender for getting punished.

The system enhances the power and position of the non-com. enormously, and undoubtedly makes for tremendous discipline—and some injustice and tyranny.

All was well this morning, however, and the great man's iron face remained impassive and his hard mouth unopened.

We took our Lebel rifles from the rack, put our bayonets in their frogs, and clattered down to the parade-ground at five-thirty, on that glorious cold morning.

The battalion marched away to field-exercises, and the recruits were formed up, told off by *escouades*, each under a corporal, and taken out to the "plateau." a vast drill-ground near the *village nègre,* for physical training, which to-day was simply steady running. It was nothing much for young athletes like us three, but a little cruel for half-starved or out-of-condition men, who had not run for some time.

On other mornings the physical culture took the form of gymnastics, boxing, or a long route-march.

On our return to barracks, wet and warm, we had our morning meal of *soupe* and bread, and a quarter-litre of good wine. Tin plates and *gamelles* were rattled out of hanging-cupboards, and we sat at the long tables that occupied the centre of the big room. There was meat as well as vegetables in my excellent stew, and the bread, though grey, was palatable, and more than sufficient in quantity.

After a rest, the recruits had a lecture, and after that, squad and company drill, while the battalion did attack-formation exercise on the plateau.

After this we were set to work with brooms and wheel-barrows at tidying up around the barracks, and were then free to go to the *lavabo* to wash and dry our white uniforms.

At five o'clock we got our second meal, exactly like the first, and were then finished for the day, save in so far as we had to prepare for the next, in the way of cleaning and polishing the leather and metal of our arms and equipment —no small task, especially with stuff fresh from store.

Here the poverty of the Legion again helped us, for no man need do a stroke more than he wishes of this kind of work, while he has a halfpenny to spare.

We soon found that it was a real and genuine kindness to let a comrade have a go at our leather and brass, our rifles and bayonets, our dirty fatigue-suits and undercloth-ing; for, to him, a job meant the means of getting a packet of *caporal* cigarettes, a bottle of wine, a postage-stamp, a change of diet, a piece of much-needed soap, or a chance to replenish his cleaning materials.

We three did not shirk our work, by any means, but very often, when weary to death, or anxious to go out of bar-racks, we gave our *astiquage* work to one of the many who begged to be allowed to do it.

The recruits progressed with astonishing speed, being practically all trained soldiers before they joined, and picked up the necessary Legion-French remarkably rapidly.

We three very soon became good soldiers, aided by our intelligence, strength, sobriety, athletic training, sense of discipline, knowledge of French, and a genuine desire to make good.

More fortunate than most, we were well-educated and had "background"; a little money (thanks to Michael's forethought), which was wealth in the Legion; good habits, self-control, and a public-school training; and we were inoffensive by reason of possessing the consideration, courtesy, and self-respecting respect for others proper to gentlemen.

Less fortunate than most, we were accustomed to varied food, comfortable surroundings, leisure, a great deal of mental and physical recreation, spaciousness of life, and above all, *privacy*.

But at first, everything was new and strange, remarkable and romantic; we were Soldiers of Fortune, we were together, and we were by no means unhappy.

But oh, how I longed to see Isobel!

And gradually, wondering thoughts as to the "Blue Water" and its whereabouts, retired to the back of my mind, for the world was too much with us altogether, for there to be time available for introspection or day-dreaming. Our days were too full and busy and our nights all too short for thought. They were scarce long enough for the deep dreamless sleep necessary to men who were worked as we were.

And how we blessed Sundays—those glorious life-saving days of complete rest.

On our first Sunday morning in the Legion, we three sat on Michael's bed and held a "Council of War," as we had so often done, in the days of the Band, at Brandon Abbas.

It was decided that I should write to Isobel, telling her where I was, and saying that I knew where Michael and Digby were, and could send them any messages or news.

Isobel was to use her discretion as to admitting that she knew where I was, but if she did admit it, she was to add—

the simple truth—that she had not the slightest idea as to where the others were.

This plan was Michael's, and as he seemed keen on it, and neither Digby nor I saw anything against it, we adopted it, and I wrote a letter which she could show to Aunt Patricia, or not, as she liked.

I wrote as follows:—

> *"Légionnaire John Smith, No.* 18896,
> *7th Company, Premier Étranger,*
> *Sidi-bel-Abbès, Algeria.*
>
> *Dear Isobel,*
> *A letter to the above address will find me. Michael and Digby know it also. I can send them any messages, or news, from Brandon Abbas. Neither of them is in England. Either of them will let me know if he changes his present address. I am in excellent health. I shall write again if I hear from you. I am so anxious to know what is happening at home.*
>
> *John."*

Michael and Digby approved of this, as it opened up a line of communication with Brandon Abbas, but made no change in the situation.

From what we had learnt, after discreet enquiries of Boldini, we had quite come to the conclusion that the English police would take no steps in pursuit of the legionary, John Smith, so long as he remained in the Legion, even though there were strong reasons for suspecting him to be John Geste who had disappeared at the time of the jewel-robbery.

But I privately inserted a scrap of paper on which was a message of undying and unalterable love to my sweetheart. This she could destroy, and the letter she could produce for Aunt Patricia's information or not, as might seem best to her in whatever circumstances arose. . . .

On a Saturday night, a fortnight later, I got a private and personal love-letter that made me wildly happy and as proud as a peacock; and, with it, a long letter that I could send to Michael and Digby if I wished to do so.

This latter said that things were going on at Brandon Abbas exactly as before.

Aunt Patricia had, so far, communicated neither with the police nor with anybody else, and had taken no steps, whatsoever in the matter.

Apparently she had accepted the fact that one of the three Gestes had stolen the ''Blue Water''—and, extraordinarily and incredibly, she was just doing nothing at all about it, but simply awaiting Uncle Hector's return.

She had released Augustus, Claudia, and Isobel herself, from the prohibition as to leaving the house, and had asked no questions of any of them since the day that I had disappeared. On that day, she had accepted the solemn assurance of Augustus, Cladudia, and Isobel, that they knew *absolutely nothing* as to where the Gestes had gone, which of them was the thief, or whether they were in league.

''I cannot understand her,'' she wrote, ''nor get at what she thinks and feels. She fully accepts, apparently, my exculpation of Gussie (and incidentally of myself at the same time) and scorns to suspect Claudia. She has told us that we are absolutely free from suspicion, and she wishes us to make no further reference to the matter at all. Gussie is, of course, unbearable. He has '*known all along that you would come to a bad end—the three of you,*' but while certain that you are all in it together, he believes that you, John, are the actual thief. I told him that I had a belief too, and when he asked what it was, I said, '*I believe that if you gave your whole soul to it, Gussie, you might possibly, some day, be fit to clean John's boots—or those of any other Geste. . . .*' I also said that if he ever uttered another word on the subject I would discover, when the police came, that I had made a mistake in thinking that it was *his* arm I had held when the light failed! . . . Am I not a beast? But he does make me so angry with his sneers and conscious rectitude, the mean little rascal.

However, as I have said, the police have not come yet, and absolutely nothing is being done. The servants haven't a ghost of an idea that anything is wrong, and life goes on just as if you three had merely gone up to Oxford for this term. Burdon must wonder that you all went so suddenly and with so little kit, but I don't suppose it interests him much.

I don't know *what* Uncle Hector will say about the delay in going to Scotland Yard! It almost looks as though Aunt wants the culprit to escape, or else feels that Uncle Hector would prefer that there should be no public scandal if it could possibly be avoided, and the sapphire recovered privately. Somehow I can't think that Aunt would have any mercy on the thief, though—and I really don't think she'd suppose Uncle Hector would prefer this delay to scandal. Surely he is not the person to care twopence about scandal, and he certainly is not the person to approve a delay that may make recovery impossible. I can't make it out *at all*.

Fancy Uncle Hector robbed of thirty thousand pounds! He'll go raving mad and kill people!

Oh, John, where *is* the wretched thing? And how long will it be before you can all come back? I shall wire to you at once if it turns up, and I shall certainly come and see you if you don't come soon—for it's my private opinion that you are all three together! . . ."

I produced this letter for Michael and Digby to read, at our Sunday "Council of War" next morning.

Michael read it without a word of comment, and with an inscrutable face.

Digby said, "The little darling! I bet she comes out to Sidi if the thing doesn't turn up!" and he bounced on the bed, with glee, at the idea.

"Wonder what Uncle Hector will do?" said Michael. "Poor Aunt Patricia will get a thin time. . . ."

"For not preventing us from pinching it?" jeered Digby.

"No—for not calling in the police at once," said Michael.

"I wonder why she didn't," I remarked.

"Yes," said Michael. "Funny, isn't it?"

And yawning and turning round from the window, out of which we had been looking, I noticed that Boldini was asleep on his bed behind us. It was curious how quietly that man could move about, with his cat-like steps and silent ways.

§ 8.

Recruit-days passed swiftly away, and we were too busy and too tired to be wretched.

From five in the morning till five in the evening we were hard at it, and after that we had plenty to do in preparing our kit and accoutrements for the morrow.

That done, or given to a needy comrade to do, we dressed in our walking-out uniforms, according to the particular *ordre du jour,* and went for a walk in tawdry hybrid Sidi, or to hear the Legion's magnificent band in the Place Sadi Carnot, or the Jardin Publique. Usually we three went together, but sometimes the two Americans and St. André would accompany us, and Boldini whenever we could not shake him off.

He stuck to us closer than a brother sticketh, and after his first usefulness was over (and paid for), as we gained experience and learnt the ropes, we certainly did not desire his society for himself alone.

But apparently he desired ours, and ardently.

The more we saw of the two Americans, the better we liked them, and the same applied to St. André—but precisely the converse was true of Boldini.

However, we were not troubled by his presence when Buddy went out with us, for the American would have none of him, and scrupled not to say so with painful definiteness.

"Get to hell outa this, Cascara Sagrada," he would say truculently. "Don' wantcha. Go gnaw circles in the meadow and keep away from me with both feet. . . . Skoot, son," or some equally discouraging address.

Painful as this was, we were glad to profit by it, for Boldini waxed more and more offensively familiar. Put into words, the message of his manner to us three (his implications, and the general atmosphere he endeavoured to create) was:

"Come—we're all scoundrels together! Why this silly

pretence of innocence and superiority? Let's be a united gang and share all loot" kind of idea.

I did not understand Buddy's virulent detestation of the man, though; and when I asked him about it one day, when he flatly refused to let Boldini join us in the canteen, all he could reply was:

"He's a rattlesnake with a silent rattle, and he's Lejaune's spy. You wanta watch out. He's on your trail fer somethin'," and Hank had confirmed this with a drawled, "Shore, Bo, watch the critter."

The first time that Boldini showed objection to Buddy's rudeness, the latter promptly invited him to come below and bring his fists—an invitation which Boldini declined (and was for ever the admitted inferior, in consequence).

Another person who most certainly watched us, and with a baleful boding eye, was Colour-Sergeant Lejaune himself, now, alas, Sergeant-Major.

We were, however, far too keen, careful, and capable to give him the opportunity he obviously desired.

When he came in for room-inspection, he made no pretence of not giving us and our kit, accoutrements, and bedding, a longer and more searching inspection than he gave to anybody else except Buddy.

When I met the long hard stare of his hot and cruel eyes, I thought of a panther or some other feral beast whose sole mental content was hate. . . .

"We're sure *for* it, pard," said Buddy to me, after one of these inspections. "Our name's mud. That section-boss makes me feel like when I butted into a grizzly-b'ar. On'y I liked the b'ar better."

"Yep," agreed Hank. "He's a grizzly-b'ar. . . . But I've shot a grizzly-b'ar, I hev.

"They ain't immortial," he added mildly.

It was also quite clear that Corporal Dupré had found that he had said the wrong thing when he replied to Lejaune's enquiry as to what sort of unspecified animals we were, by declaring that we were model recruits whose sole object appeared to be the meriting of his approval.

Corporal Dupré was not a bad fellow at heart, but "he

had got to live," and it grew clearer and clearer, as the weeks went by, that we three could do nothing right and Boldini nothing wrong.

Our chief offence was that we would commit no offence, but we felt we walked on very thin ice. . . .

In less than a couple of months we were dismissed recruit-drills and became full-blown *légionnaires*.

Above the head of my bed appeared a printed pasteboard card, bearing the legend, *John Smith, No.* 18896, *Soldat 2ème Classe,* and I was a (second-class) Soldier of Fortune, taking my place in the ranks of my battalion. In time I should be a *Soldat 1ère Classe,* if I were good.

Michael, Digby, the two Americans, Maris, and St. André came to the battalion at the same time, and our little party kept together.

We now learned what marching really is, and why the Legion is known in the Nineteenth Army Corps as the *cavalerie à pied.* The route-marches were of appalling length at an unvarying five kilometres an hour. Over English roads, in the English climate, and with the English soldier's kit, they would have been incredible. Over sand and desert stones, under the African sun, and with the much heavier kit of the legionary (which includes tent-canvas, firewood, a blanket, and a spare uniform), they were infinitely more so.

On one occasion we took a stroll of five hundred miles, marching continuously at thirty miles a day, as the Colonel thought we wanted "airing."

In addition to these marches, we had admirable training in skirmishing and scouting, plenty of company and battalion drill, first-aid, field engineering, varied rifle-range work, and the theory of infantry warfare.

By the time we three felt ourselves old soldiers, we also began to feel we were stagnating mentally, and becoming mechanical, bored, and stale. Night after night of strolling about Sidi-bel-Abbès was not good enough, and our brains were demanding exercise.

Michael decreed that we should study Arabic, both for the good of our souls and with a view to future usefulness at such time as we should be generals entrusted with diplomatic missions or military governorships.

Our Arabic proved useful before then.

We got books from the library, engaged a half-caste clerk, who worked in the *Bureau Arabe,* to meet us for an hour, four evenings a week, for conversation; and took to haunting Arab cafés instead of French ones.

We distinctly liked the dignified and courteous men with whom we talked over the wonderful coffee.

We made rapid progress and, after a time, made a point of talking Arabic to each other. It is an easy language to learn, especially in a country where it is spoken.

And still Boldini haunted us like our shadow, Corporal Dupré waited for a chance to report us, and Lejaune bided his time.

But we were wary and we were unexceptionable soldiers. Even these skilful fault-finders and fault-makers could not get an opportunity, and we were favourably noticed by our Lieutenant (Debussy) and Captain (Renouf), of whom we saw all too little. Theirs to lead us in manœuvres and war, the non-commissioned officers' to prepare us to be led. And in this the officers assisted them only by their authority. In every possible way. and some impossible ways, they upheld the power of the non-coms., backed them up on every occasion, took their word for everything, and supported them blindly.

There was no appeal. What the non-commissioned officer said, was true; and what he did, was right, as against the private soldier. The resulting discipline was wonderful— and so was the bitterness, hatred, and despair of some of the victims of injustice and personal spite.

A sergeant had only to continue punishing a victim, for the latter to earn the unfavourable notice of the officer, when the latter read the punishment book, and to find his punishment doubled—with a warning to beware lest something really serious happened to him.

The Americans were not as lucky, or not as careful, as we three. For one thing, they sometimes drank the appalling maddening filth sold in the low-class wine-shops of

the Spanish quarter or the Ghetto. Crude alcohol made
from figs, rice, or wood, and known as *bapédi, tchum-tchum,*
and *genièvre,* would make Buddy's temper explosive and
uncertain, while it rendered Hank indiscriminatingly af-
fectionate and apt to fall heavily upon the neck of the
Sergeant of the Guard, when the latter admitted him,
singing joyously, in the watches of the night.

Then was Lejaune happy, and reminded them of how
they had opened their mouths in his presence, upon the
evening of their entry into the Legion.

When they were confined to barracks, he would have
the defaulters' roll called at odd times, in the hope of their
missing it, and, when they were in the *salle de police,*
would see that the Sergeant of the Guard turned them out
hourly, under pretence of suspecting that they had tobacco
or drink.

Sometimes he would go himself to their cells, in the
middle of the night, arouse them with a sudden roar, and
give a swift, harsh order, in the hope that it would be
disobeyed through resentment or drunken stupidity.

I think he would have given a month's pay to have
succeeded in goading one of them into striking him. It
was my constant fear that Buddy would do so. And daily
we dinned this into their ears, and prayed that something
of the sort would not happen. However, they were old
soldiers and wily Americans. . . .

And so the months passed, and every week I heard from
my darling. Nothing happened at Brandon Abbas.

Gussie had gone to Sandhurst, the Chaplain was about
again, and Uncle Hector had postponed his home-coming
after all, and had gone to Kashmir to shoot bear, as he
had had poor sport with tiger in the Central Provinces.

No reference was ever made to the missing "Blue
Water," no questions had been asked of Isobel, and she had
volunteered no information as to our whereabouts and her
being in communication with me.

Also she would "come into" her money on her next
birthday, and she was then going to do a little travelling,
and intended to wander in Algeria!

"Hope she comes before we go—or that we don't go before she comes," said Digby, on learning this last piece of information—for we were full of hope that we should be among those selected for the big special draft that was going south before long.

Everyone knew that a battalion, a thousand strong, was going to "demonstrate" on the border shortly, and "demonstrating" meant further peaceful penetration with the bayonet, active service, and chances of distinction, decoration, and promotion.

If we did not go we should be bitterly disappointed, and lapse into mere bored and disillusioned victims of a monotonous soul-killing routine, daily doing the drill in which we were perfect; cursing the guard-mounting, sentry-go, and endless "fatigues"; learning the things we knew by heart; performing the exercises and operations we could do blindfold; and dragging ourselves through the killing route-marches that we hated.

But what a cruel thing if we were selected and sent off just as Isobel was coming!

On the other hand, if we were not taken (and we were still very junior soldiers), we should at any rate have Isobel's visit to Sidi-bel-Abbès to look forward to.

So great was my longing to see her that, had I been alone, I really think that I should, at times, have toyed with the idea of "going on pump," "making the promenade," which all *légionnaires* continually discuss and frequently attempt. This "going on pump," whatever that may mean, is the Legion name for deserting, and generally consists in slow preparation and swift capture, or a few days' thirst-agony in the desert, and ignominious return, or else in unspeakable torture and mutilation at the hands of the Arabs.

Less than one in a hundred succeeds in escaping, for, in addition to the patrols, the desert, and the Arabs, the native armed-police *goumiers* receive a reward of twenty-five francs a head for the return of deserters, dead or alive.

Being matchless trackers, well-armed, good shots, and brave men, they are very successful bloodhounds.

However, the attempt is frequently made by maddened victims of injustice or of sheer monotony and hardship, and their punishment, when caught, varies from leniency to cruel severity, according to the degree of *cafard* from which they were suffering, and to the amount of uniform and kit they may have lost.

One man, whom I knew personally, when under sentence to appear before the supreme court martial of Oran, which in his case meant certain death, got clean away, and was known to have escaped from the country.

Several, whom I knew, went off into the desert and were either found dead and mutilated, or never heard of more; and many either escaped and surrendered again, or were brought back running, or dragging on the ground, at the end of a cord tied to the saddle of an Arab police *goum*. . . .

However, we had come here to make careers for ourselves as Soldiers of Fortune, and to become Generals in the Army of France, as other foreigners had done, from the ranks of the Legion. And we did our utmost to achieve selection for the picked battalion that was to march south for the next forward leap of the apostles of pacific penetration (or pacification of the newly-penetrated areas) of the Sahara of the Soudan.

§ 9.

One evening, at about this period of our depôt life, Maris, the Swiss ex-courier, came to me as I lay on my cot, resting and awaiting the return of Michael and Digby from *corvée*. Said he:

"I have something to tell you, Monsieur Smith. You have done me many a good turn, and you saved me from prison when my tunic was stolen and I could not have replaced it in time for the *adjudant's* inspection. . . . Will you and your brothers meet me at Mustapha's at six to-night? It will be worth your while. We shall be safe enough there, especially if we talk in English . . ." and he glanced apprehensively round the busy room, and jerked his head towards Colonna and an Italian named Guantaio, who were working together at the table.

I thanked him and said that I would tell my brothers, and that if they returned in time, from the "fatigue" on which they were engaged, we would look in at Mustapha's.

When Michael and Digby came in from the job of sweeping and weeding, for which they had been seized by a sergeant, I told them what Maris had said.

"Better go," remarked Michael. "Maris is the clean potato, I think. No harm in hearing it anyhow."

Mustapha's was an Arab café, where we got splendid coffee very cheaply—thick, black, and sweet, with a drop of vanilla, a drop of hashish oil, or of opium, a drop of orange-essence, and other flavourings.

Here we rested ourselves on a big and very low divan, with a solid wall behind us, and awaited Maris, who came a few minutes later.

"It's like this, my friends," said he, in his excellent English, when we had got our little clay cups of coffee steaming on the floor in front of us. "I don't want to make what you call the mare's nest, isn't it? But Boldini is up to his tricks again. . . . I have heard a lot about him from Vaerren and from old *légionnaires* who served with him before. . . . He is the bad hat, that one. They say that Lejaune will get him made a corporal soon. . . . Well, I have noticed things, I.

"Yes. And last night I was sitting in the Tlemcen Gardens. It was getting dark. Behind the seat were bushes, and another path ran by the other side. Some *légionnaires* came along it, and sat down on a seat that must have been just behind mine. They were talking Italian. I know Italian well, and I always listen to foreign languages. . . . Yes, I shall be a courier again when the little trouble has blown over about the man I taught not to steal my fiancée, while I travel. Yes. . . ."

He paused dramatically, and with much eye-rolling and gesticulation continued:

"Boldini it was, and Colonna and Guantaio. He had been trying to get them to do something and they were afraid. Boldini, for some reason, also wanted Colonna to change beds with him, to make this something easier to do.

" '*Yes, and what if I am caught?*' said Colonna.

" '*You're as good a man as he is,*' said Boldini.

" '*And what about his brothers? Yes—and his friends the Americans?*' asked Colonna.

" '*And what about* YOUR *friends—me and Guantaio and Vogué and Gotto?* WHAT ABOUT SERGEANT-MAJOR LEJAUNE, *if someone makes a row, and Corporal Dupré reports the man to him and I give my humble evidence as an eye-witness—in private? Eh? . . . "Brothers," you say! Aren't Lejaune and I like brothers?*'

" '*Why not do it yourself then?*' said Guantaio.

" '*Because I'm going to be made corporal soon,*' replied Boldini, '*and I mustn't be in any rows. . . . Ah, when I'm corporal, I shall be able to look after my friends, eh?*' Then he went on to remind them of what they could do with a thousand francs—more than fifty years of their pay, for a two-minute job.

"Then Guantaio, who seems to be a pluckier dog than Colonna, said:

" '*How do you know he has got it?*' and Boldini replied, '*Because I heard them say so. They are a gang. Swell thieves. They have asked me if thieves in the Legion are given up to the police. When the third one joined at Oran, I guessed it from what they said. And they were flash with their money. They got together at night, out in the courtyard, and I crept up behind a buttress close to them and listened. I could not hear everything, but they spoke of a jewel-robbery and thirty thousand pounds. The one they call "Le Beau" said he kept it like the* CANGURO . . . *the kangaroo . . . keeps its young! I heard him plainly.*

" '*And where does the* CANGURO *keep its young? In a pouch on its stomach, and that is where this thief, Légion-naire Guillaume Brown, keeps this jewel. In a pouch. . . . He wears it day and night.*

" '*And it's a thousand francs for the man that gets me the pouch. And I'll take the chance and risk of getting the jewel sold in the Ghetto for more than a thousand. . . . Some of those Ghetto Jews are millionaires. . . . I'd put the lamp out. One man could gag and hold him, while the other got it, and they could run to their beds in the dark.'* . . .

"And much more of the same sort he talked, egging them on, and then they went away, but with nothing settled," continued Maris.

Digby and I burst into laughter at mention of the kangaroo, and Michael turned, smiling, to Maris.

When the latter stopped, Digby asked if Boldini had not also divulged that he wore a sapphire eye, and I enquired if the wily Italian had not observed a lump in Digby's cheek, where a simian pouch concealed a big jewel.

"The fool overheard an elaborate joke," said Michael to Maris; "but we're very much obliged to you."

"Oh, he is the fool all right," said Maris; "but he is also the knave.

"Knave of diamonds!" he added with a grin. "I just tell you because I like you English gentlemen, and it is just possible that they may try to steal your money-belt, if they think there is a chance of getting something valuable."

We filled the worthy Maris up with *cous-cous* and *galettes* (pancakes and honey), and strolled back to barracks.

When we were alone, I said to Michael:

"You *do* wear a money-belt, Beau. Let me have it at night for a bit—in case these gentle Italians have been persuaded, and something happens in the dark."

"Why?" asked Michael.

"Well," replied I, "you could favour them with your full personal attention, untroubled with grosser cares, if you had no property to protect. Also you could establish the fact that you don't wear a money-belt at night."

"I'd sooner establish despondency and alarm in the thief, thanks," said Michael.

"What a lark!" chuckled Digby. "I'm going to wear a brick under my sash and swear it's a ruby. Anyone that can pinch it while I slumber, can have it for keeps. . . . I must find this Boldini lad." . . .

But, personally, I did not regard the matter as precisely a lark.

I had heard of Italian knives, and it seemed to me that a man might well be found dead in his bed, with a knife —or his own bayonet—through his heart, and nobody be any the wiser. . . . And even if justice could be done, which was doubtful, that would not bring the dead man back to life.

We had been long enough in the Legion to know its queer code of morals, and on the subject of theft the law was very peculiar, very strict, and very savage.

One might steal any article of uniform, and be no thief. It was a case of "robbery no stealing." To take another man's uniform or kit was merely "to decorate oneself," and decorating oneself was a blameless pastime, regarded universally as profitable, amusing, and honourable. Public opinion was not in the slightest degree against the time-honoured practice, and the act was concealed from none save the owner of the sequestrated property.

This was all very silly, for it was a most serious matter, involving very heavy punishment, for a man to be found to be short of so much as a strap when "showing-down" kit for inspection by the *adjudant*. Nevertheless, you might "decorate yourself" with a tunic, a sash, an overcoat, a pair of boots, a pair of trousers, or the whole of a man's "washing" from the line in the *lavabo*, and no one thought one penny the worse of you, save the unfortunate whom you had robbed.

The idea was, that if you were short of an article of equipment (after all, the property of *Madame la République*, and not of the individual), you must help yourself where you could, your victim must help himself where he could, his victim must do likewise, and so on. And whoever was caught out, in the end, as short of kit, was the fool and the loser in this childish game of "beggar my neighbour" (of his uniform).

Of his uniform, public property—but of nothing else.

Anything else was private property and sacred. To steal private property was not self-"decoration" at all, but theft; and theft, in that collection of the poorest of poor men, was the ultimate horrible crime, infinitely worse than murder. The legionary did not value his life much, but he valued his few tiny possessions beyond estimation.

With the abomination of theft, the Legion itself dealt, and dealt most drastically, for it could not be tolerated where everything private was so valuable, and so easily stolen if a thief should arise in the midst.

There was no thought of appeal to Authority in a case of theft; nor was there either enquiry or comment on the part of Authority when a case occurred and was punished by the men themselves, according to Legion law and custom.

And we were soon to see the law in operation and to behold an example of the custom. . . .

Since Michael absolutely refused to let me wear his money-belt for him at night, I decided that I must think of some other plan—in view of this story told by Maris. I did not doubt its truth for one moment, as it merely confirmed, in particular, what I had thought and Buddy had voiced, in general—that Boldini's interest in our comings and goings, our conversation and habits, our antecedents and private affairs, had a sinister cause and object.

At first I thought of arranging with Digby that he and I should take turns to keep watch, but I discarded this plan as impossible. Nobody who worked as long and as hard as we did, could possibly lie awake in bed, and Michael would soon have "put an end to our nonsense" if we had sat up to guard him.

I then thought of going to Boldini and saying:

"Kangaroos have a horrible kick, my friend," or "Better not let me see you putting the light out, Boldini," or even frankly and plainly promising to kill him, if anybody attempted to rob my brother.

After pondering the matter and consulting Digby, who did not take as serious a view of it as I did, I had the bright idea of getting the advice of an older, worldly-wiser, and far cleverer person than myself—and appealed to Buddy.

What he did not know about crooks and the best ways of defeating them was not worth knowing, and his experiences in the Texas Rangers had been those of detective, policeman, watch-dog, and soldier combined.

I accordingly walked out one evening with Hank and Buddy, "set the drinks up" at the Bar de Madagascar off the Rue de Daya, and told them that I had excellent reason to believe that Boldini was arranging with Colonna and Guantaio to rob my brother, one night.

"My brother can look after himself, of course," said I; "but these curs have got hold of the idea that he has a marvellous jewel which we three have stolen. . . . What I'm wondering is whether Guantaio, who looks like a *pucca* Sicilian bandit, would stick a knife into him, to make sure of getting his belt. That's the only thing that worries me."

"Fergit it, son," was Buddy's prompt reply. "Those slobs would never do that. Don't trust each other enough, for one thing. Far too risky, for another. That sort of poor thieving boob wouldn't dare. Why, one drop of blood on his hands or shirt, or one yell outa your brother, an' he'd be taken red-handed."

"Shore," agreed Hank. "Not in barracks they wouldn't. Git him up a side-street and bash him on the head, more like. Anybody mighta done it there. Lots o' guys git done in fer their sash an' bayonet in the *village nègre*, an' them low dives an' sash-joints in the Spanish quarter. . . . Don't let him go around alone, an' he's safe enough."

This was reassuring, and it was common sense. It would, of course, take a very cool, skilful, and courageous murderer to kill a man sleeping in a room with thirty others.

"I don't know so much," I said, arguing against myself and for the sake of complete reassurance. "Suppose Guantaio or Colonna simply crept to the bed and drove a bayonet through the blankets and through his heart. There'd be no bloodstains on the murderer . . ."

"Not when he started monkeying with the belt?" put in Buddy. "And wouldn't there be no sound from your brother? Not a cheep outa him? Fergit it, I say."

"Look at here, Bo," argued Hank. "Figger it was you agoin' to stick me. How'd you know where my heart was, me curled up under the blankets, and nearly dark an' all? How'd you know as everybody was asleep all right! How'd you know there wouldn't be noise? . . . Shucks! 'Tain't horse-sense. . . . Nope. These legendaries don't stand fer murder in the barrack-room, still less fer robbery, and least of all fer bein' woke up at night outa their due and lawful sleep." . . .

"See, boy," interrupted Buddy at this point, "that barrack-room is just your brother's plumb safest place. As fer his kohinoor di'mond, I allow he can sure look after that himself."

"Shore thing," agreed Hank.

"Absolutely," said I. "If there's no fear of his being murdered in his sleep, there's an end of the matter. I'd rather like Boldini to go and try to rob him."

"I wouldn't go fer to say as much as that, Bo," demurred Buddy. "I'd undertake to clear your brother out every night of his life—every cent outa his belt—and the belt likewise also, too. . . . P'r'aps Mister Cascara Sagrada could do as much," and we smiled, both thinking of the occasion upon which Buddy had "minded" my money for me.

"Look at here, Bo," said Hank at this. "I gotta little idee. Suppose I goes to Cascara an' ses to him, '*Pard,*' I ses, '*if that English legendary, Willyerm Brown, No. 18897, gits robbed, I'm sure agwine ter do you an onjustice. I'm agwine ter beat you up most ugly. So's yer own father, if you had one, wouldn't know yer, an' yer mother'd disown yer,*' or something discouragin' like that."

I thanked this large slow person, but declined, assuring him that we could take excellent care of ourselves, and I had only wanted to know if murder were a possible contingency.

"Not inside the barracks. Not till hell pops," said Buddy.

"Sure thing," agreed Hank. "But don't let him prowl around no boweries nor hootch-joints, on his lonesome. Nope."

"An' tell him from me that I'll mind his money-belt an' be responserble, if he likes," offered Buddy. "Then he can sleep free and easy like, an' also deal faithful with any guy as comes snooping around in the night, without having to waste time feeling if his gold-dust is there all right. . . ."

I again thanked him, changed the subject, and soon afterwards got them back to barracks, "a-settin' sober on the water-waggon, a credit to all men," as Hank observed.

And, this very night, there happened that which must have given certain gentlemen of our barrack-room to think, and to think seriously, of abandoning any schemes for their quick enrichment, had they been entertaining them.

I was awakened by a crash and a shout. . . . Springing up, instantly awake, I saw two men struggling on the floor near Michael's bed. The one on top, pinning the other down with a hand on his throat, was Michael. As I leapt from my bed, I was aware that the room was alive and that men were running with angry shouts to see what, and who, had broken their sacred sleep—a horrible violation of strictest Legion law.

"Wring the sneakin' coyote's neck, Bo," shouted Buddy.

" '*Learn him to be a toad,*' Beau," quoted Digby, and with cries of "Thief! Thief!" the wave of shouting, gesticulating men swept over the two and bore one of them to the surface. It was neither Guantaio nor Colonna, neither Gotto nor Vogué—one of whom I had fully expected to see.

White-faced, struggling, imploring, in the grip of a dozen indignantly outraged and savagely ferocious *légionnaires*, was a man from the next room.

I looked around for Boldini.

He was sound asleep in his bed! And so was Corporal Dupré in his, and with his face to the wall—both of them men whom the squeak of a mouse would awaken.

"What are you doing here, *scélérat?*" shouted half a score of fierce voices as the man was pulled hither and thither, buffeted, shaken, and savagely struck.

"Speak up, you Brown. What about it?" roared

Schwartz, who had got the man by the throat. "Was he stealing?"

"On the table with him," yelled Brandt.

"Yes, come on. Crucify the swine," bawled the huge bearded Schwartz, shaking his victim as a terrier shakes a rat.

Hank, followed by Buddy, barged into the middle of the scrum, throwing men right and left.

" 'Tain't one of Boldini's outfit," I heard Buddy say.

"Give the guy a fair trial," shouted Hank. "Lynchin' fer hoss-thieves an' sich—but give him a trial," and he seized the man himself. "Cough it up quick," he said to the terrified wretch, who seemed about to faint.

"Wait a minute," shouted Michael, in French. "He belongs to me. . . . He's had enough. . . ."

The crowd snarled. Several had bayonets in their hands.

"I lost my way," screamed the prisoner.

"And found it to the bed of a man who has money," laughed a voice. "Legion law! On the table with him!"

Michael jumped on the table.

"Silence, you fools!" he shouted. "Listen!" and the crowd listened. "I woke up and found the man feeling under my pillow. I thought he was somebody belonging to the room. Somebody I have been waiting for. Well— he isn't. Let him go—he won't come again. . . ."

At that there was a perfect yell of derision and execration, and Michael was sent flying by a rush of angry men.

While he, Digby, and I were struggling to get to the table, the thief was flung on to it and held down; a bayonet was driven through each of his hands, another through each of his ears, and he lay moaning and begging for mercy. As I got to the table, sick with disgust, with some idea of rescuing the poor beast, I was seized from behind and flung away again.

"Lie there and think about it, you thieving cur," shouted Schwartz to the thief.

"Stop your snivelling—or I'll put another through your throat," growled Brandt.

Hank seized me as I knocked Haff down.

"Let be, Johnny," he said, enveloping me in a bear's hug. "It's the salootary custom of the country. They discourages thievin' in these parts. But I wish it was Boldini they was lynchin'. . . ."

I tried to shake him off, as I saw Michael spring on Schwartz like a tiger.

There was a sudden cry of *"Guard!"* a swift rush in all directions, and the guard tramped in, to find a silent room—full of sleeping men—in the midst of which were we three pulling bayonets out of a white wooden table, and a whiter whimpering man.

"What's this?" said the Corporal of the Guard. . . .

"An accident," he answered himself, and, completely ignoring me, he turned to the stolid guard, gave the curt order:

"To the hospital," and the guard partly led, and partly carried, the wretched creature away.

What his name was, whether he was incited by Boldini, or whether he was merely trying to rob a man known to have money, I did not know.

As Michael caught him feeling under the pillow, it seemed quite likely he was merely looking for a purse or coins.

On the other hand, he may have tried the shelf and *paquetage*, and then under the pillow, in the hope of finding the alleged belt and jewel, before essaying the far more risky business of rifling the pouch and money-belt.

Talking the affair over the next day, none of us could remember having seen Guantaio or Colonna in the fray, so I concluded that, like Boldini, they had decided not to be awakened by the noise.

As all the old *légionnaires* prophesied would be the case, we heard nothing whatever from the authorities about the riot and the assault upon the thief. Clearly it was considered best to let the men enforce their own laws as they thought fit, provided those laws were reasonable and in the public interest.

When the injured man came out of hospital, we took an interest in his movements. He proved to be a Portuguese named Bolidar, a wharf-rat docker from Lisbon, and quite probably an amateur of petty crime. He stuck to his absurd tale that he had mistaken the room and was feeling his way into what he thought was his own bed.

We came to the conclusion that he was either staunch to his confederates, or else afraid to implicate them. We saw more of him later at Zinderneuf.

"Leave him to me," said Buddy. "I'll loosen his tongue —the miserable hoodlum. One night that dago swine is agwine to tell me an' Hank the secrets of his lovin' heart. . . ."

"He'll sure sob 'em out," opined Hank.

But whether he was to do this under the influence of wine or of terror, I did not gather.

What we did gather, a week or two later, was that we were the most famous gang of international crooks and jewel-thieves in Europe, and had got away with a diamond worth over a million francs. With this we had sought safety in the Legion, that we might lie low until the affair was forgotten, and then sell the diamond whole, or have it cut up, as might seem best.

We were Germans pretending to be English, and we had stolen the diamond, in London, from Sir Smith, a great English general, to whom it had been presented by the Prince of Wales, who was in love with his sister. Buddy solemnly informed me that Bolidar knew all this "for certain." Bolidar had got it from a friend of ours. No —no names—but if Hank and Buddy could get the diamond—"rescue" it from the rascals—he, Bolidar, was in a position to promise them a thousand francs, *and* the protection of—someone who was in a position to protect them.

"So there you are, pard," concluded Buddy, with an amused grin. And there we were.

But only for another month. At the end of that time we found ourselves in the selected draft under orders for the south, and our chance had come of winning that distinction, decoration, and promotion which was to be our first step on the Path of Glory—which was to lead not to the grave but to fame and fortune.

CHAPTER IV

THE DESERT

WE left the depôt of Sidi-bel-Abbés in the spirit in which boys leave school at the end of the half. The thought of escape from that deadly crushing monotony and weariness, to active service, change, and adventure, was inexpressibly delightful. The bitterness in my cup of joy was the knowledge that I was going before Isobel could visit Algeria, and that if we were sent to the far south, and were constantly on the move, I could only hear from her at long and irregular intervals.

I poured out my heart to her in a long letter, the night before we marched; told her I was absolutely certain I should see her again; and begged her not to waste her youth in thinking of me if a year passed without news, as I should be dead.

Having had my hour of self-pity, and having waxed magnificently sentimental, I became severely practical, made all preparations, tallowed my feet, and, laden like a beast of burden, fell in, for the last time, on the parade-ground of the Legion's barracks at Sidi-bel-Abbès.

With a hundred rounds of ammunition in our pouches, joy in our hearts, and a terrific load upon our backs, we swung out of the gates to the music of our magnificent band, playing the March of the Legion, never heard save when the Legion goes on active service.

Where we were going, we neither knew nor cared. That it would be a gruelling murderous march, we knew and did not care. We should march and fight as a battalion, or we should be broken up into companies and sections, and garrison desert-outposts where we should be in touch with our enemies—be they raiding Touaregs, rebellious Arab tribes, *jehad*-preaching Moors, or fanatical Senussi—and in a state of constant active-service.

249

Possibly we were going to take part in some comprehensive scheme of conquest, extending French dominion to Lake Tchad or Timbuktu. Possibly we were about to invade and conquer Morocco once and for all.

Our ideas were vague and our ignorance abysmal, but what we did know was, that we were on the road, we carried "sharp" ammunition, we were a self-contained, self-supporting unit of selected men, that the barracks and their killing routine were behind us, and the freedom and movement of active service were before us, with adventure, change, fighting, and the chance of decoration and promotion.

Merrily we sang as we tramped, passing gaily from *"Voilà du Boudin"* to *"La casquette de Père Bougeaud,"* *"Pan, pan, l'Arbi,"* *"Des marches d'Afrique,"* *"Père Brabançon,"* and *"Soldats de la Légion,"* and other old favourites of the march.

Michael, Digby, and I were in one "four" with Maris, and behind us were Hank, Buddy, St. André, and Schwartz. At night, we shared the little tent, which we could build in a minute and a quarter, with the canvas and jointed tent-poles that we carried. We slept on our overcoats with our knapsacks for pillows, our rifles chained together and the chain handcuffed to a man's wrist.

We were keen, we were picked men, and nobody went sick or fell out. Had he done so, he would have died an unpleasant death, in which thirst, Arabs, and hyenas would have been involved.

We cheerfully did our utmost like men, cheerfully grumbled like fiends, cheerfully dropped like logs at the end of a forty-kilometre march, and cheerfully arose like automata, at the sound of the 2 a.m. reveillé bugle.

We had insufficient water, insufficient rice and macaroni, no meat nor vegetables, and insufficient bread, and were perfectly fit and healthy. We had no helmets and no spine-pads, we wore heavy overcoats, we had only a linen flap hanging from our caps to protect our necks, and we had no cases of sunstroke nor heat apoplexy.

And, in time, we reached Ain-Sefra and rested to recoup

and refit, the *fourrier-sergents* having a busy time, chiefly
in the matter of boots.

Here we learnt that the whole of the Sahara was fermenting in one of its periodic states of unrest, simply
asking for peaceful penetration, what with Touareg raids
on protected villages, Senussi propaganda, tribal revolts,
and sporadic outbursts of mutiny and murder.

There was also much talk of a serious concentration in
the south-east, engineered from Kufra, and a "sympathetic strike" on the part of the numerous and warlike
tribes along the Moroccan border.

When this materialised, it would be found that they
had struck simultaneously at every French outpost, fort,
and settlement, on the Saharan border from Morocco to
Tripoli.

The programme, then, was to carry fire and sword
northward to the sea, and sweep the surviving *Roumis*
into it, freeing the land for ever from the polluting presence of these unbelieving dogs.

Let Morocco, Tunisia, Tripoli, and Egypt join hands, and
under the green banner of a purified faith and the spiritual
leadership of Our Lord the Mahdi el Senussi, carry on the
good work in the name of Allah the All-Merciful, the
Compassionate, and Mahomet his Prophet, until Islam
was again free, triumphant, and conqueror of all. . . . .

This we gathered by talking to Arab *goumiers,* marabouts, camel-drivers, and villagers, in their own tongue;
as well as from orderlies and officers' servants who overheard the conversation of their masters at mess. . . .

From Ain-Sefra we marched to Douargala, where a
large force of all arms was concentrating, and from this
place we proceeded south, either to trail the French coat
in the sight of the Arab, or as a reconnaissance in force and
a protective screen behind which the brigade could make
its preparations at leisure and in security.

And, in the fullness of time, after endless desert marching, the battalion found itself strung out along a chain of
oases between which communication was maintained by
camel-patrols, which met half-way and exchanged reports,
orders, information, cigarettes, and bad language.

It was at El Rasa, the last of this chain of oases (which must have marked the course of one of those subterranean rivers which are common in Northern Africa) that our half-company came in contact with the Arabs and we had our first taste of desert warfare.

Arab *goumiers* came in at dawn one day, riding in haste, with the news that they had seen the camp-fires of a big Touareg *harka* about twenty miles to the south, where an ancient well marked the "cross-roads" of two caravan routes, as old as civilisation; routes charted by the bones of countless thousands of camels and of men who had trodden them until they died of thirst, starvation, heat, disease, or murder at the hands of Bedouin and Touareg nomads.

These are the oldest roads in the world and the grim relics that line them are those of yesterday and those of centuries ago. They were ancient when Joseph came to Egypt, and the men and beasts that venture upon them have not changed in fifty centuries.

§ 2.

We were in touch with the enemy at last. At any moment we might be fighting for our lives. We were delirious with excitement.

At once our little force in the oasis and this Arab *harka* became a microcosm of the whole war, and our Lieutenant Debussy sent out a small reconnoitring force under Sergeant-Major Lejaune, which should be to the strung-out battalion what the battalion was to the brigade at Douargala.

It was the good luck of our *escouade* to be selected for this duty, and within half an hour of the arrival of the *goumiers*, we were advancing *en tirailleur* in the direction from which they had come. Over the loose, hot sand we plodded, our scouts far in advance and our flankers far out to left and right.

"Are we the bait of a trap? Or would you call us the point of a spear?" said Michael, marching between Digby and me.

"Both," replied Digby, "a bit of meat on the end of a
spear, say."

And I wondered how many of us would be bits of meat
before nightfall.

Not that I felt in the least degree apprehensive or depressed. If I had to analyse and describe my feelings,
I should say that beneath a strong sensation of pleasurable
excitement was that undercurrent of slight nervous anxiety
which one experiences before going in to bat, or when
seated in a corner of the ring, awaiting the word *"Time"*
at the beginning of a boxing contest.

I would not have been elsewhere for worlds, but at the
same time I wondered what the smack of a bullet felt like,
and how much chance a bayonet stood against the heavy
sword or the lance of a charging Arab. . . .

There was no doubt about it that Sergeant-Major Lejaune
knew his job, and I found myself wishing that he were not
such a wholly hateful person.

I should have liked to admire him as much as I admired
his military skill, and ability as a commander, and I began
to understand how soldiers love a good leader when it is
possible to do so.

One felt that nobody could have handled the situation
with more grasp and certainty than he did, and that if any
kind of catastrophe or disaster ensued, it would be owing
to no fault in the ability, courage, and promptitude of
Sergeant-Major Lejaune.

To watch him conducting operations that day, was to
watch a highly skilled artisan using his tools with the
deftness and certainty of genius.

On a low, flat-topped rocky hill, we halted and rested,
all except Lejaune himself and the scouts whom he sent
to various distant sand-hills and low rocky eminences
which, while visible from the detachment, gave a wide
range of vision in the supposed direction of the enemy.

Among others set to similar tasks, I was ordered to
watch one particular man and to report any movement on
his part. I watched the tiny distant figure through the
shimmering heat haze, which danced over the sand and

stones, until my eyes ached and I was forced, from time to time, to close them and cover them with my hand.

Upon opening them after one of these brief rests, which were absolutely necessary, I saw that he was crawling back from his position. When below the skyline, he rose and ran, stooping, for a short distance. He then halted and signalled *"Enemy in sight."*

The moment that I had pointed him out to Corporal Boldini, Lejaune was notified, and he sent a man named Rastignac running to an eminence, well to our left rear, and a minute later we were lining the edge of our plateau on the side to which this man had disappeared.

Here we lay concealed, and waited.

A few minutes later, the man who had been sent off, fired a shot and exposed himself on the highest point of his rocky hillock.

To my surprise, I saw our scouts retiring and running— not back to us, but to him; and, a minute or two later, I saw a flutter of white on a distant sand-hill.

Rallying on the man who was firing from the top of the rock, the scouts opened fire at distant camel-mounted figures who began to appear over the sand-hills. We received no orders, save to the effect that we should lie as flat and still as the hot stones that concealed us.

Between two of these I watched the scattered fringe of Arabs increase to lines, and the lines to masses of swiftly-moving camel-riders, and soon their deep menacing cry of *"Ul-ul-ul-ul-ul-ullah Akbar,"* came to our ears like the growing roar of an advancing sea.

As they came on, the little party of our scouts fired rapidly, and after about the thousand-yard range, a camel would occasionally sprawl headlong to the ground, or a white-clad figure fall like a sack and lie motionless on the sand.

On swept the Arab *harka* at the top pace of their swift camels, the men in front firing from the saddle, the others brandishing their long, straight swords and waving their lances aloft.

Rapidly and steadily the little band of scouts fired into

the brown of them, and, by now, every bullet was hitting man or beast in the closely-packed irregular ranks of the swiftly-advancing horde.

It was thrilling. I felt I must get a grip upon myself, or I should be shaking with excitement, and unable to shoot steadily when our turn came to take part in the fight.

And then, to my amazement, I saw that our scouts were retreating. One by one, they sprang up from behind rocks and fled to their right rear, each man dropping and firing as his neighbour rose to retreat in his turn. Before long, the little band was again in position, nearer to us and still further behind us. With increased yells, the Arabs swerved to their left and bore down upon them, men and camels falling beneath the magazine-fire of their rifles.

I could scarcely keep still. How long was this unequal fight to continue? None of the scouts had been hit by the wild fire of the camel-riders, but in a couple of minutes they would be overwhelmed by this wave of mounted men, and, out-numbered by fifty to one, would have as much chance as has a fox beneath a pack of hounds.

And as I held my breath, the tiny handful again rose to their feet, turned their backs upon the Arabs, and fled as one man toward a sand-hill in our rear. With a simultaneous yell of mingled execration and triumph, the Arab *harka* swerved again, seemed to redouble their speed, and bore down upon their prey.

And then, Sergeant-Major Lejaune stood up on a rock, gave a crisp order, coolly as on parade, and, at less than fifty yards, the Arab masses received the withering blast of our magazine-fire.

Swiftly as our hands could move the bolts of our rifles and our fingers press the trigger, we fired and fired again into the surging, shrieking, struggling mob, that halted, charged, retired, and then fled, leaving quite half their number behind.

But of those who were left behind, by no means all were killed or even wounded, and our orgy of slaughter rapidly turned to a desperate hand-to-hand fight with dismounted and unwounded Arabs, who, knowing they must die, had but the one idea of gaining Paradise and the remission of sins, in the slaying of an infidel.

With a shout of *"Bayonette au canon,"* Lejaune had us to our feet, and launched us in a fierce bayonet-charge down the slope of our plateau upon the Arab swordsmen, who were rallying to the attack, on foot. Our disciplined rush swept them back, they broke and fled, and, still keeping us in hand, Lejaune quickly had a double rank of kneeling and standing men shooting down the fleeing or still defiant foot-men, and making practice at the remains of the mounted *harka* disappearing over the skyline.

Within half an hour of the first signalling of the approach of the enemy, the only Arabs in sight were those that lay singly and in little bloodstained heaps, in the shallow valley into which they had been decoyed by our scouts.

It was a neat little action, reflecting the highest credit on Lejaune and on the man who was the senior in charge of the scouts. The latter, one Gontran, was promoted corporal, in orders next day, and Sergeant-Major Lejaune made *adjudant*.

The Arabs must have lost over a hundred men in this fight, as against our three killed and five wounded.

Such was my first experience of war, my first "smelling of powder" and my blooding. I had killed a man with cold steel and I think at least three with my rifle.

Reflecting on this I was glad to remember that these Touaregs are human wolves, professional murderers, whose livelihood is robbery with violence, which commonly takes the form of indescribable and unmentionable tortures.

Nor is the *Roumi,* the infidel dog, the favourite object of their treacherous attack, save in so far as he is a more rewarding object of attention. They are as much the scourge and terror of the Arab villager, the nomad herdsman, or the defenceless negro, as they are of the wealthy caravan or their peaceful co-religionists of the town, the *douar,* and the oasis.

The man whom I had killed with my bayonet, had made it necessary to my continued existence, for he rushed at me with a great, heavy, straight-bladed sword, exactly like those used by our Crusaders of old.

Whirling this round his head, he aimed a blow at me that would have split my skull had I not promptly side-stepped, drawing back my bayonet as I did so. As the sword missed my head, I drove at his chest with all my strength, and the curved hilt of my Lebel bayonet touched his breast-bone as he fell staggering back, nearly pulling the rifle out of my hands.

I found afterwards that Digby had had his coat torn under the armpit by a spear, which, as he remarked, was not fair wear, but tear, on a good coat. He had shot his assailant at a range which he estimated as being a good half-inch, and he was troubled with doubts as to whether this would be considered quite sporting in the best Arab circles.

"Of course," he said, "the bird wasn't actually 'sitting' —though he's sitting now. . . ."

Michael, being particularly good with the bayonet, and a noted winner of bayonet *v.* bayonet competitions, had used the butt of his rifle in the mêlée, and seemed to think it unfair of the Arab to wear a turban, that diminishes the neat effectiveness of this form of fighting! However, neither of them was hurt, nor were any of our more immediate friends.

Having buried our dead and obliterated their graves, we retired slowly toward El Rasa, weary to death and thoroughly pleased with ourselves, to make our report. . . .

§ 3.

The pitched battle of El Rasa was fought next day, our battalion holding the oasis against tremendous odds until supports came from the brigade, and the Arabs learnt what quick-firing little mule-guns can do, when given such a target as a huge mob of horse and camel-men advancing *en masse* over a level plain.

As my part in this battle was confined to lying behind

the bole of a palm-tree and shooting whenever I had something to shoot at, I have no adventures to relate. I might as well have spent the day on a rifle-range.

But I saw a magnificent charge of a couple of squadrons of Spahis upon a vastly superior number of Arab cavalry, which, shaken by artillery fire, appeared to be hanging in doubt as to whether to make one of their fierce rushes, overwhelming and desperate, upon the infantry lining the edge of the oasis. It was a thrilling and unforgettable sight. . . .

After the signal victory of El Rasa, the brigade moved on southward and we preceded it, the weeks that followed being a nightmare of marching that ended in the worse nightmare of garrison duty in the ultimate, furthermost, desert outpost of Zinderneuf, where we had the initial misfortune of losing Digby and many of our friends, including Hank and Buddy.

They departed to the mounted-infantry school at Tanout-Azzal, where the gentle art of mule-handling was taught, and the speed of the swift-marching legionary increased by mounting him on a mule. A company of such men was thus rendered as mobile as a squadron.

It was a cruel blow to Michael and me, this separation from our brother and from those best of friends, Hank and Buddy.

However, we were certain to be reunited sooner or later, and there was nothing to do but to make the best of this and the other drawbacks and miseries of Zinderneuf.

CHAPTER V

THE FORT AT ZINDERNEUF

"They learn that they are not as others are,
Till some go mad, and some sink prone to earth,
And some push stumbling on without a star."

THINGS began badly and rapidly grew worse in this
ill-omened mud fort, isolated in the illimitable desert
like a tiny island in the midst of a vast ocean.

Cafard broke out early, and in a very virulent form,
both suicidal and homicidal in its nature.

It took this terrible form, I verily believe, largely by
reason of the fact that Captain Renouf, our Commandant,
shot himself after a month of life in this dreadful oven
of a place. I do not, of course, know his reason for doing
this, but it was rumoured that he found he had contracted a horrible disease. This tragedy cast a deeper
gloom over a place and a community already gloomy
beyond description.

Within a week of this disaster, for a disaster it was
to all of us, a most unusual manifestation of *cafard* was
exhibited, when a corporal killed a sergeant and then
committed suicide. What Corporal Gontran's grievance
against the sergeant was, I do not know, but this again
was an exceedingly unfortunate affair, as, like Captain
Renouf himself, both these men were on the side of the
angels, inasmuch as they were decent, fair-minded, and reasonable people.

But the Fates and the Furies had one more disaster
in store for the unhappy garrison before they were ready
to launch upon our luckless heads the final torrent of destruction.

Lieutenant Debussy, the new Commandant, sickened and
died, and his place was taken by none other than *Adjudant*
Lejaune.

From the moment in which it was known that the Lieutenant was dead, the atmosphere of Zinderneuf changed from bad to worse and rapidly from worse to the worst possible.

The lion-tamer had entered the cage, and the lions, sullen, infuriated, and desperate, knew that he held in one hand the whip that should drive them to revolt, and in the other the revolver that should instantly punish the first sign of it.

§2.

Life at Zinderneuf was not really life so much as the avoidance of death—death from sunstroke, heat-stroke, monotony, madness, or Adjudant Lejaune.

Cafard was rampant; everybody was more or less abnormal and "queer" from frayed nerves, resultant upon the terrific heat and the monotony, hardship, and confinement to a little mud oven of a fort; many men were a little mad, and Adjudant Lejaune, in the hollow of whose hand were our lives and destinies, was a great deal more than a little mad.

From the point of view of the authorities, he was sane enough, for he could maintain an iron discipline; make all reports and returns, to the minute and to the letter; and, if attacked, he could be trusted to keep the Tri-couleur flying while there was a man alive in the Fort.

From the point of view of his subordinates, he was nevertheless a madman, and a very dangerous one.

At times, I was almost glad that Digby was not with us, much as I missed him; and at those times I almost wished that Michael was not, much as I depended on him.

Danger to oneself is unpleasant enough, when it is that of being murdered by a lunatic. When to it is added the danger, and constant fear, of a similar fate overtaking people whom one loves, it becomes ten times worse.

Michael and I both begged each other not to be so foolish as to play into Lejaune's hands, by giving him the faintest chance to accuse us of any breach of duty or discipline, or of so much as an insubordinate look, even under the great-est provocation. But we felt that the time would come when Lejaune would cease to wait for an excuse, and that all we could do was to put off the evil day. . . .

"I'm positively glad, now, that Dig isn't here," said Michael to me, one terrible afternoon, as we lay gasping on our burning cots during siesta hours, in our stifling *caserne*.

"Hank and Buddy too," he added. "One word of back-chat to Lejaune would have been fatal. . . . And Dig might have done it. Buddy more so. . . . Or if Hank once lost control he'd lay Lejaune out like a pole-axed ox. . . ."

"Somebody'll do for him one of these days, if we don't soon get a new commanding officer," said I. "And a good job too."

"Not it," contradicted Michael. "It would be one degree worse than letting him live. . . . These asses would give three loud cheers, march off into the desert, and sur-vive about three days of it—if the Arabs didn't get them before they died of thirst."

"It'll happen," prophesied I. "Schwartz is getting very mysterious and important these days. Oh, it'll happen all right."

"That's what I think." said Michael, "and it's about the worst thing that *could* happen. And if no one goes and does it spontaneously, there'll be a plot to murder him—if there isn't one already, which I believe there is, as you say—and we should have the choice of fighting for Lejaune—(for *Lejaune!*)—or being two of a gang of silly, murdering mutineers with nothing but a choice of beastly deaths—thirst and Arabs in the desert, or court martial and a firing party at dawn. . . . Rotten."

"If he's promoted Lieutenant and kept in command here, he won't last a week," said I. . . . "What's going to happen if they make a plot to mutiny and we're the only two that refuse to join them?"

"We should join Lejaune instead, where dead men tell no tales, I expect," answered Michael.

"What would Sergeant Dupré and Corporal Boldini do?" I speculated.

"If it were a case of saving their skins they'd join the mutineers, I should say—if they were given the option," replied Michael. "They probably loathe Lejaune as much as we do, and neither of them is exactly the man to die for a principle. . . . If they woke to find a gang of bad men, with rifles, round their beds, they'd '*take the cash and let the discredit go,*'—'*Nor heed the rumble of a distant drum*' from Tokotu," he added.

"I doubt if they'd be given the option," I said.

"So do I," agreed Michael. "They're not loved. They've been whips and scorpions in Lejaune's hands too long and too willingly."

"And if we were 'approached' on the subject of a mutiny and did our miserable duty in warning Lejaune and the others?" I asked.

"We should promptly get thirty days' cells from Lejaune for currying favour with horrible lies, and short shrift from the mutineers for being *escrocs*," said Michael. . . .

"Let us give thanks unto the Lord and count our many blessings, my brethren," he yawned, and, at that moment, Schwartz, Haff, Brandt, Bolidar, Delarey, and Vogué entered the room and joined Guantaio, Colonna, and Gotto at the other end of it. Here they conversed in low voices, with occasional glances at us.

§ 3.

And to me, one night, came Schwartz, as I sat in a corner of the little courtyard, trying to imagine that the night was cooler than the day, and this spot, which faced north, less hot than the others.

He was a huge, powerful, hairy ruffian, who would have made a great pirate-captain, for he had brains, courage, and determination, quite unhampered by over-fine scruples of honour or mercy. He was further endowed with a magnetic personality and power of command.

"Are you enjoying life, Smith?" he asked, seating himself beside me.

"Quite as much as you are, Schwartz," I replied.

"Would you like a change?" he enquired.

"I am fond of change," said I.

A brief silence ensued.

"Have you ever seen a pig die?" he asked suddenly.

"No," I replied.

"Well, you soon will," he assured me.

"Feeling ill?" I enquired rudely. I did not like the gross Schwartz.

"You are going to see a big pig die," he went on, ignoring my vulgarity. "A sacred pig. An anointed pig. A striped pig. A promoted pig. Oh, an *adjudant* pig."

"So?" I murmured.

"Yes. *Monsieur le Cochon* is going to become *Monsieur Porc*."

"And are you going to become *Monsieur Charcutier*, 'Mr. Pork-butcher,' so to speak?" I enquired. There could be no harm in knowing all there was to know about this business.

"Aha! my friend," growled the German, "that remains to be seen. So many want a *côtelette de porc* or a *savouret de porc*. We shall have to cast lots."

He was silent for a minute and sat beside me, gnawing his knuckles. He was shaking from head to foot with fever, excitement, or diseased nerves.

"Do you want a chance to be *charcutier?*" he asked.

"I have had no experience of pig-killing," I answered.

"Look you," he growled, seizing my arm, "you will have the experience shortly, *either as pig or as butcher*, for all here will be *cochon* or *charcutier*—in a day or two. See? Choose whether you will be a pig or a butcher. . . . And tell your brother to choose. . . . Meantime, if any man comes to you and says '*porc*,' you reply '*cochon*.' Then he will know that I have spoken to you, and you will know that he is one of us. See? And you and your brother make up your minds quickly. We don't care either way. There are enough of us—oh, enough. . . ." And as somebody approached, he got up and slouched off.

That night I told Michael what I had heard.

The next day it was Guantaio. I was sitting in the same place and he crept towards me purposefully.

"Who's that?" he asked, and, hearing my name, came and sat down beside me, as Schwartz had done.

"It's hot," he said, removing his *képi* and puffing.

"It is," I agreed.

"Are you fond of hot . . . *porc?*" he enquired.

"*Cochon!*" said I playfully.

"Ah!" he replied at once. "What do you think of it all?"

"I never think," said I.

This silenced him for a minute.

"They are ten to one," he said suddenly. "Ten butchers to a pig. What chance has the big pig and one or two biggish pigs against a score of butchers?"

"Ah!" I said imitatively. "What do you think of it all?"

"I never think," said Guantaio, with a malevolent smile. I yawned and stretched and affected to settle myself to slumber.

"How would you and your brother like to be *pigs* if I could find two or three other pigs to join the big pig, and the one or two biggish pigs?" he enquired, nudging me.

I belied my statement that I never thought, and did some rapid thinking.

Had it been arranged that he should sound me as soon as Schwartz had hinted at the assassination of Lejaune? Was it his task to find out whether my name was to be put on the "butcher" list or on the "pig" list? Were all those who did not wholeheartedly join the "butchers" to be shot in their beds on the night of the mutiny?

Or, again, was the rogue trying to find out which was likely to be the stronger party, and did he intend to betray his friends to the non-commissioned officers, if he thought them likely to win?

"How should we like to become *pigs,* you say?" I temporised. . . . "I should hate to be butchered—shouldn't you?"

"Very much," he replied. . . . "But do you know," he

went on, "I have heard of pigs attacking men. *Taking them unawares* and eating them up. . . ."

"I should hate to be eaten up by a pig—shouldn't you?" I observed.

"Very much," he agreed again. "One does not want to be slaughtered by butchers nor eaten by pigs."

"No," said I. "Need either happen?"

"Not if one is a wise pig—forewarned and forearmed—who attacks the butchers, *taking them unawares*," he replied.

"Has the big pig got his eye on the butchers?" I asked.

"No," replied Guantaio. "Nor have the biggish pigs."

"And are you going to open the eyes of the blind pigs?" I enquired.

"I don't know," answered Guantaio. And I had a very strong conviction that he was speaking the truth, for there was a ring of genuine doubt and puzzlement in his voice. At any rate, if he were lying when he said it, he was lying extraordinarily well.

No—he did not know what to do, I decided, and he was simply trying to find out where his private interests lay. Would it pay him better to stand in with his friends, and assist in the mutiny and the murder of Lejaune and the non-commissioned officers? Or would he do better for himself if he betrayed his friends, warned his superiors, and assisted them to defeat the mutineers?

That he was one of the ringleaders of the plot was obvious, since he was the bosom friend of Colonna, Gotto, Vogué, and the rest of Schwartz's band, and had always been one of the circle in their recent confabulations and mutterings together.

I followed the excellent, if difficult, plan of trying to put myself in Guantaio's place, and to think with his mind.

On the one hand, if I were Guantaio, I should see the great dangers attendant on the mutiny. It might fail, and if it succeeded, it could only be the prelude to a terrible march into the desert—a march of doomed men, hunted by the Arabs and by the French alike, and certain to die of thirst and starvation if not killed by enemies.

On the other hand, if I were the excellent Guantaio, I should see the advantages attendant upon playing the part of the saviour of the situation. Reward and promotion were certain for the man who saved the lives of his superiors and the honour of the flag, and who preserved the Fort of Zinderneuf for France. And, of course, it would be the simplest thing in the world for Lejaune, Dupré, Boldini, Guantaio, and a few loyal supporters to defeat the conspirators and secure the mutineers. It would only be a matter of entering the barrack-room at night, seizing the arms, and covering the suspects with the rifles of the loyalists, while the guard arrested them. Anyone resisting, could be shot as soon as he raised a hand.

Lejaune alone could do the business with his revolver, if he entered the room while all were asleep, and shoot any man who did not instantly obey any order that he gave.

In fact, I began to wonder why Guantaio should be hesitating like this. Surely it was to his interest to betray his friends?

Certainly he would not allow any ridiculous scruples to hinder him from committing any treacherous villainy, and certainly it was far less dangerous, in the long run, to be on the side of authority—for the mutineers' real danger only *began* with the mutiny, and it steadily increased from the moment when they set forth into the desert to escape.

More and more I wondered at his hesitation.

And then a light began to dawn upon my brain. This Guantaio was the henchman of his compatriot, Corporal Boldini. Boldini might be killed when the mutineers killed Lejaune; for hate and vengeance were the mainsprings of the plot, and Boldini was hated second only to Lejaune himself. He might not be given the option of joining the mutineers when Lejaune was murdered. Suppose the Italians, Boldini, Guantaio, Colonna, and Gotto, were a united party, led by Boldini, with some sinister end of their own in view? And might not Guantaio be doubtful as to whether the rôle allotted to him were not too much that of the cat's-paw?

Suppose the Boldini party intended to fish in troubled

waters—for a pearl of great price? In other words, suppose they hoped to do what they had certainly tried, and failed, to do in Sidi-bel-Abbès, when they had induced Bolidar to attempt to rob my brother?

Most undoubtedly these rogues believed Boldini's story that we were a gang of jewel-thieves and that Michael carried about with him a priceless gem—to which they had at least as much right as he had. No—I decided—Guantaio spoke the truth when he said he did not know what to do. He was a knave all through. He would betray anybody and everybody. He was afraid that his share in the mutiny would be death, whether it failed or not, and what he really wanted to do was to follow the course most likely to lead him to the possession of two things—a whole skin and a share in the jewel—unless indeed he could get the jewel itself.

"It's a difficult problem, my friend," mused I sententiously. "One does not know which side to take. . . . One would like to be a pig, if the pigs are going to catch the butchers napping. . . . On the other hand, one would like to be a *charcutier,* if the butchers are going to act first. . . .

We sat silent awhile, the excellent Guantaio making a perfect meal of his nails.

"And—that is a point!" I went on. "When *are* the butchers going to kill?"

"*Monsieur le Grand Charcutier*" (by whom, I supposed, he meant Schwartz) "talks of waiting till full moon," was the reply. "If a new Commandant has not come by then, or if *Monsieur le Grand Cochon* has been promoted and given command before then, it would be a good date. . . . Do it at night and have full moon for a long march. . . . Rest in the heat of the day, and then another big moonlight march, and so on. . . ."

"So one has three or four days in which to make up one's mind?" I observed.

"Yes," replied Guantaio. "But I don't advise you waiting three or four days before doing it. . . . Schwartz will want to know in good time. . . . So as to arrange some butchers for each pig, you see. . . ."

"And what about Lejaune?" I asked, since we were to use names and not fantastic titles. "Suppose somebody warned him? What then?"

"Who *would?*" asked Guantaio. "Who loves that mad dog enough to be crucified, and have his throat cut, on his behalf? Why *should* anyone warn him? Wouldn't his death be a benefaction and a blessing to all?"

"Not if things went wrong," I replied. "Nor if it ended in our all dying in the desert."

"No," agreed Guantaio, gnawing away at his nails. "No . . . I hate the desert . . . I fear it . . . I fear it. . . ."

Yes—that was the truth of the matter. He feared being involved in a successful mutiny almost as much as in an unsuccessful one.

"Suppose, *par exemple,* I went and warned Lejaune?" I asked.

"Huh! He'd give you sixty days' *cellule*, and take damned good care you never came out alive," replied Guantaio, "and he would know what he knows already—that everybody hates him and would be delighted to kill him, given a good opportunity. . . . And what would your comrades do to you?"

He laughed most unpleasantly.

No—I decided—friend Guantaio would not like me to warn Lejaune. If Lejaune were to be warned, Guantaio would prefer to do the warning himself.

"How would they know that I was the informer?" I asked.

"Because I should tell them," was the reply. "If Lejaune gets to know—then you and nobody else will have told him."

So that was it? Guantaio could turn informer, having sworn that I was going to do so! Not only would he save his own skin, but Michael would soon have a friend and brother the less, when Schwartz and his merry men heard who had betrayed them.

"Of course, you and your brother would be held to have acted together, as you always do," said Guantaio.

So that was it again? Michael and I being denounced
to the mutineers as traitors, Guantaio might well be moved
to murder and rob Michael—secure in his honourable rôle
of executioner of justice upon a cowardly traitor.

The Legion knew no punishment too severe for infliction
upon any man who acted contrary to the interests of his
comrades. Guantaio need not fear the fate of Bolidar
in such circumstances.

"What would you do if you were me?" I asked.

"Join the butchers," was the prompt reply. "You and
your brother must follow Schwartz. Better the enmity of
Lejaune than of half the barrack-room led by Schwartz.
Lejaune couldn't come straight to your bed and murder
you, anyhow. Schwartz could, and would. And he *will*,
unless you join him. . . ."

Yes, undoubtedly the filthy creature was in grave doubt
about the best course to pursue, and spoke from minute
to minute as new ideas and fresh views occurred to him,
and as his fears and hopes swayed him.

At present he saw the desirability of me and Michael
being mutineers. Just now, he had seen some advantage
in our not being of their party. . . .

Probably the most puzzling and baffling thing to a tor-
tuous mind is simple truth. It is often the subtlest diplo-
macy, when dealing with such people as this. So I decided to speak the plain truth, and leave him to make
what he could of it.

"I shall talk the matter over with my brother," I said,
"and we will decide to-night. Probably we shall warn
Lejaune. You can tell Schwartz that. And I can give
him a definite answer to-morrow. Then he can do as he
pleases."

"You won't warn Lejaune until you have told Schwartz
you are going to do so, of course?" asked Guantaio, and I
had seen his eyes light up as I announced the probability of
our defying Schwartz. That seemed to suit him finely.

"No, I won't," I assured him. "Neither will my
brother. . . . Provided, of course, that nothing will be
done to-night? No mutinying, I mean. . . ."

"Oh, no," said Guantaio. "They're not ready yet. A few haven't joined. Schwartz would like to get everybody, of course; but failing that, he wants to know exactly *who* is to be killed before they start. It will prevent unfortunate accidents. . . . Also they want the full moon. . . ."

"Well—I shall decide to-night," I said. "And now please go away. I want to think—and also I'm not extraordinarily fond of you, Guantaio, really. . . ."

§ 4.

The first thing to do now was to find Michael and decide as to what line we were going to take.

He was on sentry-go, and I must wait.

Meantime, I might find St. André, Maris, Glock, and one or two others who were fundamentally decent honest men of brains and character, and less likely than some of the rest to be driven by blind hatred of Lejaune, or the dominance of Schwartz, into murderous folly that was also suicidal.

St. André was lying on his cot in the barrack-room. He looked at me as I entered. Taking my belt and a polishing-rag, I strolled in the direction of his bed, and came to a halt near him, rubbing industriously.

"Are you fond of *pork, mon ami?*" I enquired softly, without looking away from my work.

"I am something of a *cochon* about it," he replied in a low voice, and added, "Anyhow, I would rather be that than a butcher."

So he had been approached, too.

"Follow me outside when I go," I said.

A few minutes later he found me in the courtyard, and I learned that Schwartz had sounded him that day; told him that he must choose between being a pig or a butcher; and had given him a couple of days in which to make up his mind. Schwartz had concluded by informing St. André that all who were not *for* him would be treated as being *against* him, and that eighty per cent of the men had willingly taken the oath to follow him and to obey him absolutely. . . .

"What are you going to do, St. André?" I asked.

"What you and your brother do," was the immediate reply.

He went on to say that he had thought of nothing else from the moment he had learnt of the plot, and that he had come to the conclusion that he would join with Michael and me, to do what seemed the best thing.

"You see, my friend," he concluded, "one, of course, cannot join in with these poor madmen—one has been an officer and a gentleman. Even if one *had* sunk low enough to do such a thing, and one eased one's conscience by saying that Lejaune deserves death, the fact remains that these lunatics can but step from the frying-pan into the fire."

"Exactly," I agreed.

"Here we live—in hell, I admit—but we do *live,* and we are not here for ever," he went on. "Out in the desert we shall not live. Those who do not die of thirst, will die by slow torture under the knives of the Arab women."

"They will," said I.

"Besides," he continued, "I would not join them if we could march straight into the service of the Sultan of Morocco and be welcomed and rewarded with high rank in his army. . . . I am a Frenchman and have been an officer and a gentleman. . . . I am here through no fault of my own. St. André is my real name. My brother is a Lieutenant in a Senegalese battalion. . . . But you and your brother are not Frenchmen, and if you could get to Morocco, each of you could be another Kaid McLean. . . . But you could not get to Morocco on foot from here. . . . You would be hunted like mad dogs, apart from all question of food and water. . . . You could not do it. . . ."

"We are not Frenchmen and we have not been officers, St. André," I replied; "but we are gentlemen—and we do not murder nor join murder-gangs. . . . And as you say—we could not do it and would not if we could."

"No, I knew you would not join them," said St. André, seizing my hand, "and I told myself I should do just what you and your brother did."

"Well—I'll talk it over with him as soon as he comes off

duty, and we will let you know what we decide," I said, "but certainly it will not be to join them.

"Meanwhile," I added, "you get hold of Maris—he's a decent good chap, and see what he has got to say. You might try Glock, Dobroff, Marigny, Blanc, and Cordier, too, if you get a chance. . . . They are among the least mad in this lunatic asylum."

"Yes," agreed St. André, "if we can form a party of our own, we may be able to save the situation," and he went off.

I waited for Michael, sitting on a native bed, of string plaited across a wooden frame, that stood by the courtyard wall near the guard-room.

Seated here in the stifling dark, I listened to the gibberings, groans, yells, and mad laughter that came from the *cellules,* where some of Lejaune's victims were being driven more and more insane by solitary confinement and starvation.

When Michael was relieved, I followed him as he went to the barrack-room to put his rifle in the rack and throw off his kit.

"I'll be sitting on the *angareb,*" I said. "More developments."

"I'll be with you in five minutes," he replied.

When he joined me, I told him what Guantaio had said, and I added my own views on the situation, together with those of St. André.

Michael listened in silence.

"Position's this, I think," he said, when I had finished. "Schwartz and his band of lunatics proposing to murder Lejaune and anybody who stands by him, Guantaio has given the show away to Corporal Boldini because he thinks the mutiny too risky. Boldini wants to join the mutineers if they're likely to be successful—but not otherwise. Probably he, Guantaio, Colonna, Gotto, and Bolidar are in league to get the mighty 'diamond'—one way or the other—out of this mutiny. If we join the mutineers, Boldini and Co. will join, too, with the idea of killing me and robbing me in the desert and getting to Morocco with the Cullinan-Kohi-

noor. . . . Or to put it more truly, Boldini would get the
'Co.' to do the murdering and stealing, and then kill or
rob whichever of his gang brought it off. If we refuse to
join the mutineers, Boldini's plan would then be to get
Guantaio to murder me in my bed—ostensibly for being
a traitor to the noble cause of mutiny—and pinch the Great
Diamond from my belt. . . . Failing that, Boldini would
use us in helping to suppress the mutiny, hoping that, in
the scrap, I might get done in, and he could rob my corpse.
He could do more than hope it. He could arrange it. . . .''

"On the other hand," said I, "Boldini may know nothing whatever about the plot, and Guantaio may be wondering whether to let the mutiny go on, or whether to warn
his old pal Boldini and give the show away."

"Quite so," agreed Michael. "We're absolutely in the
dark in dealing with hopeless congenital bred-in-the-bone
liars like Guantaio. We can only go on probabilities, and,
on the whole, the swine seemed to be egging you on to join
the plot. . . . Well, that means he has some definite personal interest in our joining it. Obviously if he hadn't, he
wouldn't care a damn whether we joined it or not."

"What's to be done, Beau?" I asked.

"Get together an opposition-gang of non-mutineers, and
then tell Schwartz plainly that we are going to warn
Lejaune and also going to obey Lejaune's orders on the
subject," was the prompt reply.

"Exactly," said I. "Just about what I told Guantaio.
. . . And St. André will stand in with us, whatever we decide to do.

"But suppose we can get no one else," I pondered.

"Then we and St. André will warn Lejaune and tell
him he can count on us three to be true to our salt," said
Michael.

"Without warning Schwartz?" I asked.

"Certainly not," replied Michael. "We can't sneak like
that."

"Of course, Schwartz and Co. will do us in, as traitors,"
I observed.

"Probably," agreed Michael. "Try to, anyhow."

"If we can get up a strongish party, Schwartz's lot may chuck the idea of mutiny," he went on. "If they don't, it will be a case of who strikes first. We must warn Lejaune the moment we've made it quite clear to Schwartz that we're going to do so then and there, unless he gives up the whole idea. . . . Whether he gives it up, or not, will depend on the number we can get to back us."

We sat silent for a minute or two, pondering this cheerful position.

"Tell you what," he said suddenly, "we'll call a meeting. The Briton's panacea. To-morrow evening at six, the other side of the oasis, and we'll invite St. André, Blanc, Cordier, Marigny, and any other Frenchmen who'd be likely to follow St. André. Then there's Maris, Dobroff, Glock, and Ramon, among the foreigners, who might join us. . . . I wish to God that Digby, Hank, and Buddy were here."

"They'd make all the difference," said I.

"Well—if that lot will join us, we can probably turn Schwartz's murder-party into a mere gang of ordinary deserters, if go they must. . . ."

Shortly afterwards, St. André, looking for us, came to where we were sitting.

"I've spoken to Maris," said he, "and he's with you two, heart and soul. I also sounded Marigny, but he takes the line that we can't possibly be such curs as to warn the unspeakable Lejaune and betray our own comrades."

"We can't be such curs as not to do so," said Michael.

"Precisely what I tried to make him see," replied St. André. "It's a question of the point of view and of the degree of mental and moral development. . . . To us it is unthinkable that we should stand by and see murder done, the regiment disgraced, the Flag betrayed, and the fort imperilled. . . . We are soldiers of France. . . ."

He stood up and saluted dramatically, but not self-consciously, in the direction of the flagstaff.

"To Marigny and his kind," he went on, "it is just as unthinkable that, having been entrusted with a secret by a comrade, they should betray this secret and thwart and endanger the friends who have put their faith in them."

"The point of view, as you say," agreed Michael. "Personally, though, I've not been entrusted with a secret by a comrade. I have merely had a threatening and impudent message from a ruffianly blackguard named Schwartz. He tells me he is going to commit a murder. I reply that he is not going to commit a murder, and that unless he abandons the intention, I am going to warn his victim. That seems a clear issue to me."

"And to me," said St. André.

"I also found Blanc to be much of the same mind as Marigny," he went on. "Averse from promoting or even condoning murder, but even more averse from 'betraying' his comrades. . . . I've only spoken to those three so far. . . ."

"Well, look here," said Michael. "To-morrow at six, beyond the oasis. All our friends and all who are not actually of Schwartz's gang. You get Marigny, Blanc, and Cordier, and any other Frenchman you think might join us, and we'll bring Maris, Ramon, Dobroff, and Glock, and possibly one or two more. They'll come. . . . They'll come, because, obviously, it's a life-or-death matter for all of us. We must try to see that none of Schwartz's gang know about the meeting, at any rate until it's over—but if they do, we can't help it. I suppose we have as much right to lay plans as they have?"

"It's a good idea," agreed St. André. "I'll be there and bring whom I can. About six o'clock."

§ 5

Next evening, a handful of the better sort assembled near the *shaduf* in the shade of the palm-grove, out of sight of the fort. Besides Michael, St. André, Maris, and myself, there were Cordier, Blanc, Marigny, Ramon, Dobroff, Glock, Vaerren, and one or two others—fifteen or sixteen of us altogether—enough, as Michael remarked to me, to control events, provided a united party, with a common policy, could be formed.

But this proved impossible. Ideas of right and wrong, honour and dishonour, fair dealing and vile dealing, were too discrepant and probably tinctured by other thoughts and motives, such as those of fear, hatred, ennui, vengeance, and despair.

Michael addressed the meeting first.

"As you all very well know," said he, "there is a plot to murder Lejaune and the non-coms., to desert and to abandon the fort. Schwartz is the ringleader and says that those who do not declare themselves supporters will be considered as enemies—and treated as such. Personally, I do not do things because Schwartz says I must, nor do I approve of shooting men in their beds. Supposing I did, I still should disapprove of being led out into the desert by Schwartz, to die of thirst. Therefore I am against his plot—and I invite you all to join with me and tell Schwartz so. We'll tell him plainly that unless he gives up this mad scheme of murder and mutiny, we shall warn Lejaune. . . ."

Here a growl of disapproval from Marigny and Blanc, and some vigorous head-shaking, interrupted Michael's speech.

"I swear I will warn Lejaune," put in St. André, "but I will warn Schwartz first—and if he likes to drop the murder part of the scheme, he can do what else he likes. Any sacred imbecile who wants to die in the desert can go and do it, but I have nothing to do with mutinies. . . ."

"No treachery!" roared Marigny, a typical old soldier, grizzled and wrinkled; an honest, brainless, dogged creature who admired Schwartz and loathed Lejaune.

"Don't bray like that, my good ass," said Michael turning to him, "and try not to be a bigger fool than God meant you to. Where is the treachery in our replying to Schwartz, *'Thank you, we do not choose to join your murder-gang. Moreover, we intend to prevent the murder—so drop the idea at once.'* Will you kindly explain how the gentle Schwartz is thus 'betrayed'?"

"I say it *is* betrayal of comrades—to tell an anointed, accursed, nameless-named dog's-tail like Lejaune that they are plotting against him. Treachery, I say," replied Marigny.

Michael sighed patiently.

"Well—what are you going to do, Marigny—since you

must either be against Schwartz or for him?'' asked Maris.

"I'm *for* him," replied Marigny promptly.

"A slinking, skulking murderer?" asked Michael contemptuously. "I thought you were a soldier—of sorts."

"I'm for Schwartz," said Marigny.

"Then go to him," snapped Michael. "Go on. . . . Get out. . . . We should prefer it—being neither cowards afraid of Schwartz, nor creeping murderers."

Marigny flushed, clenched his fists and, with an oath, put his hand to his bayonet and made as though to spring at my brother; but he evidently thought better of it as Michael closed his right hand and regarded the point of Marigny's chin.

With a snarl of "Dirty traitors!" the old soldier turned and strode away.

"Anybody else think as he does?" asked Michael.

"I can't agree to betraying old Schwartz," said Blanc, a Marseilles seaman, noisy, jolly, brave, and debonair; a rotund, black-eyed, bluff Provençal.

"Well—say what you are going to do then," said Michael sharply. "Join Schwartz's murderers or else join us."

"I can't join Lejaune's boot-lickers," said Blanc.

"Then join Schwartz's gang of assassins. You may perhaps be safer there," said Michael, and Blanc departed grumbling.

"I must join my compatriots, I'm afraid," said Glock.

"You are 'afraid'!" mocked Michael. "You have said it! It is Schwartz you are afraid of. You needn't be. You'll be safer outside that gang of murderers."

"I can't betray my compatriots," repeated Glock.

"Well—can you go to them and say—(*what is the truth*) —'*I don't believe in murder and I am certain this business will end in the deaths of* ALL *of us. Drop it or I and my friends will make you.*' Can you do that?" asked Michael.

Big, simple Glock, with his blue eyes and silly face, could only scratch his head and shuffle awkwardly from one foot to another.

"They'd kill me," he said.

"They certainly will kill you of thirst, if you let them lead you out there," argued Michael, with a wave of his arm to the encompassing desert.

"It seems we've all got to die, either way," said Glock.

"It's what I am trying to prevent, isn't it, fat-head?" answered Michael. "If the decent men of this garrison would act together and tell Schwartz to stop his silly tricks, no one need die."

"Except those whom *Lejaune* is killing," said Cordier, a clever and agreeable Frenchman who had certainly been a doctor, and whose prescriptions and treatment his comrades infinitely preferred to those of any army surgeon. "If that pariah cur of the gutters of Sodom and Gomorrah could be shot with safety to the rest of us—I'd do it myself to-night, and write my name among those of the benefactors of the human race."

"Oh? Where do *you* stand then?" asked Michael.

"I come in with you and St. André," replied Cordier, "though I admit my sympathies are wholly with Schwartz. Still . . . one's been a gentleman. . . ."

And in the end we found that only Cordier could really be depended upon to join Michael, St. André, Maris, and myself as a staunch and reliable party of anti-Schwartz, pro-duty-and-discipline non-murderers, prepared to tell the mutineers that they must drop their assassination plot, or Lejaune would be warned.

One by one, the others went off, some apologetic and regretful, some blustering, some honestly anxious to support what they considered Schwartz's brave blow for their rights, some merely afraid to do what they would have liked to do.

When we five were at length alone, Michael said, "Well, I'm afraid we're not going to scare Schwartz off his scheme."

"No," agreed Cordier. "It looks more as though we are only going to provide him with some extra labour. More little pigs. . . ."

"There won't be any pigs if Lejaune acts promptly," said St. André.

"None," agreed Maris, "and I'm almost tempted to vote for warning Lejaune *before* saying anything to Schwartz. It would give us more chance. . . ."

"No. No. We can't do that," said Cordier. "We must give old Schwartz a fair show. If he'll cut out the murder items from his programme, we'll say nothing, of course, and he can carry on. If he won't, we'll do our duty as decent folk, and give Lejaune his chance."

"Will he take it?" I asked. "Will he listen?"

"Not to one of us alone," said St. André. "But he'd have to take notice of a deputation, consisting of the five of us, all telling the same tale."

"A deputation consisting of ourselves, coming from ourselves?" smiled Cordier.

"After all, though," asked Maris, "does it matter if he believes or not? Suppose one of us goes and tells him the truth—isn't that enough? If he likes to punish the man and ignore his warning, that's his affair."

"Quite," agreed Michael. "But it's ours too! We don't want to be shot in our beds because Lejaune won't listen to us. . . . If Schwartz isn't forestalled, every man in this fort who hasn't joined his gang by the day after to-morrow will share Lejaune's fate."

"That means us five, Boldini, Dupré, and Lejaune," said Cordier.

"Unless Boldini is in with them,—which is quite likely," put in St. André.

"Yes, seven of us," mused Michael, "even without Boldini. If Lejaune listens to our tale of woe and acts promptly, we five and the two non-coms. are a most ample force for him to work with. . . . Simply a matter of acting a night before they do—and there need be no bloodshed either."

"Fancy fighting to protect *Lejaune!*" smiled Cordier. "Enough to make *le bon Dieu* giggle."

"We're fighting to protect the Flag," said St. André. "Lejaune is incidental. We're going to fight a murderous mutiny—and another incidental is that we are probably going to save our own lives thereby. . . ."

"Who'll tell Schwartz?" interrupted Cordier.

"I will," said Michael.

"We all will," said I. "Let us five just go to him to-gether and warn him. We won't emphasise the fact that we speak for ourselves only."

"That's it," agreed St. André. "We'll tell Schwartz that we're a 'deputation' to him—and do the same when we go on to interview Lejaune—if that's necessary."

And so the five of us agreed to go in search of Schwartz then and there, to tell him that we would take no part in mutiny and murder, and to warn him that we should report the matter at once, unless he agreed to abandon the part of his scheme that included the slaughter of superiors and the coercion of comrades.

§ 6.

As we left the oasis and strolled towards the fort, we met a man carrying pails, for water. As he passed, I saw it was the Portuguese, Bolidar, the man who had been so roughly handled for attempted theft in our barrack-room at Sidi-bel-Abbès. He had always pretended that, on that melancholy occasion, he had strayed, under the influence of liquor, into the wrong room, and that, when caught, he was merely getting into what he thought was his own bed!

Warned by Hank and Buddy, however, we, on the other hand, regarded the gentleman as the miserable tool of Boldini, who had taken him up when Guantaio, Colonna, and Gotto had declined to do his stealing for him.

As he passed Michael, he half stopped, winked, made as though to speak, and then went on. Looking back, I saw that he had halted, put his pails down, and was staring after us.

Seeing me turn round, he signalled to me to come to him, and began walking towards me.

Here was a man with whom a quiet talk might be very useful, particularly as he had made the first overtures.

"I want to speak to your brother and you," he whispered. "Privately. I daren't be seen doing it. I am in Hell—and yet I am going to Hell. Yes, I am going to Hell—and yet I am in Hell now."

He was evidently in a very unbalanced state of mind.
He was trembling, and he looked terribly ill.

"Go into the oasis and wait," said I. "I'll bring my
brother along soon."

"I must hide . . . I must hide . . . I must hide," he
kept repeating.

"All right," I agreed. "You hide. I'll stroll along
whistling '*Père Bougeaud*' when I bring my brother."

"Lejaune will tear my throat out. . . . He'll eat my
heart. . . . So will Schwartz. . . . So will Boldini. . . ."

"Well, you won't feel the second two," I comforted him,
"and you haven't got three hearts. . . . You tell us all
about it," I added soothingly. "We'll look after you.
Pull yourself together now," for I thought he was going
to burst into tears.

"You won't bring anybody else? You won't tell anybody else? Not a word?" he begged.

"Not a soul. Not a word," I replied. "You wait for
us in the far clump of palms beyond the well," and I went
after Michael.

As soon as I could speak to him alone, I told him about
Bolidar.

"Good," said Michael. "We'll hear what the merchant's
got to say before we tackle Schwartz. The bold Bolidar
evidently wants to hedge a bit, for some reason. . . . 'When
rogues fall out.' . . . Let's go straight back before he
changes what he calls his mind."

Michael ran on and asked St. André and the others to
wait a little while and do nothing until he returned.

We then went back to the oasis, and as we passed near
the well, I whistling "*Avez-vous vu la casquette de Père
Bougeaud?*" Bolidar joined us, trembling with fear and
fever.

We went and sat down together with a high sand-hill
between us and the oasis.

At first, Bolidar was incoherent and almost incomprehensible, but soon it was quite clear that the wretched
creature was turning to us as a last hope and last resort
in his extremity of anxiety, suspense, and terror.

Realising what it was that drove him to unburden him
self to us—sheer cowardly fear for his own wretched skin
—we never for one instant doubted the truth of what he
said.

He oozed truth as he did abject funk, from every pore,
and he showed it in every gleam of his bloodshot rolling
yellow eyes, and in every gesticulation of his trembling
dirty yellow hands.

"My friends," he gabbled, "I must confess to you and
I must save you. I can bear it no longer. My conscience.
. . . My rectitude. . . . My soul. . . . My sense of grati-
tude. . . ."

Michael winked at me. We did not value Bolidar's conscience and gratitude as highly as we did his state of trembling fright, when estimating his motives for "confession." . . .

"On that terrible night when I was so cruelly misjudged
and so cruelly treated, you tried to save me. . . . Yes, even
though it was you whom I was supposed to be trying to rob.
. . . An absurd idea, of course . . ." and he laughed nerv-
ously.

There was no doubting the fact that the gentle dago was
in a rare state of terror. His convulsive swallowings,
drawn yellow features, tremblings and twitchings, clenched
hands and wild eyes, were really distressing.

"Most absurd idea, of course," murmured Michael.
"What is it you want to tell us?"

"Your diamond! Your diamond!" whispered Bolidar
hoarsely, gripping Michael's wrist and staring into his eyes.

"Ah—my diamond. And what about it?" said Michael
gently.

"Lejaune! Lejaune means to get it," he hissed. "And
he'll kill me! He'll kill me! If he doesn't Schwartz will.
. . . Or Boldini. . . . What *shall* I do! What *can* I do!"
he screamed.

Michael patted the poor rascal's shoulder.

"There! There! Never mind. No one's going to kill
you," he soothed him, almost as though he had been a baby.
"Now tell us all about it and we'll see what can be done.
. . . You join our party and you'll be safe enough."

"*Your* party?" asked Bolidar. "What is *your* party? And what are you going to do?"

"Oh—we are a party all right. The stoutest fellows in the garrison—and we're going to *warn* Lejaune—if Schwartz doesn't agree to give up the murder part of the plot," replied Michael.

"You're going to do *what?*" asked Bolidar, open-eyed and open-mouthed.

"Going to warn Lejaune," repeated Michael.

Bolidar threw his hands up and shook with mirthless laughter.

"*But he* KNOWS!—*He* KNOWS! *He* KNOWS ALL ABOUT IT, *and who's in it—and when it's to be—and every word that's said in the place!*" cackled Bolidar in a kind of broken, hoarse voice.

Michael and I stared at each other aghast.

"Who tells him?" asked Michael.

"*I do,*" was the proud reply of this shameless animal. "And when he has got your diamond, he will kill me," he snivelled.

I was absolutely staggered. If Lejaune knew all about it, what of our precious threat to Schwartz? And what was our position now?

"Why doesn't Lejaune do something then?" asked Michael.

"Oh, he'll *do* something all right," said Bolidar. "He'll do a good deal, the night before Schwartz and his fools intend to strike."

"Why does he wait?" we asked simultaneously.

"To see what you two are going to do," was the reply. "If you join Schwartz you'll be killed *with* Schwartz, the night before the mutiny is due—and I'm to secure the diamond. It is not really supposed that you'll join him though. And if you don't join Schwartz you are to be killed in the attack *on* him instead."

"By whom?" asked Michael.

"*By me,*" replied Bolidar. "You see, if you should join Schwartz, I am to be loyal and enter the barrack-room with Lejaune and the others on the night. As we cover the

mutineers with our rifles, mine is to go off and kill you.
. . . If you don't join Schwartz, I am to be a mutineer,
and when *you* enter the barrack-room with Lejaune and the
loyal party, in the night, I am to shoot you from my bed.
. . . Either way you are to die—and I am perfectly sure
that I shall die too. . . . Oh, God! Oh, Jesus Christ! Oh,
Holy Virgin! Oh, Saints in Heaven!'' he blubbered.

"And suppose I refuse to give Schwartz any answer, and
remain perfectly neutral?'' asked Michael.

"Then I am to harangue the mutineers and urge them
to kill you as a non-supporter! You *and* any others that
won't join them, so that it will not look as though I have
any personal motive or feeling with regard to you specially.
Then I am to offer to 'execute' you. . . . Having done it,
I am to get the diamond and give it to Lejaune. . . . Yes,''
he added with another whispered gasp, "Lejaune is going
to shoot me if you are killed without my securing the jewel
for him . . .'' and he rocked his body to and fro in despair.

"He ought to have an apron to throw over his head and
cry into—like an old peasant woman whose cow has died,''
said Michael in English.

"Yes,'' I agreed. "Let's get all we can out of the brute
before we let him go.''

"Is Boldini in this?'' Michael asked Bolidar. "I mean,
are he and Lejaune working together?''

"Well—Boldini knows that Lejaune knows,'' was the
reply. "And those two are going to use Dupré and St.
André and Cordier and Maris and you two, for the arrest
of the unarmed mutineers in the middle of the night. That
is, if you refuse to join Schwartz as they anticipate. . . .
But I doubt if Boldini and Lejaune quite trust each other.
Guantaio says they don't. He thinks that Boldini intends
to get the diamond for himself, and that Lejaune suspects
as much. At least that is what Guantaio tells me—but I
don't wholly trust him. . . .''

"Don't you really?'' said Michael.

"No. I don't think he's absolutely honest,'' said Bolidar
doubtfully.

"You surprise me,'' admitted Michael. "The dirty
dog!''

"He has made proposals to me which I have rejected with contempt," said Bolidar.

"Dangerous?" asked Michael.

"Absurdly," replied Bolidar. "Besides, how was I to know that I should get my share? It's bad enough to *have* to trust Lejaune as one is compelled to do—without risking things with a rascal like Guantaio."

"Has Boldini made—er—proposals which you rejected with contempt?" Michael enquired.

"Oh, yes. But as I pointed out to him—Lejaune is *adjudant* while Boldini is only *caporal*."

"And what did he say to that?" asked Michael.

"That a live *caporal* is better than a dead *adjudant*," was the interesting reply.

"Sounds sinister," I observed in English.

"Nice little crowd," said Michael in the same language. "One really doesn't know where one is, nor where to start on the job of making head or tail of the business."

"Let's get this clear now," he said to Bolidar. "You are Lejaune's—er—man. You warned him of Schwartz's plot to mutiny and kill him, while acting as though you were a ringleader. You have told every detail to Lejaune and kept him up to date with every development. Lejaune has given you the job of killing me. If I join Schwartz, you are to turn loyal, go over to Lejaune, and shoot me in my bed when we are arrested.

"If I refuse to join Schwartz you are to continue as a mutineer and shoot me, from your bed, when I come in with the loyal party to arrest you.

"If I decline to declare myself you are to be my executioner, self-appointed, on behalf of the worthy mutineers —who will have no neutrals about. And all this in order that Lejaune may get a diamond that is supposed to be in my possession. . . ."

Bolidar was sunk in a lethargy of miserable thought. He slowly nodded in affirmation.

"And probably Boldini has a plan of his own which involves a dead *adjudant* and leaves a live *caporal*—also in pursuit of a diamond! And Boldini's plan, I suppose, is to support Lejaune until he has got the diamond, and then withdraw the support—and the diamond? . . .''

Bolidar came out of his fit of brooding abstraction.

"That is what Guantaio said," he replied. "He wanted me to join Boldini, Colonna, Gotto, and himself. We were to plot, and kill Lejaune *and* those who stood by him against the mutineers, after those poor fools had been arrested and either shot (in 'self-defence,' of course) or put in the cells. When we had got the diamond we could decide whether to liberate the mutineers and use them in fighting our way to Morocco, or whether their mouths had better be closed. . . . We could set fire to the fort and clear out—and everything would be put down to the account of the Arabs. . . .''

"And why did you not fall in with this pretty scheme?" asked Michael.

"Well—who could trust Boldini? Or Guantaio? Or any of them, for that matter? They are not *honest* men. Once Boldini had the diamond, what would be the worth of the life of the man who had a claim on a share of it? To have the diamond would, of course, be death! To be one of a syndicate owning it would, of course, be death! Even to know who had got it would be death, for the man who had it would kill you lest you robbed him or demanded your share. . . . How *can* one work with such dishonest people?" and the speaker's voice broke with righteous indignation.

"And has Guantaio made any other proposals which you have rejected with contempt?" asked Michael.

"Oh—any number," replied Bolidar. "He seems to think I'm a fool. He actually proposed that I should rob you, and he and I should desert together, before all this mutiny business takes place. I was almost tempted—but—but——''

"Quite," said Michael. "It must be a great handicap."

"It is," agreed Bolidar. "And besides," he added, "how could two men walk across two thousand miles of desert, apart from the question of *goums* and the Touaregs? . . . And wouldn't Guantaio murder me directly we got to Morocco?"

"Unless you murdered him first," said Michael.

"Yes," agreed Bolidar, "but one might leave it too

late . . ." and he meandered on about the untrustworthiness of Italians.

"Well, now. Let's get down to business," Michael interrupted. "What have you told us all this for? What do you want us to do?"

"Why," said Bolidar, "I felt I must deal with honest men and I must get away. It is certain death for me. If I get the diamond I shall be killed for it, or for knowing that Lejaune has got it. If I don't get it, Lejaune will kill me for failing him, or else for knowing too much when there is a court martial about the mutiny. . . ."

"Well?" Michael encouraged him.

"I thought that if I told you two all about it—the real truth to honest men—you would save my life and your own, and give me a share in the diamond."

"How save our lives?" Michael asked.

"All desert together before the mutiny, and you give me a third-part share in the diamond when we are safe."

"How do you know we should keep our promise?" asked Michael.

"Because you are English. . . . In Brazil, we say, '*Word of an Englishman!*' and '*Word of an American!*' when we are swearing to keep faith. If you promise, I know you will perform."

"This is very touching," said Michael. "But suppose I give you my word that I haven't got a diamond and never possessed a diamond in my life?"

Bolidar smiled greasily, as at one who must have his little jest.

"Oh, *Señor!*" he murmured, waggling his head and his hands idiotically.

"One knows of the little parcel in your belt-pouch," he said.

"Oh, one does, does one?" smiled Michael. "Fancy that now!"

Silence fell.

"Well—as you just said, two or three people can't march off into the desert and expect to live for more than a day or two," observed Michael after a while.

"We might make a party," suggested Bolidar. "It is known that St. André, Maris, Cordier, and one or two more more refuse to listen to Schwartz's plan to kill Lejaune."

"Nor are they deserters," said Michael.

"No—but when they know that they are to be killed by the mutineers if they don't join them, or to be killed by Lejaune if they do—what then? . . . Tell them the truth —that Lejaune is going to have no survivors of this mutiny —whichever side they may be on. No. He's going to have the diamond and the credit and glory of suppressing the mutiny and saving the fort single-handed. He'll teach *les légionnaires* to mutiny! Their mutiny shall end in death for the lot of them—and in wealth and promotion for Lejaune. He sees himself an officer and a rich man on the strength of this fine mutiny. . . . And what happens to the men who told him about the diamond—the men who helped him and risked their lives for him? What, I ask you? . . . Death, I tell you. *Death! Death! Death!*" he screamed, trembling and slavering like a trapped beast.

"And who *did* tell him about this wonderful diamond?" asked Michael.

"Boldini," replied Bolidar. "As soon as he rejoined, he told him of the gang of famous London jewel-thieves who had fled from the English police to the Legion. He and Guantaio and Gotto were to get it and give it to Lejaune, who would protect them and who would either place it and share with them, or keep it until they had all served their time. . . . I don't know."

"And they put you up to steal it in Sidi, eh?" asked Michael. "Why you?"

But Bolidar spurned such an unworthy suggestion.

"Anyhow, we're getting away from the point," Michael interrupted him. "What's to be done? We're certainly not going to desert. I wonder if one could possibly persuade the gentle Lejaune that there's no such thing as a diamond in Zinderneuf?"

"What—pretend you hid it and left it—at Sidi-bel-Abbès?" said Bolidar. "That's an idea! . . ."

Michael laughed.

"Did you leave it at Sidi?" asked Bolidar.

"I most certainly have not got a diamond here," replied Michael.

"Do you swear it by the name of God? By your faith in Christ? By your love of the Blessed Virgin? And by your hope for the intercession of the Holy Saints?" asked Bolidar.

"Not in the least," replied Michael. "I merely say it. I have not got a diamond—'*Word of an Englishman.*'"

"It's a chance," whispered Bolidar. "Dear Christ! It's a chance. Oh, lovely Christ, help me! . . . I'll tell Lejaune you left it at Sidi."

"Tell him what you like," said Michael.

Bolidar pondered.

"Huh! Anyhow, he'll *make sure* you haven't got it," he said darkly, and rose to his feet. "But I'll try it. I'll try it. There is a small hope. . . . I'll tell you what he says," he added.

"You'll tell us *something,* I've no doubt," replied Michael, as the heroic Portuguese took up his pails and slunk off.

§ 7.

"Well, my son—a bit involved, what?" smiled my brother as we were left in solitude.

"What *can* one do?" I asked feebly.

"Nothing," replied Michael promptly and cheerfully. "Just await events and do the straight thing. I'm not going to bunk. And I'm not going to join any beastly conspiracy. But I think I'm going to 'beat Bolidar to the draw' as Hank and Buddy would say—when he tries to cover me with his rifle."

"In other words, you're going to shoot friend Bolidar before friend Bolidar shoots you?" I said.

"That's it, my son. If he's cur enough to do a dirty murder like that, just because Lejaune tells him to, he must take his little risks," replied Michael.

"And if that happens—I mean if I see him cover you and you shoot him—Lejaune is going with him. It is as much Lejaune's murder as it is Bolidar's," I said.

"You're going to shoot Lejaune, eh?" asked Michael.

"I am," said I, "if Bolidar covers you. Why should he cover *you*, in particular, out of a score of so of men, unless he has been told to shoot you?"

"Well—we'll tell Bolidar just what's going to happen, and we'll invite him to tell Lejaune too. It would be fairer, perhaps," said Michael.

"Golly," I observed. "Won't it make the lad gibber! One more slayer on his track!"

"Yes," smiled Michael. "Then he'll know that if neither Lejaune nor Boldini nor Schwartz kills him, *I* shall. Poor old Bolidar. . . ."

"What about poor old us?" I asked.

"We're for it, I should say," replied Michael. "Of course, Lejaune won't believe that this wonderful diamond they are talking about has been left at Sidi, and he'll carry on."

"I'm mudlded," I groaned. "Let's get it clear now:

"*One:* We tell Schwartz we won't join his gang, and that we will warn Lejaune of the plot to murder him . . ."

"Or shall we tell Schwartz that *Lejaune knows all about it?*" Michael interrupted.

"Good Lord, I'd forgotten that," I said. "I suppose we'd better."

"Then they'll crucify poor old Bolidar for good, this time," grinned Michael. "Serve him right too. Teach him not to go about murdering to order. . . ."

"We need not say who told us that Lejaune knows," I observed.

"And then they *will* know that you and I are beastly traitors!" said Michael. "Of course, they will at once think that we told him ourselves."

"Probably Guantaio has told them that, and done it himself, meanwhile," I suggested.

"Oh, damn it all—let's talk about something else," groaned Michael. "I'm sick of their silly games."

"Yes, old chap. But it's pretty serious," I said. "Let me just go over it again:

"*One:* We tell Schwartz that we won't join his **gang**. And that Lejaune knows all about his plot.

"*Two:* Lejaune acts before Schwartz does, and he raids the barrack- room the night before the mutiny. We shall either be in bed as though mutineers, or we shall be ordered to join the guard of loyal men who are to arrest the mutineers.

"*Three:* In either case, Bolidar is to shoot you. But directly he raises his rifle in your direction, you are going to shoot him. (You'll have to take your rifle to bed with you if Lejaune is going to pretend that you are a mutineer.)

"*Four:* If I see that Bolidar is out to murder you, I shall shoot Lejaune myself. (I shall take my rifle to bed too, if we are left with the mutineers.)

"*Five:* If . . ."

"Five: The fat *will* be in the fire, nicely, then," interrupted Michael. "What can we do but bolt into the desert with the rest, if you kill Lejaune? You'd be the most badly-wanted of all the badly-wanted mutineers, after that. . . . They'd get us too, if they had to turn out a desert-column of all arms. . . ."

We pondered the delightful situation.

"Besides," Michael went on, "you couldn't do it. Of course you couldn't. It would be a different thing if Lejaune were raising a rifle to shoot you, as Bolidar will be doing to me, if I shoot Bolidar. You couldn't just blow Lejaune's head off, in cold blood. That is exactly what Schwartz is going to do. . . . And what we object to."

And it was so, of course. I might just as well go to Schwartz and offer to be the butcher.

"Well," said I, "suppose I cover Lejaune with my rifle and tell him I'll blow his head off the moment he moves—and then I tell him to . ."

"Consider himself under arrest?" jeered Michael. "And what are you then, but the rankest mutineer of the lot? Besides, it's quite likely that Lejaune won't be there. He's brave enough—but he'd like to survive the show. In fact, he intends to be the sole survivor, I should say."

"Looks as though we've simply *got* to join Schwartz then," I said.

"Damned if I do," replied Michael. "I'm certainly

going bald-headed for anyone who goes for me, but I'm not going to join any mutineers, nor commit any murders.''

"Nor are you," he added, as I stared glumly out into the desert.

"What *is* to be done then?" I asked once again.

"*Nothing,* I tell you," repeated Michael. "We've got to 'jump lively when we do jump,' as Buddy says; but we can only wait on events and do what's best, as they arise. Meanwhile, let's hold polite converse with the merry Schwartz. . . . Come on."

And we got up and strolled through the starlit darkness to the Fort.

"I suppose we can take it that Sergeant Dupré knows all about the plot?" I said, as we passed into the stifling court-yard.

"No doubt of it," replied Michael. "I am inclined to think Lejaune would try to keep a nice compact 'loyal party' to deal with the mutineers, and hope they'd be like the Kilkenny cats, mutually destructive. . . . Say, Dupré, Boldini, and five or six *légionnaires.* . . . Some of whom would be killed in the scrap. . . . Of course, one doesn't know *what* his plans really are—except that he means to get a diamond, a lot of kudos, and a nice little vengeance on his would-be murderers. . . ."

As we entered the barrack-room, we saw that a committee-meeting of the "butcher" party was in session. They stared in hostile fashion at Michael and me as we went to our cots and got out our cleaning-rags from the little bags.

I sat down on my bed and began melting wax on to my belt and pouches, preparatory to *astiquage* labours.

The conspirators' heads drew together again.

Michael went over to where they were grouped at the end of the long table.

"Have you come with your answer to a question I asked you about some *cochons?*" growled Schwartz, scowling at him.

"I have come with some news about a *cochon,* my friend," replied Michael.

Half a dozen pairs of eyes glared at him, and I strolled

over. So did St. André from his cot. Just then Maris and Cordier entered, and I beckoned to them.

"He knows *all* about it," said Michael.

Schwartz sprang to his feet, his eyes blazing, his beard seeming to bristle, and his teeth gleaming as he bared them. He was a dangerous savage-looking ruffian.

"*You* have told him!" he shouted, pointing in Michael's face. "You treacherous filthy cur, you have betrayed us!" and he glanced to where a bayonet hung at the head of his bed.

"And come straight here and told you?" sneered Michael coldly. "If you were as clever as you are noisy, you might see I should hardly do that. You're a pretty leader of a gang of desperate mutineers, aren't you?"

Schwartz stared in amazement, struck dumb by the cool daring of the person who had the courage and effrontery to taunt and insult *him*.

Michael turned to Brandt, Haff, Delarey, Guantaio, Vogué, and the rest of Schwartz's familiars.

"A remarkable leader," he said. "Here you are, the gang of you, making your wonderful plans, *and Lejaune knows every word you say,* and precisely what you are going to do—almost as soon as you know it yourselves! . . . *Join* you? No, thanks. You have talked cleverly about 'pigs' and 'butchers'—but what about a lot of silly *sheep?* You make me tired," and Michael produced a most convincing and creditable yawn.

"Well, what are you going to do?" he asked as they sat open-mouthed. "Whatever it is, Lejaune will do it first," he added, "so you'd better do nothing."

"And Lejaune will do it first," I put in.

Michael's coolness, bitter contempt for them, and his obvious sincerity, had won. They knew he spoke the truth, and they knew he had not betrayed them to Lejaune.

I watched Guantaio, and decided that save perhaps for a little courage, he was another Bolidar. Certainly Boldini would hear of Michael's action, if Lejaune did not, as soon as Guantaio could get away from his dupes.

"What to do!" murmured Schwartz. "What to do! If Lejaune knows everything! . . ."

"Declare the whole thing off," said Michael, "and then the noble soul who has told Lejaune so much, can tell him that too," and Michael's eye rested on Guantaio.

It rested so long upon Guantaio, that that gentleman felt constrained to leap to his feet and bluster.

"Do you *dare* to suggest . . ." he shouted and stopped. (*Qui s'excuse s'accuse.*)

"I did not know I had suggested anything," said Michael softly. "Why *should* I suggest anything, my friend?"

"If it were you—I'd hang you to the wall with bayonets through your ears, you yellow dog," growled Schwartz, glaring at Guantaio.

"He lies! He lies!" screamed Guantaio.

"How do you know?" asked Michael. "How do *you* know what Lejaune knows?"

"I meant that you lie if you say that I betrayed the plot," blustered Guantaio.

"I haven't said it," replied Michael. "It is only you who have said it. . . . You seem to be another of the clever ones. . . ."

Michael's coolness and superiority were establishing a kind of supremacy for him over these stupid creatures, driven and bedevilled as they were by *cafard* and by Lejaune.

They stared at each other and at us.

"What's to be done?" said Schwartz. . . . "By God! When I catch the traitor . . ." he roared and shook his great fists above his shaggy head.

"Nothing's to be done," replied Michael again, "because you can *do* nothing. You are in Lejaune's hands absolutely. Take my advice and drop this lunacy, and you may hear nothing more of it. . . . There may be a new Commandant here in a week or two . . ."

"Yes—and his name may be Lejaune," answered Schwartz.

"Anyhow—he *knows*, and he's got us," put in Brandt. "I vote we all join in the plot and then all vote it abandoned. Then he can't punish one more than another. He can't put the whole blasted garrison in his cursed cells can he?"

"You're right," said Haff. "That's it. Abandon the whole scheme, I say. *And* find out the traitor and give him a night that he'll remember through eternity *in* Hell. . . ."

But the ferocious Schwartz was of a different fibre, and in his dogged and savage brain the murder of Lejaune was an *idée fixe.*

"Abandon nothing!" he roared, springing to his feet. "I. tell you I . . ." And then Michael laid his hand on his arm.

"Silence, you noisy fool," he said quietly. "Don't you understand *yet* that whatever you say now will go straight to Lejaune?"

Schwartz, foaming, swung round on Guantaio.

"Get out of this," he growled menacingly, and pointed to the door.

"I swear I . . ." began Guantaio indignantly.

"Get out, I say!" bawled Schwartz, "and when the time comes for us to strike our blow—be careful. Let me only *suspect* you, and I'll hang you to the flagstaff by one foot. . . . By God, I will. . . . *Go!*"

Guantaio slunk off.

"Now listen to me again," said Michael. "As I told you, Lejaune knows all about your plot to murder him and desert at full moon. I did not tell him. But I was going to tell him, if, after I had warned you, you refused to abandon the scheme."

Schwartz growled and rose to his feet again.

"Oh yes," Michael went on, "I was going to warn you first, to give you a chance to think better of it—in which case I should have said nothing, of course. . . . But now get this clear. If I know of any *new* scheme, or any change of date or method, or anything that Lejaune does not already know—I shall tell him. . . . Do you understand? . . ."

"You cursed spy! You filthy, treacherous hound! You . . ." roared Schwartz. "Why should *you* . . ."

"Oh, don't be such a noisy nuisance, Schwartz," interrupted Michael. "I and a party of my friends don't choose *to give Lejaune the chance he wants.* and we don't really like murder either. . . . We have as much right to live as you, haven't we?''

"*Live*," snarled Brandt. "D'you call *this* living?"

"We aren't dying of thirst, anyhow," replied Michael. "And if we are chivvied and hunted and hounded by Lejaune, it's better than being hunted to our deaths by a camel-company of *goums* or by the Touaregs, isn't it?"

"And who *are* your precious friends?" asked Haff.

"There are five of them here, for a start," said St. André.

"And how many more?" asked Schwartz.

"You'll find that out when you start mutinying, my friend," said Maris. "Don't fancy that all your band mean all they say."

"In fact," put in Cordier, "you aren't the only conspirators. There is also a plot *not* to mutiny, d'you see? . . . And some good 'friends' of yours are in it too."

"So you'd better drop it, Schwartz," I added. "None of us is a spy, and none of us will report anything to Lejaune without telling you first and inviting you to give it up. And if you refuse—Lejaune is going to know all about it. You are simply surrounded by *real* spies, too, mind."

"You cowardly hounds!" growled Schwartz. "There isn't a *man* in the place. . . . *Cowards*, I say."

"Oh, quite," agreed Michael. "But we've enough pluck to stick things out while Lejaune is in command, if *you* haven't. . . . Anyhow—you know how things stand now," and he strolled off, followed by St. André, Maris, Cordier, and myself.

"This is a *maison de fous*," observed St. André.

"A corner of the lunatic asylum of Hell," said Cordier.

"Some of us had better keep awake to-night, I think," observed Maris.

"Especially if Bolidar is not in his bed," I added.

Michael drew me aside.

"We'll have another word with that sportsman," he said. "I think he'll have the latest tip from the stable, and I fancy he'll believe any promise we make him."

§ 8.

After completing our *astiquage* and other preparations
for the morrow, Michael and I strolled in the courtyard.

"What'll Schwartz do now?" I asked.

"Probably act to-night," said Michael, "unless he swallowed our bluff that our party consists of more than us five.
He may be wondering as to how many of his supposed
adherents will really follow him if he starts the show. . . ."

"He may see how many will take a solemn oath to stand
by him and see it through, if he gives the word for to-
night," I suggested.

"Quite likely," agreed Michael. "And if neither Guantaio nor Bolidar knows about it, Schwartz may pull it off
all right."

"I don't somehow see Lejaune taken by surprise, when
he knows what's brewing," I said.

"No," replied Michael. "But he may be relying on
Bolidar giving him the tip."

"What are we going to do if we wake up and find that
the show has begun?" I asked.

"Stand by Lejaune," replied Michael. "France expects
that every halfpenny legionary this day will do his dooty."

"It'll be too late to save Lejaune if we're awakened by
rifle-shots and 'alarums and excursions without,' won't it?"
I observed.

"That won't be our fault," said Michael. "If they murder Lejaune and the others, all we can do is to decline to
join the mutineers."

"If we survive and they desert, I suppose the senior
soldier will carry on as Commandant of the fort," I mused.
That will take some deciding if only St. André, Maris,
Cordier, you, and I are left. . . ."

"St. André has been a French officer," observed Michael.

"Yes—but they'll select you, old chap," I said.

"Then I'll use my powers to appoint St. André," smiled
my brother.

Someone passed and repassed us in the dark, and then

waited near the lantern by the quarter-guard, to identify us by its light.

It was Schwartz.

"See here, you," he said as he recognised us. "Come with me. . . . Now. . . . What are you going to do if someone kills Lejaune without doing himself the honour of consulting your lordships?"

"Nothing," replied Michael, as we walked away from the light. "We shall continue in our duty as soldiers. We shall obey the orders of the senior person remaining true to his salt and the Flag."

"The devil burn their filthy Flag!" snarled Schwartz. "I spit on it."

"A pity you came under it, if that's what you think," said Michael.

"Then you and your gang of cowards and blacklegs will not interfere?" asked Schwartz.

"If you will desert, you will desert," replied my brother. "That is not our affair. If we know what you are going to do, we shall report it, if we can't stop it. If we can prevent mutiny and murder we shall. . . . As for deserting —I should say the Legion would be well rid of you."

"Oh, you do, do you, Mr. Preacher?" replied Schwartz, who was evidently putting great and unwonted restraint upon himself. "What I want to know is whether you are going to fight us or not?"

"Certainly—if ordered to," replied Michael.

"And if there is no one to order you?" sneered Schwartz.

"Then obviously we shall not be ordered to, my good ass," was the unsoothing reply. "And we certainly shan't hinder your departure. . . . Far from it," he added.

Schwartz turned to go.

"Look to yourselves! I warn you! Look to yourselves," he growled.

"Oh, we shall. Don't you worry," replied Michael.

"They'll do it to-night," he added, as we watched Schwartz disappear. "We must secure our rifles and we must keep awake."

I wondered how much longer we should be able to stand

this intolerable strain, in addition to the terrific heat and monotony of hardship.

"Go and look for Bolidar," said my brother after a brief silence. "I'll hunt round too. Bring him here if you find him. We'll ask him what's likely to happen if they mutiny to-night. Then we can fix up a plan of action with St. André and the others."

I went back to the barrack-room.

Bolidar was deep in conclave with Schwartz, Brandt, Haff, Vogué, Delarey, and one or two others, round Schwartz's bed.

I pretended to go to my *paquetage* for something, and then retired and reported to Michael.

"That's all right then," he said. "Whatever the fools fix up for to-night will be reported to Lejaune to-night, and he will know what to do.

"We'll have a word with Bolidar though, by and by," he added. "Nothing like knowing what's going to happen."

Half an hour later, we returned to the reeking, stifling room. Most of the men were lying on their cots. Bolidar was sitting on a bench, polishing his bayonet.

"Will you polish mine too?" I said, going over to him. "Follow me out," I whispered, as I gave him my bayonet.

I strolled back to my cot, began to undress, and then, taking my mug, went out of the room as though for water.

Watching the lighted doorway I waited in the darkness. Ten minutes or so later, Bolidar came out.

"Well?" I asked.

"Lejaune does not believe a word about the diamond not being here," he said, "and the mutineers are going to shoot him and all the non-coms. on morning parade to-morrow instead of at night. They think he will be expecting it at night, as some informer must have told him that is the plan. . . . He'll be off his guard. . . . They are going to kill Dupré and Boldini simultaneously with Lejaune. . . . If your party is a big one they are going to leave you alone, if you leave them alone. They will load themselves up with water, wine, food, and ammunition, and march out at sunset.

"Blanc, who has been a sailor, is going to lead them straight over the desert to Morocco, by Lejaune's compass. . . . Schwartz is to be Captain; Brandt and Haff, Lieutenants; Delarey and Vogué, Sergeants; and Glock and Hartz, Corporals. . . . There will be twenty privates. . . .

"They are going to court martial Guantaio, and if he is found guilty they are going to hang him. . . . *I* know enough to get him hung, the dirty traitor. . . ."

"And you?" I asked.

"I am to shoot Lejaune," he replied, "to prove my sincerity and good faith. If I don't, I am to be shot myself. . . . Guantaio has been maligning me to Schwartz."

"Have you told Lejaune this?" I asked this astonishing creature.

"*I am just going to do so now*," he replied, and I gasped.

"And I suppose he'll arrest them to-night?" I asked.

"Probably. *If he believes me*," was the interesting answer.

"What if he doesn't?" I enquired, and, at that, the wretch had another "nerve-storm" or hysterical fit of trembling, with demented gesticulations and mutterings.

"What *shall* I do? What *shall* I do?" he kept on. "What *will* become of me? God help me! Help me! Help me!"

"Look here," said I. "You tell me and my brother everything—the absolute truth, mind—and we'll save you all right, provided you do nothing against us. No covering with your rifle, mind!"

He clutched my hand in his hot shaking fists.

"You stand in honestly with our party, and you'll be safe," I went on. "We'll prevent the mutiny, and nobody will be killed. Neither you nor anybody else."

I hoped I spoke the truth. Perhaps if I now told Schwartz that I knew about the new morning scheme, and assured him that Lejaune knew it too, he'd own himself defeated and give it all up. On the other hand, he might run amok, yelling to his gang to follow him. . . . Lejaune's perarranged plans would probably settle their business promptly. Would Lejaune then go and shoot whomsoever else he thought might be better dead?

Bolidar slunk off, and I went back to the barrack-room.

Taking my Arabic copy of the Q'ran from the shelf above my bed, I winked at Michael, and opening the book, seated myself beside him, and began to read in Arabic, as we often did.

Having read a verse, I went on in the same monotone, as though still reading, and said in Arabic:

"To-morrow. Morning. They will kill. One now goes to give information," and then went on with the next verse. I then gave the book to Michael, who followed the same plan. Soon I heard between actual verses:

"We have warned them. Say nothing. He will strike to-night. Do not sleep. I will tell our friends," and then another verse of the wisdom of the Prophet, before closing the book.

Soon after this, Bolidar entered the room and began to undress.

"What about my bayonet, you, Bolidar?" I called across to him.

"Oh—half a minute, Smith," he replied, and began polishing it.

A little later he brought it over, and as he bent over my bed to hang the weapon on its hook, whispered:

"I have not told him. . . . To-morrow," and went back to his place.

Under cover of the "Lights out" bugle, I repeated this to Michael.

"That's all right then," said he. "We shall have a quiet night."

And then perfect silence descended on the room as usual.

§ 9.

It was an unpleasant night for me, nevertheless, for I by no means shared Michael's faith in its quiet.

What more likely, I thought, than that Lejaune should choose to-night for his anticipatory counter-stroke? He must have an iron nerve or very great faith in his spies, otherwise he could hardly continue thus to sit on the powder-barrel when the fuse was alight.

Or had he other and surer sources of information, than the tales of Bolidar, and Guantaio's reports to Boldini? Was one of Schwartz's most trusted lieutenants merely Lejaune's *agent provocateur?*

Could Schwartz himself be Lejaune's jackal? No, that was nonsense, and this horrible atmosphere of treachery and suspicion was poisoning my mind. Whereas Lejaune himself was wholly evil and was probably after Michael's fabulous jewel—patiently and remorselessly creeping towards it along a path that led through quagmires of treachery and rivers of blood—Schwartz was a comparatively honest and honourable brute, madly thirsting for vengeance upon a savage beast-tamer who had driven him to utter desperation by injustice and savage cruelty. And, save for Bolidar and Guantaio, his followers were like him, brave men of average character, de-humanised by an inhuman system and the more inhuman monster who applied it.

And why did not the monster strike? For what was he waiting, when every hour increased his danger? Surely it could not be merely the love of the fearless man for prolonging a terribly menacing and precarious situation?

Could it be that, before taking action, he really wished to know absolutely for certain what Michael and I were going to do when the mutineers rose?

Or was he waiting to be surer of Boldini or Dupré?

Of course, if he felt that in the presence of the "diamond" no reliance could be placed on either of these two colleagues, and if, as a shrewd and experienced judge of men, he estimated Bolidar and Guantaio at their true worth, or worthlessness—perhaps it was quite impossible for him to act at all. If practically every one in the garrison belonged to one of two parties—the "honest" mutineers determined to desert, or the rascally thieves determined to steal the great jewel and get away with it—what could the man do?

Was he hoping to use the thieves to fight the mutineers and to deal with the surviving party himself? Hardly that, for the mutineers greatly outnumbered the thieves.

On the other hand, could he not quite easily secure the

arms of the mutineers, and arrest the men in their beds by employing the thieves? He could—but what then? The thieves would murder him and escape with the jewel— probably releasing the mutineers and organising them as the "diamond's" unsuspecting escort to Morocco. And each man of the thief-party (Boldini, Guantaio, Colonna, Gotto, and quite probably Vogué and Dupré) would hope that by good luck—or more likely by good management— he would be sole survivor of the thief-party.

I tried to put myself in Lejaune's place.

What should I do if I were he, in such circumstances? If I wished first to save my life, and secondly to secure a gem of great price which I believed to be reposing in the pouch of one of the two or three men upon whom I could depend in time of trouble?

And I found it easier to ask the question than to answer it, since one party wanted my life and the other party wanted the jewel.

Having tried to put myself in Lejaune's place, I began to understand his delay in acting. He did nothing because he *could* do nothing.

I almost began to pity the man as I realised his position. He had not a soul to turn to in his loneliness and danger. Well—he was now reaping the reward of his consistent brutality to all who were his subordinates, as well as of his beastly avarice.

Hitherto he had always been backed by the immeasurable power and authority of his superiors, and could inevitably rely upon their inalienable support and unswerving approval. Now he had no superiors, and, face to face with the men whom he had so long outraged, bedevilled, and wronged, he must stand or fall alone.

And it looked as though he must fall.

Then an idea occurred to me. *Had he sent for outside help?* Was a column already on its way from Tokotu, where there were Senegalese as well as a mule-mounted company of the Legion? Was that what he was waiting for?

No. In the first place he would sooner, I felt absolutely certain, lose his life than send out an appeal for help against the very men he was supposed to command, the very men whose trembling disciplined fear of him was his chief pride and loudest boast. It would certainly be the end of all promotion for Adjudant Lejaune if he had to do such a thing as that. In the second place it might also destroy this chance of getting the fabulous gem. It was only in very troubled waters that he, in his position, could fish for that.

I decided that there had been no S.O.S. appeal from Zinderneuf to Tokotu.

I tossed and turned in my hot and uncomfortable bed as the problem tossed and turned in my hot uncomfortable brain; and my attempt to decide what I should do in Lejaune's place ended in my deciding that I simply did not know what I *could* do.

It almost seemed best for Lejaune to put himself at the head of the "honest" mutineers, arrest the thief-party, and then appeal to the others with promises of amendment in his conduct and reform of their condition. . . . But arrest the thieves for what? . . . And suppose the mutineers laughed at the promised amelioration of their lot?

It was a hopeless *impasse*. I gave it up and turned once more on to my other side. This brought my face toward the door and there, in the doorway, stood—Lejaune.

There stood Lejaune—looking from bed to bed. He was quite alone and he held a revolver in his hand. . . . Whom was he going to shoot?

Was this the beginning of the end?

Without thinking, I raised myself on my elbow.

He saw me at once, and, first placing a finger to his lips, beckoned to me.

I stared in amazement.

Frowning savagely, he beckoned again, with a swift and imperious movement of his arm.

What was the idea? Was he going to murder me outside? Or was he going to tell me to fetch Michael out? In that case, had I better refuse or just spring on him, get the revolver, and . . . and what? Neither murder nor mutiny was going to improve our precarious position.

As these thoughts flashed through my mind, I seized my trousers and tunic, struggled into them, and tiptoed to the door.

"Follow me," said Lejaune, and led the way to his quarters.

Closing the door of his bare, comfortless little room, and seating himself at the table, Lejaune stared at me in silence, his hot arrogant eyes glaring beneath heavy eyebrows contracted in a fierce evil-tempered frown.

"Do you and your miserable brother want to live?" he suddenly growled. "Answer me, you dog."

"On the whole, I think so, *mon Adjudant*," I replied, trying to strike a note between defiant impudence and cringing servility.

"Oh—on the whole, you do, do you?" sneered Lejaune, and again stared in silence. "Well—if you do, you'd better listen carefully to what I say, for only I can save you. D'you understand? Answer me, you swine."

"Yes, *mon Adjudant*," I replied.

"See here then, you infection," he went on, "there's some talk among those dogs, of a jewel. A diamond your gang of jewel-thieves got away with, in London. Also there is a plot among them to murder you both and steal it, and desert with it."

"Is that so, *mon Adjudant?*" said I, as he stopped.

"Don't you answer me! God smite you, you unspeakable corruption!" he roared. "Yes, it is so," he went on, mimicking me savagely, "and I know all about it, as I know everything else that is done, and said, and thought too—*thought,* I say—in this place. . . . Now I don't care a curse what you stole, and I don't care a curse what becomes of you and that anointed thief, your brother; but I won't have plots and plans and murders in any force under *my* command. Understand *that!* D'you hear me, sacred animal? Answer me."

"I hear you, *mon Adjudant*," I admitted.

"Very well, then," he growled. "I am going to teach these sacred curs to attend to their duty and leave diamonds and plots alone. By God, I am! To that end, I am going to detail you and your brother and a few more—say, Légionnaires St. André, Cordier, and Maris, as a Corporal's guard to arrest the ringleaders among those impudent swine. And I myself am going to attend to the business. You'll act at my personal orders, under my personal command, and you'll shoot down any man whom I tell you to shoot—as mutineering mad dogs *should* be shot. D'you hear me, you fish-faced, cod-eyed, bug-eating, dumb *crétin!* Answer me!"

"I hear you, *mon Adjudant*," I replied.

"Well—say so then, grinning imbecile. And to put an end to this thrice-accursed nonsense, and prevent any more disturbances of this sort, your brother will hand over this diamond to me. I'll put it where no plots and plans will trouble it. . . . You and your cursed jewels! Wrecking discipline and causing trouble! You ought to be doing twenty years in gaol, the pair of you. . . . D'you hear me, blast your soul? Answer me, damn you."

"I hear you, *mon Adjudant*," I replied.

"Very well. To-morrow morning, you and your brother and the others will have duties assigned you. You'll be given ammunition. You or your brother or both, will be put over the magazine, and will shoot anyone, except myself, who approaches it. *Anyone*, you understand, whether non-commissioned officer or *légionnaire*. . . . I'll teach the swine—by God, I'll teach them! . . . Now then . . . it was your brother I wanted, but you happened to be awake and I saw no point in entering that cage of treacherous hyenas —go and tell your brother what I have said, and as soon as I have that diamond locked for safety in the Company treasure-chest, I'll give you a chance to save your worthless lives. . . .

"Listen carefully now. Creep back and wake your brother, St. André, Maris, and Cordier, and tell them to get up and steal silently from the room with their rifles. . . . I shall be at the door with that revolver and I'll shoot *anybody*—on the first movement that I don't like. . . . Go! . . ."

I saluted and turned about.

So the hour had come! And Lejaune was about to act! Moreover he was going to act on Bolidar's information that Michael, Maris, St. André, Cordier, and I had refused to join the mutineers, and so belonged to neither party. He was going to make us five loyal soldiers the executioners of the rebels.

He had a perfect right to order us to seize any mutineer and to shoot the man if he resisted arrest. Also it was our plain duty to obey him. . . .

But Michael? What would happen when Michael denied any knowledge of a diamond? How would he fare at Lejaune's hands when the mutiny had been suppressed? Lejaune's bare word was sufficient to send him to join the defeated mutineers—whether they were in the next world or in that antechamber of the next world, the Penal Battalion. . . .

"Make a sound—or a false move, and you'll be the first that dies—the first of many, I hope," growled Lejaune, as I crept down the passage between thick mud walls, and I felt the muzzle of his revolver jabbed into the small of my back.

The blood surged to my head, and I all but sprang round. One second's space of time for a drive at the point of his jaw—and I asked no more.

But he wouldn't give me that second, and I couldn't do much for Michael with my spine shattered by a .450 expanding bullet. Lejaune would think as much of shooting me as he would of putting his foot on a scorpion. . . . And if, by any wild chance, I succeeded, and knocked him out and secured the revolver—how should we be any the better off? Boldini and his gang, and probably Dupré too, were after the "diamond," and would kill Michael to get it. . . .

With Lejaune following, I reached the door of our barrack-room. Here the *adjudant* halted, his revolver raised, and whispered:

"Your brother, Maris, Cordier, St. André—quick. . . ."
I crept to Michael's bed.

What would happen if he sprang up with a shout, and roused the snoring sleepers around him? Could Lejaune overawe the lot, or would they, empty-handed, have the courage to rush him? Probably they would not. Everybody waits for a lead in a case like that.

I began whispering in Michael's ear.

"Beau, old chap! . . . It's John. . . . Don't make a noise. . . . Beau, old chap! . . . It's John. . . . Hush! Don't make a noise. . . ."

He woke, and was instantly alert.

"What's up?" he whispered.

"Take your tunic and trousers and boots, get your rifle, and go out. Lejaune is relying on our party. Take your bayonet. . . ."

He saw Lejaune in the doorway, near which was the night-lamp, and got off his cot.

I crept to St. André, and woke him in the same way.

"The *adjudant* wants us," I whispered. "He's at the door."

"Good!" said St. André. "It is time he did something."

Maris also woke quietly, and soon grasped what was wanted of him.

By the time I had roused Cordier, Michael was creeping from the room, dressed, his rifle in his hand. I saw Lejaune give him some cartridges from his bulging side-pockets. I crept out too, taking my rifle and bayonet, and Lejaune gave me ten cartridges.

"Go outside and load," he whispered. "Quick. . . . Then shoot any man, at once, if he sets his foot on the floor, after a warning."

We charged our magazines and stood behind Lejaune in the doorway, rifles at the ready. St. André joined us and received the same orders. Lejaune shook his fist at Maris and Cordier, and beckoned to them angrily. Not one of the sleepers stirred.

When the other two joined us, Lejaune said:

"St. André and Cordier—remain here until relieved. If any man wakes, order *silence*, cover him with your rifle, and say you'll shoot him if he leaves his bed. *Do* it at once, to any man and every man, who disobeys. Fail, and I'll

shoot you myself. . . . Follow me, you others," and he
quietly returned to his quarters.

"Guard the door, you," he said to Maris, "and shoot
anybody who approaches. *Anybody*, I say."

"Now you, *quick*," he said, entering the room and closing the door. "Give me this wretched diamond that is the
cause of all this trouble."

He glared at Michael.

"You jewel-thieves have corrupted the whole of this
garrison, and are a menace to discipline. I'll take charge
of it now; and then I'll take charge of some of those swine
who think they can plot murder and robbery and desertion
in *my* Company, by God! . . . Out with it, you thieving
gaol-bird. . . . *Quick*. . . . Unless you want your throat
cut by those mad dogs of mutineers who've fixed *your*
business for this morning, at parade. . . . Oh yes, I know
all about it. . . . *Quick*, I say—the Devil blast your dirty
soul . . ." and he shook his fist.

Michael stared back, as one lost in astonishment and
wonder.

" 'Diamond,' *Monsieur l'Adjudant?*" he murmured.

Lejaune's swarthy face was suffused, his eyes bulged and
blazed.

"You try any tricks with me and I'll blow your filthy
head off—here and now!" he roared, picking up his revolver from the table where he had laid it.

"Give me that diamond, you scurvy hound, and I'll keep
it until I know whose property it is. D'you think I'm going
to have the discipline of this fort spoiled by every cursed
run-away jewel-thief that chooses to hide here with his
swag, and tempt honest men? . . . Out with it, you gallows-
cheating gaol-breaker, before I put you where you belong.
. . . *Quick!*"

"I have no diamond, *mon Adjudant*," replied Michael
quietly, and giving back look for look.

"As I could have told you, *mon Adjudant*," I put in,
"my brother has never had a diamond in his life and neither
have I."

Words failed Lejaune.

I thought (and hoped) that he was going to have an apoplectic fit. His red face went purple and his eyes bulged yet more. He drew back his lips, baring his cruel-looking teeth and causing his moustache to bristle.

He raised and pointed the revolver, and I was just about to bring up my rifle, but had the presence of mind to realise that he could shoot twice with the lifted revolver, before I could even bring my rifle up to cover him. Michael did not turn a hair, and I was thankful that I, too, had sufficient restraint to stand motionless at attention. A movement would have been mutiny, and probably—death.

I felt certain that Lejaune would have shot us both, then and there (and would have searched Michael's body), but for the precarious position in which he himself stood, and the fact that he needed us alive—for the present.

At any moment we might hear the rifles of St. André and Cordier, as the mutineers rushed them. Or, at any moment, for all that Lejaune knew, the mutineers might burst into the room, headed by St. André, Cordier, and Maris, to kill him. He believed that, like Michael and me, these three were faithful—but he did not *know* they were.

He was a brave man. Situated as he was, his life hanging by a thread, he still attended to the business in hand. He turned his heavy glare from Michael to me.

"Oh? You would talk, would you?" he said, in a quiet and most sinister tone of terrible self-repression. "Well! Well! You haven't *much* more time for talking. Not *many* more words to say. . . . Would you like to make another remark or two before I shoot you? . . . No? . . . Won't you speak again, gaol-bird? A little prayer, perhaps? . . ." and the scoundrel turned the revolver from Michael's face to mine, and back again to Michael's.

It was most unpleasant, the twitching finger of an infuriated homicidal maniac on the hair-trigger of a loaded revolver, a yard from one's face—a maniac who longed for our deaths that he might enrich himself beyond the dreams of his own avarice!

He began to swear blasphemously, horribly, foully. All that he had learnt of vileness among the vile with whom he had consorted, he poured over us. He literally and actually foamed.

We stood like statues. He put the revolver down in front of him, the better to tear his hair with both hands.

I thought of the aborigines of the Congo over whom his power had been absolute, and whose lives and deaths were in his hand and mere questions of his profit and loss . . .

And then suddenly, a thought which had ben clamouring for attention for some minutes suddenly occupied my mind and brought comfort and a curious sense of security.

Of course, Lejaune would do nothing to us until the mutiny was quelled, and he was again unthreatened and supreme.

We five were his only defence, the sole support of his authority, his one chance of saving not only his life, but his reputation and career. Obviously he would not kill two-fifths nor one-fifth of his loyal troops at the moment of his greatest need. It was absurd.

And then, without thought, I did what would have been the bravest thing of my life if it had been done consciously, and with intent. I defied, insulted, and outfaced Lejaune!

"Look here, Lejaune," said I coolly, and in the manner of an Oxford undergraduate addressing an extortionate cabman or an impudent servant. "Look here, Lejaune, don't be a silly fool. Can't you understand that in about two minutes you may be hanging on that wall with bayonets through your hands—and *left* there, in a burning fort, to die? Or pinned out on the roof with the sun in your face? Don't be such an ass. We've got no diamond and you've got five good men to fight for you, more's the pity! Stop gibbering about jewels and be thankful that we five know our duty if you don't. . . ."

"*Very* Stout Fella," murmured my brother. "*Order of Michael* for you, John."

What would happen if the meanest slave in his palace went up to the Emperor of Abyssinia and smacked his face? . . . I don't know. Nor did Lejaune, or he would have done it, I think.

Probably the Emperor would begin by gasping and feeling faint. Lejaune gasped and looked faint.

Then he sprang to his feet with a sound that was a mixture of a roar, howl, and scream. As he did so, Michael's left hand made a swift, circling swoop, passed under Lejaune's hand, and swept the revolver to the floor.

Almost as it clattered to the ground, my bayonet was at Lejaune's throat and my finger was round my trigger.

Whether Lejaune had been going to shoot or not, I do not know, but he certainly looked as though rage had destroyed the last of his sanity, and our death was all he cared about.

Anyhow, he couldn't shoot now.

"Move—and I'll kill you," I hissed dramatically, feeling like a cinema star and an ass.

Michael picked up the revolver.

"So you *are* mutineers, you beautiful loyal lying grandsons of Gadarene swine, are you?" panted Lejaune, moving his head from side to side, and drawing deep breaths as though choking.

"Not at all," said Michael calmly. "We're decent soldiers wishing to do our duty properly—not to babble about diamonds two minutes before a mutiny breaks out. . . . Man, don't you know the fort will be burnt, the garrison gone, and you dead (if you are lucky), in an hour's time—unless you do your job while you've a chance? . . ."

" '*Cré bon sang de bon jour de bon malheur de bon Dieu de Dieu de sort,*" swore Lejaune, "and I'll deal with you after this *chien d'une revolte*. But wait! You wait, my clever little friends. Hell's bells! I'll teach you one of my little lessons. . . . If you don't both die *en crapaudine*, by God, you shall live *en crapaudine*. . . ."

"Reward for saving your valuable life, I suppose," said Michael.

"You'll do that as your simple duty, my little friend. Oh, you love your duty. You are '*decent soldiers wishing to do your duty properly and not babble about diamonds,*' I believe? . . . Good! Come and do your duty then. We'll see what you'll babble about afterwards, with your

mouths full of salt and sand, *en crapaudine,* eh? Perhaps
you'll prefer drops of water to diamonds then, eh? . . .
You wait. . . ."

He turned to me.

"And you talked about hanging on walls. And being
pinned out in the sun, my little friend, eh? Will you
kindly wait until I have you strapped up in a cell, *of which
I alone have the key?* Perhaps it will not be I who *'jabbers
about jewels'* then, eh? . . . You wait. . . ."

"Your turn to jabber now, anyhow, Lejaune," said I
wearily. "You're a fatiguing fellow. What about doing
something *now,* and less of this 'waiting' business?"

The man pulled himself together, exerted his undeniably
powerful will, and got the better of his immediate impulse.

"Come with me," he said quietly, and with a certain
dignity. "Our real conversation is postponed until I have
dealt with a few other unspeakables. We will then see what
happens to those that threaten officers and point rifles at
them. . . . Put that revolver down. . . ."

"Open the door, John," said Michael. I lowered my rifle
and did so.

Maris, on guard outside, looked at me enquiringly. Presumably he had heard Lejaune's roars of rage.

Michael put the revolver on the table.

Lejaune took it up and strode to the open door.

"Follow me, you three," he said, and led the way to the
barrack-room, without hesitating to turn his back to us.

Apparently he had complete faith in our loyalty to duty,
and knew that he could depend upon us to obey any proper
military order. At the door of the barrack-room stood
St. André and Cordier, *faisant sentinelle.*

"Any trouble?" growled Lejaune, as they silently sprang
to attention.

"No one has moved, *mon Adjudant,*" replied St. André.

"Put down your rifles," said Lejaune to us three, "and
bring all arms out of this room, quickly and silently. You
other two will shoot any man who leaves his bed."

We set to work, emptying the arms-rack of the Lebel

rifles first, and then going from bed to bed and removing the bayonet from its hook at the head of each.

A steel bayonet-scabbard struck a tin mug, and a man sat up. It was Vogué.

"Cover him," said Lejaune, and the two rifles turned toward the startled man. He looked in the direction of the voice.

"Lie down, man," I whispered. Vogué fell back instantly and closed his eyes.

It was remarkable with what speed slumber claimed him.

On my last journey to the door, with a double armful of bayonets, the inevitable happened. One slipped and fell. As it did so, I shot out my foot. The bayonet struck it and made little noise, but my foot knocked against a cot and its occupant sprang up, blinking.

"*Himmel!* What's that?" he said.

It was Glock.

"Lie down, Glock," I whispered. "Look," and I nodded my head toward the door.

"Shoot him if he moves," said Lejaune calmly.

Glock lay down again, staring at Lejaune, as a hypnotised rabbit at a snake.

I passed on, and in another minute there was not a weapon in the room, nor was there a sound. None slept so deeply as Corporal Boldini, who was nearest to the door.

Lejaune took a key from his pocket. "Into the armoury with them, St. André, Cordier, and Maris, quick!" he said. "You, St. André, mount guard. Send the key back to me with Cordier and Maris, and shoot *instantly* any living soul that approaches the place, other than one of these four men.

"Now then," he continued to Michael and me, as the others crept off, laden with rifles, "some of these swine are awake, so keep your eyes open. . . . If several jump at once, shoot Schwartz and Brandt. Then Haff and Delarey. If only one man moves, leave him to me. . . ."

A very, very faint lightening of the darkness outside the windows showed that the false dawn was breaking. As

I stared into the room, I found myself trying to recall a
verse about "Dawn's left hand" being in the sky and,

> *"Awake! for morning in the bowl of night*
> *Has flung the stone that puts the stars to flight;*
> *And lo! the Hunter of the East has caught*
> *The Sultan's turrets in a noose of light."*

I tried to put it into Arabic, and wondered how the
original sounded in the liquid Persian. . . . Was it "tur-
rets" or "terrace"? . . .

What sort of a stone was Lejaune about to fling into the
bowl of night? . . .

Would he order the five of us, when the other three returned, to open fire and begin a massacre of sleeping men?
—an indiscriminate slaughter? . . .

He was quite capable of it. These were mutineers who
had threatened his life, and, worse still, his sacred authority
and discipline.

Why should he wait, he would argue, for a court martial
to do it?   Besides, if he waited, there would never be a
court martial. He could not permanently arrest the whole
lot with only five men, and guard his prisoners, garrison his
fort, carry on all the work of the place, and mount sentries,
with five men. What would happen when the five slept, ate,
cooked, mounted guard on the roof? It couldn't be done. It
was their lives or his, and the very existence of the fort.

Perhaps he'd only shoot the ringleaders?

What should I do if Lejaune ordered me to open fire
on unarmed men in their beds? What would Michael do?

What was my duty in such a case, with orders from such
an officer?   Private conscience said, "Absolutely impossible! Sheer murder! You are not an executioner. . . .
Not the public hangman."

Military conscience said, "Absolutely necessary. These
men are guilty of the greatest military crime. It is Lejaune's duty to save the fort at any cost. *Your* duty is
to obey your officer implicitly. If you refuse, you are a
mutineer, as criminal as they."

The windows grew lighter.

Maris and Cordier crept back, their work completed. Maris gave Lejaune the key of the armoury.

"St. André is on guard over the magazine, *mon Adju-dant*," whispered he, saluting.

"Good!" said Lejaune. "Maris, Brown, and Cordier, remain here. Shoot instantly any man who puts his foot to the ground. If there's a rush, shoot Schwartz first. Your own lives depend on your smartness. They're all unarmed, remember. . . . Come with me, you, Smith, and I'll disarm the guard and sentries. . . . Use your wits if you want to see daylight again."

He glared round the room.

"Aha, my little birds in a trap," he growled. "You'd plot against *me*. *Me, l'Adjudant Lejaune*, would you? . . . Ah! . . ."

I followed him down the passage.

"I'll clear that dog of a sentry off the roof first," he said. "Then there'll be no shooting down on us when I disarm the guard. . . ."

Leading the way, he went up the stairs that opened on to the flat roof, round which ran a thick, low, crenellated wall, embrasured for rifle-fire.

A sentry patrolled this roof at night, though the high look-out platform was not occupied, for obvious reasons, during the hours of darkness.

Lejaune relieved the sentry and posted me. He then took the man's rifle from him and ordered him to go below to the guard-room and request Sergeant Dupré to come up to the roof.

"Now," said he to me as the man went, "come here. Look," and he pointed down into the courtyard to the open door of the guard-room. "I shall order Sergeant Dupré to take the rifles of the guard and sentries, and then to send one man out of the guard-house with the lot. If any man comes out with only one rifle, shoot him at once. Shoot anybody who comes through that doorway, except a man with half a dozen rifles. And shoot to kill too."

I raised my rifle and covered the lighted doorway below me, at the other side of the courtyard.

"*You* understand," growled Lejaune. "The moment Sergeant Dupré enters that guard-room, after I've spoken to him, you shoot anybody who carries one rifle. A man with a rifle is a proclaimed and confessed mutineer. . . ."

I felt that he was right, and that it was my duty to obey him, little as I relished the idea of shooting comrades like bolting rabbits.

Should I shout, "*Drop that rifle!*" before I fired, and shoot if the man did not do it? I wondered if Lejaune would kill me if I did so.

I saw the relieved sentry cross the courtyard and enter the guard-room, and a moment later Sergeant Dupré came out.

"Watch!" growled Lejaune. "That sentry will talk, and they may make a rush."

Nothing stirred below.

Sergeant Dupré came up the stairs, out on to the roof, and saluted Lejaune.

"I want the rifles of the guard and sentries, Sergeant Dupré," said Lejaune. "Send one man, and only one, to me here, with the lot. Shoot instantly any man who hesitates for a second. No man is to leave the guard-room (except the one who carries all the rifles), or he'll be shot as he does so. . . ." And he pointed at me, standing with my rifle resting in an embrasure and covering the doorway below.

Sergeant Dupré saluted and turned about with a quiet, "Very good, *mon Adjudant.*"

He descended the stairs and emerged into the courtyard, crossed it to the gate beneath the gate-house, and took the rifle from the sentry there. The man preceded him to the guard-room. Dupré visited the other sentries, repeating the procedure.

A minute after the Sergeant's last visit to the guard-room, a man came out. I was greatly relieved to see that he carried three or four rifles over each shoulder, the muzzles in his hands.

"Watch," growled Lejaune. "They may all rush out together now. Open rapid fire if they do," and he himself also covered the doorway with the rifle he had taken from the sentry.

The man with the rifles, one Gronau, a big stupid Alsatian, came up the stairs. I did not look round, but kept my eyes fixed on the doorway through which a yellow light (from "where the great guard-lantern guttered") struggled with that of the dawn.

I heard a clattering crash behind me and then I did look round, fully expecting to see that the man had felled Lejaune from behind.

Gronau had released the muzzles of the rifles, they had crashed down on the roof, and he was standing pointing, staring, his silly eyes goggling and his silly mouth wide open.

So obviously was he stricken by some strange vision, that Lejaune, instead of knocking him down, turned to look in the direction of his pointing hand.

I did the same.

The oasis was swarming with Arabs, swiftly and silently advancing to attack!

Even as I looked, a huge horde of camel-riders swept out to the left, another to the right, to make a detour and surround the fort on all sides. There were hundreds and hundreds of them already in sight, even in that poor light of early dawn.

Lejaune showed his mettle instantly.

"Run like Hell," he barked at Gronau. "Back with those rifles," and sent him staggering with a push. "Send Sergeant Dupré here, quick."

"Down to the barrack-room," he snapped at me. "Give the alarm. Take this key to St. André and issue the rifles. Send me the bugler. Jump, or I'll . . ."

I jumped.

Even as I went, Lejaune's rifle opened rapid fire into the advancing hordes.

Rushing down the stairs and along the passage, I threw the key to St. André, who was standing like a graven image at the door of the magazine.

"Arabs!" I yelled. "Out with the rifles and ammunition!"

Dashing on, I came to the door of the barrack-room.

Michael was pointing his rifle at Boldini's head. Maris was covering Schwartz, and Cordier was wavering the muzzle of his rifle over the room generally. Everybody was awake, and there was a kind of whispered babel, over which rose Michael's clear and cheerful:

"Show a foot anybody who wants to die. . . ."

Nobody showed a foot, though all seemed to show resentment, especially Boldini, with a loaded rifle a yard from his ear.

Taking this in at a glance, I halted, drew breath and then bawled, *"Aux armes! Aux armes! Les Arbis! Les Arbis!"* and, with a shout to Michael and the other two, of:

"Up with you—we're surrounded," I turned to dash back, conscious of a surge of unclad men from the beds, as their gaolers rushed after me. Whoops and yells of joy pursued us, and gleeful howls of:

"Aux armes! Les Arbis!" as the delighted men snatched at their clothes.

St. André staggered towards us beneath a huge bundle of rifles.

Dupré and the guard were clattering up the stairs.

As we rushed out on to the roof, Lejaune roared:

"Stand to! Stand to! Open fire at once! Rapid fire! Give them Hell, you devils! Give them Hell!" and, ordering Dupré to take command of the roof, he rushed below.

A couple of minutes later, a constant trickle of men flowed up from below, men in shirt-sleeves, men bareheaded and barefooted, men in nothing but their trousers—but every man with a full cartridge-pouch and his rifle and bayonet.

Lejaune must have worked like a fiend, for within a few minutes of Gronau's dropping of the rifles, every man in the fort was on the roof, and from every embrasure rifles poured their magazine-fire upon the yelling, swarming Arabs.

It had been a very near thing. A very close shave indeed.

But for Gronau's coming up and diverting attention from the inside of the fort to the outside, there probably would not have been a man of the garrison alive in the place by now—except those of the wounded sufficiently alive to be worth keeping for torture.

One wild swift rush in the half-light, and they would have been into the place—to find what? A disarmed garrison!

As I charged my magazine and fired, loaded and fired, loaded and fired, I wondered if these things were "chance," and Gronau's arrival and idle glance round, at the last moment that gave a chance of safety, pure accidental coincidence.

A near thing indeed—and the issue yet in doubt, for it was a surprise attack. They had got terribly close, the oasis was in their hands, and there were many hundreds of them to our little half-company.

And they were brave. There was no denying that, as they swarmed up to the walls under our well-directed rapid-fire, an Arab falling almost as often as a legionary pulled the trigger.

While hundreds, along each side, fired at our embrasures at a few score yards' range, a large band attacked the gate with stones, axes, heavy swords, and bundles of kindling-wood to burn it down.

Here Lejaune, exposing himself fearlessly, led the defence, controlling a rapid volley-fire that had terrible effect, both physical and moral, until the whole attack ceased as suddenly as it had begun, and the Touaregs, as the sun rose, completely vanished from sight, to turn the assault into a siege and to pick us off, in safety, from behind the crests of the sand-hills.

I suppose this whirlwind dawn attack lasted no more than ten minutes from the moment that the first shot was fired by Lejaune, but it had seemed like hours to me.

I had shot at least a score of men, I thought. My rifle was hot and sweating grease, and several bullets had struck the deep embrasure in which I leaned to fire.

Below, the plain was dotted over with little heaps of white or blue clothing, looking more like scattered bundles of "washing" than dead ferocious men who, a minute before, had thirsted and yelled for the blood of the infidel, and had fearlessly charged to drink it.

Our bugler blew the ''Cease fire,'' and on the order, ''Unload! Stand easy,'' I looked round as I straightened myself up, unloaded my rifle, and stood at ease.

It was a strange sight.

At every embrasure there was a caricature of a soldier— in some cases almost naked—at his feet a little of spent cartridges, and, in one or two instances, a pool of blood. As I looked, one of these wild figures, wearing nothing but a shirt and trousers, slowly sank to the ground, sat a moment and then collapsed, his head striking with a heavy thud. It was Blanc, the sailor.

Lejaune strode over from his place in the middle of the roof.

''Here,'' he shouted. ''No room nor time, yet, for shirkers,'' and putting his arms round the man, dragged him from the ground and jerked him heavily into the embrasure.

There he posed the body, for Blanc appeared to be dead. Into the embrasure it leaned, chest on the upward sloping parapet, and elbows wedged against the outer edges of the massive uprights of the crenellation.

Lejaune placed the rifle on the flat top of the embrasure, a dead hand under it, a dead hand clasped round the small of the butt, the heel-plate against the dead shoulder, a dead cheek leaning against the butt.

''Continue to look useful, my friend, if you can't *be* useful,'' he jeered; and as he turned away, he added:

''Perhaps you'll see that route to Morocco if you stare hard enough.''

''Now then, Corporal Boldini,'' he called, ''take every third man below, get them fed and properly dressed, and double back here if you hear a shot, or the 'Assembly' blown. If there's no attack, take below one-half of the rest. . . . Then the remainder. . . . Have all *klim-bim* and standing-to again in thirty minutes. . . . You, St. André, and Maris, more ammunition. A hundred rounds per man. . . . Cordier, pails of water. Fill all water-

flasks and then put filled pails there above the gate. . . .
They may try another bonfire against it. . . . Sergeant
Dupré, no wounded whatsoever will go below. Bring up
the medical panniers. . . . Are all prisoners out of the
cells?'' . . .

He glared around, a competent, energetic, courageous
soldier. "And where's the excellent Schwartz?'' he went
on. "Here, you dog, up on to that look-out platform and
watch those palm trees—till the Arabs get you. . . . Watch
that oasis, I say. . . . You'll have a little while up there
for the thinking out of some more plots. . . .'' And he laid
his hand on the butt of his revolver, as he scowled menacingly at the big German.

Schwartz sprang up the ladder leading to the high look-
out platform that towered far above the roof of the fort.
It was the post of danger.

"Now use your eyes, all of you," bawled Lejaune, "and
shoot as soon as you see anything to shoot at.''

Ten minutes or so later, Boldini returned with the men
whom he had taken below, now all dressed as for morning
parade. They took their places and the Corporal hurried
round the roof, touching each alternate man on the
shoulder.

"Fall out, and go below," he ordered.

Ten minutes or so later they were back, fed, clothed,
and in their right minds. Gone like magic were all signs
of *cafard*, mutiny, and madness. These were eager, happy
soldiers, revelling in a fight.

With the third batch I went, hoping to be back before
anything happened. Not a rifle-shot broke the stillness,
as we hastily swallowed *soupe* and coffee, and tore at our
bread.

"Talk about 'They came to curse and remained to
pray,' '' murmured Michael, with bulging cheeks. "These
jolly old Arabs removed our curse and remained for us to
slay. There'll be no more talk of mutiny for a while.''

"Nor of anything else, old bean," I replied, "if they
remain to prey.''

"Never get in here," said Michael. "They couldn't take
this place without guns.''

"Wonder what they're doing?" I mused.

"Diggin' themselves in on the crests of the sand-hills," said Michael. "They can't rush us, so they're going to do some fancy shooting."

"Yes. What about a regular siege?" I asked. "And killing only one of us to a score of them that we kill? We should be too few to man the four walls eventually."

"What about relief from Tokotu?" suggested Michael.

"Over a hundred miles away!" I replied, "and no wires. Nor any chance to heliograph across a level desert, even if they could see so far."

"Chance for the *médaille militaire*," grinned Michael. "Go to Lejaune and say, '*Fear not! Alone I will walk through the encircling foe and bring you relief.*' Then you walk straight through them, what?"

"Might be done at night," I mused.

"I *don't* think," said Michael. "These merry men will sit round the place in a circle like a spiritualists' *séance*, holding hands, rather than let anyone slip through them."

"Full moon too," I observed. "Anyhow, I'm very grateful to the lads for rolling up. . . ."

"Shame to shoot 'em," agreed Michael, and then Boldini hounded us all back to the roof, and we resumed our stations.

All was ready, and the Arabs could come again as soon as they liked.

Lejaune paced round and round the roof like a tiger in a cage.

"Hi you, there!" he called up to Schwartz. "Can you see nothing?"

"Nothing moving, *mon Adjudant*," replied Schwartz.

A moment later he shouted something, and his voice was drowned in the rattle and crash of a sudden outbreak of rifle fire in a complete circle all round the fort. The Arabs had lined the nearest sand-hills on all sides of us, and lying flat below the crests, poured in a steady independent fire.

This was a very different thing from their first mad rush up to the very walls, when they hoped to surprise a sleeping fort and swarm up over the walls from each other's shoulders.

They were now difficult to see, and a man firing from his embrasure was as much exposed as an Arab lying flat behind a stone or in a trench scooped in the sand.

There was a man opposite to me, about a hundred yards distant, who merely appeared as a small black blob every few minutes. He must have been lying on a slope or in a shallow sand trench, and he only showed his head for a few seconds when he fired. I felt that either he or I would get hurt, sooner or later, for he, among others, was potting at my embrasure.

It was certainly "fancy shooting" as Michael had said, waiting for the small object, a man's head, to appear for five seconds at a hundred yards' range, and get a shot at it. It was certainly interesting too, and more difficult than rifle-range work, for one's nerves are not steadied nor one's aim improved by the knowledge that one is also being shot at oneself, and by several people.

With unpleasant frequency there was a sharp blow on the wall near my embrasure and sometimes the high wailing song of a ricochet, as the deflected and distorted bullet continued its flight at an angle to the line of its arrival.

The morning wore on and the sun gained rapidly in power.

Unreasonably and unreasoningly I did not expect to be hit, and I was not hit, but I was increasingly conscious of the terrific heat and of a severe headache. I wondered if high nervous tension made one more susceptible, or whether the day was really hotter than usual. . . .

Suddenly, the man on my right leapt back, shouted, spun round and fell to the ground, his rifle clattering at my feet.

I turned and stooped over him. It was the wretched Guantaio, shot through the middle of his face.

As I bent down, I was suddenly sent crashing against the wall, as Lejaune literally sprang at me.

"By God!" he roared. "You turn from your place again and I'll blow your head off! *Duty*, you dog! Get to your duty! What have you to do with this carrion, you cursed, slinking, cowering, hiding shirker . . ." and as I turned back into my embrasure, he picked up the choking,

moaning Guantaio and flung him into the place from where
he had fallen.

"Stay there, you rotten dog," he shouted, "and if you
slide out of it, I'll *pin* you up with bayonets through you,"
and he forced the dying wretch into the embrasure so that
he was wedged in position, with his head and shoulders
showing through the aperture between the crenellations on
either side of him.

"I'll have no skulking malingerers here," he roared.
"You'll all stay in those embrasures alive or *dead,* while
there's an Arab in sight. . . ."

Suddenly the Arab fire dwindled and slackened and then
ceased. Either they had had enough of our heavy and
accurate fire, or else some new tactics were going to be
introduced. I imagined that a camel-man had ridden all
round the sand-hills, out of sight, calling the leaders to
colloquy with the Emir in command.

Our bugles sounded the "Cease fire."

"Stand easy! . . . Wounded lie down where they are,"
rang out Lejaune's voice, and some half-dozen men sank
to the ground in their own blood. I was thankful to see
that Michael was not among them.

Sergeant Dupré with Cordier, who had been a doctor,
went to each in turn, with bandages and stimulants.

"Corporal Boldini," barked Lejaune, "take the men
down in three batches. Ten minutes for *soupe* and a half-
litre of wine each. Come back at the '*pas gymnastique*' if
you hear the 'Assembly' blown. . . . St. André, replenish
ammunition. Each man to have a hundred. . . . Stop that
bandaging, Cordier, and stir yourself. . . ."

When my turn came, later, to go below, I was more
thankful for the comparative darkness and coolness of the
caserne than for the *soupe* and wine even, for my head was
splitting.

" ' *Moriturus te saluto,*' " said Cordier, as he raised his
mug of wine.

"Don't talk rot," said I. "You're no more *moriturus*
than—*Madame la République.*"

"I shall be dead before sunset," replied Cordier. "This
place will be a silent grave shortly . . . '*Madame la Ré-*

publique—morituri te salutant! . . ." and he drank again.

"He's fey," said Michael. "Anyhow, better to die fight-ing than to be done in by Lejaune afterwards. . . . If I go, I'd like to take that gentle *adjudant* with me. . . ."

"He's a topping soldier," I said.

"Great," agreed Michael. "Let's forgive him."

"We will, if he dies," said I. "I am afraid that he'll see to it that he *needs* some forgiving, if he and we survive this show, and he gets control again. . . ."

"Yes," said Michael. "Do you know, I believe he's torn both ways when a man's hit. The brute in him says, *'That's one for you, you damned mutineer,'* and the soldier in him says, *'One more of a tiny garrison gone.'* "

"He's a foul brute," I agreed. "He absolutely *flung* two wounded, suffering men back into their embrasures—and enjoyed doing it."

"Partly enjoyment and partly tactics," said Michael wiping his lips, and lighting a cigarette. "He's going to give the Arabs the idea that not a man has been killed. Or else that he has so many men in the fort that another takes the place of each one that falls. . . . The Touaregs have no field-glasses, and to them a man in an embrasure is a man. . . ."

"What about when there are too few to keep up any volume of fire?" I asked.

"He may hope for relief before then," hazarded Michael.

"He does," put in St. André, who had just joined us and taken a seat at the table. "Dupré told me so. The wily beggar has kept the two *goums* outside every night lately—presumably ever since he knew of the conspiracy. They had orders to go, hell for leather, to Tokotu, and say the fort was *attacked,* the moment they heard a rifle fired, *inside or out.*"

"By Jove!" I exclaimed. "Of course! He wouldn't send to Tokotu to ask for help in quelling a mutiny of his own men, before it happened—but he wouldn't mind a column arriving because a *goum* had erroneously reported an attack on the fort."

"Cunning lad!" agreed Michael. "And he knew that

when the conspiracy was about to bloom and he nipped it in the bud, he'd be pretty shorthanded after it, if he should be attacked—even by a small raiding party out for a lark!"

"Yes," said Cordier. "He saved his face and he saved the fort too. If a shot had been fired at the mutineers, the *goums* would have scuttled off as ordered, and the relief-column from Tokotu would have found an heroic Lejaune cowing and guarding a gang of mutineers. . . . As it is, they'll know to-morrow morning, at Tokotu, that the place is invested, and they'll be here the next day."

"Question is—where shall *we* be by then?" I observed.

"In Hell, dear friends," smiled Cordier.

"Suppose the *goums* were chopped in the oasis?" said Michael. "Taken by surprise, as we were."

"What I said to Dupré!" replied Cordier. "But Lejaune was too old a bird. They camped in the oasis by day, but were ordered to be out at night, and patrol separately, one north to south on the east and the other on the west, a half-circle each, from sunset to sunrise, Dupré says . . . Likely they'd have been chopped in the oasis in the daytime all right, sound asleep—but they wouldn't be caught at dawn. They were well outside the enveloping movement from the oasis when the Arabs surrounded the place, and the *goums* would be off to Tokotu at the first shot or sooner. . . . By the time . . ."

"Up with you," shouted Boldini, and we hurried back to the roof and resumed our stations. The wounded were again in their places, one or two lying very still in them, others able to stand.

On either side of me, a dead man stood wedged into his embrasure, his rifle projecting before him, his elbows and the slope of the parapet keeping him in position.

I could see no sign of life from my side of the fort. Nothing but sand and stones over which danced the blinding aching heat-haze.

Suddenly there was a cry from Schwartz on the look-out platform.

"The palms," he shouted and pointed. "They're climbing them." He raised his rifle and fired.

Those were his last words. A volley rang out a minute later, and he fell.

Bullets were striking the wall against which I stood, upon its *inner* face. Arab marksmen had climbed to the tops of the palms of the oasis, and were firing down upon the roof. From all the sand-hills round, the circle of fire broke out again.

"Rapid fire at the palms," shouted Lejaune. "Sergeant Dupré, take half the men from the other three sides to that one. Bring those birds down from their trees quickly. . . . Brandt, up with you on to the look-out platform. Quick. . . ."

I glanced round as I charged my magazine afresh. Brandt looked at the platform and then at Lejaune. Lejaune's hand went to the revolver in the holster at his belt, and Brandt climbed the ladder, and started firing as quickly as he could work the bolt of his rifle.

Michael was still on his feet, but, as I turned back, I saw his neighbour spin round and crash down, clutching with both streaming hands at his throat.

When I took another swift glance later, the man had been wedged into the embrasure and posed by Lejaune as a living defender of the fort.

Soon afterwards I heard a shout from above, and turning, saw Brandt stagger backwards on the high platform. He struck the railing, toppled over, and came with a horrible crash to the roof.

"Find a good place for that carrion, Sergeant Dupré," shouted Lejaune. "Make him ornamental if he can't be useful."

I then heard him call the name of Haff.

"Up you go, Haff," he shouted. "You're another of these brave *risque touts*. Up you go!"

Schwartz, Brandt, Haff! Doubtless the next would be Delarey and Vogué. . . . And then Colonna, Gotto, and Bolidar. . . . Guantaio was dead. . . . Why didn't he send Michael up there? Presumably he hoped to keep him, St. André, Cordier, Maris, and me alive until the mutineer ringleaders and the diamond-stealers were dead. . . . He wouldn't want to be left victorious over the Arabs, only to find himself defenceless in the hands of the mutineers and the thieves.

I glanced up at Haff and saw that he was lying behind Schwartz's body, and firing over it as though it were a parapet along the edge of the platform.

I wondered how long this second phase of the fight had lasted, and whether we could hold out till night fell and the Arabs could not see to shoot. . . . Would they shoot by moonlight? It was unlikely, the Arab being, as a rule, averse from any sort of night work except peaceful travelling. A dawn rush is his favourite manœuvre . . .

It was agony to fire my rifle, for my head ached with one of those terrible eye-strain heat-stroke pains that give the feeling that the head is opening and shutting, exposing the brain. Every explosion of my rifle was like a blow on the head with a heavy hammer. I had almost come to the end of my tether when once again the fire of the Arabs slackened and dwindled and died away.

On the "Cease fire" bugle being ordered by Lejaune, I straightened up. I looked round as the words, "Unload! Stand easy!" rang out.

Michael was all right, but a good half of the garrison was dead or dying, for quite half the men remained partly standing, partly lying, wedged into their embrasures as the others obeyed the orders shouted by Lejaune.

Among the dead were both Sergeant Dupré and Corporal Boldini, and both had been stuck up to simulate living men. Haff must be dead too, for Delarey had been sent up to the platform, and was lying flat behind a little pile of bodies.

St. André was alive, for Lejaune called out:

"St. André, take rank as Corporal. One half the men to go below for *soupe* and coffee. Double back quick if you hear the 'Assembly' blown . . ." and St. André passed round the roof, touching each alternate man of those who were standing up, and saying, "Fall out, and go below."

In many embrasures was a man whom he did not touch.

Poor Cordier had spoken truly as concerned his own

fate, for he remained at his post, staring out with dead eyes across the desert.

Maris was dead too. There were left three men—St. André, Michael, and myself, upon whom Lejaune could rely if the Arabs now drew off and abandoned the siege of the fort.

But this, the Arabs did not do.

Leaving a circle of what were presumably their best marksmen, to pick off any of the defenders of the fort who showed themselves, the bulk of them retired out of sight behind the oasis and sand-hills beyond it.

By Lejaune's orders, the embrasures were occupied only by the dead, the living being ordered below in small parties, for rest and food.

St. André was told to see that every man left his bed and *paquetage* as tidy as for inspection, and that the room was in perfect order. Lejaune himself never left the roof, but had *soupe*, coffee, and wine brought up to him.

To the look-out platform he sent Vogué to join the bodies of his fellow-conspirators, Schwartz, Haff, and Delarey.

Except for a crouching sentry in the middle of each wall of the roof, those who were not below, feeding and resting, sat with their backs to the wall, each beside his embrasure.

The fire of the Arab sharpshooters did no harm, and they wasted their ammunition on dead men.

And so the evening came and wore away and the moon rose.

Where we were, we lay, with permission to sleep, St. André having the duty of seeing that two sentries patrolled each wall and were changed every two hours.

By Lejaune's orders, Vogué, in the dusk before moon-rise, pushed the bodies of Schwartz, Haff, and Delarey from the look-out platform to fall down to the roof. They were then posed in embrasures, as though living defenders of the fort. It seemed to give Lejaune special pleasure to thrust his half-smoked cigarette between Schwartz's teeth, and pull the dead man's *képi* rakishly to one side.

"There, my fine conspirator," said he when the body was arranged to his liking. "Stand there and do your duty satisfactorily for the first time in your life, now you're dead. Much more useful now than ever you were before.''

"He's a devil! He's a devil! He's mad—*mad!* . . .'' groaned Vogué as he dragged the body of Delarey past me.

"Up with him! Put him over there,'' growled Lejaune, when Vogué had got the body in his arms. "I'll allot your corpse the place next to his, and your pipe shall be stuck between your teeth. You are fond of a pipe, friend Vogué! Helps you to think out plots, eh? . . . Up with him, you dog . . .'' and he kept his hand on the butt of his revolver as he baited the man. He then sent him back to the look-out platform, to be a target for the Touaregs when the moon rose, or the sun, if he lived to see it. . . .

I had a talk with Michael when our turn came to go below for a rest and food.

"Looks like a thin time to-morrow,'' said Michael. "If they pot a few of us and then rush, they should get in.''

"Yes,'' I agreed. "They ought to keep up a heavy fire while their ammunition lasts, and then charge on camels in one fell swoop. And then climb up from the backs of the camels. A lot would be killed but a bigger lot would get in.''

"Don't give them the tip, anyhow,'' grinned Michael. "Two or three hundred of the devils inside the place, and it would be a short life and a merry for the half-dozen or so of us who were left by that time. . . .''

"If we can stand them off to-morrow, the relief from Tokotu ought to roll up the next morning,'' I said.

"If either of those *goums* got away and played the game,'' agreed Michael. "They may have been pinched though. . . . The relief will find a thin house here, if they do come. . . . It'll mean a commission for Lejaune all right.''

"Nice if he's confirmed in command here, and we survive!'' I remarked.

"Yes,'' said Michael, "and talking of which, look here, old son. If I take the knock and you don't, I want you to do something for me. . . . Something *most* important . . . what?''

"You can rely on me, Beau," I said.

"I know I can, John," he replied. "There's some let‧ters. A funny *public* sort of letter, a letter for Claudia, and one for you, and one for Digby, in my belt—and there's a letter and a tiny packet for Aunt Patricia. If you possibly can, old chap, get that letter and packet to Aunt. No hurry about it—*but get it to her.* See? *Especially the letter.* The packet doesn't much matter, and it contains nothing of any value, but I'd die a lot more comfortable if I knew that Aunt Patricia was going to get that letter after my death. . . ."

"Oh, shut it, Beau," I said roughly. "Your number's not up yet. Don't talk rot."

"I'm only asking you to do something *if* I'm pipped," said Michael.

"And, of course, I'll do it if I'm alive," I replied. . . "But suppose we're both killed?"

"Well—the things are addressed and stamped, and it's usual to forward such letters and packets found on dead soldiers, as you know. Depends on what happens. . . . If we die and Lejaune survives, I doubt their being dispatched. Or rather, I don't doubt at all. . . . Or if the Arabs get in, there's not much chance of anything surviving. . . . But if we're both killed and the relief gets in here before the Arabs do, the officer in charge would do the usual thing. . . . Anyhow, we can only hope for the best. . . .

"Anything I can do for you if it's the other way round, John?" he added.

"Well, love to Dig, you know, and there's a letter for Isobel, and you might write to her if ever you get back to civilisation and say we babbled of her, and sang, '*Just before the battle, Mother,*' and '*Bring a flower from Maggie's grave,*' and all that. . . ."

Michael grinned.

"I'll say the right things about you to Isobel, old son," he said, "and if otherwise, you'll see that Aunt gets my letter, eh? Be sure I'm dead though. . . . I mean if I were captured alive by Arabs, or anything humorous like that, I don't want her to get it while I'm alive. . . . Of

course, all five of the letters are important, but I *do* want
Aunt to get hers. . . ."

And then St. André ordered our little party up to the
roof, and brought down the other one.

The Arabs had ceased their desultory firing, and might
have been a hundred miles away. Only the sight of a little
smoke from their camp-fires and the occasional scent of the
burning camel-dung and wood betrayed their presence, for
none were in sight, and they made no sound. No one
doubted, however, that a very complete chain of watchful
sentries ringed us round, and made it utterly impossible
for anyone to leave the fort and bring help to his besieged
comrades.

The fact that Lejaune sent no one to make the attempt
seemed to confirm the story that Dupré had told Cordier as
they bandaged the wounded, and to show that Lejaune believed that the *goums* had got away.

It would be a wellnigh hopeless enterprise, but there was
just a chance in a thousand that a daring and skilful scout
might be able to crawl to where their camels were, and get
away on one. Nor was Lejaune the man to take any count
of the fact that it was almost certain torture and death for
the man who attempted it.

I decided that, on the one hand, he felt pretty sure the
goums had got away to Tokotu directly the Arabs appeared,
and that, on the other hand, the two or three men whom
he could trust were just the men whom he could not spare.

Unless St. André, Michael, and I were with him, his fate
would be the same whether he drove the Arabs off or not,
and doubtless he would rather go down fighting Arabs,
than be murdered by his own men.

I was ordered on duty as sentry, and, for two hours,
patrolled my side of the roof with my eyes on the moonlit
desert, where nothing moved and whence no sound came.

When relieved, I had a little chat with St. André after
he had posted my relief.

"Dawn will be the dangerous time; they'll rush us then,"
he said, "and it will want quick shooting to keep them
down if they come all together and on all four sides at

once. They must be a hundred to one. . . . I wonder if they'll bring ropes and poles, or ride their camels right up to the walls. . . ."

"If they don't count the cost, I don't see how we can keep them out," I said.

"Nothing could keep them out," replied St. André. "But if they fail at dawn they won't try again until the next dawn. They'll just pepper us all day and tire us out. . . . They think they have all the time they want."

"Haven't they?" I asked.

"No," replied St. André. "Lejaune is certain that one of the *goums* got away. The Arabs couldn't get them *both*, he says, as they were at opposite sides of the fort, and half a mile apart always, at night."

"What about their ammunition?" I asked. "The Touaregs', I mean."

"The more they spend the more determined they'll be to get ours, and the more likely to put their money on a swift dawn-rush with cold steel. . . ."

I lay down and fell asleep, to be awakened by the bugle and Lejaune's shout of *"Stand to!"*

There was no sign of dawn and none of the Arabs.

From the centre of the roof, Lejaune addressed the diminished garrison of Fort Zinderneuf.

"Now, my merry birds," said he, "you're going to *sing*, and sing like the happly joyous larks you are. We'll let our Arab friends know that we're not only awake, but also merry and bright. Now then—the *Marching Song of the Legion* first. All together, you warbling water-rats— *Now.*" And led by his powerful bellow, we sang at the tops of our voices.

Through the Legion's extensive repertoire he took us, and between songs the bugler blew every call that he knew.

"Now *laugh*, you merry, happy, jolly, care-free, humorous swine. *Laugh.* . . . You, Vogué, up there—roar with laughter, or I'll make you roar with pain, by God. . . . Out with it. *Now.* . . ."

A wretched laugh, like that of a hungry hyena, came down from the look-out platform.

It was so mirthless a miserable cackle, and so ludicrous, that we laughed genuinely.

"Again, you grinning dog," roared Lejaune. "Laugh till your sides ache, you gibbering jackal. Laugh till the tears run down your horrible face, you shivering she-ass. Laugh! . . . *Now*. . . ."

Again the hideous quavering travesty of a laugh rang out, and the men below roared heartily at the ridiculous noise.

"Now then, you twittering, sniggering *soupe*-snatchers, laugh in turn," shouted Lejaune. "From the right—you start, Gotto."

Gotto put up a pretty good roar.

"Now beat *that*, next. Out with it, or, by God, I'll give you something to laugh at," Lejaune continued.

And so round that circle of doomed men, among the dead men, ran the crazy laughter, the doomed howling noisily, the dead smiling secretly out to the illuminated silent desert.

"Now all together with me," roared Lejaune, and great guffaws rang out, desecrating the silence and the beauty of the moonlit scene.

It was the maddest, most incredible business—that horrible laughter among the dead, from men about to die.

Certainly the Arabs must have thought us mad and certainly they were not far wrong. Anyhow, they knew we were awake and must have gathered that we were cheerful and defiant.

For Lejaune was justified of his madness, and no dawn attack came.

Whether the Touaregs regarded us as "The afflicted of Allah," and feared to rush the place, or whether they realised that there could be no element of surprise in the attack, I do not know, but it was never made.

And when the sun rose and they again lined the sand-hills and opened their heavy fire upon the fort, every embrasure was occupied by an apparently unkillable man, and every Arab who exposed himself paid the penalty.

But not all those who lined the walls of Zinderneuf were beyond scathe by Arab bullets. Now and then there would be a cry, an oath, a gurgling grunt or cough, and a man would stagger back and fall, or die where he crouched, a bullet through his brain.

And, in every case, Lejaune would prop and pose and arrange the body, dead or dying, in the embrasure whence it had fallen, and to the distant Arab eyes it must have seemed that the number of the defenders was undiminished.

As the morning wore on, Lejaune took a rifle, and, crouching beside each dead man in turn, fired several shots from each embrasure, adding to the illusion that the dead were alive, as well as to the volume of fire.

Later still, he set one man to each wall to do the same thing, to pass continually up and down, firing from behind the dead.

When the Arab fire again slackened and then ceased, toward midday, and our bugle blew the *"Cease fire,"* I hardly dared to turn round.

With a sigh of relief, I saw Michael among the few who rose from their embrasures at the order *"Stand easy."*

It was a terribly tiny band. Of all those who had sprung from their beds with cries of joy, at the shout of *"Aux armes!"* yesterday morning, only Lejaune, St. André, Michael, Colonna, Marigny, Vogué, Moscowski, Gotto, Vaerren, and I were still alive.

The end was inevitable, unless relief came from Tokotu before the Arabs assaulted the place. All they had to do now, was to run in and climb. Ten men cannot hold back a thousand.

If we survived to see the arrival of a relieving force, it would be the dead who saved us, these dead who gave the impression of a numerous, fearless, ever-watchful garrison, who would cause an attack across open ground to wither beneath the blast of their rifles like grass beneath a flame.

"Half the men below, for *soupe* and coffee and half a litre of wine, Corporal St. André," ordered Lejaune. "Back as soon as you can—or if the *'Assembly'* is blown . . ." and St. André took each alternate man.

Soon coffee and *soupe* were ready, although the cook

was dead, and we sat at table as though in a dream, surrounded by the tidy beds of dead men.

"Last lap!" said Michael, as I gave him a cigarette. "Last cigarette! Last bowl of *soupe!* Last mug of coffee! Last swig of wine! Well, well! It's as good an end as any—if a bit early. . . . Look out for the letter, Johnny," and he patted the front of his sash.

"Oh, come off it," I growled. "Last nothing. The relief is half-way here by now."

"Hope so," replied Michael. "But I don't greatly care, old son. So long as you see about the letter for me."

"Why *I*, rather than you, Beau?" I asked. "Just as likely that you do my posting for me."

"Don't know, Johnny. Just feel it in my bones," he replied. "I feel I'm in for it and you're not, and thank the Lord for the latter, old chap," and he gave my arm a little squeeze above the elbow. (His little grip of my arm, and squeeze, had been one of my greatest rewards and pleasures, all my life.)

As we returned to the roof at the end of our meal, Michael held out his hand to me.

"Well, good-bye, dear old Johnny," he said. "I wish to God I hadn't dragged you into this—but I think you'll come out all right. Give my love to Dig."

I wrung his hand.

"Good-bye, Beau," I replied. "Or rather, *au 'voir*. . . . Of course, you didn't 'drag' me into this. I had as much right to assume the blame for the theft of the 'Blue Water' as you and Dig. . . . And it's been a great lark. . . ."

He patted my shoulder as we clattered up the stairs.

Lejaune assigned one side of the roof to Michael and the opposite one to me. Vogué and Vaerren respectively were sent to the other two. Our orders were to patrol the wall and shoot from behind a dead man, if we saw an Arab.

St. André took Colonna, Marigny, Moscowski, and Gotto below.

Lejaune himself went up to the look-out platform with his field-glasses and swept the horizon in the direction of Tokotu. Apparently he saw no sign of help.

Nothing moved on the sand-hills on my side of the fort, and I watched them over the heads of my dead comrades. . . .

How much longer could this last?

Would the Touaregs draw off from this fort-with-an-inexhaustible-garrison?

Would the relief come in time? If not, would they be in time to avenge us? It would be amusing if the Arabs, having got into the fort, were caught in it by the Senegalese and mounted troops from Tokotu—a poetic justice—for not a man of them would escape!

Where *did* all the flies come from? . . . Horrible! . . .

St. André and his party returned to the roof, and now two men were posted to each wall, St. André and Lejaune remaining in the centre of the roof to support whichever side of the fort should need it most when the attack came.

When it did come, it was a repetition of the siege-tactics and attrition warfare, a desultory fire of sharpshooters, and most of it aimed at the dead.

Up and down his half of the wall, each of the defenders hurried, firing from a different embrasure each time.

The Arabs must have been completely deceived, for they came no nearer, and fired impartially at the silent corpse-guarded embrasures and at those from which our eight rifles cracked.

Glancing round, as I darted from one embrasure to another, I saw that both Lejaune and St. André were in the firing-line now, and that Lejaune had one wall of the fort to himself. There were only seven of us left. Michael was among them.

The Arab fire died down.

Lejaune himself picked up the bugle and sounded the "*Cease fire.*" I saw that Vogué, Moscowski, and Marigny were dead and propped up in their places. St. André was dabbing his face with a rag, where a bullet had torn his cheek and ear.

Colonna, Gotto, and I were sent below to get food, and we spoke not a single word. When we returned, Michael, Vaerren, and St. André went down in their turn.

Lejaune walked up and down the roof, humming "*C'est la reine Pomaré,*" to all appearance cool and unconcerned.

Not an Arab was to be seen, and not a shot was fired.

I wondered whether they withdrew for meals or for prayers—or whether they fired so many rounds per man from their trenches on the sand-hills, and then awaited their reliefs from the oasis.

Certainly it was a leisurely little war—on their side; and no doubt they were well advised to conduct it so. They must have lost terribly in their first attack, and they had learnt wisdom.

A shot rang out.

"Stand to!" shouted Lejaune, and blew the *"Assembly"* two or three times, as though calling up reserves from below to the already well-manned walls.

That fort and its garrison must have been a sore puzzle to the gentle Touareg.

The firing recommenced and grew hotter, and an ominous change took place in the Arab tactics.

While a heavy fire was maintained from the crests of the sand-hills, men crawled forward *en tirailleur* and scratched shallow holes in the sand, behind stones. . . . Nearer and nearer they came. . . . They were going to assault again.

I rushed from embrasure to embrasure, up and down my side of the roof, pausing only just long enough to bring my fore-sight on to an Arab. Time after time I saw that I hit one of the running or crouching crawling figures drawing ever closer to the wall.

Lejaune was like a man possessed, loading and firing, dashing from place to place, and rushing from one side of the fort to the other, to empty the magazine of his rifle. . . .

Why from one side to the other? . . . As I loaded and fired, emptied and recharged my magazine, I found myself asking this question.

Glancing round, I saw the reason. There was no one defending the two walls that ran to left and right of mine.

Lejaune was firing a burst from one, and then dashing across to the other—defending two walls at once.

Only one man was defending the wall behind me. Swiftly I looked across.

It was not Michael. . . .

Only Lejaune, St. André, and I were on our feet.

This was the end. . . .

Michael was gone—but I should follow him in a minute.

Cramming another clip of cartridges into my hot rifle, I looked across again.

The opposite wall was now undefended.

Rushing across the roof from left to right, Lejaune shouted:

"Both walls, damn you! To and fro, curse you! Shoot like hell, blast you!" and I dashed across and emptied my magazine from that side, a shot from a different embrasure each time.

Back again I ran and got off a burst of fire along the opposite wall.

And so Lejaune and I (*Lejaune and I!*) held Fort Zinderneuf for a while, two against a thousand.

And when I was nearly spent, panting like a hunted fox, dripping with sweat, and nearly blind with eye-strain and headache, the Arab fire again dwindled and died, and there was perfect silence—an incredible dreadful silence, after those hours of deafening racket.

"Go below, you, quick!" shouted Lejaune, pointing to the stairs. "Boil coffee and *soupe,* and bring them here. Double back, quick, the moment a shot is fired. They may be at us again in a few minutes. . . . If we keep them off till dark, we're saved. . . ."

"Hurry, you swine," he roared, as I stood staring at where Michael lay on his face in a pool of blood.

I dragged myself to the stairs as Lejaune cursed me.

As I went down them I heard him merrily blowing the *"Cease fire,"* and bawling fierce orders to imaginary defenders of the fort.

I stumbled to the cook-house.

"Keep them off till dark and we're saved," did he say?

I hadn't the very faintest desire to be saved. Why should I be saved when Michael lay there so still?

As I struck a match to light the oil-stove, I thought I heard a shot. Rushing back up the stairs, I saw that Lejaune was posing a corpse in an embrasure. One body still lay where it had fallen.

It was Michael's.

I must have been mistaken as to hearing the sound of a shot. At any rate all was silent now, and Lejaune, his back to me, was fitting the dead man's rifle to his shoulder and clasping the dead left hand round the barrel.

I turned and crept back to my duties as cook, placed twigs and wood beneath the *soupe*-kettle, and turned up the wick of the oil-stove. . . .

And as I watched the fire burn up, I imagined Lejaune posing Michael's body—perhaps long before life was out of it. . . . The thought was unbearable.

He might be in agony.

He might be so wounded that his life could be saved if he lay flat. Not all the killed had been killed outright—though many of them had died immediately, as only their heads were exposed and their wounds were in the brain or throat.

There was really no more reason why Michael should be spared than any of the others should be—but he was my dearly-loved brother, and I simply could not bear it. I could not have his poor wounded body flung about like a sack of potatoes, and stuck up by the jeering Lejaune with indignities and insults.

He might not yet be dead, and his life might depend on what I did now! I turned to run upstairs.

Was I then going to mutiny after all? Was I going to defy my superior officer and tell him what he should, and what he should not, do in the fort that he commanded? Was I going to tell him that Michael was of superior clay and not to be treated as all the others had been treated?

I was.

And as I ran up the stairs, another thought struck me.

Michael's last request and instructions! I must get those letters and the little packet that he had spoken about. I must say to Lejaune:

"I'll fight till I drop, and I'll obey you implicitly—but leave my brother's body alone—leave it to me. . . .

After all, things were a little different now.

Lejaune and I were the only survivors. We had passed through Hell unscathed, and, at the last, two against a thousand, had kept the Flag flying.

Surely he could be decent now, unbend a little, and behave as a man and a comrade. . . .

As I came out on to the roof, Lejaune was bending over Michael.

He had unfastened my brother's tunic, torn the lining out of his *képi*, removed his sash, and opened the flat pouch that formed part of the money-belt that Michael wore.

Lying beside Lejaune, were three or four letters, and a torn envelope. In his hands were a tiny packet, bound up in string and sealing-wax, and an opened letter.

I sprang toward him, seeing red, my whole soul ablaze with indignant rage that this foul vulturous thief should rob the dead, rob a soldier who had fought beside him thus —a brave man who had probably saved his life, before the fight began.

"So he '*had no diamond*,' had he? Didn't know what I meant, didn't he?" the ruffian jeered, holding up the packet and the letter in his left hand.

"You damned thief! You foul pariah-dog!" I shouted, and, in a second, his revolver was at my face.

"Stand back, you swine," he growled. "Back further. Back, I say. . . ."

One movement, and I should be dead.

And a good thing too, but I had a word or two to say first. As I stepped back, he lowered the revolver and smiled horribly. . . .

"I didn't know that *men* crept round robbing the dead, after a fight, Lejaune," I said. "I thought that was left to Arab women—of the vilest sort. . . . You dirty, thieving cur —you should be picking over dust-bins in the Paris gutters, not defiling an honourable uniform—*chiffonnier!* . . ."

Lejaune bared his teeth and laughed unpleasantly.

"A fine funeral oration from a jewel-thief!" he snarled. "Any more grand sentiments before I blow out what brains you have? No? Well, I think I promised you that I would attend to you, all in good time. Now I'm going to do it. . . . I am going to shoot you now, where you stand. Half a dozen through the stomach, shall we say? I don't want to hurry you unduly out of this pleasant world. . . . Oh, no, don't think I want you any longer. The Arabs

won't attack again to-day, and they've settled all my mutineers nicely for me. . . . And a relief-column will arrive at
dawn. . . . Then you and the rest of these cursed dogs will
be given a hole in the sand for the lot of you—and I shall
get the Cross of the Legion of Honour, a Captain's commission, and a trip to Paris to receive thanks and decoration. . . . And at Paris, my chatty little friend, I shall dispose of this trifle that your gang so kindly brought to the
Legion for me!'' and he again held up the little packet in
his left hand.

"A rich man, thanks to you—and to *this* . . .'' and as
he said the last word, he actually kicked Michael's body!

Even as I snatched at my sword-bayonet, and leapt forward—in the instant that my dazed and weary mind took
in the incredible fact of this brutal kick—it also took in
another fact even more incredible—*Michael's eyes were
open, and turned to me.*

Michael was alive! . . . I would live too, if possible. . . .
My hand, still grasping my bayonet, fell to my side.

"Good!'' said Lejaune. "Armed attack on a superior
officer—and in the face of the enemy! . . . Excellent! I
court martial you myself. I find you guilty and I sentence
you to *death.* . . . I also carry out the sentence myself.
. . . *Thus* . . .'' and the revolver travelled slowly from
my face to the pit of my stomach.

"*There!* . . .''

As Lejaune had spoken, Michael's right hand had moved.
As the last word was uttered, the hand seized Lejaune's
foot, jerking him from his balance, as he pulled the trigger
in the act of looking down and of stumbling.

Blinded, deafened, and dazed, I leapt and lunged with all
my strength and drove my bayonet through Lejaune. I
stumbled, and it was torn from my hand. When I could
see again (for I must have ducked straight at the revolver
as he fired it, or else he must have raised it as his foot was
pulled from under him), he was lying on his back, twitching, the handle of the bayonet protruding from his chest,
the blade through his heart.

Lejaune was dead, and *I* was the mutineer and murderer
after all! *I* was the "butcher'' and *Lejaune* the "pig.''

CHAPTER VI

A "VIKING'S FUNERAL"

"All night long, in a dream untroubled of hope,
He brooded, clasping his knees."

I STOOPED over Michael, whose eyes were closed again. Was he dead—his last act the saving of my life?

I don't think I felt very much, at the moment. My mind was numb or blank, and I wasn't certain that the whole affair was not a nightmare. . . .

Michael opened his eyes.

"Stout Fella," he whispered. "Got the letters?"

I told him that he would deliver them in person. That we were the sole survivors. That the relief would come soon and we should be promoted and decorated.

"For stabbing Lejaune?" he smiled. "Listen, Johnny. . . . I'm for it, all right. Bled white. . . . Listen. . . . I never stole anything in my life. . . . Tell Dig I said so, and *do* get the letter to Aunt Patricia. . . . You mustn't wait for the relief. . . . Lejaune's body. . . . They'd shoot you. . . . Get a camel and save yourself. . . . In the dark to-night. . . . If you can't get away, say I killed Lejaune. . . . I helped to, anyhow . . ."

I do not know what I said.

"No. Listen. . . . Those letters. . . . You are to leave one on me. . . . Leave it in my hand. . . . Confession. . . . Do the thing thoroughly. . . . No need for you and Dig to carry on with the game now. . . . You must get the confession published or it's all spoilt. . . ."

"You've nothing to confess, Beau, old chap," I said. . . . "Half a minute, I'm going to get some brandy. . . ."

His fingers closed weakly on my sleeve.

"Don't be an ass, Johnny," he whispered. "Confession's
344

the whole thing. . . . Leave it where it'll be found or I'll haunt you. . . . Gnaw your neck and go '*Boo*' in the dark. . . . No, don't go. . . . Promise. . . . God! *I'm going blind*. . . . John . . . John. . . . Where are you? . . . Promise. . . . Confession. . . . John . . . John . . ."

Within two minutes of his seizing Lejaune's foot and saving my life, my brother was dead. . . . My splendid, noble, great-hearted Beau. . . .

I have not the gift of tears. I have not cried since I was a baby, and the relief of tears was denied me now.

No. I could not weep. But I looked at the revolver, still clutched in Lejaune's right hand. . . . It was only a momentary temptation, for I had something to do for Michael. His last words had laid a charge on me, and I would no more fail Michael dead, than I would have failed him when he lived.

Michael's affairs first—and if the Touaregs rushed the place while I attended to them, I would just take Lejaune's revolver and make a good end. I ought to get five of them, and perhaps might grab one of their heavy straight swords and show them something. . . .

I turned to the letters.

One of them was addressed to Lady Brandon. She should get it, if I had the ingenuity, courage, and skill to keep myself alive long enough. One was addressed to Claudia. That too. . . . There was one for me, and one for Digby. And there was another, crushed up in Lejaune's left hand. The envelope from which he had torn it lay near. It was addressed to *The Commissioner of Police, Scotland Yard, London, England*. Poor Michael's "confession" of something he had never done! I was sorely tempted to destroy it, but his words were still in my ears, urgent and beseeching. *I was to see that the "confession" was published.*

Well—let it remain where it was. It would get a wide-enough publicity if it were found in the dead hand of the murdered Commandant of a beleaguered fort. . . . I picked up the packet that Lejaune had dropped when I struck him, and put it with the three letters into my pocket. I then opened the one addressed to me. It ran as follows:—

"My dear John,

When you get this, take the letters that are with it to Brandon Abbas, as soon as you can. Send them if you can't take them. The one for Aunt Patricia solves the Mystery of the 'Blue Water,' at any rate to HER *satisfaction, and she can publish the solution or not, as she thinks fit, later on. . . . After Uncle Hector's death, for example. . . . Meanwhile, I beg and beseech and instruct and order you, to see that the letter addressed to the Chief of Police is not burked. It is exactly what we all bolted for—this averting suspicion from innocent people (including your Isobel, don't forget, Johnny boy!). We took the blame between us, and the first of us to die should shoulder the lot, of course, so that the other two can go home again. You or Dig would do this for his brothers, and so will I, if I pip first. So off with the home letters—*HOME, *and see that the other one gets into the papers and into the hands of the police and all that. I have written an absolutely identical letter to this for Digby too, so I am sure that one or both of you will see that my wishes are carried out. No nonsense about '*DE MORTUIS NIL NISI BONUM,*' mind. It is the living we have to think about, so do exactly as I tell you. You'll be doing the best for me, as a matter of fact, as well as for the living, if you carry out what I ask—so* GO TO IT, PUP.

If I outlive you, I shall do the same by you or Dig, SO GO TO IT.

You spoilt my plans by your balmy quixotic conduct in bunking from home—now put them right by doing exactly as I say.

Good-bye, dear old stoutest of Stout Fellas. See you in the Happy Hunting Grounds.

Beau.

P.S.—Don't come near me there, though, if you destroy that confession."

I put the letter down and looked at his face. Peaceful, strong, dignified, and etherealised beyond its usual fineness and beauty. . . . I closed his eyes and folded his hands upon his chest. . . .

How *could* I let this thing happen—let the world have

confirmation of the suspicion that Michael was a despicable mean thief? Or rather, how could I publish to a world that knew little or nothing about the affair, that Michael had done such a miserable deed?

I looked at his face again.

How could I disobey his last instructions, refuse his last request?

Nor was it a request made impulsively, on the spur of the moment. He had thought it all out, and written it down long ago, in case of just such an event as had happened— his predeceasing us. . . .

What would Digby do in my position? Would he take that paper from Lejaune's hand and destroy it? I felt he would not. He *could* not, had he been present at Michael's death, and heard his dying words. . . . Not having done so, would he blame me if I left that confession there, to be found by the relieving force?

Well—if he did, he must, and I must act according to my own light—if I could find any. . . .

And suppose the Arabs assaulted again, before the relief arrived?

That would settle the problem quite finally, for they would loot the place, mutilate the dead, and then make the fort the funeral pyre of the mangled corpses. . . .

I found myself wishing they would do so, and then saw the cowardice of my wish.

No, it was my affair now to—to—to . . . I actually found that I was nodding, and had all but fallen backwards as I sat!

In fact, a heavy faintness, an unspeakable weariness, formed the only sensation of which my mind or body was now conscious. I had seen too much, done too much, suffered too much, felt too much, in the last few hours, to have any other feeling left, save that of utter exhaustion. I felt that I could die, but could not sleep.

In the very act of pulling myself together and saying that *this* would not do, I must have fallen into a state of semi-coma that was not sleep.

I shook it off, to find that a new day was dawning, and, for a minute, I gazed around at the extraordinary sight that met my eyes—the bloodstained roof, the mounds of cartridge-cases, the stiff figures crouching in the embrasures, the body of Lejaune with the handle of my bayonet protruding from his chest; and Michael's calm smiling face, as noble in death as in life. . . .

"I must go, Beau, old chap," I said aloud, "if I am to get your letter and parcel to Aunt Patricia and tell them of your heroic death."

I knelt and kissed him, for the first time since babyhood.

And only then, actually not till then, I remembered the Arabs!

There was no sign of them whatsoever, alive or dead, which may partly account for my having completely forgotten their existence. . . .

I should not be doing much toward carrying out Michael's wishes if I walked straight into their hands. Nor was death any less certain if I remained in the fort till relief came, and Lejaune's body was found with my bayonet in it.

Idly I supposed that I might remove it and replace it by that of another man, and blame him for the murder. I had not the faintest intention of doing so, of course, nor would my tale have been very convincing, since I was alive and everybody else neatly disposed and arranged, *after* death. It did occur to me that perhaps I could pretend that I was the hero of the whole defence, and had posed all these corpses myself, including that of the man who had murdered Lejaune, but, of course, I did not seriously consider the idea.

No. Unless I wanted to die, I must evade both the Arabs and the relieving force from Tokotu. If I could do that, I must, thereafter, evade the entire population of the desert between Zinderneuf and safety, as well as evading any avenging search-party that might be sent out after me. There were also the little matters of thirst, starvation, and exposure. All I could do in the way of preparation in that direction would be to load myself with food, water, spare boots, and ammunition.

Rising to my feet, I wearily dragged myself down the stairs and filled and relit the oil-stove. While the kettle was boiling for coffee, I foraged round, filled my water

bottle with water and three big wine-bottles with the same
liquid. Water was going to be infinitely more precious than
any wine, before I was much older. I also emptied my
knapsack and haversack of everything but a pair of boots,
and filled them to bursting, with bread, coffee, and the bottles of water.

I thought my best plan would be to load myself up to the
weight I was accustomed to, but to let my burden consist
of food and water. This would grow lighter as I grew
weaker—or I should grow weaker as it grew lighter. Anyhow, it seemed the best thing to do, but how I longed for
a camel! The thought occurred to me that if the relief did
not arrive that day, I could remain in the fort till night,
and then try to get one of the Arabs' camels when it was
dark. A moment's reflection, however, made it clear that
if the relief did not enter the fort pretty soon, the Arabs
would.

The sooner I got away, the better chance I should have
of doing it successfully.

I ate and drank all I could, shouldered my burdens and
returned to the roofs for a last look round. If I could see
anything of the Arabs in one direction I could, at least,
try to get away in the opposite quarter. If not, I must
simply trust to luck, and crawl off in the direction opposite
to the oasis, as being the likeliest one to offer a chance of
escape.

I gazed round in all directions. There still was no sign
of an Arab, though, of course, there might have been any
number beyond the oasis, or behind the sand-hills that surrounded the fort.

I glanced at Lejaune. Should I remove my bayonet from
its place in his evil heart?

No. My whole soul revolted from the idea. . . . And as
for any hope of concealing the manner of his death, it
would still be perfectly obvious that he had been stabbed
by a comrade and not shot by the enemy.

Besides, I had killed him in self-defence—self-defence
from as cold-blooded, dastardly, and criminal a murder as
a man could commit.

No. Let the righteously-used bayonet stay where it was

—and incidentally I had quite enough to carry without the now useless thing. . . .

"Good-bye, Beau," I said, crossing to where he lay—and, as I spoke, I almost jumped, for the brooding silence was broken by a shot, followed by several others. . . .

The Arabs? . . . No—these were neither rifle shots nor fired towards the fort. The sound of them made that quite evident.

Crouching, I ran to the side of the roof and looked.

On a distant sand-hill was a man on a camel, a man in uniform, waving his arm above his head and firing his revolver in the air.

It was a French officer.

The relief had arrived from Tokotu, and I must escape or be tried, and shot, for the murder of my superior officer in the very presence of the enemy. . . .

Yes—but what about this same enemy? Where were they? Was that fine fellow riding to death and torture? Straight into an ambush, a trap of which the uncaptured fort with its flying flag was the bait? That might well be the explanation of there having been no dawn-assault that morning, while I slept. They might, with Arab cunning, have decided that it would be a much better plan to maintain the siege, unseen and unheard, and lure the relieving force, by an appearance of peace and safety, into marching gaily into an oasis covered by hundreds of rifles lining neighbouring sand-hills. They could massacre the relief-column and then turn to the fort again. If no relief-force came, they could still assault the fort whenever they thought fit. . . .

As these thoughts flashed through my mind, I decided that I must warn that man, riding gaily to his death, deceived by the peaceful quiet of the scene, and the floating Tri-couleur at the flagstaff top.

Seeing the walls lined, as they were, with soldiers, the Flag floating above them, and no sign of any enemy, he would at once conclude that we had long since driven them off.

Obviously this must be the case, or he would have heard sounds of rifle-fire, miles away, he would think.

I must warn him, for I had no doubt, in my own mind, that hundreds of Arab eyes were watching him.

Nor was it this man alone. rejoicing there in our safety. A whole column must be close behind him. Comrades of ours who had marched day and night to our relief. Of course, I could not let them walk into the trap, deceived by the very ruse that had deceived the Arabs. . . .

This officer was no fool, doubtless, but how was he to know that the fort was a whited sepulchre, tenanted by the dead, unable to signal to him that he was walking into an ambush with his column? Naturally he would assume, that since the apparently crowded fort gave him no warning of danger, there *was* no danger, and he and his column could come gaily marching into the fort from which its foes had fled.

This being so, I must warn him myself. I was certain that Michael would approve, and that he would have done so himself had he been in my place. It might mean death instead of escape, but death was certainly preferable to sneaking off while a whole column of one's comrades marched to a destruction one had the power to avert.

What to do? Should I lower the Flag? Run it up and down a few times? Wave my arms and dance about, up on the look-out platform? . . .

As likely as not, he would take any such signals as signs of joy and welcome. If I were he, approaching a fully-manned fort over whose crowded walls floated the Flag, I should certainly see nothing of warning about such demonstrations as those.

Until I was actually fired upon, I should certainly suppose I was safe and being welcomed to the fort by those whom I had been too late to assist in their victory over some impudent little raiding-party.

Exactly! *Until fired upon!* That would surely give him something to think about—and, moreover, would give me a chance of escape, even yet. . . . Long before he came within shouting-distance he would be rushed by the Arabs. I would do the firing.

Kneeling down and resting my rifle in an embrasure, I aimed as though my life depended on hitting him. I then raised my fore-sight half an inch, and fired. Rushing to another embrasure, I took another shot, this time aiming to hit the ground, well in front of him.

He halted.

That was enough.

If he walked into an ambush now, he was no officer of the Nineteenth Army Corps of Africa. . . .

Rushing across to the side of the roof furthest from his line of approach, I dropped my rifle over, climbed the parapet, hung by my hands and then dropped, thanking God that my feet would encounter sand. . . . Snatching up my rifle, I ran as hard as I could go, to the nearest sand-hill. If this were occupied I would die fighting, and the sounds of rifle-fire would further warn the relief-column. If it were not occupied, I would hide and see what happened. Possibly I might be able to make a very timely diversion upon the Arab flank if there were a fight, and, in any case, I might hope to escape under cover of darkness. . . . The sand-hill was not occupied, I was safely out of the fort, and a chance of getting safely away existed, whether the Arabs attacked the column or not.

I crept into an Arab trench and set to work to make a hole in it, that I might be as inconspicuous as possible should anybody come, or look, in my direction.

From between two stones on the edge of the parapet of my trench, I could watch the fort and the oasis. I was conscious of an uneasy sensation as I watched, that I myself might be under the observation of enemies in my rear. . . .

As soon as I saw what the Arabs and the approaching column were going to do, I would consider the possibilities of a safe retreat in the most likely direction. . . .

I began to wish something would happen, for the situation was a little trying, and there was too strong a suggestion of leaving an Arab frying-pan on the one hand, to step into the French fire on the other . . . an Arab torture by frying . . . a French firing-party at dawn.

While I lay gazing to my front and wondering what might be happening behind me, I was astonished to see the French officer come round the corner of the fort, alone, and proceeding as unconcernedly as if he were riding in the streets of Sidi-bel-Abbès! . . .

Well! I had done my best for him and his column. I had risked my own safety to warn him that things were not what they seemed—and if the Arabs got him and his men, it was not my fault.

He could hardly call *being shot at* a welcome from the fort? . . . Round the walls he rode, staring up at the dead defenders.

I wondered if the shade thrown by the peaks of their caps would so hide and disguise their faces that, from below, it would be impossible to see that the men were dead. . . .

What were the Arabs doing? . . . Leaving him as further bait for the trap, and waiting for the whole column to walk into it?

Ought I to warn them again? Surely once was enough? It would mean almost certain capture for me, by one side or the other, if I fired again. . . . Apparently this officer was unwarnable, moreover, and it would be nothing but a vain sacrifice to proclaim my existence and my position, by firing again. . . . And while I argued the matter with my conscience, I saw that all was well—the relieving force was approaching *en tirailleur,* preceded by scouts and guarded by flankers.

Slowly and carefully the French force advanced, well handled by somebody more prudent than the officer who had arrived first, and by no means disposed to walk into an Arab ambush.

A few minutes later, I heard the trumpeter summoning the fort, blowing his calls to dead ears.

I could imagine the bewilderment of the officer standing before those closed gates, waiting for them to open, while the dead stared at him and nothing stirred.

As I waited for him to climb up into the fort or to send somebody in, to open the gates for him, I came to the conclusion that the Arabs must have abandoned the siege and departed altogether. I wondered whether this had been due to Lejaune's ruse and the fort's apparently undiminished garrison, or to news, from their scouts, of the approach of a strong relief force. Anyhow, gone they were, and very probably they had raised the siege and vanished after moonrise the previous night. . . .

The officer, his *sous-officier,* the trumpeter, and a fourth man, stood in a little group beneath the wall, some three hundred yards or so from where I lay. . . . I gathered that the fourth man was refusing to climb into the fort. There was pointing, there were gesticulations, and the officer drew his revolver and presented it at the face of the man who had shaken his head when the officer pointed up at the wall.

The trumpeter, his trumpet dangling as he swung himself up, climbed from the back of his camel to a projecting water-spout, and through an embrasure into the fort.

I expected to see him reappear a minute later at the gate, and admit the others.

He never reappeared at all, and, about a quarter of an hour later, the officer himself climbed up and entered the fort in the same way.

As before, I expected to see the gates opened a minute later—but nothing happened. There was silence and stillness. The minutes dragged by, and the men of the relief-column stood still as statues, staring at the enigmatical fort.

Presently I heard the officer bawling to the trumpeter, the men outside the fort began to move towards it in attack-formation, another squadron of the relief-column arrived on mules, the gates were thrown open from within, and the officer came out alone.

He gave some orders, and re-entered the fort with his second-in-command. No one else went in.

A few minutes later, the officer's companion reappeared, called up a sergeant, and gave orders, evidently for camping in the oasis.

It occurred to me that my situation was about to become an unwholesome one, as, before long, there would be vedettes posted on all four sides of the fort in a big circle, to say nothing of patrols.

I must be going, if I wished to go at all, before I was within a ring of sentries. . . .

After a good look round, I crawled painfully and slowly

to the next sand-hill, trusting that the two in the fort would
find too much of interest, within its walls, to have time to
look over them and see me on my brief journey from cover
to cover. Apparently this was the case, for when I reached
the next sand-hill and looked back from behind its crest,
there was no sign that I had been seen.

I rested, regained my breath, and then made another
bolt to the sand-hill behind me, keeping the fort between the
oasis and my line of retreat, and a good look-out for the
vedette which, sooner or later, was certain to come more
or less in this direction.

My best plan would be to creep from cover to cover,
between the sand-hills, as I was doing, until beyond the
vedette-circle, and then hide and rest till night fell. A
good night's forced marching and I should be thirty miles
away before the sun gained full strength, on the morrow.
As though for a prize—and, of course, my life *was* the
prize—I carried out this careful scouting retirement until
I was half a mile from the fort and among the big stones
that crowned a little hill of rock and sand. Here I was
safe enough for the present. I could lie hidden and see
where the vedettes were posted; sleep in what shade there
was; eat, drink, rest, and gather strength; and set forth,
when the moon rose, on my fairly hopeless journey. . . .
Fairly hopeless? . . . Absolutely hopeless—unless I could
secure a camel. . . . And then and there, I firmly rejected
the idea that entered my mind—of killing a vedette to get
his beast. That I could regard as nothing better than cold-
blooded murder.

A more acceptable notion was that of trying to creep
into the oasis, during the night, and stealing a camel from
there. It would be an extremely difficult thing to do successfully, for there would be brilliant moonlight, a very
sharp look-out for Arabs, and a horrible row from the
camel when one disturbed it. . . . Yes, very difficult and
dangerous, but just possible, inasmuch as I was in uniform
and might be believed if, challenged by the camel-guard, I
pretended I was an orderly in search of his camel, for
duty. Or if I walked up boldly and announced that I had
been ordered to take a camel and ride back to Tokotu with

a dispatch. . . . Distinctly possible, I considered. With really good luck and a really good bluff, it might be done. The good luck would lie in the camel-guard being unaware that I wasn't a member of the relief-force at all.

If I were not recognised, if my bluff were convincing, if I were not caught in the act by the very officer whom I should be pretending to have sent me for a camel; or if, on the other hand, there were a chance of simply stealing the camel unseen—I might get away with it. But there seemed to be a good many *ifs*. . . .

However, after thinking the matter over from all points of view, and weighing the chances impartially, I came to the conclusion that there was more likelihood of Michael's letter reaching Aunt Patricia if I had a shot at getting a camel, than if I did not. A thousand-mile stroll across the Soudanese Sahara did not strike me as one that would lead me home, in view of the fact that it takes a good man to do it under the somewhat more favourable conditions of preparation, organisation, and the protection of numbers and of the law (such as it is).

I decided to wait until night, see what happened, and reconnoitre the oasis with a view to deciding whether theft, bluff, or a combination of the two, offered the greater possibilities of success in securing a mount.

And the more I could concentrate my thoughts upon problems and considerations of this sort, the longer could I postpone and evade the on-rushing realisation of my loss . . . the longer could I keep myself numb and insensate beneath the hammer-blows of the terrible Fact that lurked and struck, lurked and struck; the longer deafen myself to the waxing Voice with its . . . *Michael is dead* . . . *Michael is dead. . . . Listen and heed—Michael is dead. . . .*

In spite of the terrific heat and my unutterable misery and wretchedness, I fell asleep, and slept soundly until towards evening.

§ 2.

When I awoke, I realised that I had been lucky. The nearest vedette was quite a thousand yards to my right, and

so placed that there was no fear of my being seen, so long
as I exercised reasonable precaution.

The sun was setting, the appalling heat of the day was
waning in fierceness, and the fort and oasis presented a
scene of normal military activity—or rather inactivity—
for nothing whatever moved in or around the fort, and there
was but little coming and going about the oasis. Here and
there, a sentry's bayonet gleamed, a man led a mule or
camel; a little column of smoke rose from among the palms,
as a cooking-fire was lighted or replenished.

So far as I could see, the fort had not been taken over by
a new garrison, nor, to my surprise, had the dead been removed from the walls. Those motionless figures could not
be living soldiers, for no Commandant would have kept his
whole force on duty like that—particularly after a day-
and-night march such as this one had just made.

I should have expected to see that the dead had been
buried, the fort occupied, the look-out platform manned,
and the sentry-posts occupied. However, it didn't matter
to me what they did, so long as they left their camels in
the oasis. . . .

As I watched, a small party, preceded by an officer on
a mule, crossed from the oasis and entered the fort. I
expected to see them remove the dead from the embrasures,
but they did not do so. From where I was, I could not see
on to the roof, but I should have seen them at work, had
they come to the wall and begun their labours as a burial
fatigue-party. . . .

Before long, the party returned to the oasis, the officer
remaining in the fort. I wondered what they made of
the *adjudant* with a French bayonet in him, of the dead
légionnaire with his eyes closed and his hands crossed upon
his breast, of the men dead upon their feet, of the complete
absence of life in the uncaptured fort from which two
warning shots had come. . . . Some of the superstitious
old legionaries would have wonderful ideas and theories
about it all!

The evening wore on, the sun set, and the great moon
rose. In the brief dusk, I crept nearer to the fort and
oasis, crouching and crawling from sand-hill to sand-hill.

I would wait until everybody who was not on duty would
be asleep; and then work round and enter the oasis,
walking up boldly as though sent from the fort with a message. If challenged, I would act precisely as I should have
done if dispatched by an officer to get my camel and hasten
back to Tokotu. . . .

I imagined myself saying to a sentry who was disposed
to doubt me, "All right, you fool, you hinder me—go on.
. . . Don't blame *me,* though, when I say what delayed
me! . . ." and generally showing a perfect willingness to
be hindered, provided I was not the one to get the blame. . . .

From the crest of the next sand-hill, I saw that the men
of the relieving-column were parading outside the oasis,
and I wondered what this portended.

As I watched, they marched towards the fort, halted,
faced into line, with their backs towards me, and stood
easy. I concluded that their officer had given them an
"off" day after their long march, and was now going to
work them all night at clearing up the fort, burying the
dead, and generally re-establishing Zinderneuf as a going
concern among the military outposts of Empire-according-
to-a-Republic.

This might be very favourable to my plans. If I marched
boldly up to the oasis, as though coming from the fort,
when everybody was very busy, and demanded a camel, I
should probably get one. . . .

The Commandant rode out from the oasis on a mule, and
the men were called to attention. He was evidently going
to address them—probably to congratulate them on the excellence of their forced march and refer to the marvellous
defence put up by the garrison of the fort, who had died
to a man in defence of the Flag of their adopted country.

Suddenly, the man standing beside him cried out and
pointed to the fort. Instinctively I looked in the direction
of his pointing finger—and very nearly sprang to my feet
at what I saw.

The fort was on fire!

It was very much on fire, too, obviously set alight in
several places and with the help of oil or some other almost
explosive combustible. . . . And what might *this* mean?

Surely it was not "by order"? Not the result of official decision?

Of course not. . . . Could it be the work of some superstitious legionary left alone in the place as watchman? No. If there were anybody at all on duty there, he would have been up on the look-out platform, the emptiness of which had puzzled me. . . .

How was this going to affect my chance of escape? Ought I to make a dash for the oasis while all hands were engaged in an attempt to put the fire out?

And, as I stared, in doubt and wonder, I was aware of a movement on the roof of the fort!

Carefully keeping the gate-tower between himself and the paraded troops, a man was doing precisely what I myself had done! I saw his cap as he crept crouching along below the parapet, I saw his arm and rifle come through an embrasure, I saw the rifle fall, and a minute or so later, as a column of smoke shot up, I saw him crawl through the embrasure and drop to the ground. By good luck or by skill, he had chosen a spot at which he was hidden from the vedette that had been a thousand yards to my right. . . .

And who could he be, this legionary who had set fire to the fort of Zinderneuf? He certainly had my sympathy and should have my assistance. I must see that he did not crawl in the direction of the vedette. He might not know that he was there. I began creeping in a direction that would bring me on to his line of retreat in time to warn him.

A few minutes later he saw me, and hitched his rifle forward. Evidently he did not intend to be taken alive. Very naturally, after setting fire to one of *Madame la République's* perfectly good forts. . . . I drew out what had been a handkerchief, and from the safe obscurity of a sand-valley, waved it. I then laid my rifle down and crawled towards him. I noticed that he was wearing a trumpet, slung behind him.

As I came closer to the man, I was conscious of that strange contraction of the scalp-muscles which has given rise to the expression "his hair stood on end with fright."

I was not frightened and my hair did not stand on end, but I grew cold with a kind of horrified wonder as I saw what I took to be the ghost or astral form *of my brother* there before me, looking perfectly normal, alive, and natural.

It *was* my brother—my brother Digby—Michael's twin. . . .

"Hullo, John," said Digby, as I stared open-mouthed and incredulous, "I thought you'd be knocking about somewhere round here. Let's get off to a healthier spot, shall us?"

For all his casual manner and debonair bearing, he looked white and drawn, sick to death, his hands shaking, his face a ghastly mask of pain.

"Wounded?" I asked, seeing the state he was in.

"Er—not physically. . . . I have just been giving Michael a '*Viking's Funeral,*'" he replied, biting his lip.

Poor, poor Digby! He loved Michael as much as I did (he could not love him more), and he was further bound to him by those strange ties that unite twins—psychic spiritual bonds, that make them more like one soul in two bodies than separate individuals. Poor, poor Digby!

I put my arm across his shoulders as we lay on the sand between two hillocks.

"Poor old John!" he said at length, mastering his grief. "It was you who laid him out, of course. You, who saw him die. . . . Poor Johnny boy! . . ."

"He died trying to save my life," I said. "He died quite happily and in no pain. . . . He left a job for us to do. . . . I've got a letter for you. Here it is. . . . Let's get well off to the flank of that vedette and lie low till there's a chance to pinch a camel and clear out . . ." and I led the way in a direction to bring us clear of the vedettes and nearer to the oasis.

A couple of minutes after our meeting, we were snugly ensconced behind the crest of a sand-hill, overlooking the parade of our comrades, the oasis, and the burning fort. A higher hillock behind us, and to our right, screened us from the nearest vedette.

"*And,*" said Digby, in a voice that trembled slightly, "they're not going to spoil Michael's funeral. Nor are they going to secure any evidence of your neat job on the foul Lejaune. . . . They're going to be attacked by Arabs . . ." and he raised his rifle.

"Don't shoot anybody, Dig," I said. It seemed to me there had been enough bloodshed, and if these people were now technically our enemies and might soon be our executioners, they were still our comrades, and innocent of offence.

"Not going to—unless it's myself," replied Digby. "Come on, play Arabs with me . . ." and he fired his rifle, aiming high.

I followed his example, shooting above the head of the officer as I had done once before that day.

Again and again we fired, vedettes to left and right of us joining in, and showing their zeal and watchfulness by firing briskly at nothing at all—unless it was at each other.

It was a sight worth seeing, the retreat of that company of legionaries. At a cool order from the officer, they faced about, opened out, doubled to the oasis, and went to ground, turning to the enemy and taking cover so that, within a couple of minutes of our first shots, there was nothing to be seen but a dark and menacing oasis, to approach which was death. . . .

"Good work!" said Digby. "And they can jolly well stop there until the fort is burnt out. . . . We'll go in and get camels, as vedettes whose camels have been shot by these attacking Arabs, later on. . . . If we swagger up to the sentry on the camels, and pitch a bold yarn, it ought to be all right. . . ."

"Yes—better if one of us goes," said I. "Then, if he doesn't return, the other can clear off on foot, or try some other dodge."

"That's it," agreed Digby. "I'll have first go."

"Now tell me all that happened," he added, "and then I'll bring you up to date."

I did so, giving him a full account of all our doings, from the time he had left us to go to the mounted company.

"Now tell me a few things, Dig," I said, when I had finished, and he knew as much as I did.

He then told me of how his *escouade* had suddenly been ordered from Tanout-Azzal to Tokotu. Here they had

found, of all people on this earth, the Spahi officer who had
once visited Brandon Abbas, now Major de Beaujolais, seconded from his regiment for duty with mounted units in
the *Territoire Militaire* of the Soudan, where the mobile
Touaregs were presenting a difficult problem to the peaceful penetrators towards Timbuktu and Lake Tchad.

The Major had not recognised Digby, of course, nor
Digby him, until he heard his name and that he was a Spahi.

(And it was at him that I had been shooting that day, or
rather it was he at whom I had not been shooting. It was
this very friend of boyhood's days whom I had been trying
to warn against what I thought was an ambush! . . . Time's
whirligig! . . .)

At Tokotu, news had been received that Zinderneuf was
besieged by a huge force of Touaregs, and de Beaujolais
had set off at once.

The rest I knew until the moment when I had seen
Digby, who was de Beaujolais' trumpeter, climb into the
fort. . . .

"Well—you know what I saw as I got on to the roof,"
said Digby, "and you can imagine (can you, I wonder?)
what I felt when I saw Beau lying there. . . . I dashed down
below and rushed round to see if you were among the
wounded, and then realised that there *were* no wounded,
and that the entire garrison was on that awful roof. . . .
That meant that you had cleared out, and that it was your
bayonet ornamenting Lejaune's chest, and that it was you
who had disposed Michael's body and closed his eyes.
Someone must have done it, and it wasn't one of those
dead men. . . . Who else but you would have treated
Michael's body differently from the others? As I have
told you, I was mighty anxious, coming along, as to how
you and Michael were getting on, and whether we should be
in time, and I had been itching to get up on to the roof
while de Beaujolais was being dramatic with Rastignac.
. . . You can guess how anxious I was *now*. . . . What with
Michael's death and your disappearance. . . .

"I could almost *see* you killing Lejaune, and felt certain
it was because he had killed Michael and tried to kill you
for that cursed 'diamond.' . . . I tell you I went dotty. . . .

" '*Anyhow—he shall have a "Viking's Funeral,*' ' I swore, and I believe I yelled the words at the top of my voice, '*and then I must find John.*' . . . You know, it was always Beau's constant worry that harm would come to you. It was the regret of his life, that he was responsible for your bolting from home. . . . You young ass. . . .

"Anyhow, my one idea was to give him a proper funeral and then to follow you up. I guessed that you had stuck there, the sole survivor, until you saw de Beaujolais, and then slipped over the wall. . . .

"Then I heard someone scrambling and scraping at the wall, climbing up, and I crept off and rushed down below, with the idea of hiding till I got a chance to set fire to the beastly place, if I could do nothing better for Beau. . . . I saw the door of the punishment-cell standing open, and I slipped in there and hid behind the door. There was just room for me, and I should never be seen until someone came in and closed the door of the cell—which wasn't likely to happen for a long while. . . .

"Soon I heard de Beaujolais bawling out for me, and by the sound of his voice he wasn't much happier than I was. . . . The sight upstairs was enough to shake *anybody's* nerve, let alone the puzzle of it all. . . . By and by I heard him and the Sergeant-Major talking and hunting for me. They actually looked into the cell once, but it was obviously empty—besides being a most unlikely place for a soldier to shut himself in voluntarily! . . . I gathered that old Dufour was even less happy than de Beaujolais, who certainly wasn't enjoying himself. . . . Presently they went away, and the place became as silent as the grave. It occurred to me that whatever else they made of it they must be certain that Lejaune had been killed by one of his own men and that the man must have bolted. If I could also vanish in this mysterious place, it would give them something more to puzzle over; and if I could absolutely destroy it, there would be no evidence for them to lay before a court martial. . . . Mind, I had been marching for twenty-four hours and was all but sleeping on my feet, so I wasn't at my brightest and best, by a long way—apart from what I had just seen. . .

"When I felt pretty certain that there was no one about, I crept up on to the roof again and took a look round.

"There was a sentry at the gate, and the company was evidently going to camp in the oasis, and have a sleep before entering the fort.

"I pulled myself together, crawled over to where Beau lay, heaved him up in my arms and carried him below to his own bed in the barrack-room. All round his cot I laid piles of wood from the cook-house and drenched it with lamp oil. I did my best to make it a real '*Viking's Funeral*' for him, just like we used to have at home. Just like he used to want it. My chief regret was that I had no Union Jack to drape over him. . . .

"However, I did the best I could, and covered the whole pyre with sheets of canvas and things. . . . All white, more or less. . . . There was no sign of the wood and oil. . . . He looked splendid. . . . Then, after thinking it over, I took the spare Tri-couleur and laid that over all. . . . It wasn't what I would have liked, but he had fought and died under it, so it served. . . . It served. . . . Served. . . ."

Digby's head was nodding as he talked. He was like a somnambulist. I tried to stop him.

"Shut up, John. . . . I must get it clear. . . . *Oh, Beau! Beau! . . . I did my best for you, old chap. . . . There was no horse, nor spear, nor shield to lay beside you. . . . But I put a dog at your feet though. . . . And your rifle and bayonet was for sword and spear. . . .*"

He must be going mad, I feared.

"A dog, old chap?" I said, trying to get him back to realities. "You are not getting it right, you know. . . ."

"Yes, a dog. . . . A dog at his feet. . . . A dog lying crouching with his head beneath his heels. . . ."

This was getting dreadful.

"I did not carry it down, as I carried Beau. I took it by one foot and dragged it down. . . ."

"*Lejaune?*" I whispered.

"Yes, John. Lejaune—with your bayonet through his heart. *He* won't give dumb evidence against you—and Beau had his '*Viking's Funeral*' with a dog at his feet. . . ."

I think I felt worse then than I had felt since Michael

died. I gave Digby a sharp nudge in the ribs with my elbows.

"Get on with it and don't drivel," I said as though in anger.

"Where was I?" said Digby, in the tone of a man waking from a nap.

"Oh, yes. And when all was ready, John, I sat and talked to Beau and told him I hadn't the faintest idea as to what he'd been up to in this 'Blue Water' business, but what I *did* know was that, far from being anything shady, it was something quixotic and noble. . . . And then what do you think I did, John? . . . *I fell asleep*—and slept till the evening. . . .

"I was a bit more my own man when I woke up. I went up on the roof to see what was doing. . . . Creeping to the wall and peeping over, I saw that the Company was parading, and that I had cut it very fine. I thanked God that I had awakened in time, for in a few minutes they would be marching in, to clean up and take over.

"I crept back and set fire to Beau's funeral pyre. Then I rushed off and poured a can of oil over the pile of benches and furniture that I had heaped up in the next room. I set light to that and knocked another can over at the foot of the stairs. I lit it and bolted up to the stair of the look-out platform. At the bottom of this, I did the same, and by that time it would have taken more water than there is in the Sahara to put the place out. . . . I decided that Beau's funeral was all right, the evidence against you destroyed, and the time arrived for me to clear out. . . ."

He yawned prodigiously.

"So I came to look for you, John. . . . To look for . . . for . . ."

Digby was asleep.

Should I go to sleep too? The temptation was sore. But I felt that if we were to save ourselves, we must do it at once. We could hardly hope to lie there all night and escape detection in the morning, when the place would be swarming with scouts and skirmishers.

I decided to watch for an hour or two, while poor Digby slept. At the end of that time I would wake him and say that I was going to make the attempt to get a camel. . . .

It was extraordinarily silent. . . . It seemed impossible that the oasis, lying there so black and still, was alive with armed men. Even the camels and mules were behaving as though aware that the night was unusual. Not a grunting gurgle from the one or a whinnying bray from the other broke the brooding stillness of the night. I wondered if every man had been made responsible for the silence of his own animal, and had muzzled and gagged it. I smiled at the idea.

Not a light showed. Was the idea to make the smoulder-ing fort a bait for the Arabs whom de Beaujolais would suppose to be in the neighbourhood—a bait to attract them to his lead-and-steel-fanged trap? . . .

How would it be possible, after all, for me to approach that silvered black oasis, across the moonlit sands, without being challenged, seized, and exposed for what I was? I had anticipated approaching a normal, somnolent camp—not a tensely watchful look-out post, such as the oasis had become from the time Digby and I had fired our rifles.

Would it be better, after all, to sleep all night and try to bluff the camel-guard on the morrow, when the whole place would be buzzing with life and activity? It seemed a poor look-out anyway. And how bitterly one would regret not having made the attempt on foot, if one were seized in the effort to take a camel. . . .

Having decided that Digby had slept for about a couple of hours, I woke him up.

"What about it, Dig?" I said. "Are we going to have a shot at getting a camel, or are we going to march? We must do one or the other, unless you think we might do any good here by daylight. . . ."

"Oh, quite," replied Digby. "I'm sure you're right, John," and went to sleep again, in the act of speaking.

This was not exactly helpful, and I was trying to make up my mind as to whether I should give him another hour, or knock him up again at once, when I saw two camel-riders leave the oasis. I rubbed my eyes.

No. There was no doubt about it. A patrol was going out, or dispatches were being sent to Tokotu.

Here were two camels. Two well-fed, well-watered camels were coming towards us.

I did not for one moment entertain the thought of shooting their riders, but I certainly toyed for a moment with the idea of offering to fight them, fair and square, for their beasts! If we won, we should ride off and they would tramp back to the oasis. If they won, they'd continue about their business and we should be where we were. . . . A silly notion. . . . About two seconds after revealing ourselves, we should be looking into the muzzles of their rifles, and have the option of death or ignominious capture. . . . Why *should* they fight us? . . . I must really pull myself together and remember who I was and where I was. . . .

The camels drew nearer and I decided, from their direction, they were on the way to Tokotu.

I crawled down the reverse slope of my sand-hill and ran along the valley at its base. Climbing another hillock, I saw that a repetition of the manœuvre would bring me on to their line. I did not know what I was going to do when I got there, but I felt there would be no harm in trying to find out who they were and where they were going. If we followed them and got a chance to steal their camels while they were not too far from the oasis to return on foot, I had an idea that we might take that chance. The temptation would be very strong, as it was a matter of life and death to us, while to them it would be merely a matter of a long day's march and a fearful tale of terrific combat with the horde of Arabs who had shot their camels. . . .

Suddenly a well-known voice remarked conversationally:

"We sure gotta put them nigs wise, Buddy. . . . We don' want nawthen to eventooate to the pore boobs through us not taking 'em by the hand. . . ."

"Hank!" I yelped in glee and thankfulness, and he and Buddy turned their camels towards me.

"Here's *one* of the mystery boys, anyhow," went on Hank. "I allowed as how you'd be around somewheres when we see you all three gone missin' from the old home. . . ."

In a valley between two sand-hills, Hank and Buddy brought their camels to their knees and dismounted. Both wrung my hand in a painful and most delightful manner.

"No offence, and excusin' a personal and dellikit question, Bo," said Buddy, "but was it you as had the accident with the cigar-lighter an' kinder caused arsonical proceedins'? . . ."

"Sort of 'arson about' with matches like?" put in Hank solemnly.

"No," I said. "It was Digby set fire to the fort."

"Then I would shore like to shake him by the hand, some," said Hank. "Is he around?"

"Having a nap over there," I replied.

"The other bright boy too?" asked Buddy. "An' where's Lejaune? Havin' set fire to the home, hev you taken Poppa by the ear an' led him out into the garden for to admire? . . ."

As quickly as possible I told him what had happened— of Michael's death and "funeral."

"He was a shore white man, pard. 'Nuff said," commented Hank.

"He was all-wool-an'-a-yard-wide, Bo," said Buddy, and I felt that Michael might have had worse epitaphs.

A brief silence fell upon us.

"Gee!" said Hank after a while. "Wouldn't it jar you? It shore beats the band. Such nice quiet boys too—always behavin' like they was at a party, an' perlite as Hell—an' one of 'em kills the Big Noise an' the other sets the whole gosh-dinged outfit afire an' burns out the dod-gasted burg. . . . *Some* boys, I allow. . . ."

I greatly feared that our deeds of homicide and arson had raised us higher in the estimation of these good men than any number of pious acts and gentle words could ever have done.

As I led the way to where I had left Digby sleeping, I asked the Americans where they were going.

"Wal—we was sorta sent lookin' fer some nigs from Tokotu," replied Hank. "Ole Man Bojolly allows they'll run into an Injun ambush if they ain't put wise. We gotta warn them there's Injuns about, fer all the location's so quiet an' peaceful-lookin' . . .

"I wonder they didn't git you two boys when they shot us up," he added.

"We *were* the Arabs," I confessed with modest pride.

"Gee!" admired Buddy. "Can you beat it! . . . I shore thought there was thousands come gunnin' fer us. . . . Oh, *boy!* You quiet perlite young guys. . . . *Mother! . . .*"

"How many guns did you shoot then?" enquired Hank.

"Two," I replied. "Rapid fire. And then the vedettes obligingly joined in."

Buddy gave a brief hard bark, which may, or may not, have been meant for laughter.

"Sunday pants of Holy Moses!" he observed. "And that lyin' son of a skunk of a Schneider swore he shot seven of you himself—and the rest of you carried away their bodies as he retired in good order! Thinks he oughta get the *médaille militaire* or somethin'. . . ."

"Yep," confirmed Hank, "an' Ole Man Dupanloup estimates the lot that was agwine ter rush the parade, when he held 'em up, at from a hunderd to a hunderd an' fifty. He lost count of the number he killed—after a score or so. . . . Gee! At them north outposts there was *some* bloody battle, son. . . ."

"*And* some bloody liars," observed Buddy, who had sojourned in London.

I had difficulty in awaking poor Digby, but when he realised that Hank and Buddy were actually present in the flesh, he was soon very much awake and on the spot.

"Say, boys," he went on, after greeting them and hearing their tale of the Battle of the Vedettes, "it's a lot to ask, I know. But *do* you think you could be attacked, like Dupanloup, by about a hundred and fifty of us, and lose your camels? . . . They'd be shot beneath you, or on top of you, if you like,—while you fought desperately—one to seventy-five, isn't it? . . . You would have peace with honour, and we'd have a chance to save our lives. We don't pretend that they're very valuable, but we've got something we really must do for our brother. . . . And I promised Mother I'd bring the Baby home," he added, indicating me.

"Fergit it, son," replied Hank to Digby, but he looked at Buddy.

"Couldn't you possibly let us have them?" I said. "If we went a mile or two further on, we could kick up a fearful row with our four rifles, and you could go back and collect a medal when old Dupanloup gets his. . . . Stroll home doing a rear-guard stunt, and we'd pepper the scenery in your direction before we rode off. . . . The Senegalese are safe enough. There are no Arabs and no ambush. . . . And we simply shan't have a little dog's chance without camels."

"*We* want 'em, Bo," replied Hank with quiet finality.

"Shore," agreed Buddy, eyeing him.

I was surprised and disappointed. Even more disappointed at the attitude of my friends than at the loss of the camels.

"Well—all right then! We won't *fight* you for them," said Digby, "but I wish it had been someone else."

"I don't get your drift. Snow again, Bo," said Buddy, who seemed pained.

"Why someone else? Don't you admire our low and vulgar ways, pard?" asked Hank. "Don't you like us?"

"Yes, but to be honest, at the moment I like your camels better," replied Digby.

"Well, then—you got the lot, ain't you?" asked Hank. "What's bitin' you now, Bo?"

"Do you mean *you're coming with us?*" I asked, a great light dawning upon me, a light that so dazzled my eyes that I was afraid to look upon it.

"You shore said a mouthful, Bo," replied Hank. "Why, what did you figger? That we'd leave you two innercent children to wander about this yer sinful world all on your lone? . . ."

"After you bin and killed their Big Noise? And obliterised their nice little block-house?" put in Buddy. " 'Twouldn't be right, boy. *'Course* we're comin' along."

I really had to swallow hard as I took their horny hands.

"But look here, boys," Digby remonstrated, after following my example and trying to express thanks without words, "there's no need for that. Give us your camels and anything else you can safely spare, and go back in modest glory. There's nothing against *you*. If you're caught escaping with us and helping us, you'll be shot with us. It will be 'desertion in the face of the enemy when sent on reconnaissance' when it comes to the court martial.''

"Go back nawthen," said Buddy. "Look at here. This is what Hank wants to say.... Is there any Injuns around? Nope. Is those nigs from Tokotu in any danger? Nope. Hev you had a square deal in this Madam Lar Republichouse stunt? Nope. Didn't you and your brother stand by your dooty in this mutiny game? Yep. Wasn't you two scrapping all the time and doing your damnedest till everybody else had handed in their checks? Yep. And then didn't this Lejaune guy start in to shoot you up? Shore. And what'll happen to you now if they get you? Shoot you up some more. Shore. 'Tain't a square deal. . . .

"Well, we figger that these nigs from Tokotu aren't on the chutes fer the bow-wows. Nope. They're marchin' on right now fer Zinderneuf—like John Brown's body—or was it his soul?—safe enough. . . . We allow you ain't got no chance on a lone trail. Not a doggoned smell of one. You're two way-up gay cats an' bright boys, but you're no road-kids. You don't know chaparral from an arroyo nor alkali sage-brush from frijoles. You couldn't tell mesquite from a pinto-hoss. Therefore Hank says we gotta come along. . . .''

"Shore thing," agreed Hank, "and time we vamoosed too, or we'll hev these nigs a-treadin' on us. They'll go fer a walk on empty stummicks—ours. . . .''

A minute later each of the camels bore two riders, and we were padding off at a steady eight miles an hour.

"Any pertickler direction like?" said Hank, behind whom I was riding. "London? N'York? Morocker? Egyp'? Cape Town? All the same ter me.''

Buddy drove his camel up beside ours.

"What about it, Dig?" said I to my brother. "We've got to get out of French territory. . . . Morocco's north-west; Nigeria's south-east. . . .''

"And where's water?" replied Digby. "I should say the nearest oasis would be a sound objective.''

"If there's a pursuit, they'd take the line for Morocco for certain, I should say," I pointed out. "I vote for the opposite direction and a beady eye on our fellow-man, if we can see him. Where there are Arabs there'll be water somewhere about, I suppose."

"Shore," said Hank. "We'll pursoo the pore Injun. What's good enough fer him is bad enough for us. You say wheer you wants ter go, an' I allow *we'll see you there* —but it may take a few years. What we gotta do first is turn Injun, see? . . . Git Injun glad rags, and live like they does. We're well-armed and got our health an' strength an' hoss-sense. When in the desert do as the deserters does. . . . Yep. We gotta turn Injun."

From which I gathered that Hank the Wise firmly advocated our early metamorphosis into Arabs, and the adoption of Arab methods of subsistence in waterless places.

"Injuns lives by lettin' other folks *pro*-juce an' then collectin'," put in Buddy.

"We gotta collect," said Hank.

"From the collectors," added Buddy.

From which I gathered further that our friends were proposing not only that we should turn Arab, but super-Arab, and should prey upon the Touareg as the Touareg preyed upon the ordinary desert-dweller. It seemed a sound plan, if a little difficult of application. However, I had infinite faith in the resourcefulness, experience, staunchness, and courage of the two Americans, and reflected that if anybody could escape from this predicament, it was these men, familiar with the almost equally terrible American deserts.

"I vote we go south-west," said Digby. "We're bound to strike British territory sooner or later and then we're absolutely safe, and can easily get away by sea. We're bound to fetch up in Nigeria if we go steadily south-west. If we could hit the Niger somewhere east of Timbuktu— it would lead us straight to it."

"Plenty o' drinkin' water in the Niger, I allow," observed Buddy. "But there don't seem ter be no sign-posts to it. It shore is a backward state, this Sahara. . . ."

"Anyhow it's south-west of us now, and so's Nigeria," Digby insisted.

"Starboard yer hellum," observed Hank. "Nigeria on the port bow—about one thousand miles."

And that night we did some fifty or sixty of them without stopping, by way of a good start—a forced march while the camels were fresh and strong.

As we padded steadily along, we took stock of our resources.

With my bottles of water, and the regulation water-bottles, we had enough for two or three days, with careful rationing.

Similarly with food. I had a haversack full of bread, and the other three had each an emergency ration as well as army biscuits.

Of ammunition we had plenty, and we hoped to shoot dorcas gazelle, bustard, and hare, if nothing else.

Had Michael been with us, I should have been happy. As it was, the excitement, the mental and physical activity, the hopes and fears attendant on our precarious situation, and the companionship of my brother and these two fine Americans combined to help me to postpone my defeat by the giants of misery, pain, and grief that were surely only biding their time, lurking to spring when I could no longer maintain my defences.

Digby, I think, was in much the same mental condition as myself, and I wondered if I, too, had aged ten years in a night.

As we jogged steadily on, the monotony of movement, of scene, and of sound, sent me to sleep, and every now and then I only saved myself from falling by a wild clutch at Hank, behind whom I was sitting.

No one spoke, and it is probable that all of us slept in brief snatches—though they must have been very brief for those who were driving the camels.

I came fully awake as the sun peered over the far-distant edge of the desert to our left.

I longed for a hot bath and hotter coffee, for I ached in every nerve and muscle.

" ' "They'll have fleet steeds that follow," quoth young Lochinvar,' " said Digby.

"They've got 'em," replied Buddy, looking behind as we topped a ridge of rock.

On we drove, south-west, throughout what was, very comparatively speaking, the cool of the morning, until Hank thought we should be making more haste than speed by continuing without resting the camels.

"I don't perfess ter know much about these doggoned *shammos,* as they call 'em," observed Hank, "but I allow you can't go very far wrong if you treats 'em as hosses."

"Shore," agreed Buddy, " 'cept that they got more control of their passions like. . . . Fer eats, and fer settin' up the drinks, anyhow. . . . They can live on nawthen. An' as that's just what we pervided for 'em, they oughta thrive."

"We'll have to find *something* for them," said Digby, "if it's only newspaper or the thatch of a nigger's hut."

"I hev heard of 'em eatin' people's hats at dime shows and meenageries," said Hank. "My Aunt 'Mandy went to Ole Man Barnum's show on her golden weddin' day, an' a camel browsed her hat and all her back hair, an' she never knowed it until she felt a draught. . . . Yep. They kin hev our *képis* if they wait till we got some Injun shappos an' pants an' things. . . ."

I was aware that camels had meagre appetites and queer, limited tastes, embracing a narrow selection ranging from bran to the twigs of dead thorn-bush, but I agreed with Digby that we should have to give them something, and something other than our caps. Our lives depended upon these two ugly, unfriendly beasts, for without them we should either be quickly recaptured or else we should die of thirst and starvation, long before we could reach any oasis.

In the rapidly narrowing shadow of a providential great rock in this thirsty land, we lay stretched on our backs, after an ascetic meal of bread and water.

"What's the programme of sports, Hank?" I asked, as we settled ourselves to sleep.

"Another forced march ter git outta the onhealthy location o' Zinderneuf," he replied. "Then we gotta scout fer Injuns or an oasis. Spread out in a four-mile line an' peek over every rock and hill. . . . We'll shore fix it . . ." and he went to sleep.

Personally I slept till evening without moving, and I was only then awakened by the grumbling, gurgling roar of the camel that Hank was girthing up, one of his feet pressed against its side and all his weight and strength on the girth-rope.

Having put the camel-blanket on the other animal, lifted the wooden framework regulation saddle on to it, girthed it up, taken the nose-reins over the beast's head and looped them round the pommel, he bawled "All aboard," and stood with his foot on the kneeling camel's near fore-knee, while I climbed into the rear part of the saddle. He then vaulted into the front seat and the camel, lurching heavily, came to its feet with an angry hungry roar.

Buddy and Digby mounted the other beast, and once more we were off, not to stop until we estimated that there were at least a hundred miles between us and Zinderneuf.

This was, of course, too good to last—or too bad, from the camels' point of view. At the end of this second ride they must have food and a day's rest, if not water.

Again I slept spasmodically, towards morning, especially after Hank had insisted upon my embracing him round the body and leaning against him.

I was awakened from a semi-slumbrous state of coma by an exclamation from Buddy, to realise that it was day again, the camels were standing still, and their riders gazing at what Buddy was indicating with outstretched arm.

Over the level stretch of unblown sand which we were crossing, ran a broad and recent trail of camel footprints.

This trail crossed ours, though not at right angles. If we were going south-west I should think the riders were going south—or north.

Hank and Buddy brought the camels to their knees, with the gentle insistent *"Oosha, baba, oosha; adar-ya-yan!"* which is about the only order that a camel obeys without cavil or protest.

Following the footmarks and regarding them carefully, they decided that there were about twenty camels in the party, that they were going south, and that they had passed quite recently.

"What we bin lookin' for!" observed Hank with grim satisfaction, as he swung himself back into the saddle. "The nearer we kin git to them Injuns, the quicker—but we don' wanta tread on 'em. Keep yer eyes skinned, boys." And the others having remounted, on we went.

I should think we followed this trail for three or four hours, without seeing anything but the eternal desert of sand and rock.

For some time I had been wondering how much longer we were to go on without resting the camels, when a grunt of satisfaction from Hank renewed my waning interest in life. He brought the camel to a halt and pointed, as Buddy ranged up beside us.

We had come to the bank of a very wide and rather shallow dry river-bed, whose shelving sides led down to gravel and stones which at one time must have been subject to the action of running water. The place looked as though a river had flowed along it ten thousand years ago.

But what Hank was pointing to was the spot to which the footprints led.

Beneath a huge high rock, that rose from the middle of the river-bed, was a dark inviting shadow around which were dry-looking tufts of coarse grass, stunted dwarf acacias, and low thorn-bushes.

The camels were perceptibly eager to get to this spot.

"Water," said Hank. "May have to dig."

But there was no need to dig. Beneath and around the rock was a pool, fed presumably from a subterranean source. It wasn't the sparkling water of an English spring, bubbling up among green hills, by any means. The green was rather in the water, but we were not fastidious, and certainly the camels were not. On the contrary, we were delighted and deeply thankful.

Here were shade, water, and camel-food, giving us a new lease of life, and encouragement on our way. It was evident that a party of travellers had recently halted here.

"Good old Touaregs," said Digby, as we dismounted in the glorious shade. "Obliging lads. We'll follow them up just as long as they are going our way home."

"We gotta do more'n foller 'em up," said Hank. "We gotta *catch* 'em up. They gotta lend us some correc' desert-wear striped gents' suitings. Likewise grub-stake us some."

"Shore," agreed Buddy. "An' we ain't no hoss-thieves

neither, but I allow they gotta lend us a couple o' good camels too.''

From the first, the Americans had been anxious to secure Arab dress, both on account of possible pursuit from Zin-derneuf, and as being less conspicuous and less likely to bring every wandering Arab band down upon us, directly they caught sight of us and recognised us for hated *Roumis*.

They were doubly anxious to procure the disguise on learning that, in the south, towards Nigeria, there were numerous forts and outposts of the French Niger Territory, garrisoned by Senegalese, and that between these posts, numerous patrols would carefully watch the caravan-routes, and visit such Arab towns and settlements as existed.

It would certainly be better to encounter a patrol in the rôle of Arabs than in that of runaway soldiers from the Foreign Legion.

Accordingly Hank decreed that we must push on, only enough time being spent here for the camels to eat and drink their fill. He was of opinion that the party we were following was an offshoot of the big band that had at-tacked Zinderneuf and was on its way to "gather in" some village which they visited periodically.

Here they would appropriate its harvest of dates or grain, such camels as might be worthy, those of the sons and daughters who might be suitable for slaves, and any goats, clothing, money, and useful odds-and-ends that they might fancy.

These Touareg bands make an annual tour and visit the villages of an enormous area, in the spirit of somewhat arbitrary and undiscriminating tax-collectors. What they want, by way of tax, is everything the villagers possess that is portable, including their young men and maidens.

If the villagers are reasonable and relinquish everything with a good grace, there need not be any bloodshed—or very little, just in the way of fun and sportive merriment.

The Touaregs do not wish to destroy the village and slaughter the inhabitants, because they prefer to find a peaceful and prosperous community here, again, next year.

All they wish to do, is to clean them out absolutely and leave them alone to amass some more. But if the villagers choose to be uppish and truculent, giving their visitors trouble—they must take the consequences—which are fire and sword and torture.

Or, if the band is off its regular beat and not likely to come that way again, it combines sport with business, and leaves no living thing behind it, nor any roofed dwelling in what was a village—scarcely one stone upon another of what was a little town.

After about three hours' rest, we pushed on again, and rode for the remainder of the day and right through the night. The fact that we did not come up with our quarry seemed to confirm the theory that they were a war-party on raiding business. Peaceful caravans and travellers would never go at such a pace, and we should have over-taken such a party easily. . . .

On this side of the river, or rather river-bed, the scenery began to change. The earth grew greyer in colour, cactus and acacia began to appear, and there were numerous great rock *kopjes*. The change was from utterly lifeless sand-desert to rock-desert, having a sparse vegetation.

Suddenly we heard distant rifle-fire to our front—a few scattered shots. Simultaneously, Hank and Buddy brought the camels to their knees among the rocks, and we dis-mounted, unslinging our rifles as we did so.

"Mustn't get the *shammos* shot up," said Hank to me. "You hold 'em, Bo, while we rubber around some," and they skirmished forward.

Nothing further being heard and nothing seen, they re-turned, and we rode on again.

Rounding a great rock, a mile or two further on, a rock that reminded one of a Dartmoor tor, we saw an ugly sight.

A woman had been tied to an acacia tree and horribly mutilatel. I need say no more about the sight and its effect upon us, although I might say a good deal.

It was evident that she had been herding a flock of goats. . . .

"Village near," said Hank, and he and Buddy again simultaneously wheeled the camels round, and we retired behind the tor and dismounted.

"We'll corral the hosses here, and scout some," said

Hank. "It'll be worth dollars to see these darned coyotes before they see us."

This time the camels were tied with their *agals*, and left. We advanced *en tirailleur*, as though to the attack of an Arab *douar*, a manœuvre with which our training had made us only too familiar.

Gradually we approached what appeared to be a completely deserted village by an oasis at the edge of a deep ravine. I should think there had been a village on this spot for thousands of years, though the present buildings were wretched mud huts crowning the basements of ancient stone houses of great strength. It was as though a tribe of gipsies, encamped permanently on an Ancient British hut-circle site on Dartmoor, had used the prehistoric stones in the construction of their rude dwellings.

Into this village, evidently very recently abandoned, we made our way with due precaution.

In one of the huts, on a rough *angareb*, lay a wounded man. As we entered, he drew a curved dagger from his belt and feebly struck at us.

"We are friends," said I in Arabic. "Tell us what has happened. We want to help. . . ."

Digby also aired his Arabic, and the man was convinced.

He appeared to understand all we said, and I understood him about as well as an English-speaking Frenchman would understand a Devonshire yokel.

I gathered that the usual village tragedy had developed as follows:

A woman, minding goats, had seen a band of Touaregs approaching (this man called them "The Veiled Ones, the Forgotten of God"), and had foolishly, or bravely, got up on a rock and screamed the news to a youth, who was working nearer the village. They had both then started running, but the Touaregs had caught the woman. The youth had roused the village and the men had rushed out with their rifles to some rocks near by, ready to fire on the Touaregs, and hoping to give the impression of a large and well-armed force, fully prepared to give them a warm reception. The women and children had scuttled to the big ravine behind the village, down which they would make their way to their usual hiding-place.

A couple of lads had been sent off to warn the men who had taken the camels out to graze.

The speaker had been one of these men, and while he and one or two others were collecting the camels and driving them to the ravine, a Targui scout had come upon them and shot him. The rest of the Touaregs had come straight to the spot, circled round, fired a volley, and closed in on the camels.

He himself had been left for dead. When he came to his senses he was alone with the corpses of the other camel-guards, and he had slowly crawled to his hut to die.

The Touaregs had camped and were calmly enjoying a well-earned rest. Apparently the village men were still watching events from their place among the rocks, the women and children were in hiding down the ravine, and the camels were captured.

I gathered that it would have been less calamitous had the camels been in hiding down the ravine, and the women and children captured.

We explained the situation to Hank and Buddy.

"Sport without danger, and business with pleasure," was their view, but we must give the Touaregs the shock of their lives.

We held a council of war, and it was decided that the wounded man should get in touch with the villagers and tell them that we were friends of theirs. More, we were deadly enemies of the Touaregs, and (most) we'd get the camels back and give them those of the Touaregs too—if they'd play the man and do as we bade them.

Having told his tale and grasped that we really wished to befriend him, the wounded man seemed to be farther from death than he had thought. He was shot through the chest, but I did not think that his lungs had suffered, as there was no hæmorrhage from the mouth.

After a drink of water and a pill, which Digby gave him with the assurance that it would do *wonders* for him (though I doubted whether they were wonders suitable to the situation), he got off the *angareb* and staggered to the doorway of the hut. From here he peered beneath his hand for a while, and then tottered out and did some signalling.

Very pluckily he stuck to it until an answering movement among the rocks, unseen by us, satisfied him, and he returned to the hut.

Shortly afterwards, a hail brought him to the door again, and this time he walked off fairly steadily, and disappeared into the ravine.

He returned with a big, dirty squint-eyed Arab, who, he said, was the headman of the village, which was called Azzigig (or sounds to that effect).

The headman was in the mental condition of one who sees men as trees walking, when he found himself in the presence of four armed and uniformed *Roumis,* two of whom spoke Arabic to him, and all of whom wished him to put up a fight for Azzigig, Home, and Beauty.

His own idea was to thank Allah that things were no worse, and to lie low until the Touaregs chose to depart, praying meanwhile that they would do so in peace, without troubling to hunt out the villagers, burn the houses, slaughter the goats, and have a little torture-party before doing so.

When I asked if he felt no particular resentment about the mutilated woman and the slaughtered camel-guards, to say nothing of the loss of the entire stock of camels, he replied that it was doubtless the will of Allah, and who should dispute that?

When I pointed out that it was obviously the will of Allah that we should arrive in the nick of time, and that the Touaregs should camp and rest instead of riding off, he said he would go and talk with his brethren.

This he did, and returned with a deputation of very dirty, suspicious, evil-looking Arabs, who evidently did not believe what he had told them, and had come to see for themselves.

"Gee!" observed Buddy. "Watta ugly bunch o' low-lifer hoboes."

"*Some* stiffs," agreed Hank.

However, I harangued the stiffs, offering them a chance

of recovering their camels and teaching the Touaregs a lesson. I fumbled for the Arabic for "catching a Tartar" as I tried to get these fatalists to see they had as much "right to life, liberty, and the pursuit of happiness" as Touaregs, and that the latter had no God-given privilege to torture, murder, and rob. As for the "Will of Allah," let them follow us and show a little pluck, and they'd soon see what was the will of Allah in the matter.

In support Digby said, "Anyhow, we're going to attack them, whether you do or not. Those who help us will share the loot."

As the loot would include excellent rifles and incomparable camels, this gave the poor wretches something to think about. In the end, they agreed that if we would really fight for them, and with them, and give them all the loot, except a couple of camels, as we had promised, they would fight their hardest.

We began by reconnoitring the Touareg camp.

Absolutely certain of their complete security, the robbers had merely lighted fires and lain down to rest, leaving one of their number to guard their own camels and two to guard those stolen from the villagers.

Presumably these guards were more herdsmen than sentries, as the Touaregs had nothing to fear. Villagers do not attack victorious Hoggar robbers. It simply is not done. All that was necessary was to prevent the camels from straying, and to have a rest before proceeding on the tax-gathering journey—with or without a little sport in the village before starting. . . .

Our plan was simple for our job was easy.

Half a dozen selected heroes of Azzigig were to deal with the somnolent loafing camel-guards—silently if possible. Every rifle that Azzigig could boast was then to be discharged into the Touareg camp, from as close a range as it was possible to wriggle to.

When the Touaregs bolted to the ravine, as they certainly would do, to take cover from this blast and organise their defence—they would find their way blocked by the entire French army, in uniform, with a bugler blowing calls to bring up thousands more! . . .

I must say that the villagers behaved very well. They were, of course, born desert fighters, and we had put heart into them.

After a tremendous volley, at about forty yards' range, they charged like fiends, and when we four arose from behind rocks and the Touaregs recoiled in astounded terror, they surrounded them like a pack of wolves.

In a brief, mad, happy minute of hacking, stabbing, and shooting, they worked off a good deal of the personal and ancestral grudge of centuries. As they outnumbered the Touaregs by five or six to one, had them at a complete disadvantage, and knew we were behind them, they made a short job of it and a clean one.

From another point of view it was not a clean one.

At any rate, we prevented torture even if we could not save life. For once it was the under-dog's turn, and he used his teeth. . . .

Digby, not unreasonably, claimed that the bugle really won the battle.

The upshot of the business was that we left Azzigig, each riding a splendid *mehari* camel, and each clad in the complete outfit of a Touareg raider—newly washed for us by the grateful dames of the village. Nor could the lads-of-the-village do enough for us. What they could, and did, do, was to provide us with a guide and a spare camel laden with food and water, to help us on our way to the next village and oasis in the direction of our goal.

A desperate band of ruffians we looked, Touareg to the last detail of dress, weapons, and accoutrement.

Lean and leathery hawk-faced Hank and Buddy made splendid Arabs, and seemed to enjoy "playing Injun" like a pair of boys.

They soon learned the uses and arrangings of the *serd* and *jubba* vests, the *kaftan* inner coat, the *hezaam* sash, the *jelabia* overall, the *sirwal* baggy trousers, the *ma-araka* skull cap with the *kafiya* head-dress bound round with the *agals*, ropes of camel-hair.

The blue veils which the Touaregs wear, were the chief trouble, but in time we grew accustomed to them.

I do not know whether these veils are a centuries-old

relic of the days when the Touaregs were a white race and took care of their complexions; whether they were a sudden bright idea for keeping the sand from the lungs in windy weather; whether they were invented for purposes of mystery and playing bogey with their enemies and victims; or whether they simply evolved as useful desert-wear for people always on the move, against cutting sand-filled winds and a burning glare that smites upward as well as downward. Anyway, it is curious that only the Touaregs evolved them.

On our camels we carried *zemzimayas* full of water, and *jaafas,* or leather sacks, which our hosts filled with *hubz,* or native bread, and *asida,* horrible masses of dough mixed with oil and onions, flavoured with *fil-fil,* a sort of red pepper.

On the spare camel were huge *khoorgs,* or saddle-bags, filled with *alafs* of fodder for the camels, as well as *girbas* full of water.

We discarded our two military saddles and replaced them with Arab *sergs,* and, in fact, "went native" altogether, retaining nothing European but our rifles and Digby's bugle.

And in doing this, even, we were not guilty of any anomaly. I had been interested to note that, along with heavy swords of Crusader pattern, and lances and knives of a type unchanged since the days of Abraham, the Touaregs carried splendid magazine-rifles of the latest pattern.

Both these and their ammunition were of Italian make, and I wondered whether they had been captured in Tripoli, or smuggled by the Chambaa rifle-runners of Algeria. As two men had Turkish rifles and cartridges of .450 calibre, I thought it likely that the former was the source. The useful bugle was, of course, concealed.

Before we departed, the village pulled itself together, and, evidently trying to show us "what Todgers' could do" in the way of a *diffa,* or feast, regaled us upon *fatta,* a mess of carrots, bread, and eggs, and a quite decent *couscous* of goat.

For wassail, the headman brought up from the "cellar" (under his bed) a magnum (leather) of *laghbi*, a rare old vintage palm-juice, which had lain mellowing and maturing in bottle for quite a week.

I found that my names for things of this sort were not always the same as the names I had learned in Algeria, but by any other name they smelled as remarkable.

I asked Hank what he thought of the "liquor."

"Fierce, ain't it?" replied he, and left me to apply mine own evaluation to the word.

"Guess we could stop here to be the Big Noise of the tribe," remarked Buddy, endeavouring to feed himself gracefully with his fingers—not an easy thing to do when a spoon is the indicated instrument.

"Yep. Shakers and emus," agreed Hank, with hazy memories of sheikhs and emirs perhaps.

"And a harem-scarum," added Buddy.

"Why don' the gals jine the hash-party?" he enquired, looking round to where the women, in their long *barracans*, sat afar off and admired the prandial performances of their lords.

"Shut up. Take no notice of the women-folk," said Digby. "Sound plan among Mussulmans of any kind."

"No doubt yore right, pard," agreed Buddy, "but there shore is a real little peach over there jest give me the glad eye like a Christian gal as knowed a hill o' beans from a heap o' bananas. Cute an' cunnin'. . . . Still, we don't want no rough stuff from the Injuns. . . . My, but it was a cinch . . ." and he sighed heavily. . . .

CHAPTER VII

ISHMAELITES

*"Greater love hath no man than this,
That a man lay down his life for his friends."*

I COULD fill a large volume with the account of our adventures, as Touaregs of the Sahara, on this ride that began at Azzigig, in the French Soudan, and ended (for some of us) at Kano in Nigeria, in British West Africa.

It was perhaps the longest and most arduous ride ever achieved by Europeans in the Sahara—few of whom have ever crossed the desert from north to south without an organised caravan.

We rode south-west when we could, and we rode north-east when we must, as when, north of Aïr, we were captured by Touaregs on their way to their own country on the borders of Morocco.

During one terrible year we made an almost complete circle, being at one time at El Hilli, within two hundred miles of Timbuktu, and, at another, at Agadem, within the same distance of Lake Tchad—and then later finding ourselves at Bilma, five hundred miles to the north.

Sometimes thirst and hunger drove us to join salt-caravans, and sometimes slave-caravans (and we learnt that slavery is still a very active pursuit and a flourishing business in Central Africa). Generally these caravans were going in the direction opposite to ours, but we had to join them or perish in the waterless desert.

Sometimes we were hunted by gangs larger than our own; sometimes we were met at villages with volleys of rifle-fire (being taken, naturally, for what we pretended to be); sometimes we reached an oasis only to find it occupied by a patrol of French Senegalese troops—far more dangerous to us than the nomadic robbers for whom we were a match when not hopelessly outnumbered.

Whether we did what no Europeans have ever done before, I do not know, but we certainly went to places where Europeans had never been before, and "discovered" desert cities which were probably prehistoric ruins before a stone of Damascus was laid.

We encountered no Queens of Atlantis and found no white races of Greek origin, ruled by ladies of tempestuous petticoat, to whom it turned out we were distantly related.

Alas, no. We found only extremely poor, primitive, and dirty people, with whom we sojourned precisely as long as untoward circumstance compelled.

Of course, we could never have survived for a single month of those years, but for the desert-skill, the courage, resourcefulness, and experience of Hank and Buddy.

On the other hand, the ready wits of Digby, and our knowledge of Arabic, saved the situation, time after time, when we were in contact with our fellow-man.

On these occasions we became frightfully holy. Hank and Buddy were *marabouts* under a vow of silence, and we were Senussi on a mysterious errand, travelling from Kufra in the Libyan desert to Timbuktu, and visiting all sorts of holy places on the way.

Luckily for us, there were no genuine Senussi about; and the infinite variety of sects, with their different kinds of dervishes, and the even greater variety of people who spoke widely differing dialects of Arabic, made our task comparatively easy.

Probably our rifles, our poverty, and our obvious truculence did still more in that direction.

We suffered from fever, terrific heat, poisonous water, bad and insufficient food, and the hardships of what was one long campaign of active warfare to live.

At times we were very near the end, when our camels died, when a long journey ended at a dried-up well, when we were surrounded by a pack of the human wolves of the desert, and when we were fairly captured by a *harka* of Touaregs, suspicious of our *bona fides*. . . .

As I have said, an account of our *katabasis* would fill a volume, but the description of a few typical incidents will suffice to give an idea of it, without rendering the story as wearisome as was the journey.

For example, our discovery of the place where there certainly ought to have been *"a strange fair people of a*
civilisation older, and in some ways higher, than our own;
ruled over by a woman, so incredibly beautiful, so mar-
vellously . . ." etc.

One day we rode over the crest of a long ridge of sand-
covered rock—straight into a band of armed men who outnumbered us by ten to one, at least, and who were ready
and waiting for us with levelled rifles.

We did as we had done before, on similar exciting occasions. The Holy Ones, Hank and Buddy, fell dumb, and
Digby became the emissary of the Senussi Mahdi; I, his
lieutenant.

Digby rode forward.

"Salamoune aleikoumi Esseleme, ekhwan" (Peace be
unto you, brothers), said he, in solemn, sonorous greeting,
to which a fine-looking old man replied, to my great relief,
"Aselamu, alaikum, marhaba, marhaba" (Greetings to you
and welcome), in a different-sounding Arabic from ours.
It turned out later that the old gentleman took us for an
advance-party of a big band of Touaregs who were near,
and was only too charmed to find us so charming.

Digby then proceeded with the appropriate account of
ourselves, alluding to the dumb forbidding Hank and
Buddy, as most holy men, *khouans, hadjis, marabouts,*
under a strict vow of silence that it would be ill work for
any man to attempt to break. Himself and me he described
as *m'rabets,* men hereditarily holy and prominent in faith
and virtue.

How much of this our hearers understood, and how much
of what they understood, they believed, I could not tell,
but they were obviously relieved to find us friendly and not
part of a larger force.

We were promptly invited to come along, and thought it
best to comply, there being little reason against doing so
and much against refusing. In any case they had "got
us," from the moment we came upon their levelled rifles,
our own slung behind us; and we were at their mercy. As
we rode along, nominally guests, but feeling we were prisoners, I was interested to hear Digby assuring the old

sheikh that though we were as holy as it is given to mere men to be, we were nevertheless good hefty proselytisers who carried the Q'ran in one hand and the sword in the other, fighting-men who would be pleased to chip in, if the Touaregs attacked his band.

The old gentleman returned thanks and said that, once home, they did not fear all the Touaregs in the Sahara, as the place was quite impregnable. This sounded attractive, and proved to be perfectly true.

What did trouble them, was the fact that when they set off with a caravan of camels for sale at Tanout, it was more than likely that they would, for months, have to fight a series of pitched battles or lose the whole of the where-withal to purchase grain for their subsistence, for there was nothing a Touareg robber desired more than camels.

"It is the only wealth that carries itself," observed Digby sententiously.

After riding for some three or four hours towards some low rocky mountains, we reached them and approached a narrow and lofty pass. This we threaded in single file, and, coming to the top, saw before us an endless plain out of which arose a *gara*, an abrupt and isolated plateau, looking like a gigantic cheese placed in the middle of the level expanse of desert.

Toward this we rode for another hour or two, and discovered it to be a precipitous mountain, sheer, cliff-sided, with a flat top; the whole, I suppose, about a square mile in area.

Apparently it was quite inaccessible and untrodden by the foot of man, or even of mountain sheep or goat. Only an eagle, I imagined had ever looked upon the top of that isolated square mile of rock.

I was wrong, however, the place proving to be a gigantic fort—a fort of the most perfect kind, but which owed nothing whatever to the hand of man.

Circling the cliff-like precipitous base of the mountain, we came to a crack in the thousand-foot wall, a crack that was invisible at a hundred yards.

Into this narrow fissure the sheikh led us in single file, and, squeezing our way between gigantic cactus, we rode along the upward-sloping bottom of a winding chasm that was not six feet wide.

Suddenly our path was cut by a deep ravine, some three yards wide, a great crack across the crack in which we were entombed. Bridging this was laid a number of trunks of the *dôm* palm, and over these a matting of palm-leaf and sand made a narrow but safe path for camels.

Obviously this bridge could easily be removed if necessary, and the place defended with the greatest ease, if any enemy were foolish enough to attempt to bridge the abyss while the defenders dropped boulders from terrific heights, and fired their rifles at point-blank range from behind the strong stone wall that faced the chasm.

Having crossed the bridge, we rode on upward to where this narrow slit in the mountain opened out into a big rock-enclosed square like a landing on a staircase—beyond which camels could not go.

In this natural *serai* we dismounted and left our beasts, continuing our climb on foot.

It was, indeed, an impregnable place, and I did not see how the best troops in the world could capture it, so long as there remained a stout-hearted defender in any one of the invisible places that commanded the path up which two men could nowhere climb abreast and where, in many places, only one could squeeze with difficulty.

And on the plateau was a walled city, a city built of blocks of dressed stone, blocks larger than any I have ever seen put to such purpose, and obviously of such an age in this use as must have left them old there when the world, as we know of it, was young.

It was a great and melancholy place, containing, I should think, at least three times as many dwelling-places as there were dwellers. Personally, I lost any sense of our precarious position and all feeling of danger and anxiety, in interest and wonderment at this "walled city set upon a hill," and such a hill.

But, as I have said, there was no wonderful white race here for us to restore to touch with modern civilisation. Nor was there any wonderful black race either. The inhabitants of this strange city were just ordinary Arabs, I believe, though I am no ethnologist, and, so far as they knew, they had "always" lived there.

Nevertheless, I felt perfectly certain that no ancestor of theirs had placed those incredible monoliths in position, nor made for themselves doorways twelve and fifteen feet in height, leading into chambers ten feet higher.

These people were undoubtedly the long-established dwellers in this city, but none the less were they dwellers in someone else's city, and merely camping in it at that, even if for a few thousand years.

However, they were very interesting people, living simply and austerely under the benign sway of their patriarchal sheikh, and quite hospitable and friendly. They knew but little of the outside world, though they realised that there were *Roumis* and infidels of all kinds, other cities than their own, holy places besides Mecca and Medina, and greater sheikhs, sultans, and emperors than their own. They apparently regarded the world, or at any rate their world, as divided up into Touareg robbers on the one hand, and the enemies and victims of Touaregs on the other.

In their marvellous rock fastness they were safe, but out on the desert they were at the mercy of any nomadic robber-band stronger than themselves.

Water they had in plenty, as their mountain contained an apparently inexhaustible well and spring, and they had goat-flesh and a little grain, vegetables, and dates, but were compelled to make the six months' caravan journey to Tanout for the grain that formed the staple of their food, as well as for ammunition, salt, and cooking-vessels—for which commodities they exchanged their camels as well as dressed goatskins, and garments beautifully woven and embroidered by their women-folk.

With these good folk we stayed for some days, a pleasant restful oasis in the weary desert of our lives, receiving genuine Arab hospitality, and repaying it with such small gifts as were of more value to them than to us, and by offering to scout for, and fight with, their caravan then about to set out across a notoriously dangerous tract of country to the east.

We must have puzzled the simple souls of this inbred dying people, for though we were obviously of strict piety, and observed the same hours of prayer as themselves from the *fedjer* at dawn to the *asha* at night, we would not pray in company with them, nor, as we sat and *faddhled* (or gossiped) round the sheikh's fire at night, would we say one word on religious subjects. We ran no unnecessary risks. A dignified *"Allahou akbar"* or *"In châh Allah,"* showed our agreement with the speaker and our pious orthodoxy, and it had to suffice. As puritanical protestant reforming Senussi, we had a higher and purer brand of Islamism than theirs, but refrained from hurting their feelings by any parade of it. . . .

Digby was great, and his descriptions of Mecca and Medina, Baghdad, Constantinople, and Cairo, Fez, Timbuktu, and Kufra, held his hearers spellbound and left them little time for questions.

Hank and Buddy were equally great, in what they did not say and the manner in which they did not say it.

Nevertheless, it was well we could make the departure of the caravan our opportunity for going, and it was well that our hosts were what they were, and even then the ice, at times, was very thin.

We descended from this extraordinary and apparently absolutely unknown prehistoric city, and set off with the caravan, rested and in better case than we had been in for months.

We were going in the right direction, we were approaching Aïr, we should then be near a caravan-route on which were wells; and if our danger from our fellow-men, Arab and French, were likely to increase, our danger from the far more terrible enemy, the desert, would decrease.

With luck, we might parallel the caravan-route and make dashes for water when opposite the oases on the route, trusting that we should be able to evade French patrols (of Senegalese infantry and Arab *goumiers*) and Touareg raiding-parties alike.

We said our *"Abka ala Kheir"* (good-byes) to our late hosts and heard their *"Imshi besselema"* (Go in peace) with real regret, at the last oasis on our common route, pressed on in good heart and high hopes, did very well for a month, and then fell straight into the hands of the rascally and treacherous Tegama, Sultan of Agades, when we were only four hundred miles from the frontier of Nigeria and safety.

§ 2.

Our visit to Agades was a very different affair from that to the impregnable city on the hill. In the latter place we felt no real fear and little anxiety. In Agades we walked very warily, our hearts in our mouths and our heads loose upon our necks. To the old sheikh we had been objects of wonder and interest. To the Sultan Tegama we were objects of the most intense suspicion.

There was nothing of the simple out-of-the-world dweller-apart, about the swashbuckling ruffians of this City of the Plain, nor about the arch-ruffian Tegama, their leader (executed later by the French for treachery), nor would the pose of pious Senussi emissaries have been of any avail in these circumstances. In the idiom of Buddy, there was no moss upon the teeth of the Sultan Tegama and his gang. In the idiom of Digby there were no flies upon these gentlemen.

We owed our lives to the fact that we escaped before the worthy Tegama had quite placed us, and was quite certain that we were not what we pretended to be—seditious mischief-makers from the north, bent upon raising the desert tribes of the centre and south against the French in a great pan-Islamic *jehad*.

Not that Tegama had the slightest objection to being so "raised"; far from it. Nothing would have suited him better, for there was nothing he enjoyed more; and if to rapine and slaughter, fire and sword, robbery and massacre, he could add the heaven-gaining merit of the destruction of the Unbeliever and the overthrow of his empire in Africa, the cup of his happiness would be full. . . .

But we puzzled him undoubtedly. Our accent, manners, habits, ignorance, eyes, complexions, faces, and everything about us puzzled him.

Certainly we spoke Arabic fluently and knew men and cities; we seemed to be *hadjis* all right; we inveighed with convincing bitterness against the French; we were upstanding desert fighting-men with nothing whatsoever European about our clothing and accoutrements; we were too small a party to be dangerous, and there was no earthly reason why we should be French spies (for the emissaries of France came perfectly openly in the shape of extremely well-equipped military expeditions, pursuing the well-worn way of all peaceful penetrators, and were a source of fear and bitter hatred to the Sultan)—*but*, we had no credentials; we gave absolutely no information whatsoever about the strength, disposition, and movements of the French forces; we had no cut-and-dried play for an on-fall; and the dumbness of two of us did not seem to mark them out as born emissaries of sedition, unrest, and rebellion!

When Tegama voiced these suspicions, Digby, with fine courage, took the high hand and, as tactfully as possible, hinted that there might be things in the minds of the Great Ones, our masters, that were not to be comprehended by every petty desert chieftain, and that one thing about their minds was the certainty of a powerful and dangerous resentment against anybody who hindered the free movements of their messengers, or behaved as though they were the friends of the very Infidels from whom these Great Ones were endeavouring to free Islam. . . .

And the gentle Tegama halted long between two opinions, whether to impale us out of hand, or whether to put off till to-morrow what he would like to do to-day, in case we were what we said we were.

It was an unpleasant time, and though we were not ill-treated nor imprisoned, our rifles and camels were "minded" for us, and we never found ourselves alone—particularly when we walked abroad, although it was obvious that no one could escape from Agades on foot.

We felt that at any moment Tegama might decide that we were genuine delegates and emissaries from those who were then so busily stirring the fermenting brew of pan-Islamic discontent in northern Africa—and let us go; and also that at any moment we might so betray ourselves that he would decide we were impostors—and forthwith impale us, living, on the sharpened stump of a young tree. . . .

We had been caught at dawn, in an oasis south-west of the Baguezan mountains, by a *harka* of Tegama's that had evidently been raiding and robbing to the north, and, for a week or so, we rode south as the prisoner-guests of the emir in command, a magnificent specimen of the best type of desert Arab.

Him Digby had told the same tale that he had told to the old sheikh and many another inquisitive wayfarer, but he had decided to alter his tale for the private ear of the Sultan as soon as we learnt that it was to so important and well-informed a person that we were to be taken.

Whispering together at night, we decided that Hank and Buddy must of course remain dumb, and that we must put up a terrific bluff of mystery. It would be worse than hopeless to pretend to be Senussi from Kufra, in a place like Agades, where it was quite probable there were specimens of the genuine article, and where our stories would rapidly be tested and found wanting.

And so we took the high hand with Tegama, so far as we dared ; told him that we had no definite message for him *yet*, but that on our return journey he would hear things that would surprise him, and so forth. . . .

Agades proved to be a very ancient, clay-built, sand-buried walled town, containing a remarkable mosque with a tower like a church spire, and although so utterly lost in the very heart of the Sahara, still in touch with the outside world by reason of being on the pilgrim-route to Mecca, and on the great caravan-route that crosses Africa.

The only other building that was not insignificant was the Sultan's palace, a big two-storied building of baked clay, surrounded by a high thick clay wall, the gateway through which was practically a short tunnel.

Through this tunnel, and past very strong gates made of palm-trunks nailed solidly together upon cross-pieces, we were led into a dirty square of desert sand and stones, two sides of which were formed by mud huts that backed against the high enclosing wall.

One side of the square was occupied by the palace and another by a mosque. Camels, goats, chickens, and dirty men ornamented this palace courtyard or back-yard.

We were invited to enter the palace, and through another small tunnel came into a big windowless hall, with unornamented clay walls. clay ceiling, and clay floor.

Here we were kept waiting with our escort, and stood in haughty silence until conducted across a small inner court-yard to the presence-chamber of the Sultan of Agades.

This was another windowless clay room with great arched ceiling beams and a door, ten feet from the ground, up to which ran a clay staircase. In the middle of the wall opposite the door by which we entered, was a throne, also of clay—a base material for so exalted a symbol, but at least it was of honest clay, which its occupant was not.

Cross-legged on this bed-like throne, in dirty white robes sat Tegama, who carried on his face the stamp of his ruling passions, greed, cruelty, lust, savagery, and treachery. Around him stood a small group of wazirs, sheikhs, soldiers, and what I uncomfortably took to be executioners.

The Sultan glared at us and I felt sorrowful to the tips of my toes. I knew by now all the ways that such gentlemen have of putting to death those of whom they do not approve, and I liked none of them at all. Impaling, a favourite one, I liked, perhaps, the least. . . .

Digby took the bull by the horns, greeted Tegama politely, hoped he was well, professed pleasure at seeing him, and said he had a good deal to say to him later on, when he had made some arrangements further south and had taken the political temperature of one or two places in Damerghou and Damergrim.

Digby took it for granted that we were honoured guests, and that nothing so silly as the idea of molesting us would ever occur to so wise and great a ruler as the good Tegama of Agades.

The good Tegama of Agades continued to eye us coldly.

"And who might *you* be, with your talk of El Senussi?" he enquired contemptuously.

"That is for your ear alone," replied Digby. "I have told the sheikh whom we—er—*met*, in the Baguezan oasis, such things as are fitting to be told to underlings. I come from those whose business is not shouted in every *douar* and *quasr* and chattered about to every wayfarer."

And here I boomed:

"No, indeed! Allah forbid!" and smiled at the idea.

"Oh, you can talk, can you?" sneered Tegama, who had evidently been told that some of us were dumb.

"*Salaam aleikum wa Rahmab Allah,*" I intoned piously.

"Our Master in the north—*Rahmat ullahi Allahim*—(and he may be in Morocco, and he may be in Algiers, and he may be near here with a mighty army of the Faithful)—is not one of whose affairs his messengers babble, nor is he one whose messengers are delayed."

"And what is his message?" asked Tegama, with, I thought, less sneer in his voice.

"That comes not here *yet*," replied Digby. "The word comes to the great and good Sultan of Agades later, when the time is ripe . . ." and much more of bluff and mystification that sufficiently impressed Tegama to lead him to wait and see.

He waited but he did not see, for we escaped—this time, I must admit, thanks to Buddy's irrepressible interest in "squaws."

What he could have achieved had he had the free use of his tongue I cannot say. In this case, although love was not only blind, but dumb as well, it contrived to laugh at locksmiths, and we other three benefited by the laughter.

We got away and on good camels, but we had not a rifle among us, nor any other weapon of any sort whatever.

I am tempted to tell, in full, the story of this evasion, for it was a most romantic business, with all the accessories of fiction and melodrama. I have said that the story of this journey alone would fill a large volume, and it would be small exaggeration to say that a complete account of our sojourn in Agades would fill another.

I wish I had space in which to tell of the incredible things we saw in this place, whose atmosphere and ways and deeds were those of a thousand years ago.

I have read that the first Europeans to set foot in Agades were the members of the French Military Mission (which came with the great annual salt-caravan from the south in 1904), but I could tell of a fair-bearded man who stared at us with blazing *grey* eyes, a man whose tongue had been cut out, whose ears and fingers had been cut off, and who was employed as a beast of burden.

I could also tell of a Thing that sat always in the Sôk, mechanically swaying its body to and fro as it crooned. Its lips, eyelids, ears, hands, and feet had been cut off, it was blind, and it crooned in *German*.

I could tell of such scenes as that of the last hours of a very brave man, who was bound face downwards on a plank that was thrust over the edge of an enormously deep dry well. At the other end of the plank was a big stone and a jar of water that slowly leaked, either by reason of a crack or its porosity. When the water had leaked away to such an extent that the weight of the jar and stone was less than that of the man, he and the plank would go headlong down into the dark depths from which he would never return.

There he lay staring down into the horrible place, while round about sat citizens of leisure who told him to hurry with his last prayers, for the water was nearly gone, while others bade him to heed them not, for he had hours longer to wait. . . .

I should like to tell of Tegama's executioners, four negroes who were the most animal creatures I ever saw in human form, and not one of whom was less than seven feet in height. The specialty of their leader was the clean, neat flicking-off of a head or any required limb, from a finger to a leg, with one stroke of a great sword; while that of another was the infliction of the maximum number of wounds and injuries without causing the death of the victim.

They were skilled labourers and their work was their hobby. . . .

I could tell of some very remarkable adventures, risks, dangers, and escapes in Agades, and of some very strange doings in that horrible "palace" with its plots and intrigues, jealousies and hatreds, factions and parties, if space permitted.

And when our time and opportunity came (and we were led one dark night to where four camels, with water and food for two or three days, awaited us) we would not have taken advantage of the chance, being weaponless, had we not felt that we ran a greater danger by remaining.

Tegama was growing more suspicious and more truculent, and I rather think that the dumb Hank and Buddy had been overheard in fluent converse. Probably we gave ourselves away too (whenever we ate, drank, prayed, sat, stood, sneezed, or did anything else whatsoever), as the weirdest kind of weird Mussulmans who ever said, *"Bismillah arahman arahmim. . . ."*

It was time to go and we went, aided by a young person of magnificent physique, magnificent courage, and negroid ancestry—probably the daughter of some negro slave-woman from Lake Tchad. . . .

Unfortunately it was utterly impossible for her to get us weapons.

§ 3.

We escaped from Tegama, but not from the consequences of our encounter with him. He did not destroy us, but it was to him that we owed our destruction.

Riding as hard as we could, we followed the tactics of our escape from Zinderneuf, feeling sure that if Tegama pursued and recaptured us, our fate would be sealed and our deaths lingering and unpleasant.

We therefore avoided the caravan-route that runs from Agades, and struck out into the desert, hoping that, as hitherto, we should, sooner or later, discover someone or something that would lead us to water.

After three days of painful wandering, we chanced upon the wretched encampment of some aboriginal Beri-Beri bushmen, black, almost naked, and armed only with bows and arrows. They apparently lived by trapping ostriches by means of tethered foot-traps concealed beneath the bushes and trees, thorns and acacias, on which the birds feed.

These primitive people were camped beside an inexplicable pool of water among colossal boulders as big as cathedrals.

Here we rested ourselves and our camels for a day or two, and then again set out, with our leather water-skins filled and our food-bags nearly empty.

A couple of days later we were riding in a long line, just within sight of each other, and scouting for signs of human beings or water.

Hank was on the right of the line, I next to him and half

a mile away, having Buddy on my left, with Digby at the far end.

Looking to my right, I saw Hank, topping a little undulation, suddenly wheel towards me, urging his camel to its topmost speed.

As I looked, a crowd of riders swarmed over the skyline, and, two or three of them, halting their camels, opened fire on us.

Buddy rode at full speed toward me and Hank. Digby was cut off from view by a tor of rocks.

"Dismount and form sqar'," yelled Hank, riding up.

I knew what he meant.

We brought our camels to their knees, made a pretence of getting out rifles from under the saddles, crouched behind the camels, and levelled our sticks as though they were guns, across the backs of the animals, and awaited death.

"This is war we gits what's comin' to us," said Buddy.

"The durned galoots may not call our bluff," growled Hank.

The band, Hoggar or Tebu robbers by the look of them, bore down upon with yells of *"Ul-ul-ul-ul-ul-ullah Akbar,"* on pleasure and profit bent—the pleasure of slaughtering us and the profit of taking our camels—brandishing swords, lances, and rifles as they swent along.

I could have wept that we had no rifles. Steady magazine fire from three marksmen like ourselves, would have brought the yelling fiends crashing to earth in such numbers as might have saved us and provided us with much that we sorely needed.

The feeling of utter impotence was horrible, and like the impotence of nightmare. . . . To be butchered like sheep without striking a blow. . . . Could Digby possibly escape? . . . Or would they see his tracks and follow him after slaughtering us? . . . There was an excellent chance that they would pass straight on without crossing his trail. . . . Would they swerve from our apparently levelled rifles? No, On they came. . . . Digby might be well away by now. . . .

And then from somewhere, there rang out loud, clear, and (to these Arabs) terrible, *a bugle-call*—that portentous bugle-call, menacing and fateful, that had been almost the last thing so many desert tribesmen had heard, the bugle-call that announced the closing of the trap and preluded the hail of bullets against which no Arab charge could prevail.

The effect was instant and magical. The band swerved to their right, wheeled, and fled—fled to avoid what they thought a terrible trap, so neatly baited and into which they had so nearly fallen!

As the bugle-call died away, Hank roared orders in French at the top of his enormous voice, and away to the left a man was apparently signalling back with excited energy, to the French forces behind him, *"enemy in sight."*

Evidently the panic-stricken mob of raiders thought that the danger was behind the spot on which they had first seen Hank, for they fled in a direction to the right of the rocks behind which Digby had blown his bugle. . . .

Suddenly my heart leapt into my throat, as one of the robbers, perhaps their leader or a candidate for leadership, swerved to the left from the ruck of the fleeing band, and, either in a spirit of savage vengeance, or the desire, not uncommon with these people, for single combat in the presence of many onlookers, rode at the man who had exposed himself to signal back to the French force of which he was evidently the scout. . . .

"Quick!" I shouted. "He'll get him," and I found myself yelling Digby's name.

We scrambled on to our camels, Hank bawling commands in French, and Buddy yelling devilish war-whoops.

Digby stooped and then poised himself in the attitude of a javelin-thrower. As the Arab raised his great sword, Digby's arm shot forward and the Arab reeled, receiving the stone full in his face, and jerking the camel's head round as he did so. Digby sprang at the man's leg and pulled him down, the two falling together.

They rose simultaneously, the Arab's sword went up, Digby's fist shot out, and we heard the smack as the man reeled backwards and fell, his sword dropping from his hand. Digby seized it and stood over the half-stunned robber, who was twitching and clawing at the sand. . . .

And then we heard another sound.

A rifle was fired, and Digby swayed and fell.

An Arab had wheeled from the tail of the fleeing band, fired this shot at thirty yards' range, and fled again, we three on our galloping camels being not a hundred yards from him.

   .   .   .   .   .   .

Digby was dead before I got to him, shot through the back of the head with an expanding bullet. . . .

We tied the Arab's feet, and I blew bugle-calls to the best of my ability.

I am going to say nothing at all about my feelings.

Digby was dead. Michael was dead. I felt that the essential *me* was dead too.

I lived on like an automaton, and—like a creature sentenced to death—I waited for the blow to fall, the moment of collapse to come.

§ 4.

We buried Digby there, although we expected the return of the Arabs at any moment.

"He shore gave his life for ourn," said Hank, chewing his lips.

" '*Greater love hath no man,*' " I was able to reply.

Buddy said nothing, but Buddy wept. He then untied the completely-recovered Arab, a huge, powerful young fellow, twice his size, and without weapons on either side, fought him and beat him insensible.

Discussing the question of this robber's future, I suggested we should bind his hands, put him on his camel, and make him our guide—bidding him lead us first to the oasis from which the band had come.

"Lead us not into temptation," said Buddy. "He'd shore lead us where he wanted us."

Speaking to the man in his own tongue, when he had recovered from Buddy's handling of him, I asked him what he was prepared to do to save his life. . . . Could he lead us south, parallel with the caravan route, from one oasis or water-hole to another, if we agreed to set him free as soon as we were in the Kano territory?

He replied that he would willingly lead us to Hell and

cheerfully abide there himself, so long as he got us there too. He was undoubtedly a brave man.

I told him that in that case we should take his camel and weapons (unfortunately for us he had no rifle), and leave him where he was, to die of thirst.

"*El Mektub Mektub*" (What is written is written), he replied, with a shrug, and that was all we could get out of him.

In the end we took him with us, bound, on his camel, which was tied to Buddy's, and left him at the first water-hole to which we came. This we found by following the track made by his friends as they had come northward.

From here we rode on with filled water-skins and half the food-supply of the Arab whom he had abandoned. . . .

Digby's death proved to be the first tragic catastrophe of a series of disasters that now overtook us.

First we encountered a terrible sand-storm that nearly killed us, and quite obliterated all tracks.

Then we missed the caravan-route when we reluctantly decided to return to it, either crossing it in ignorance, where the ground was too rocky for there to be any footprints, or else riding over the road itself at a spot where all traces of it had been wiped out, or buried, by the sand-storm.

Next, nearly dead with thirst, we reached a water-hole, and found it dried up!

Here our starving camels ate some poisonous shrub or other, speedily sickened, and within thirty-six hours were all dead.

We thus found ourselves stranded in the desert, not knowing whether the caravan-route was to the east or to the west of us, without rifles, without food, without camels, and with one goat-skin containing about a pint of water.

This we decided not to drink until we must literally drink or die, though it seemed that we must surely do that in any case.

For a day we struggled on, incredibly, without water, and at the end of the day wondered whether we were a day's march further from the caravan-road on which were oases, wells, water-holes, and villages.

Once we found it (if ever), we would risk the French patrols until we could again get camels. On the caravan-route, death was probable, here in the desert, on foot, it was certain.

Night found us unable to speak, our lips black, and cracked in great fissures, our tongues swollen horribly, our throats closed, and our mouths *dry*. (It is an incredibly horrible thing to have one's mouth literally and really *dry*, like hard leather.)

I pointed at the precious water-skin and raised my eye-brows interrogatively.

Hank shook his head and pointed at the setting sun and then at the zenith. We must drink to-morrow when we should, if possible, be in worse case than now.

We reeled on through the night, for our lives depended on reaching the "road."

Towards morning, I could go no further and sank down without meaning to do so. I tried to rise and failed. Seeing that I could do no more, the other two lay down beside me, and we fell asleep.

The sun woke me to see Buddy, with a face like death, staring at a scrap of paper torn from a pocket-book.

He passed it to me. On it was scrawled:

> "*Pards,*
> *Drink up the water slow and push on quick. Good old Buddy, we bin good pards.*
>
> *Hank.*"

Hank was gone. . . .

Buddy untied the neck of the goat-skin and filled his mouth with water. He held the water in his mouth for a minute and then swallowed it slowly.

"Take a mouthful like that and then swaller," he croaked hoarsely.

"We gotta do what Hank ses," he added, as I shook my head. I could not drink the water.

"We gotta hike," wheezed Buddy. "We don' wanta make what he done all for nix. All no good, like. He won't come back an' drink it. . . . Yew ain't goin' to *waste* his life, pard? . . . He done it fer *you*. . . ."

I filled my mouth and swallowed—but I could not swallow the lump in my throat. . . .

We staggered on through that day and the next, moistening our mouths at intervals, and just before sunset, on the second day, saw a mirage of palm trees, a village, a little white mosque, and—the mirage was real.

We stayed at this village for months, scouring the desert for Hank, working as cultivators, water-carriers, watchmen, camelmen, and at any other job that offered, and we were never both asleep at the same time.

When French patrols visited the place, we hid, or fled into the desert, with the entire sympathy of the villagers. We could have joined more than one south-bound caravan, but I would not urge Buddy to leave the place.

He had such faith in the indestructibility of Hank, that he hoped against hope, until hope deferred made his heart sick.

At first it was:

"He'll come mushin' in here ter-morrer, a-throwin' his feet like the Big Buck Hobo, rollin' his tail like a high-fed hoss, an' grinnin' fit ter bust. . . ."

Then it was:

"Nobody couldn't kill Hank. . . . He's what you call ondestructible. . . . Why, back in Colorado, he shore chased a man over the Panamint Mountains an' right across Death Valley once, an' inter the Funeral Mountains t'other side. A hoss-rustler, he was, and when ole Hank got him, he was stone dead with heat an' thirst, an' Hank turned right round an' hiked back and come out alive! . . ."

And at last, when a caravan came from the north actually going south to Zinder (the military headquarters of the *Territoire Militaire*) and comparative civilisation, he proposed that we should join it as camelmen and guards.

"You can't stop here fer keeps, pard," he said. "I reckon I bin selfish. But I couldn't leave old Hank while there was a chance. . . ."

But for Michael's letter (and my longing to see Isobel), I would have urged Buddy to stay, for that was what he really wanted to do.

Nothing could destroy his faith in his friend's superiority

to the desert and to death. We joined the caravan as fighting-men, one dumb, and later (as we neared Zinder) we left it though we had little fear of getting into trouble there. Still, it was just possible that some non-com. of the big garrison there might know and recognise us, and possible that a well-equipped desert-party of *goumiers* might have come along the caravan-road from Zinderneuf.

Our adventures between Zinder and the British border at Barbera, where we first saw Haussas in the uniform of the West African Field Force, were numerous, and our hardships great; but Fate seemed to have done its worst—and now that I had lost Digby, and Buddy had lost Hank, and neither of us cared very much what happened, our luck changed and all went fairly well.

And one day we rode, on miserable donkeys, into the great city of Kano, and I revealed myself to an astounded Englishman as a compatriot.

He was kindness itself, and put me in communication with a friend, or rather a friend of Aunt Patricia's, a Mr. Lawrence of the Nigerian Civil Service. This gentleman sent me money and an invitation to come and stay with him at his headquarters and to bring Buddy with me.

And when I told Buddy that on the morrow he was actually going to ride in a train once more—I found that he was not.

He had only come to Kano to see me safe, and, having done so, he was going straight back to look for Hank!

Nothing would shake his determination, and it was waste of words to try. Nor was it pleasant to strive to persuade him that his friend was dead.

"Would *you* go if it was yore brother that was lost, pard?" he said.

"Nope. . . . Hank give his life fer us. . . ."

All I could do was to see him fitted out with everything procurable in Kano—a fine camel, a spare one for food, water, ammunition, and a small tent, and a Haussa ex-soldier as servant and guide, recommended by the Kano Englishman, an official named Mordaunt.

The latter made it clear to the Haussa that he was to go north with this American "explorer," obey him in all things, receive half his pay before starting, and the other half, with a bonus depending in value upon his merit, when he returned to Kano with his master, or honourably discharged.

Mordaunt was good enough to accept my word that if he would be my banker in this matter, I would adjust things as soon as I saw Mr. Lawrence, who was an old friend of his.

I hated parting with the staunch, brave, great-hearted little Buddy, and I felt that he would never return to Kano unless it was with Hank, and I had no hope whatever of his doing that. . . .

I wondered if I should ever have had the cold iron courage to go voluntarily back into that Hell, after escaping it by a miracle, on such a ghost of a chance of finding a friend. . . .

§ 5.

I took the train at Kano to some place of which I have forgotten the name, and Lawrence met me on the platform I remembered his face as soon as I saw it, as that of the quiet, rather dour and repellent man who had been to Brandon Abbas two or three times when we were there.

He came nearer to showing excitement, while he listened to my story, than I thought was his wont. When I had finished he said:

"I should like to know when fiction was much stranger than this piece of truth! . . . And you *still* do not know the rights of this 'Blue Water' mystery?"

"No," I said. "I only know that my brother Michael never stole anything in his life."

"Quite so," he replied. "Of course. . . . And now I have something to tell *you*. Your Major de Beaujolais was sent down to Zinder and from there he went home on leave *via* Kano—and on Kano railway-station platform I met him, and he told me the whole of the story of Zinderneuf Fort from *his* side of the business, and about finding your brother's 'confession.' I went on to Brandon Abbas and told Lady Brandon what he told me—and it really did not seem to interest her enormously!"

It was my turn to feel excited now.

It was incredible to sit there in a hammock-chair under

the African stars, outside this man's tents, a whiskey-and-soda in my hand and a cheroot in my mouth, and hear him tell how *he* had taken our Zinderneuf story to *Brandon Abbas!*

I think I was soon past wonder and all power to feel astonishment.

What did strike me and what did give me endless food for speculation, from then until I saw her, was his account of how Aunt Patricia had received his incredible news. Apparently she did not seem even to *want* to get the wretched jewel back. Her attitude had puzzled Lawrence, and it puzzled me as he described it. . . .

When Lawrence had finished his tale he gave me much Brandon Abbas news.

Sir Hector Brandon was dead. He had died miserably, alone in Kashmir, of cholera—his servants and coolies having fled as soon as the disease was recognised for what it was.

The Chaplain had died of what was apparently a paralytic stroke. Claudia had married one of the richest men in England, nearly old enough to be her grandfather.

Augustus, always a poor horseman, had fallen off his hunter and been dragged until he was very dead indeed.

Isobel was quite well. No, she had not married. How long was it since Mr. Lawrence had heard from Lady Brandon? Oh, quite recently, only a month or so ago. She wrote more frequently nowadays. Seemed to have no one to turn to for advice, now the Chaplain was dead. . . .

Isobel was well and unmarried! (I was conscious that I was breathing more freely and my heart functioning more regularly than it had done since this grave austere official had mentioned Claudia's marriage.) . . .

Did she feel towards me as she had done that morning when I did not say good-bye to her—that morning that seemed so long ago that it might have been in a previous existence, that morning that *was* so long ago?

And so Aunt Patricia knew! Yet what did she know after all? Merely that Michael professed and confessed to be the single-handed thief of the "Blue Water," and that he, and he alone, was to blame. . . .

Did she yet know *the truth* as to the theft?

§ 6.

I had been feeling horribly ill for some time, and now I collapsed altogether with a combination of malarial fever and dysentery—that ill-omened union after whose attack a man is never quite the same again.

Had I been Lawrence's own son, he could not have done more for me, and the Government doctor, who came post-haste by rail and horse, was splendid. It was a close call and a long, slow recovery, but the day came at last when I found myself weak, shaky, and emaciated on Maiduguri platform *en route* for Lagos and home.

George Lawrence was with me, having sworn not to let me out of his sight until he had delivered me safe and sound at Brandon Abbas. I put aside the unworthy thought which occurred to me—that it was himself he yearned to see safe and sound at that house! The idea occurred to me when I found that whatever I said about Michael interested him to the extent that it bore upon Michael's relations to Aunt Patricia, and that his interest in the mystery of the "Blue Water" was limited to its bearing upon Aunt Patricia's affairs.

And so, one day, I found myself on the deck of a steamer, breathing glorious sea-air, and looking back upon the receding coast of horrible Africa, and almost too weak to keep my eyes from watering and my throat from swelling, as I realised that I was leaving behind me all that was mortal of two of the best and finest men that ever lived—my brothers, Michael and Digby. Also two more of the finest men of a different kind, Hank and Buddy, possibly alive, probably dead (for no word had come to Kano)—and, but for Isobel, I should have wished that I were dead too.

But I was glad to be alive, and in my selfishness let my joy lay balm upon my grief for my brothers and my friends —for in my pocket were cables from Isobel, cables dispatched as soon as Lawrence's letter reached Brandon Abbas, announcing my appearance in Nigeria, and the deaths of Michael and Digby.

§ 7.

I will not write of my meeting with her. Those who love, or ever have loved, can imagine something of what I felt as I walked to the Bower, which she had elected to be our meeting-place rather than a railway-platform, or a steamer's deck.

There was my darling, more beautiful than ever, and, if possible, more sweet and loving. . . .

Well, joy does not kill, or I should not have survived that hour. Aunt Patricia was coldly kind, at first.

I was made to feel that she had sent for me one day, and I had refused to come, and had further disobeyed her by leaving the house, against her expressed desires!

After lunch, in the drawing-room, the room from which the "Blue Water" had disappeared, I gave her, in the presence of Isobel and George Lawrence, the letter and packet that had been Michael's charge to me.

She opened the letter first and read it, and then read aloud in a clear and steady voice:

"My most dear and admired Aunt Patricia,

When you get this, I shall be dead, and when you have read it I shall be forgiven, I hope, for I did what I thought was best, and what would, in a small measure, repay you for some of your great goodness to me and my brothers.

My dear Aunt, I knew you had SOLD *the 'Blue Water' to the Maharajah (for the benefit of the tenants and the estate), and I knew you must* DREAD *the return of Sir Hector, and his discovery of the fact, sooner or later.*

I was INSIDE ONE OF THE SUITS OF ARMOUR *when you handed the 'Blue Water' over to the vizier or agent of the Maharajah. I heard everything, and when once you had said what you said and I had heard it—it was pointless for me to confess that I knew—but when I found that you had* HAD *a* DUPLICATE MADE, *I thought what a splendid thing it would be if only we* HAD A BURGLARY *and the 'Blue Water' substitute were stolen! The thieves would be nicely done*

in the eye, and your sale of the stone WOULD NEVER BE DIS-
COVERED *by* SIR HECTOR.

*Had I known how to get into the Priests' Hole and open
the safe, I would have burgled it for you.*

*Then Sir Hector's letter came, announcing his return,
and I knew that things were desperate and the matter*
URGENT. *So I spirited away that clever piece of glass or
quartz or whatever it is, and I herewith return it (with
apologies). I* NEARLY *put it back after all, the same night,
but I'm glad I didn't. (Tell John this.)*

Now I do beg and pray you to LET SIR HECTOR GO ON
THINKING THAT I AM A COMMON THIEF AND STOLE THE
'BLUE WATER'—*or all this bother that everybody has had
will be all for nothing, and I shall have failed to shield you
from trouble and annoyance.*

*If it is not impertinent, may I say that I think you were
absolutely right to sell it, and that the value is a jolly sight
better applied to the health and happiness of the tenants
and villagers and to the productiveness of the farms, than
locked up in a safe in the form of a shining stone that is
of no earthly benefit to anyone.*

*It nearly made me regret what I had done, when those
asses, Digby and John, had the cheek to bolt too. Honestly,
it never occurred to me that they would do anything so silly.
But I suppose it is selfish of me to want all the blame and
all the fun and pleasure of doing a little job for you.*

*I do so hope that all has gone well and turned out as I
planned. I* BET UNCLE HECTOR WAS SICK!

*Well, my dear Aunt, I can only pray that I have helped
you a little.*

With sincerest gratitude for all you have done for us,
            Your loving and admiring nephew,
                        'Beau' Geste.''

.   .   .   .   .   .

"A *beau geste,* indeed,'' said Aunt Patricia, and for the
only time in my life, I saw her put her handkerchief to her
eyes.

*   *   *   *   *   *

Extract from a letter from George Lawrence, Esq., C.M.G.,
of His Majesty's Nigerian Civil Service, to Colonel Henri

de Beaujolais, Colonel of Spahis, XIXth (African) Army
Corps:

.   .   .   .   .   .

"... And so that is the other side of the story, my
friend. Alas, for those two splendid boys, Michael and
Digby Geste. ...

And the remaining piece of news is that I do most sincerely hope that you will be able to come over to England
in June.

You are the best man I know, Jolly, and I want you to
be my Best Man, a desire heartily shared by Lady Brandon.

Fancy, old cabbage, after more than thirty years of devotion! ... I feel like a boy!

And that fine boy, John, is going to marry the 'so beautiful child' whom you remembered. Lady Brandon is being
a fairy godmother to them, indeed. I think she feels she is
somehow doing something for Michael by smoothing their
path so. ..."